INTERNATIONAL ORGANIZATIONS SERIES
Edited by Jon Woronoff

1. *European Community,* by Desmond Dinan. 1993
2. *International Monetary Fund,* by Norman K. Humphreys. 1993
3. *International Organizations in Sub-Saharan Africa,* by Mark W. DeLancey and Terry M. Mays. 1994
4. *European Organizations,* by Derek W. Urwin. 1994
5. *International Tribunals,* by Boleslaw Adam Boczek. 1994
6. *International Food Agencies: FAO, WFP, WFC, IFAD,* by Ross B. Talbot. 1994
7. *Refugee and Disaster Relief Organizations,* by Robert F. Gorman. 1994

Historical Dictionary
of
INTERNATIONAL TRIBUNALS

by
BOLESLAW ADAM BOCZEK

International Organizations Series, No. 5

The Scarecrow Press, Inc.
Metuchen, N.J., & London
1994

British Library Cataloguing-in-Publication data available

Library of Congress Cataloging-in-Publication Data

Boczek, Boleslaw Adam.
  Historical dictionary of international tribunals / by Boleslaw
Adam Boczek
    p. cm. -- (International organizations series ; no. 5)
    ISBN 0-8108-2903-7 (acid-free paper)
    1. International courts--History--Dictionaries. 2. Arbitration,
International--Cases. I. Title. II. Series: International organizations
series (Metuchen, N.J.) ; no. 5.
JX 1990.A2B58 1994
341.5'5'03--dc20   94-15331

CONTENTS

Series Editor's Foreword (Jon Woronoff) vii

Preface ix

Abbreviations and Acronyms Used in the Text xiii

Glossary xvii

Chronology xxiii

Introduction: International Courts and Tribunals in
 Historical Perspective 1

The Dictionary 11

Annex I. Judgments of the PCIJ 219

Annex II. Advisory Opinions of the PCIJ 223

Annex III. Judgments of the ICJ 225

Annex IV. Cases Pending before the ICJ as of 15 July 1993 230

Annex V. Contentious Cases before the ICJ Filed But
 Removed from the List without Any Judgment 232

Annex VI. Advisory Opinions of the ICJ 234

Bibliography 237

About the Author 361

SERIES EDITOR'S FOREWORD

One of the most positive trends on a not always encouraging world scene has been the growing number of international tribunals accompanied by an increasing use thereof. More states are resorting more often to these bodies which have handed down some very significant judgments and awards. Most apply only to states but individuals are also involved in some cases. The areas covered are gradually expanding, from traditional matters like territorial disputes, diplomatic protection, and the law of the sea, to more recent concerns such as economic relations, human rights and the environment. All of this makes at least a modest contribution to bolstering the rule of law on the international level where it is most fragile and also most needed.

It is therefore important for both professionals and laypersons, whether jurists, diplomats, international and national civil servants, educators, journalists or ordinary citizens, to know more about international courts and tribunals. That is the purpose of this book. In a compact and handy volume, it provides information on the world and regional tribunals, crucial rulings and awards, pathbreaking cases, famous international judges, and some basic features of international law as interpreted in the decisions of international courts and tribunals. The underlying trends are further highlighted in the Introduction and Chronology. No less useful is the comprehensive and carefully organized multilingual bibliography, the first of its kind in the literature of the subject. All this makes the *Historical Dictionary of International Tribunals* a unique tool.

This tool was fashioned by Boleslaw Adam Boczek, Professor Emer. of Political Science at Kent State University and a member of the Adjunct Faculty of Case Western Reserve University School of Law. Born and raised in Poland, he obtained law degrees (LLM and SJD) at Jagiellonian University in Cracow. In this country he studied at Harvard University where he received a PhD in Political Science in 1960. After a stint as an advisor at the United Nations he spent six years at Harvard Law School as research associate. At Kent State

University for over 25 years, he has been teaching courses in international law, organization, and relations. He has written extensively on international law, co-authoring, among other works, *The International Law Dictionary*.

Jon Woronoff
Series Editor

PREFACE

This *Dictionary* is the first comprehensive treatment of international courts and tribunals and related aspects of adjudication in international relations. While Manley O. Hudson's classic *International Tribunals* can still be useful as an account of the PCIJ era, it has long been outpaced by developments since its publication half a century ago in 1944. Furthermore, although major international courts, and especially the ICJ, have been analyzed in abundant literature, information on less known tribunals is frequently difficult to locate. Moreover, some of the most recently created tribunals have not yet generated any literature at all.

The nearly 200 entries of this *Dictionary* are preceded by a chronology providing a convenient overview of the historical development of international adjudication. This is followed by an introduction which briefly outlines the evolution of international courts and tribunals as one method of peaceful settlement of disputes in international relations.

International courts and tribunals, past and present, including "non-starters" and now defunct judicial bodies, are the first substantive area covered by the *Dictionary*. Second, a considerable number of entries are devoted to the digesting and appraisal of selected significant judicial and arbitral decisions. In view of the central role of the ICJ in international judiciary, the book includes entries on all its judgments except the most recent judgment of 14 June 1993 in the maritime delimitation case between Denmark and Norway and the 1988 judgment on jurisdiction and admissibility in the case between Nicaragua and Honduras removed from the Court's List in 1992. In addition, a number of entries deal with selected advisory opinions of the ICJ and decisions of the first "World Court," the PCIJ. It may be added here that the six Annexes list all the judgments and advisory opinions of the two Courts, the cases pending before the ICJ as of 15 July 1993, and those cases which have been removed from the Court's List without any judgment. A number of entries examine selected leading decisions of the CJEC and the

ECHR. Major arbitral awards are also included. Certain concepts relative to the structure, jurisdiction, and procedure of international tribunals constitute the third category of entries. Finally, the *Dictionary* contains concise entries on selected major figures in international judiciary, mainly members of the PCIJ and the present World Court. Some entries may be considerably longer than others, but an effort has been made to maintain the proportion between the length of individual entries and their significance for the subject matter of the *Dictionary*. Overall, repetition and overlap are hopefully limited to the minimum, with "q.v." references leading the reader to other entries. For the reader's convenience, the text includes, where appropriate, citations of primary sources. A selective but comprehensive Bibliography (on which more in its Introduction) provides the interested reader with guidance on further research in various aspects of international tribunals.

The subject of international tribunals forms an integral part of international law, an area with which the general public and even many readers with legal education are not sufficiently acquainted. Hence an attempt is made in the text to employ a language that would both be understandable to casual readers and not appear simplistic to those familiar with the concepts and institutions of international law. Incidentally, a short Glossary of foreign, mainly Latin, terms and phrases forms part of the front matter of the book. As a reference work, the *Dictionary* should be a valuable addition to library collections, both in institutions serving the general public and in colleges and universities, especially in the libraries of schools of law. It can also be included in the reading list of courses in international law and international organization as a study guide or supplement to textbooks and casebooks used in law schools and political science departments. Also professionals and scholars in the area of international law and relations will find this *Dictionary* a convenient and unique source of information on various aspects of international adjudication. The author claims sole responsibility for any errors and omissions and encourages the readers to alert him to any that they may discover and, in general, to share with him any criticism concerning the contents of this *Dictionary*. Finally the author wishes to thank Dr. Sanqiang Jian for his professional help in the word processing of the challenging text of this work.

It is hoped that in the 1990s, the "UN Decade of International

Law," this book will make a modest contribution to greater awareness of the role of international tribunals in promoting the rule of law and a truly new world order in international relations.

Boleslaw Adam Boczek
July 1993

ABBREVIATIONS AND ACRONYMS
USED IN THE TEXT*

AAA	American Arbitration Association
Adv. Op.	Advisory Opinion
AJIL	American Journal of International Law
ARAMCO	Arabian American Oil Company
art.	article
arts.	articles
ASIL Proc.	Proceedings of the American Society of International Law
Benelux	Belgium-Netherlands-Luxemburg (or BENELUX)
Benelux EUCJ	Benelux Economic Union Court of Justice
BP	British Petroleum
BYIL	British Yearbook of International Law
CACJ	Central American Court of Justice
CACM	Central American Common Market
CAOC	California Asiatic Oil Company
CAS	Court of Arbitration for Sport
CJAEC	Court of Justice of the African Economic Community
CJCA	Court of Justice of the Cartagena Agreement
CJEC	Court of Justice of the European Communities
CJECCAS	Court of Justice of the Economic Community of Central African States
Co.	Company
Corp.	Corporation
CSCE	Conference on Security and Cooperation in Europe
CTS	Consolidated Treaty Series
Dpt.St.Bull.	Department of State Bulletin
EC	European Community, European Communities
ECHR	European Court of Human Rights

---

* For bibliographical abbreviations see Bibliography.

ECOWAS	Economic Community of West African States
ECR	European Court Reports (Reports of the CJEC)
ECSC	European Coal and Steel Community
EEC	European Economic Community
EEZ	Exclusive Economic Zone
EFTA	European Free Trade Association
ELSI	Elettronica Sicula
EYb	European Yearbook (= Annuaire Européen-*AE*)
FAO	Food and Agriculture Organization
GATT	General Agreement on Tariffs and Trade
I-ACHR	Inter-American Court of Human Rights
IAEA	International Atomic Energy Agency
IBRD	International Bank for Reconstruction and Development
ICAO	International Civil Aviation Organization
ICC	International Chamber of Commerce
ICJ	International Court of Justice
ICJ Rep.	International Court of Justice Reports
ICSID	International Centre for Settlement of Investment Disputes
ILC	International Law Commission
ILM	International Legal Materials
ILO	International Labor Organization
ILOAT	International Labor Organization Administrative Tribunal
ILR	International Law Reports
IMCO	Intergovernmental Maritime Consultative Organization
IMO	International Maritime Organization
IMT	International Military Tribunal
IOC	Inter-Governmental Oceanographic Commission
ISA	International Sea-Bed Authority
ITLOS	International Tribunal for the Law of the Sea
I-USCT	Iran-United States Claims Tribunal
LIAMCO	Libyan American Oil Company
LNTS	League of Nations Treaty Series
NATO	North Atlantic Treaty Organization
No.	Number
OAPEC	Organization of Arab Petroleum Exporting

	Countries
OAS	Organization of American States
OAU	Organization of African Unity
OECD	Organization for Economic Cooperation and Development
PCA	Permanent Court of Arbitration
PCIJ	Permanent Court of International Justice
q.v.	*quod vide* (which see)
RCADI	Recueil des Cours--Académie de Droit International
SADC	Southern African Development Community
Sec.	section
Ser.	series
Stat.	Statutes at Large
Suppl.	Supplement
TIAS	Treaties and Other International Acts Series (1945———)
TOPCO	Texaco Overseas Petroleum Company
TS	Treaty Series (US treaties up to 1945)
UK	United Kingdom
UN	United Nations
UNCITRAL	United Nations Commission on International Trade Law
UNEP	United Nations Environment Programme
UNESCO	United Nations Educational, Scientific and Cultural Organization
UNRIAA	United Nations Reports of International Arbitral Awards
UNTS	United Nations Treaty Series
UP	University Press
UPU	Universal Postal Union
US	United States
USC	United States Code
USSR	Union of Soviet Socialist Republics
v.	versus
vol.	volume
vols.	volumes
WEU	Western European Union
WEUT	Western European Union Tribunal
WHO	World Health Organization

| WMO | World Meteorological Organization |
| *Yb* | Yearbook |

GLOSSARY

ab initio	from the beginning
ad hoc	for a particular purpose only, as a tribunal set up to adjudicate a specific dispute or a judge appointed by a party to form part of the bench dealing with a case
ad interim	in the meantime or temporarily. Used to describe temporary appointments
aimable compositeur (French)	an arbitrator attempting an equitable resolution of a dispute, not necessarily according to the strict rule of law. Used in commercial arbitration
amicus curiae	literally: friend of court. A person that is permitted to call to the court's attention a point of law or fact bearing upon the case but not representing the interests of any party to the proceedings
animus	intention, state of mind
bellum justum	just war
casus foederis	a situation or event causing an ally to honor the obligations under a treaty of alliance
certiorari	in American law: a writ of a higher court to an inferior court calling up the records of a case for review
compromis (French)	an agreement between states to submit a dispute to arbitration or judicial settlement
corpus juris gentium	the body or system of public international law (the law of

nations)

de facto
in fact. Used to distinguish something that actually exists from what may exist only in law

de jure
by virtue of law. Used in contrast to *de facto*

de lege ferenda
relating to or according to the law which should or is to be adopted

de lege lata
according to the law actually in force

delictum juris gentium
offense against the law of nations

dictum (plural: *dicta*)
see obiter dictum

erga omnes
valid against all

ex aequo et bono
according to what is equitable and good, as opposed to what is strictly according to the law in force

ex injuria non oritur jus
the principle that no person can benefit from an illegal act

ex officio
by virtue of a person's office, in official capacity

ex post or *ex post facto*
after the fact; retroactively

in camera
in closed session

in personam
proceedings or right with reference to or directed against a person, as opposed to *in rem*

in rem
proceedings or right with reference to a specific thing, as opposed to *in personam*

inter alia
among other things

inter se
among themselves; between the parties to an agreement or other transaction

ipso facto
by the very fact; automatically

jure gestionis
relating to a state's activities in a non-sovereign capacity, such as commercial activities

jure imperii
relating to a state's traditional functions in its sovereign capacity, such as administration and defense

jus ad bellum	the right to resort to war
jus belli	the law of war (international humanitarian law)
jus cogens	peremptory norms of general international law, that is, norms accepted and recognized by the international community of states as a whole as norms from which no derogation is permissible and which can be modified only by a subsequent peremptory norm. Examples: prohibition of force; of genocide.
jus dispositivum	law that may be modified by contrary agreement
jus gentium	today: the Latin term for the law of nations or international law
jus sanguinis	the principle that nationality by birth is acquired by parentage
jus soli	the principle that nationality by birth is determined by the territory in which the birth took place
locus delicti	the state, and more generally, the jurisdiction within which a wrong was committed
locus standi	the right to apply to a tribunal for a remedy; having sufficient legal interest in the matter at issue
ne bis in idem	no one can be proceeded against twice over the same offense or, more generally, the same matter
nemo dat quod non habet	no one can give what he does not have; no one can transfer a greater interest than that which he himself has
nullum crimen sine lege or *nulla poena sine lege*	no act can be considered to be a crime or no punishment can be imposed unless the act is qualified as a crime punishable under a pre-

existing law

obiter dictum (plural: *obiter dicta*)	an opinion expressed by a tribunal or its individual member on a matter which is not essential for the principal matter at issue
opinio juris et necessitatis	the psychological ingredient of customary international law: recognition that certain states' practice is required by, or consistent with, international law
pacta sunt servanda	agreements must be observed
pacta tertiis nec nocent nec prosunt	agreements impose no burdens nor confer any benefits upon third parties
prima facie	at first sight, presumptively
proprio motu	on one's own initiative
ratione materiae	when referring to a court's jurisdiction: by reason of the subject matter
ratione personae	when referring to a court's jurisdiction: by reason of the person concerned
rebus sic stantibus	as long as the circumstances remain the same. A doctrine, recognized in international law under certain very strictly defined conditions, that a treaty is binding only as long as there is no fundamental change of circumstances which occurred with regard to those existing at the time of the conclusion of the treaty
res communis	a thing that cannot be subjected to the sovereignty of any state and whose usage is common to all states, such as the high seas and celestial bodies
res inter alios acta	a matter which in law concerns only

	other persons; a matter of no legal concern to a person
res judicata	the principle that an issue decided by a court should not be reopened
res nullius	a thing that belongs to nobody; something that is outside the sovereignty of any state and is susceptible of appropriation
restitutio in integrum or *restitutio ad integrum*	in the international law of responsibility: specific restitution or restitution in kind, as opposed to pecuniary compensation or damages
stare decisis	the principle followed in the common-law countries that in cases of the same character the courts must follow past decisions of equal or superior courts. This principle does not apply in international law
status quo or *status quo ante*	the existing state of affairs
terra nullius (*see also res nullius*)	land territory under no state's sovereignty
Thalweg (German)	the main navigable channel of a river
travaux préparatoires (French)	preparatory work relating to the drafting of a treaty, such as drafts and minutes of conferences
ultra vires	exceeding one's authority
uti possidetis or *uti possidetis juris*	a principle, applied to Latin American states, that their boundaries should correspond to the administrative boundaries between different parts of the former Spanish empire. This principle can be applied by analogy in other post-colonial areas, such as Africa
versus	against

CHRONOLOGY

1794   Jay Treaty signed
1799   Jay Treaty mixed claims commissions start functioning
1804   Jay Treaty mixed claims commissions end their activities
1862   Three US-Great Britain mixed courts of justice in slave trade matters set up in Sierra Leone
1868   US-Mexican mixed claims commissions established
1871   US-Great Britain Treaty of Washington provides for arbitration of claims
1872   *Alabama* arbitration (US-Great Britain)
1874   Treaty creating Universal Postal Union, with arbitration clauses
1875   Arbitration regulations suggested by Institute of International Law
1890   Convention on International Transport by Rail, with arbitration clauses
1892   Arbitral Tribunal of Union for International Transport by Rail established
1893   *Behring Sea* Arbitration (Great Britain-US)
1895   Proposal of Interparliamentary Union to create a permanent international court of arbitration
1899   First Hague Peace Conference: Convention on the Pacific Settlement of International Disputes
        Foundation of PCA
1902   First arbitral tribunal set up within the framework of PCA: The *Pious Fund* case (US-Mexico)
1903   France-Great Britain Arbitration Treaty, first to include the reservation of vital interests, independence or honor of the parties
1907   Second Hague Peace Conference: Revision of 1899 Convention; Abortive Hague Convention XII providing for creation of an International Prize Court
        Skeleton project for an International Court of Arbitral Justice

1908   CACJ starts its activities
1909   *Casablanca* Arbitration (France-Germany)
        Canada-US Permanent International Joint Commission established
1910   *North Atlantic Coast Fisheries* Arbitration (Great Britain-US)
1911   Abortive Taft Arbitration Treaties of the US with France and Great Britain
1912   Institute of International Law unanimously recommends establishment of a Court of Arbitral Justice
1918   CACJ ceases to exist
1919   Peace Treaty of Versailles with Germany signed, with Covenant of the League of Nations providing for the creation of a Permanent Court of International Justice and for setting up mixed arbitral tribunals
        Peace Treaties of Saint-Germain with Austria and Neuilly with Bulgaria provide for setting up mixed arbitral tribunals
1920   Peace Treaty of Trianon with Hungary provides for setting up mixed arbitral tribunals
        Statute of PCIJ adopted by League of Nations Assembly in the Protocol of Signature
1921   Statute of PCIJ enters into effect
1922   PCIJ begins its functions; renders its first advisory opinion
        Upper Silesia Arbitral Tribunal established between Germany and Poland
        US-Germany Mixed Claims Commission established
        US-Austria and Hungary Tripartite Claims Commission established
        ICC Court of Arbitration established
1923   Peace Treaty of Lausanne with Turkey provides for setting up mixed arbitration tribunals
        First PCIJ judgment (*Wimbledon* case)
        US-Mexican Convention setting up mixed claims commissions
1924   Second US-Mexican Convention setting up mixed claims commissions
        League of Nations Assembly adopts General Protocol for Pacific Settlement of International Disputes
1927   Administrative Tribunal of League of Nations established

(continues as Administrative Tribunal of ILO)
Lotus Case before PCIJ

1928 General Act on the Pacific Settlement of International Disputes
Palmas Arbitration (US-Netherlands)

1929 Protocol revising Statute of PCIJ adopted by League of Nations Assembly
General Treaty of Inter-American Arbitration signed

1931 PCIJ Advisory Opinion on *Customs Régime between Germany and Austria*

1935 Last advisory opinion of PCIJ (*Danzig Legislative Decrees*)
Draft Protocol on US accession to PCIJ Statute, defeated in Senate

1936 Revised text of Statute of PCIJ enters into effect

1937 Abortive Convention of Geneva Conference on Terrorism providing for establishment of an International Criminal Court
Upper Silesia Arbitral Tribunal terminates its activities

1939 Last judgment of PCIJ (*Société Commerciale de Belgique*)

1940 PCIJ interrupts its activities because of German invasion of the Netherlands

1945 UN Charter with Statute of ICJ adopted and in effect
IMT at Nuremberg established

1946 Judgment of IMT at Nuremberg
IMT for Far East established
Connally Reservation (Amendment) adopted by US Senate

1947 Conciliation Commissions under Peace Treaty with Italy established

1948 First judgment of ICJ (*Corfu Channel*)
First advisory opinion of ICJ (*Conditions of Admission*)
Judgment of IMT for Far East

1949 Revision of General Act of 1928
UN Administrative Tribunal established

1950 European Convention for the Protection of Human Rights and Fundamental Freedoms signed

1951 Property Commissions under Peace Treaty with Japan established

1952 ECSC Court of Justice established

1953 Arbitral Tribunal and Mixed Commission established under

London Agreement on German External Debt

ILC adopts Draft Convention on Arbitral Procedure

1954   Establishment of Arbitral Commission on Property, Rights and Interests in Germany under Settlement Convention forming part of the Bonn (1952) and Paris (1954) Agreements on Germany

1957   CJEC established under Treaty of Rome

European Convention for the Peaceful Settlement of Disputes signed

Austro-German Property Arbitral Tribunal established

1958   Benelux Economic Union College of Arbitrators established

ILC adopts Model Rules of Arbitral Procedure

New York Convention on the Recognition and Enforcement of Foreign Arbitral Awards signed

1959   Court of Arbitration of French Community established

ECHR effectively set up

1960   Central American Common Market Arbitration Tribunal established under Treaty of Managua (now defunct)

1961   European Convention on International Commercial Arbitration signed

1964   OAU arbitration procedures established

1965   Benelux Economic Union Court of Justice established (in force 1974)

ICSID established

1967   East African Community Court of Appeal and Common Market Tribunal established (inactive, now defunct)

1968   ICJ adopts its Internal Judicial Practice

1969   American Convention on Human Rights signed

1972   ICJ Rules amended

1975   ECOWAS Tribunal established

Inter-American Convention on International Commercial Arbitration signed

1976   ICJ Internal Judicial Practice revised

UNCITRAL Rules adopted

1978   American Convention on Human Rights enters into effect

OAPEC Judicial Board established

ICJ Rules thoroughly revised

1979   I-ACHR effectively set up; its Statute adopted

CJCA (Andean Court) established

1980 I-ACHR adopts its Rules of Procedure
World Bank Administrative Tribunal established
1981 I-USCT established
1982 UN Convention on the Law of the Sea provides for an
ITLOS, with a Sea-Bed Disputes Chamber; for arbitral
tribunals; and for special arbitral tribunals
1983 Court of Justice of Economic Community of Central African
States established
1984 First judgment by a Chamber of ICJ (*Gulf of Maine, Canada/US*)
Court of Arbitration for Sport (CAS) established
1985 US announces termination of its acceptance of ICJ optional
clause
UNCITRAL Model Law on International Commercial
Arbitration adopted
1986 US acceptance of ICJ optional clause terminated
1987 Canada-US Free Trade Agreement with dispute settlement
procedures
1989 Court of First Instance of EC set up
1990 Court of Justice of African Economic Community established
1992 SADC Tribunal established
CSCE Court of Conciliation and Arbitration established
1993 UN Security Council votes to set up an international criminal
tribunal to try war criminals in the Yugoslav conflict

INTRODUCTION

International Courts and Tribunals in Historical Perspective

Compulsory settlement of disputes by an independent judiciary according to the law in force has long been recognized as a major hallmark of civilized political societies at the level of individual states where a hierarchically structured system of courts routinely enforces the law following the established procedures and irrespective of the parties' consent. In international relations judicial settlement of disputes is a relatively exceptional phenomenon in an environment characterized by legally independent and sovereign states whose consent is, as a rule, necessary before a dispute can be submitted to adjudication by an international court or tribunal.

Conceptually, procedures of peaceful settlement of international disputes may be either diplomatic (non-adjudicative), where the parties concerned agree on terms of settlement for themselves, or adjudicative, where a third party resolves the dispute by means of a legally binding decision. The process of settlement by diplomatic procedures may either take the form of direct negotiation between the disputants without any intercession of third parties or it may be aided by a friendly third party interceding in the dispute. In the latter case participation of a third party, always to be regarded as a friendly act, may vary in impact from the so-called good offices when that party, serving as a channel of communication ("shuttle diplomacy") tries to bring the disputing parties to the negotiating table, through mediation when a third party actively participates in the negotiating process by offering substantive suggestions concerning terms of settlement, to conciliation, a more formal procedure in which an impartial commission, appointed by the parties, objectively elucidates the facts and issues a report containing a concrete proposal of settlement. The three procedures, frequently combined with an inquiry into the facts of the dispute by an impartial investigative body ("commission of inquiry"), cannot sometimes be rigidly separated and merge into one process of attempts by a friendly third party to facilitate a solution of the dispute. However, in their nature good offices, mediation, and conciliation are political and diplomatic processes, and the disputing parties are under no legal obligation to accept any proposed terms of settlement. It is mainly this feature that distinguishes these methods of settlement from adjudicative procedures of arbitration and judicial settlement in the strict sense of the word.

Despite the terminological distinction, arbitration and judicial settlement are closely related. They have the same legal value and in substance arbitration can be considered as only a kind of judicial settlement. In both cases the organs involved have the competence to pronounce on the preliminary matters of jurisdiction and admissibility as well as on the merits of a dispute. Both an arbitration tribunal and an international court or tribunal are judicial bodies whose decisions are legally binding upon the parties.

Although in the prevailing English terminology the term "court" refers to a permanent (standing) court of justice and "tribunal" often means an *ad hoc* body of arbitrators, in practice the terms are interchangeable. It is not uncommon to refer to a "court" of arbitration as, for example, in the case of PCA and the *ad hoc* courts established within its framework. On the other hand, a permanent court may be called "tribunal," as is the case of the International Tribunal for the Law of the Sea (ITLOS) projected in the 1982 Convention on the Law of the Sea. The terms "claims commission" or "mixed claims commission" or even -- very misleadingly -- "conciliation commission" have also been employed in practice to denote what is an arbitration court or tribunal.

In its strict meaning, international adjudication, that is, settlement of international disputes by international tribunals, implies the existence of a standing court of general or specialized jurisdiction, established pursuant to a multilateral, global or regional, treaty, in which independent and impartial judges render legally binding decisions on the basis of international law according to previously set rules and procedures, usually spelled out in the court's statute, which guarantee the parties' right to submit their views on the basis of full equality. The International Court of Justice (ICJ), the Court of Justice of the European Communities (CJEC), and the European Court of Human Rights (ECHR) are examples of this first major category of tribunals adjudicating international disputes. The permanent nature of such tribunals allows them to develop a certain jurisprudential consistency and build up judicial tradition in their respective areas of jurisdiction.

The various kinds of international arbitration bodies, known as tribunals, courts, or commissions and set up on an *ad hoc* basis, are the second major category of international tribunals. Although their composition and procedure are determined by the parties, they are also international courts in the wider sense of the term since their decisions are legally binding upon the parties and are handed down by impartial arbitrators (or one arbitrator) on the basis of respect for international law and full equality of the parties.

In the aftermath of major international conflicts the practice of the 20th century has developed a third category of tribunals, notably semi-permanent specialized judicial bodies which are set up by treaty for the specific purpose of dealing with disputes resulting from the conflict, such as private claims taken over by governments. Such tribunals or commissions are dissolved, having performed the judicial task assigned to them by the parties. The post-World War I mixed arbitral tribunals and mixed claims commissions, and the various commissions and tribunals established after World War II to consider claims against former enemy states were such semi-permanent judicial bodies. The I-USCT, created to adjudicate claims in Iran-US relations in the aftermath of the hostage crisis and still active in 1993, also belongs to such tribunals.

The international administrative tribunals of international organizations constitute a unique category of international tribunals. They do not decide disputes between states but serve as a kind of labor court for disputes between an international organization and its staff members.

Historically, international adjudication by institutionalized standing courts developed from the much longer experience of arbitration which in the modern era was initiated by the US-Great Britain Jay Treaty in 1794 providing for settlement of various legal issues between the two countries by temporary mixed arbitral commissions. Three stages can be distinguished in the history of international tribunals in the arbitration era of 1794-1919 which preceded the emergence of the first World Court in 1920. The first stage, 1794-1871, was characterized by the use of the mixed claims commission model adjudicating mainly private claims, albeit in some cases inter-state territorial disputes were also involved. The semi-permanent but fairly long lasting African slave trade mixed tribunals were an interesting example of semi-permanent tribunals of specialized jurisdiction in the 19th century.

The famous *Alabama* arbitration of 1872 introduced the second period in the evolution of arbitration which lasted until the First Hague Peace Conference of 1899. This arbitration inaugurated the model of a truly third-party arbitral body, in some cases a head of state, which was applied in almost a hundred disputes involving the US and European and Latin American states. Introduction of compromissory clauses in bilateral and multilateral treaties and the appearance of general arbitration treaties were a further testimony to the growing international popularity of the institution of arbitration in the waning decades of the 19th century. Moreover, national parliaments and the Interparliamentary Union in 1895 suggested in their resolutions that the time was ripe for creating a permanent international arbitral tribunal. In fact, a specialized tribunal was set up in 1892 within the framework of the Union for International Transport by Rail.

The third stage in the classical arbitration era, 1899-1919, began with the First Hague Peace Conference of 1899 whose Convention on the Pacific Settlement of International Disputes provided for the creation of the Permanent Court of Arbitration (PCA). While only a framework for *ad hoc* arbitrations and neither permanent nor a real court, this institution represented a further advance toward a really permanent international tribunal. For some three decades the PCA served as an organizational framework for arbitration of international disputes, but arbitration by tribunals outside of its framework continued to be used. The network of general arbitration treaties, of which more than 120 were concluded in the years 1900 to 1914, developed further, but not many of them led to actual arbitration, especially in view of the clauses excepting disputes affecting "the vital interests, the independence or the honor" of the parties.

The increase in the popularity of the arbitration idea led the US Secretary of State Elihu Root to instruct the American delegates at the Second Hague Peace Conference in 1907 to work for the development of the PCA into a permanent tribunal. However, attempts to this effect failed and only a skeleton project for an "International Court of Arbitral Justice" was promulgated by the Conference. Attempts to create a specialized International Prize

Court also ended in failure. On the other hand, the Hague Peace movement inspired the Central American countries in 1908 to establish the Central American Court of Justice (CACJ) which, albeit short-lived, occupies an important place in the history of international tribunals as the first permanent international court in the world.

A new era in the history of international tribunals opened in 1920 with the adoption of the Statute for the first global permanent international court of general jurisdiction, in whose name the adjective "arbitral" was characteristically omitted. This Permanent Court of International Justice (PCIJ) held its first session at The Hague in 1922 and continued its activities until 1940. This predecessor of the present ICJ delivered 32 judgments and 27 advisory opinions and issued more than 200 orders. However, lack of compulsory jurisdiction was its main handicap, as it still remains for the ICJ today. While the PCIJ was the most prestigious international tribunal in the inter-war period, in quantitative terms the mixed arbitral tribunals established in the aftermath of the war and mixed claims commissions, such as the ones established in US-Mexican relations, dealt with by far more cases than the PCIJ. Thousands of claims of private parties were decided upon by these commissions and tribunals. Arbitration within the framework of the PCA was largely eclipsed by the foundation of the PCIJ; only four cases were dealt with within this framework.

The decades following World War II have witnessed a remarkable increase in the number and variety of standing international courts and tribunals. At the global level, the ICJ, an integral part of the United Nations (UN), is in practice a continuation of the PCIJ, suffering, as its predecessor, from lack of compulsory jurisdiction but recently showing signs of increased activity, with 11 cases pending on 15 July 1993. Attempts to create a global international court of criminal jurisdiction on the foundations of the law of the International Military Tribunal (IMT) at Nuremberg and the IMT at Tokyo were abandoned because of lack of political support. On the other hand, another court of specialized jurisdiction, a global UN-sponsored ITLOS with a special Sea-Bed Disputes Chamber, created under the 1982 UN Convention on the Law of the Sea, is expected to start functioning following the entry into effect of the Convention. Furthermore, in 1993 the UN Security Council resolved to set up an international criminal tribunal to try violators of international humanitarian law in the Yugoslav conflict.

However, it is at the regional level that the idea of international tribunals has found unprecedented practical application, beginning with Western Europe where broad consensus on fundamental social and political values has largely contributed to the success of the two best known and most active standing international tribunals: the CJEC created to ensure observance of the law of the European Community and the Council of Europe-sponsored ECHR which functions as the protector of human rights and fundamental freedoms in Europe. Other less known and not so active international tribunals in Europe include the Benelux Economic Union Court of Justice (Benelux-EUCJ) and Benelux Economic Union College of Arbitrators, and the European Tribunal in Matters of State Immunity. More recently, the CJEC has been complemented by the Court of First Instance of the European Community, and in 1992 a Court of Conciliation and Arbitration was established under the auspices of the CSCE.

In other parts of the world, the institution of international tribunals met with some success in America where the I-ACHR, modeled on the ECHR, has already started to exercise its contentious jurisdiction. Another international tribunal on the American continent, the Court of Justice of the Cartagena Agreement (CJCA), established as part of the Andean Common Market integration scheme, has also been inaugurated. However, in the Central American region which once could boast of a permanent tribunal, the CACJ, attempts to create a viable arbitral tribunal ended in failure, sharing the fate of the abortive Central American Common Market.

It is noteworthy that in purely quantitative terms Africa has recently emerged as a region with a growing number of international tribunals, set up as organs of the proliferating regional and subregional organizations of predominantly economic character. These tribunals are largely inactive, and it remains to be seen whether the Organization of African Unity (OAU) arbitration procedures and the various African-based tribunals, such as the Court of Justice of the African Economic Community (CJAEC), the Tribunal of the Economic Community of West African States (ECOWAS), the Court of Justice of the Economic Community of Central African States (CJECCAS) and the Southern African Development Community (SADC) Tribunal will become viable judicial bodies in their respective regions. Their future is likely to be determined by the success or failure of the integration scheme undertaken in the region concerned and progress in enhancing the member countries' political culture and respect for international rule of law. In this respect the failure of the East African integration scheme and its Tribunal in the 1970s did not establish a promising precedent for other regional institutions, including international tribunals, on the African continent.

While proposals for an Arab Court of Justice under the auspices of the League of Arab States never materialized, an interesting addition to the roster of international tribunals is the OAPEC Judicial Board which has the competence to decide, according to international and Islamic law, disputes over petroleum operations involving not only states members of the Organization of Arab Petroleum Exporting Countries (OAPEC) but also private companies in such states in disputes with member states.

The first decades of the post-war era witnessed the activities of the already mentioned semi-permanent tribunals disposing of claims in the aftermath of World War II: Arbitral Commission on Property, Rights and Interests in Germany; Austro-German Property Arbitral Tribunal; "Conciliation" commissions under the Peace Treaty with Italy; London Agreement on German External Debt Arbitral Tribunal; and Property Commissions under the Peace Treaty with Japan. The Iran-United States Claims Tribunal (I-USCT), set up in 1981 with jurisdiction over private claims in the aftermath of the hostage crisis, is an important and still very active tribunal of semi-permanent nature.

A significant trend in international adjudication in recent times has been arbitration of international commercial and investment disputes between governments and foreign companies. Investment disputes of this category can be adjudicated by arbitral tribunals operating within the framework of the International Centre for Settlement of Investment Disputes (ICSID) associated with the World Bank.

The roster of international tribunals would not be complete if no mention were made of international arbitration between private enterprises. This private-law international commercial arbitration, sponsored by numerous arbitral institutes, has emerged as an important institution contributing to settling legal disputes in international commercial relations. The Court of Arbitration for Sport (CAS), established in 1984 by the International Olympic Committee, is another example of an international arbitral tribunal settling non-governmental disputes.

While it has not played a significant part in resolving major political conflicts, adjudication of disputes between states has become a recognized method of settling international disputes, and judicial settlement is specifically named as such in art. 33 of the UN Charter. Since, except for certain regional tribunals in Europe (CJEC, ECHR) and the projected Sea-Bed Disputes Chamber of the ITLOS, jurisdiction of international courts remains voluntary, states are reluctant to submit to adjudication disputes when their perceived vital interests are at stake and prefer to resort to more familiar, diplomatic techniques rather than to the less flexible and normally final judicial settlement. With the World Court in focus, one can more readily understand the reasons for states' reluctance to use the judicial method. Apart from the lack of compulsory jurisdiction which is a serious but not fatal flaw of the ICJ, the major reason for this reluctance is that because of often uncertain rules of international law, as evidenced by many individual dissenting opinions, the outcome of the proceedings may be unpredictable and there is more room to doubt the impartiality of judges susceptible to political considerations when the law is unsettled. Thus in disputes between developing and developed countries the latter may be hesitant to bring a case before the Court, believing that some members of the bench are too radical and bent on changing the law that currently favors these countries while the former may be hesitant to use the Court, perceiving the bench to be generally conservative and upholding the *status quo.* Apart from these considerations, countries may not be willing to risk adverse judgment if their cases are not based on solid legal grounds.

Yet despite the problems adversely affecting resort to international courts and tribunals, the idea of international adjudication is now firmly established and slowly but steadily implemented both at the global and especially the regional level of international relations.

THE DICTIONARY

A

Abu Dhabi Arbitration, 1951. This case (18 ILR 144) between
Petroleum Development (Trucial Coasts) Limited and the Sheikh
of Abu Dhabi was decided in 1951 by the sole arbitrator (*see*
Arbitration), Lord Asquith of Bishopstone. It concerned the
interpretation of a concession agreement of 1939 granting
Petroleum Development the exclusive right to explore and exploit
mineral oil in Abu Dhabi and "the sea waters which belong to that
area." At issue was the question whether the 1939 agreement also
included the submarine area lying beyond the territorial waters
with respect to which the Sheikh had, in 1949, granted a fresh
concession to another company.

The arbitrator held that the area in question was not covered by
the agreement since the legal concept of the continental shelf
under which the coastal state has exclusive rights to the seabed
and subsoil of the shelf beyond the territorial sea had been
unknown in 1939 and was not accepted in international law even
in 1951; hence it could not be read back into the 1939 agreement
between Petroleum Development and the Sheikh of Abu Dhabi.

The award is also of interest in that it interpreted an agreement
between a state and a private foreign company in the light of
general principles of law of civilized nations, a sort of modern law
of nature, and not according to the municipal (domestic) law of
the contracting state or any other municipal law. (*See also*
ARAMCO Arbitration, 1958).

Ad Hoc **Judge** *see* **Judge** *Ad Hoc*

Administrative Tribunals of International Organizations. Tribunals
established by public international organizations, that is,
intergovernmental organizations whose function is to adjudicate,
mainly in accordance with the internal administrative law of the
respective organization, disputes concerning alleged breaches of
the terms of employment of the members of the staff of the

organization. The need for such tribunals arose with the emergence of international organizations employing international staff independently of national control. Apart from an *ad hoc* tribunal set up by the League of Nations in 1925, the Administrative Tribunal of the League of Nations created in 1927 was the first administrative tribunal of international organizations. It had the competence to adjudicate claims of employees and ex-employees of the League of Nations and International Labor Office. The League of Nations Tribunal continues today as the Administrative Tribunal of the ILO and since 1949 it has also been used as a tribunal for staff disputes of IAEA and a number of UN specialized agencies, such as WHO, UNESCO, FAO, WMO, GATT and UPU, and some European-based international agencies.

The UN created its own Administrative Tribunal in 1949. It hears applications alleging non-observance of contracts and, generally, terms of employment of members of its staff. Furthermore, under its statute the competence of the Tribunal may be extended to any UN specialized agency. This was done with regard to ICAO and IMO and pension disputes involving some other organizations, but most of these agencies have preferred to use the services of the ILO Tribunal. The World Bank created its own Administrative Tribunal in 1980. In a number of other international organizations, such as the OAS, the Council of Europe, NATO, OECD, and WEU, staff disputes are dealt with either by a tribunal or a special Appeal Board respectively. The European Communities do not have any special administrative tribunal although such a body has been proposed by the EC Commission. Disputes between the EC and its employees are within the jurisdiction of the CJEC (q.v.) which adjudicates them in accordance with its statute and the laws and regulations governing the service of the EC employees.

The administrative tribunals of international organizations are usually composed of persons appointed in some tribunals by the member states and in others by the organization concerned. Judicial training is usually required for at least one member of the tribunal. The number of judges varies. For example the ILO Tribunal has three and that of the UN seven judges; each of them must be of different nationality.

Proceedings before administrative tribunals are initiated by the staff member or other persons entitled to rights under the contract of employment. They are normally in written form. The oral phase, which may be held in public (UN and ILO Tribunals) or in secret, serves only to clarify written statements. In some tribunals an employee may file an application only after his claim has been dismissed by the appropriate authority of the organization. Judgments must be accompanied by reasons and must be given within a period of eight days to one month, depending on the tribunal's rules. Under the rules of the UN Tribunal judges may issue individual (dissenting) opinions (q.v.).

While the decisions of the administrative tribunals are final and there is no ordinary appeal procedure, it must be noted that judgments of the UN and ILO Tribunals may be reviewed by the ICJ (q.v.) at the request of the executive body of the organization concerned or by a special screening committee, depending on the organization. In response to an application for review of a judgment of the UN or ILO Tribunal the ICJ may hand down an advisory opinion (q.v.) according to the rules governing its advisory jurisdiction. Three such advisory opinions have been handed down by the ICJ (*see* ANNEX VI). Whether the advisory opinion of the ICJ in the review of a judgment of an administrative tribunal is legally binding depends on the relevant rules of the organization concerned. In the UN, the Secretary General may implement the opinion if it confirms the decision of the administrative tribunal, or he may ask the tribunal to confirm its judgment or reconsider it in accordance with the advisory opinion.

Advisory Jurisdiction *see* **Advisory Opinions**

Advisory Opinions. Opinions given by an international tribunal at the request of an authorized organ of an international organization. Under art. 96 of the UN Charter and art. 65 of the Statute of the ICJ (q.v.) the ICJ may give an advisory opinion on "any legal question" at the request of the UN General Assembly, the Security Council, or other organs of the UN, and its specialized agencies authorized by the General Assembly to make a request for an advisory opinion on legal questions arising within the scope of their activities. The General Assembly has granted such authorization to the Economic and Social Council, the Trusteeship Council, the Interim Committee of the General Assembly, the Committee on Applications for Review of Judgments of the UN Administrative Tribunal (*see* **Administrative Tribunals of International Organizations**), and all the specialized agencies except the UPU. It must be added that under art. 191 of the UN Convention on the Law of the Sea (1982) the Sea-Bed Disputes Chamber of the International Tribunal for the Law of the Sea (q.v.) shall give advisory opinions at the request of the Assembly or the Council of the International Sea-Bed Authority established by the Convention to manage the resources of the deep sea-bed (the "Area"). Such opinions must be given as a matter of urgency.

The institution of advisory opinions of the World Court originated in the PCIJ (q.v.) and had its basis in art. 14 of the Covenant of the League of Nations. It is now associated primarily with the ICJ, but it is also known in some regional tribunals. Thus jurisdiction to give advisory opinions has been conferred by the relevant treaties on the ECHR (q.v.), the I-ACHR (q.v.) where-- unlike the case of the ICJ--states can also petition for an advisory opinion, the Benelux-EUCJ (q.v.), the CJAEC (q.v.) and the CJEC (q.v.). In the last-mentioned court an advisory opinion on the compatibility with the EC Treaty of any agreement proposed to be concluded with a non-member state or an international organization may be requested by the EC Council, the EC Commission, or a member state.

The procedure in advisory jurisdiction follows, wherever applicable, the rules governing contentious jurisdiction. In their nature, the advisory opinions, while having a strong persuasive force as a statement of the meaning of the law by a prestigious tribunal and carrying considerable political weight, lack any legal binding force of a judgment even for the body requesting the opinion. However, in view of arts. 228 and 236 of the EC Treaty of Rome (1957), in the EC system the CJEC decisions known as "opinions," which that Court may give on the compatibility of proposed EC treaties with the EC Treaty, have legally binding consequences for the Community organs. Furthermore, within the framework of the UN, a state may by treaty undertake in advance to be legally bound by advisory opinions of the ICJ in certain questions. For example the Convention on the Privileges and Immunities of the UN (1946) has a clause to this effect.

In the history of the World Court (PCIJ-ICJ) a controversy has arisen concerning the exercise by the Court of its advisory jurisdiction in respect of an issue in dispute between parties which refuse to take part in any proceedings before the Court. In such cases an advisory opinion could be considered an exercise by the Court of disguised contentious jurisdiction which would conflict with the fundamental principle of international law and adjudication that the contentious jurisdiction (q.v.) of the ICJ derives from the parties' consent. It is for this reason that in 1923 the PCIJ refused to give an opinion on the *Status of Eastern Carelia* (q.v.) since that question directly concerned an actual dispute between Finland and the Soviet Union, the latter state not bound by the League of Nations Covenant and objecting to the Court's jurisdiction. However, this point of view has been significantly eroded by the UN Court in its advisory opinion on *Interpretation of Peace Treaties with Bulgaria, Hungary and Romania (I)* (1950) (*see* ANNEX VI: ADVISORY OPINIONS OF THE ICJ) and especially in the opinion in the *Western Sahara* case (1975) (q.v.). In the latter case the Court gave its opinion on the legal nature of the territory in question at the time of its colonization, despite Spain's objections. The Court noted in that opinion that, unlike the PCIJ case of *Eastern Carelia*, the state concerned, that is Spain, had, by its becoming a member of the UN and a party to the ICJ Statute, given its consent in general to the exercise of advisory jurisdiction by the ICJ. The Court also stressed that the UN organ requesting the opinion (the General Assembly) was concerned with the exercise of its own functions and not the settlement of the dispute, and--in any case--the Court's opinion, otherwise aiming at assisting the General Assembly in the decolonization process, would not affect Spain's rights as the state administering the territory of Western Sahara.

The use of advisory jurisdiction by the ICJ has declined as compared with the recourse to such jurisdiction of its predecessor, the PCIJ. Whereas the PCIJ delivered 26 advisory opinions, all within a period of 13 years, the ICJ had, by June 1993, handed down only 20 opinions in more than 47 years of its existence. All the advisory opinions of the PCIJ (*see* ANNEX II: ADVISORY

OPINIONS OF THE PCIJ) were requested by the Council of the League of Nations, and most related to the aftermath of World War I. As far as the ICJ is concerned, 12 opinions were delivered at the request of the UN General Assembly, one at the request of the Security Council, one originated in the Economic and Social Council, one was requested by the Intergovernmental Maritime Consultative Organization (IMCO), now known as the International Maritime Organization (IMO), one by UNESCO, one by WHO, and three by the Committee on Applications for Review of Judgments of the UN Administrative Tribunal (*see* **Administrative Tribunals of International Organizations**).

Most of the requests for an advisory opinion to the ICJ involved issues concerning the functioning of the body requesting the opinion. Five were delivered within the context of reviewing decisions of the UN and ILO Administrative Tribunals. Three opinions, handed down in the 1950s, concerned matters connected with the Cold War, such as admission of states to the UN, and five dealt with decolonization: four on South-West Africa (Namibia) and one on Western Sahara.

Although politically the advisory opinions of the ICJ have not been an effective tool in influencing states' policies, the advising procedure has contributed to clarifying and developing international law on such issues as the capacity of the UN to advance an international claim in respect of the damage suffered (*Reparation for Injuries Suffered in the Service of the United Nations*, Adv. Op. 1949) (q.v.) and reservations to multilateral conventions (*Reservations to the Convention on the Prevention and Punishment of the Crime of Genocide*, Adv. Op. 1951) (q.v.).

In the EC system the CJEC has delivered a number of opinions on the compatibility with the EC Treaty of international agreements entered into with outside states and international organizations. The I-ACHR has also exercised its advisory jurisdiction, which has not been the case of the ECHR, however.

Aegean Sea Continental Shelf (Greece v. Turkey), ICJ 1976-1978. This case had its origin in the dispute between Greece and Turkey over the delimitation of the maritime boundary of the continental shelf in the Aegean Sea in the area of certain Greek islands situated in the close vicinity of Turkey. After Turkey, against

Greek protests, began to explore for oil the disputed shelf area, Greece appealed to the Security Council and referred the matter to the ICJ (q.v.), requesting the Court to delimit the boundary and the two countries' rights in their respective maritime zones. As the basis of the ICJ jurisdiction, Greece invoked the General Act of 1928 (q.v.) and a joint communiqué issued by the two states in Brussels in 1973 which allegedly constituted an agreement to submit the dispute to the ICJ. Greece also requested the Court to indicate interim measures of protection (q.v.) under art. 41 of the ICJ Statute, which would bar Turkey from further oil exploration in the disputed areas and order it to desist from further military measures which might endanger peace. For its part, Turkey refused to take part in the proceedings, denying the Court's jurisdiction on the ground that negotiations between the disputing parties were in progress and that the dispute had a political character and was not justiciable (*see* **Justiciability of International Disputes**). Consequently, Turkey asked the Court to dismiss all the requests of Greece.

Before examining the question of its jurisdiction, the ICJ, by its order of 11 September 1976 (1976 ICJ Rep. 3), rejected, by a vote of 12 to two, the Greek request for interim measures on the ground that no irreparable damage was imminent to Greece as a result of the Turkish exploratory measures. As to the possible military threat to Greece, the Court found that in this respect the Greek request was not connected with Greece's claims on the merits, and ruled that no action on the part of the ICJ was needed because the Security Council in its Resolution 395 (1976) had already called upon Greece and Turkey to resolve their dispute peacefully.

After rejecting Turkey's preliminary objections (q.v.), the Court, in its judgment of 19 December 1978 (1978 ICJ Rep. 3) held, by a vote of 12 to two, that it lacked jurisdiction to hear the merits of the case because, first, a Greek reservation to the General Act of 1928 (q.v.), excluding disputes relating to the territorial status of Greece, had removed disputes over the continental shelf from the Court's jurisdiction and, second, the Brussels communiqué of 1973 did not constitute a commitment of the parties to submit the dispute to the ICJ.

The dispute between Greece and Turkey over the Aegean

continental shelf continues unresolved.

Aerial Incident of 27 July 1955 (Israel v. Bulgaria), ICJ 1957-1959.
Following the shooting down by the Bulgarian air defense of an Israeli airliner which intruded into the Bulgarian air space on 27 July 1955, Israel, having failed to obtain compensation from Bulgaria, instituted proceedings against that country before the ICJ (q.v.).

In its judgment of 26 May 1959 (1959 ICJ Rep. 127) the ICJ, by 12 votes to four, found that it lacked jurisdiction in the case.

Israel's contention was that the Court did have jurisdiction because Israel had accepted it under the optional clause (q.v.) in 1956 and Bulgaria had accepted the clause in 1921 for purposes of the PCIJ (q.v.). As claimed by Israel, that acceptance was still valid by virtue of art. 36(5) of the Statute of the ICJ which stipulates the continued validity of such declarations for purposes of the new World Court, that is the ICJ. The ICJ rejected this reasoning, holding that the intention of art. 36(5) was to apply it only to the original members of the UN and thereby parties to the Statute, that is the states represented at the San Francisco Conference on International Organization at the time when the Statute of the PCIJ was still in force. On the other hand, as reasoned by the ICJ, the optional clause declaration of Bulgaria of 1921, a country which did not become a member of the UN until after the dissolution of the PCIJ, terminated upon the end of the PCIJ.

It may be noted that both the US and the UK also instituted proceedings against Bulgaria with regard to damages for the losses suffered by their respective nationals as a result of the destruction of the Israeli airliner in 1955. In both cases the proceedings were discontinued by orders of the Court (1959 ICJ Rep. 264; 1960 ICJ Rep. 146) at the request of the applicant government concerned (*See* ANNEX V: CONTENTIOUS CASES BEFORE THE ICJ FILED BUT REMOVED FROM THE LIST WITHOUT ANY JUDGMENT).

African Slave Trade Mixed Tribunals. International tribunals set up in the 19th century by treaties for the suppression of African slave trade. Initiated by Great Britain in the early 19th century, such "mixed commission courts" functioned with the cooperation of Argentina, Bolivia, Brazil, Chile, Ecuador, the Netherlands, Portugal, Spain, and Uruguay. The task of these courts was to adjudicate upon seizures of vessels suspected of slave trade. The US joined this trend in 1862 by signing a treaty with Great Britain which provided for the establishment of "mixed courts of justice" to pronounce on the legitimacy of seizures of US and British vessels. Three such courts were established: in Sierra Leone in West Africa, at Cape of Good Hope in South Africa, and in New York, each composed of two judges, one appointed by each government, and two arbitrators similarly appointed available as umpires. The two latter courts were abolished in 1870 without having disposed of any cases. However, the courts sitting in Sierra Leone adjudicated 535 cases in the period 1819-1866, being instrumental in the emancipation of some 55,000 slaves. The activities of the African slave trade mixed tribunals declined after 1866 and they were all abolished toward the end of the century.

Ago, Roberto (1907-). Italian national. Member of the ICJ (q.v.) since 1979; in terms of age the oldest judge on the bench in 1993. Before being elected to the Court, he was professor of public and private international law at the Universities of Catania (1934-1935), Genoa (1935-1938), Milan (1938-1956), and Rome (1956-1982). In the period 1956-1979 Ago was member and subsequently Chairman of the International Law Commission (ILC), a subsidiary organ of the UN General Assembly charged with the codification and development of international law. He prepared eight reports to the Commission in the years 1969-1972. Ago was also Head of the Italian delegation to International Labor Conferences, 1946-1978, and Chairman of the ILO's Governing Body, 1954-1955 and 1967-1968. He represented Italy at numerous international conferences. Ago is author of many publications on international law, including contributions to *RCADI*.

The *Alabama* Arbitration, 1872. This most famous arbitration (q.v.) case concerned a dispute between the United States and Great Britain. It originated in the failure of Great Britain during the American Civil War (1861-1865) to observe its duties as a neutral, in particular by permitting the vessel *Alabama* and her supply ship

The Georgia and some other vessels to be built and fitted out in British shipyards, officially for private owners but in reality for use by the Confederate States whose belligerent status under international law Great Britain had recognized against the Union's protests. As a Confederate raider *The Alabama* inflicted a very heavy toll upon the Union's ships, but was eventually sunk off the French coast by a Union warship in 1864.

Following the Civil War, negotiations between the United States and Great Britain led to the conclusion of the Treaty of Washington, 8 May 1871, (143 CTS 145), which provided for arbitration of the US claims against Great Britain by an arbitral tribunal meeting in Geneva. It consisted of five arbitrators, namely one member appointed by each litigant, the King of Italy, the "President" of Switzerland, and the Emperor of Brazil. The arbitrators were to apply the rules governing the duties of neutrals in maritime warfare, annexed to the text of the Treaty. These rules, subsequently known as the Three Rules of Washington, in general required a neutral state to exercise "due diligence" in order to prevent breaches of its obligations as a neutral in maritime warfare. The Three Rules of Washington largely represented the American point of view on neutrality in maritime warfare. For its part, Great Britain, while consenting to the rules binding the arbitration, declared that they imposed much more stringent duties upon the neutrals than those generally observed during the American Civil War when the *Alabama* claims originated.

On 14 September 1872, the Tribunal, by a vote of four to one (the vote of the British-appointed arbitrator who did not sign the award), rendered the award (1 Moore, I. Arb. 653) against Great Britain which was found to have failed, by omission, to use due diligence in the performance of its neutral obligations. As a compensation, the Tribunal awarded the United States a lump sum of $15.5 million in gold, which sum was eventually distributed by the US to individual claimants.

The *Alabama* case represents the beginning of a new phase in the development of the institution of modern arbitration. The award was a significant event, both as a model for future arbitral tribunals and as a stimulus for resort to this method of settling international disputes. And indeed, arbitration increased considerably following the success of the *Alabama* award. The case proved that arbitration was possible between great powers even when the issue affected their honor as was initially claimed by Great Britain.

Unlike arbitration by heads of state or by mixed claims commissions (q.v.) under the Jay Treaty (q.v.), the *Alabama* dispute was decided by a collegial international body which established a pattern for future arbitral tribunals. Some of the procedures applied in the case eventually received general acceptance and were codified in the 1899 Hague Convention for the Pacific Settlement of International Disputes (q.v.). In this way the *Alabama* arbitration paved the way for the establishment of the PCA (q.v.) and eventually the PCIJ (q.v.) and the ICJ (q.v.).

Ambatielos (Greece v. United Kingdom), ICJ 1951-1953. This protracted litigation between Greece and Great Britain eventually came before the ICJ (q.v.). It originated in the claims of Ambatielos, a Greek national who in 1919 purchased nine steamships, then under construction, from the British government and subsequently, in 1921, claimed that he had suffered loss through the failure of the British government to fulfill the contract in time. Ambatielos failed to win the case before English courts but considered it futile to appeal to the House of Lords. The Greek government espoused his claim in the exercise of the right of diplomatic protection of its national. In 1939 Greece contended that Great Britain had an obligation to submit the dispute to arbitration (q.v.) under a treaty of 1886 between the two countries. The British government denied this claim.

The matter was reopened following the Second World War, with Greece applying to the ICJ for a ruling that Great Britain had to agree to arbitration and that the ICJ had jurisdiction in the Ambatielos case, "sitting as an arbitral tribunal."

In its judgment of 1 July 1952 (1952 ICJ Rep. 28) on the British preliminary objections (q.v.), the ICJ decided, by a vote of 13 to two, that it could not deal with the merits of the Greek claim because its jurisdiction dated only from 1926 when another treaty between Greece and Great Britain replaced the original treaty of 1886 which was the only basis for examining the Ambatielos claim on its merits. On the other hand, in the same judgment the ICJ found, by a vote of ten to five, that it did have jurisdiction to decide whether Great Britain was under an obligation to submit to arbitration because a declaration attached to the 1926 treaty provided for the arbitration of "claims based upon the provisions of the [1886] treaty," including the Ambatielos claim which was brought under the 1886 treaty but after the conclusion of the treaty of 1926. Otherwise, as noted by the ICJ, such claims would not be subject to arbitration under either treaty. The ICJ judgment of 1952 is frequently quoted to confirm that in interpreting a treaty the principle of effectiveness is resorted to in order to give effect to provisions in accordance with the intentions of the parties.

In its judgment on the merits of 19 May 1953 (1953 ICJ Rep. 10) the ICJ ruled that Great Britain must enter into arbitration with Greece over the Ambatielos claim. In the resulting arbitration a commission of five arbitrators delivered an award on 6 March 1956 (12 UNRIAA 83) whereby, by a vote of five to one (the Greek arbitrator), it rejected the Greek claim on the grounds that despite receiving access to British courts under the equality of treatment principle Ambatielos failed to utilize the local, that is, British, remedies by not calling a vital witness and not exhausting his right of appeal. Hence this arbitration is usually invoked to illustrate the principle of the exhaustion of local remedies (q.v.).

American Arbitration Association (AAA). The AAA is a major US private non-profit organization administering international commercial arbitration (q.v.) services according to its own, optional, commercial arbitration rules. The AAA adopted such new rules in 1991. While the bulk of AAA arbitration involves domestic companies, a growing number of foreign companies, comprising mainly firms from US major trading partners such as Canada, the UK, Japan, and the Netherlands, have used the AAA arbitration system. In 1990 more than 200 such international cases were administered by the AAA.

Amministrazione delle Finanze dello Stato v. Simmenthal S. p. A., CJEC 1978. One of the landmark cases before the CJEC (q.v.) in which the Court proclaimed the supremacy of Community law over any inconsistent law of the member states (*see also* **Van Gend en Loos**).

In the facts of the case, Simmenthal, an Italian stock company (*società per azioni*) importing meat from France, sued the Italian government (its finance administration) for refund of health inspection fees collected under an Italian law of 1970 which Simmenthal claimed to be contrary to art. 30 of the Treaty of Rome of 25 March 1957 establishing the European Community, which prohibits "quantitative restrictions on imports and all measures having equivalent effect." The Italian magistrate (*pretore*) referred the question of the validity of the fees under the EC law to the CJEC which, in a preliminary ruling, held that they were invalid under art. 30. In accordance with this ruling, the Italian court ordered a refund of the fees, whereupon the Italian government appealed, contending that it had to apply Italian national law since the 1970 law in question had not been repealed by the Italian legislature or invalidated by the Italian Constitutional Court. The Italian court then referred the matter to the CJEC, asking it two questions designed to ascertain what consequences flowed from the direct applicability of a provision of the Community law in the event of incompatibility with a subsequent law of a member state, such as the Italian law of 1970 imposing fees on imports of meat.

In its decision of 8 March 1978 (Case 106/77 [1978] ECR 629) the CJEC held that a national court was called upon to apply the Community law and must give full and uniform effect to that law disregarding, of its own motion, any conflicting provisions of national legislation, even if adopted subsequently, and without waiting until such conflicting legislation has been repealed by the national legislature or declared unconstitutional.

Andean Court of Justice *see* **Court of Justice of the Cartagena Agreement**

Anglo-Iranian Oil Co. (United Kingdom v. Iran), ICJ 1951-1952. This case had its origin in a concession agreement concluded in 1931 between Iran and the British-owned Anglo-Iranian Oil Company under which the company was granted exclusive rights to explore and exploit oil in a defined area. Following the nationalization of the oil industry by Iran in 1951 the UK, espousing the company's claim, instituted proceedings before the ICJ (q.v.) on the basis of the optional clause (q.v.). It asked the Court to declare that Iran had the duty to submit the dispute to arbitration (q.v.), as stipulated by the concession agreement, or alternatively that the nationalization was in violation of this agreement and international law. Iran disputed the Court's jurisdiction (q.v.).

On 5 July 1951 the ICJ, at the request of the UK, indicated, in an order (1951 ICJ Rep. 89), interim measures of protection (provisional measures) (q.v.), which order was ignored by Iran, however. Subsequently, in its judgment of 22 July 1952 (1952 ICJ Rep. 93) the ICJ ruled, by nine votes to five, that it lacked jurisdiction, and terminated the interim protection order. In the judgment the Court upheld Iran's contention that the Iranian optional clause declaration, ratified on 19 September 1932, covered only disputes arising under treaties entered into by Iran after that date, whereas the British claim relied on treaties concluded prior to 1932. The Court also rejected the British contention that the concessionary agreement constituted an international act in the sense of a treaty governed by public international law.

Anzilotti, Dionisio (1867-1960). Italian national. Member of the PCIJ (q.v.) in the years 1922-1939. He was the most eminent Italian scholar in the area of international law and professor of international law at the Universities of Palermo (1902-1904), Bologna (1904-1911), and Rome (1911-1937). In the years 1920-1922 Anzilotti was Assistant Secretary General of the League of Nations. He was an influential scholar whose many works, including a popular treatise on international law, were translated into other languages. Anzilotti's individual opinions (q.v.), written during his tenure as a judge of the PCIJ, are of enduring value for the present World Court and the literature of international law.

Appeal Relating to the Jurisdiction of the ICAO Council (India v. Pakistan), ICJ 1971-1972. Following the unilateral suspension by India of overflights of its territory by Pakistani aircraft in 1971, Pakistan filed a complaint against India before the Council of the ICAO on the grounds that India had committed breaches of the

Chicago Convention of 1944 on International Civil Aviation and the related International Air Services Transport Agreement. The ICAO Council assumed jurisdiction by virtue of the relevant clauses of these treaties, but India claimed that the Council lacked jurisdiction (q.v.) because India had suspended these treaties as a result of a material breach by Pakistan, specifically Pakistan's compliance in the highjacking of an Indian plane.

On the basis of the appeal procedures of the two above-mentioned international agreements, India applied to the ICJ (q.v.) for a ruling that the ICAO Council lacked jurisdiction to deal with the case. Pakistan raised some objections to the Court's jurisdiction, but asked the Court to confirm the ICAO decision.

The ICJ, in its judgment of 18 August 1972 (1972 ICJ Rep. 46), decided, by a vote of 14 to two, that it had jurisdiction to determine whether or not the ICAO Council was competent to hear Pakistan's complaint and ruled, by 13 votes to three, that the dispute should go before the Council. The matter was, however, eventually settled by negotiations between the parties.

The Court's judgment in the case is of interest in that it contains considerations of the more general question of the right to unilaterally terminate or suspend a treaty on the ground of material breach by the other party.

Application for Revision and Interpretation of the Judgment of 24 February 1982 in the Case Concerning the Continental Shelf (Tunisia/Libyan Arab Jamahiriya) (Tunisia v. Libyan Arab Jamahiriya), ICJ 1984-1985. Following the ICJ (q.v.) judgment of 1982 in the case of *Continental Shelf* between Tunisia and Libya (q.v.), in 1984 Tunisia applied to the ICJ for an interpretation of a part of the judgment and revision of an alleged error in the judgment, related to the boundaries of an oil concession granted by Libya.

In its judgment of 10 December 1985 (1985 ICJ Rep. 192) the Court unanimously found inadmissible Tunisia's request for a revision of the 1982 judgment, but found admissible its request for interpretation. The ICJ then interpreted the relevant portions of the judgment, but ruled Tunisia's request for correcting an error without object.

Application of the Convention of 1902 Governing the Guardianship of Infants (Netherlands v. Sweden), ICJ 1957-1958. This case, brought before the ICJ (q.v.) under the parties' acceptance of the optional clause (q.v.), concerned a dispute between the Netherlands and Sweden over the compatibility with the Hague Convention of 12 June 1902 on the Guardianship of Infants (191 CTS 264) of the regime of protective upbringing, instituted with respect of a child of Dutch nationality. After the child's father had lost his appeal before the Swedish Supreme Court of Administrative Justice against the action of the Swedish authorities, the Netherlands espoused his claim, bringing the dispute before the ICJ.

The Netherlands claimed that the Swedish decision instituting the regime of protective upbringing with regard to the child was contrary to the Hague Convention which made the national law of the infant, that is the Dutch law, applicable to the child.

In its judgment of 28 November 1958 the Court, by 12 votes to four (1958 ICJ Rep. 55), rejected the Netherlands' claim on the ground that the Hague Convention did not include within its scope the protection of children as understood by the Swedish law concerned and, consequently, there was no violation of the Convention on the part of Sweden.

Three years following the ICJ judgment, the Convention of 1961 on the Protection of Infants (658 UNTS 143) settled the controversial issues underlying the dispute between the Netherlands and Sweden.

Arab Court of Justice. A judicial body for the League of Arab States the creation of which has been considered by the League. Drafts of a statute for such a court, modeled on the ICJ (q.v.), were submitted for consideration in 1951 and were discussed by Arab summit conferences, but so far no court has been established.

ARAMCO Arbitration, 1958. The dispute underlying this arbitration (q.v.) between Saudi Arabia and Arabian American Oil Co. (ARAMCO) originated in 1954 when, under an agreement with Saudi Arabia, an Onassis tanker company, SADCO, obtained a right of priority for transporting Saudi Arabian oil. In reaction to this, ARAMCO claimed that the agreement was in breach of its exclusive right to explore, exploit and transport Saudi oil, granted to ARAMCO under a concession agreement concluded in 1933 with the King of Saudi Arabia by Standard Oil Co. of California which, under that concession, assigned all its rights and obligations to ARAMCO. Unable to reach agreement, ARAMCO and Saudi Arabia submitted the matter to arbitration pursuant to the arbitration clause of the 1933 concession agreement.

In its award of 23 August 1958 (27 ILR 117), the arbitration tribunal of three arbitrators, sitting in Geneva, decided in favor of ARAMCO. It ruled that ARAMCO's exclusive rights acquired under the agreement of 1933, including the right to transport oil within and outside the Saudi Arabian territory, prevailed over those granted to the Onassis company in 1954.

The consideration by the tribunal of the question which law should govern the arbitration process and the merits of the case respectively is of considerable interest from the viewpoint of international law. As far as the former is concerned, the arbitration agreement (*compromis*) (q.v.) referred to the law of Saudi Arabia and--for matters beyond that state's jurisdiction--to other law as deemed appropriate by the tribunal. The tribunal decided that, under the circumstances of the case, international law should govern the arbitration process.

There were no provisions in the concession agreement of 1933 concerning which system of law should govern the interpretation and application of the agreement. The tribunal reached the conclusion that in accordance with principles of private international law and taking all the circumstances of the case into consideration, including the nature of the economic environment in which international oil transport operates, the concession agreement of 1933 should be governed by the law of Saudi Arabia interpreted and supplemented by general principles of law and customs prevailing in the oil business. This meant that the matters relating to international transport of oil at sea should be governed by international law in all those areas where ARAMCO's rights could not be safeguarded by the law of Saudi Arabia.

Like the *Abu Dhabi* Arbitration, 1951 (q.v.), the *ARAMCO* award is significant in that it deals with a concession agreement between a state and a foreign company and, in the absence of any clause governing the applicable law, recognizes the role of international law as a supplementary source in the interpretation of such agreements.

Arbitral Award Made by the King of Spain on 23 December 1906 (Honduras v. Nicaragua), ICJ 1950-1960. This dispute concerned the question of validity of a past arbitral award delivered in 1906 by the King of Spain, which delimited a disputed section of the border between Honduras and Nicaragua. The border had been delimited earlier by a mixed commission established under a treaty of 1894 which also provided for arbitration (q.v.) by Spain of the disputed sections. Nicaragua contested the validity of the award and after many years the dispute was brought before the ICJ (q.v.), Honduras asking the Court to declare that Nicaragua should give effect to the 1906 award and Nicaragua alleging its nullity on the grounds of error and inadequate reasons in support. Nicaragua also alleged that the King of Spain had not possessed the quality of arbitrator and, in any case, exceeded his jurisdiction.

In its judgment of 18 November 1960 (1960 ICJ Rep. 192) the ICJ, by 14 votes to one, decided in favor of Honduras. It ruled that the award was valid and legally binding and had no errors or omissions; that Nicaragua had agreed to the arbitration without raising any objections as to the legal capacity of the arbitrator; and had recognized the award as binding both by express declaration and its conduct.

Like some other judgments of the ICJ (for example *Temple of Preah Vihear* (q.v.)), the *Arbitral Award* case illustrates the principle of acquiescence in international law.

Arbitral Award of 31 July 1989 (Guinea-Bissau v. Senegal), ICJ 1989-1991. The proceedings in this case were instituted in 1989 by Guinea-Bissau against Senegal on the basis of the optional clause (q.v.) declarations of the two countries. At issue was the existence and validity of an arbitral award (*see* **Arbitration**) handed down on 31 July 1989 by the Arbitration Tribunal for the Determination of the Maritime Boundary between the two states.

Guinea alleged that the award in question was "inexistent" because the President of the Tribunal had attached a declaration to his vote allegedly contradicting his otherwise affirmative vote; that the award as a whole was null and void as the Tribunal had not given a complete answer to the twofold question raised by the Arbitration Agreement (*compromis*) (q.v.), and thus had not arrived at a single delimitation line to be recorded on a map which had not been provided; and that Senegal was not justified in seeking to require Guinea-Bissau to apply the controversial award.

Claiming that the Senegalese navy interfered with foreign fishing vessels in the disputed area, Guinea-Bissau requested the Court to indicate provisional measures (q.v.) under art. 41 of the Statute and art. 74 of the Rules of Court. The ICJ dismissed this request in the order of 2 March 1990, adopted by 14 votes to one (1990 ICJ Rep. 64), primarily because the alleged rights sought to be made the subject of provisional measures were not the subject of the proceedings before the Court on the merits of the case.

In its judgment of 12 November 1991 (1991 ICJ Rep.; 31 *ILM* 32 (1992)) the ICJ rejected all the submissions of Guinea-Bissau, finding, by the votes on the three questions ranging from unanimity to 12 to three, that the controversial arbitral award of 31 July 1989 did exist and was valid and binding for the two states which had the obligation to apply it.

It must be added that before the ICJ delivered its judgment, Guinea-Bissau had, on 12 March 1991, brought a new, still pending (*see* ANNEX IV: CASES PENDING BEFORE THE ICJ AS OF 15 JULY 1993), case against Senegal, asking the Court to determine the line delimiting the whole of the maritime territories appertaining respectively to Guinea-Bissau and Senegal.

Arbitral Commission on Property, Rights, and Interests in Germany. An international arbitral commission set up after the Second World War under the Convention on the Settlement of Matters Arising out of the War and Occupation (322 UNTS 219), the "Settlement Convention," and the annexed Charter, a part of the Bonn (1952) and Paris (1954) Agreements on Germany, whose function was to decide cases concerning recovery and restitution of property and rights of nationals of the allied countries, seized by Nazi Germany or its allies. The commission acted mainly as an appeal organ from German courts and administrative authorities. It consisted of nine members from allied and neutral countries and from Germany and Italy. Under its Charter, the Commission applied primarily the provisions of the Settlement Convention and related legislation, but principles of international law and justice and equity (*see* **Ex Aequo et Bono and Equity**) could also be applied where necessary. During its existence (1956-1969) the Commission dealt with 432 appeals. It rendered 162 decisions and otherwise disposed of the remaining 270. It is interesting to note that most of the decisions favored the Federal Republic of Germany.

Arbitral Tribunals under Annex VII of the UN Convention on the Law of the Sea of 1982. These are tribunals in one of the four categories of procedure of compulsory settlement of disputes concerning the application and interpretation of the UN Convention on the Law of the Sea of 1982 (*see* **International Tribunal for the Law of the Sea**). According to Annex VII of the Convention, any party to a dispute, whether a state or an entity other than a state, may submit a dispute to arbitration (q.v.) by a tribunal constituted in accordance with the Convention. Under the complex provisions of Annex VII, an arbitral tribunal is made up of five members, one chosen by each party and the remaining three chosen jointly from a panel of individuals with experience in maritime affairs, maintained by the UN, to which each state party to the Convention is entitled to nominate four potential arbitrators. If no agreement is reached on choosing the three arbitrators, they are appointed by the President of the ITLOS. Unless otherwise agreed upon by the parties, the award of an arbitral tribunal is final. As of 31 December 1993, the Convention of 1982 was not yet in force.

Arbitration. A peaceful method of legally binding settlement of international disputes by one or more arbitrators of the parties' choice, according to procedures set forth by the parties and, to a certain extent, according to the law indicated by them, and on the basis of voluntary submission and respect for law. In a general sense, arbitration is a method of judicial settlement of international disputes (*see* INTRODUCTION) and an arbitral decision ("award") is legally binding. Arbitration differs, however, from the judicial settlement in the strict sense of the term in that the disputing parties normally have the freedom to select arbitrators and, to some extent, determine the procedure and the law to be applied. Arbitration differs from conciliation (q.v.) in that the arbitral award is legally binding upon the parties whereas the conciliation report only suggests the terms of settlement because conciliation does not belong to the judicial methods of settling international disputes. An agreement between states formally called "conciliation agreement" is, in fact, an agreement submitting a dispute to arbitration, if the parties agree to be legally bound by the conciliator's decision.

In general, arbitration may be between states over matters governed by public international law; it may be between states and private persons, normally juridical persons (*see* for example **Abu Dhabi Arbitration; ARAMCO Arbitration**) or it may be international commercial arbitration (q.v.) involving commercial disputes between enterprises from different states, private or state-owned. This entry deals primarily with disputes between states; it is with such disputes that international arbitration is mainly associated.

Arbitration of a dispute which has arisen between parties always requires their consent, usually formalized in an international agreement known as *compromis* (q.v.) or *compromis d'arbitrage* which sets forth the terms of reference for the tribunal or court, whatever the term may be, such as the applicable procedure and law, possibly the right to decide *ex aequo et bono* (*see* **Ex Aequo et Bono and Equity**), that is, generally speaking, on extralegal grounds of equity and justice; and any other provision deemed desirable by the parties. The tribunal is competent to decide upon matters not addressed by the *compromis*, including its competence to determine its own jurisdiction (q.v.), a principle dating back to the arbitration commissions established by the Jay Treaty (q.v.) of 1794.

Consent to submit to arbitration an international dispute that may arise in the future is expressed either in a general arbitration treaty, whereby the parties undertake to submit to arbitration all disputes or a specific class of disputes, or in a clause in some other treaty which provides, *inter alia*, that disputes arising in regard to its interpretation and application will be settled by arbitration. However, in international practice, a *compromis* is usually required as a precondition for submitting a dispute covered by the treaty to arbitration.

An arbitral tribunal may consist of a single arbitrator (for example in the *Palmas* Arbitration) (q.v.), sometimes a head of a third state who delegates his charge to experts, or it may be a collegial body. In the latter case it is usually a mixed commission of odd number, made up of arbitrators or "commissioners" selected in equal number by the parties, and an umpire named by the arbitrators (commissioners) or appointed by the parties.

Although in a number of arbitration cases in the 19th century the tribunals were directed by the parties to resort to principles of justice and equity, by the end of the century the arbitration tribunals decided cases according to international law. That is why the distinction between arbitration and judicial settlement by international tribunals and courts in the strict sense of the terms has become formal rather than substantive.

As a rule, arbitration procedure follows some generally accepted rules on the subject, such as those in the Hague Convention for the Pacific Settlement of International Disputes (q.v.) or model rules prepared by an international organization such as those in the General Act for the Pacific Settlement of International Disputes of 1928 (q.v.), or the European Convention of 1957 for the Peaceful Settlement of Disputes (320 UNTS 243).

Unless otherwise agreed upon by the parties, an arbitral award is final and binding. There is, however, a possibility of revision because of discovery of new decisive facts. The validity of an arbitral award may be challenged by either party, but what precisely the grounds of a challenge may be is not a settled issue. There have been few instances of repudiating an arbitral award. The US rejection in 1911 of the arbitral award in the *Chamizal* case (q.v.) and the rejection by Argentina of the 1977 arbitration award in the *Beagle Channel* (q.v.) case are among the few such instances. In general, the following grounds for invalidation have been invoked in arbitral practice, as stated by the International Law Commission (ILC), a subsidiary organ of the UN General Assembly charged with the codification and development of international law, in its Model Rules of 1958: 1. that the undertaking to arbitrate or the *compromis* was invalid; 2. that the tribunal exceeded its powers, for example by deciding on an issue not submitted to it or by applying a kind of law not authorized by the *compromis*; 3. that there has been failure to set forth the reasons for the award or a serious departure from a fundamental rule of procedure; and 4. that there was corruption or fraud on the part of a member of the tribunal. In the last-mentioned situation, extreme corruption of commissioners on both sides caused setting aside an award rendered by the US-Venezuela commission in 1868. The definition of "essential" or "manifest" error as a ground for nullity is not entirely clear.

The history of arbitration between states dates back to ancient Greece where arbitration was practiced in relations between city-states. To a certain degree, arbitration was also known in the Middle Ages in Europe, but subsequently fell into disuse in the early centuries of the modern European state system, although arbitration clauses were occasionally included in treaties in the 17th and 18th centuries.

The history of modern arbitration is usually traced back to the Jay Treaty of 1794 (q.v.) (52 CTS 243) between the US and Great Britain which provided for arbitration of claims for war damage sustained by British and US nationals respectively. The commissions established under the Treaty rendered more than 500 awards and inaugurated a widespread practice of arbitration in the 19th century. State responsibility for injury to aliens was the most common subject matter treated by these "mixed claims commissions" (q.v.), the 19th century forerunners of the post-World War I "mixed arbitration tribunals" (q.v.).

The *Alabama* Arbitration (q.v.) award of 1872 in the dispute between the US and Great Britain represents a turning point in the history of arbitration between states because, in a departure from the mixed claims commission model, it inaugurated a parallel institution of a truly third-party collegial arbitral body made up preferably of jurists familiar with international law.

Apart from an interesting permanent machinery set up by the UPU in 1874 for arbitral settlement of disputes between states members of the Union, the next important landmark in the history of arbitration was the First Hague Peace Conference of 1899 which codified the methods of pacific settlement, including arbitral procedure, in the Hague Convention for the Pacific Settlement of International Disputes (q.v.) (187 CTS 410), subsequently revised (205 CTS 277) by the Second Hague Peace Conference in 1907.

The Convention created a "Permanent Court of Arbitration" (q.v.) which, however, was only a roster of potential arbitrators. Attempts to create a real permanent tribunal or to secure acceptance by states of a firm obligation to submit their disputes to arbitration ended in failure. Moreover, since the first standing arbitration treaty was concluded between France and Great Britain in 1903, non-legal or "political" disputes were not arbitrable (*see* **Justiciability of International Disputes**) according to such treaties. Under special "restrictive clauses," disputes affecting "vital interests, the independence, or the honor of the two Contracting Parties" were excluded from the duty to arbitrate. There were also other reservations, such as those concerning interests of third states, territorial integrity, sovereign rights, and matters of domestic jurisdiction. Some of the reservations in effect virtually eliminated the parties' obligation to submit their disputes to arbitration.

Following the First World War the establishment of the PCIJ (q.v.) overshadowed the institution of arbitration. Still, various "mixed arbitral tribunals" (q.v.) settling disputes resulting from claims of private individuals affected by the war became very common. The number of "mixed claims commissions" (q.v.) of the 19th century type had declined, however; the nine such commissions dealing with US-Mexican claims are the best known.

As part of its work on codifying the system of the peaceful methods of settling international disputes, in 1924 the League of Nations adopted the General Protocol for Pacific Settlement of International Disputes (19 *AJIL* 9 (1925 Supp.)) which provided for referral of political disputes to arbitration and conciliation (q.v.), and in 1928 drafted the General Act for the Pacific Settlement of International Disputes (q.v.) which envisaged arbitration of political disputes as one method of settlement. In America, the General Treaty of Inter-American Arbitration of 5 January 1929 (130 LNTS 135) followed a similar path. A number of bilateral and subregional treaties required reference of legal disputes to arbitration. However, apart from the mixed arbitral tribunals (q.v.) dealing with private claims, not much use was made of arbitration between states in the inter-war period. The US-Netherlands *Palmas* (q.v.) case and the Portugal-Germany *Naulilaa* (q.v.) dispute were the major arbitrations of that period.

Under the UN Charter, arbitration is recognized in art. 33 as one of the methods of pacific settlement of disputes. In 1949 the UN General Assembly revised the 1928 General Act for the Pacific Settlement of International Disputes and adopted optional Model Rules of Arbitral Procedure. In addition, in 1990 the UN Secretary General prepared a Draft Handbook on Pacific Settlement which, among other subjects, elaborates on arbitration.

References to arbitration have been included in numerous post-World War II bilateral treaties and multilateral instruments such as the European Convention for the Pacific Settlement of Disputes of 27 April 1957 which provides for arbitration of non-legal disputes and the Report of 8 February 1991 of the CSCE meeting of experts on settlement of disputes.

While international commercial arbitration (q.v.) has proliferated in the post-World War II era, especially in the past two decades, arbitration of disputes between states has not been very common. Among the latter, mainly *ad hoc*, arbitrations were: the *Rann of Kutch* (q.v.) case between India and Pakistan concerning the determination of a section of their common border, 1968 (17 UNRIAA 1); the arbitration over the delimitation of the continental shelf between the UK and France, 1977 (18 UNRIAA 3) (q.v.), with an interpreting award in 1978 (18 UNRIAA 271); another arbitration between the UK and France of 1978 concerning the interpretation of the Air Services Agreement (54 ILR 304); an arbitration of 1980 concerning the interpretation of the Agreement on German External Debt between Belgium, France, Switzerland, the UK, and the US on the one hand and West Germany on the other (19 ILM 1357 (1980)); an arbitration between Guinea and Guinea-Bissau of 1985 concerning delimitation of their maritime boundary (25 ILM 251 (1986)); the arbitration of 1988 between Egypt and Israel concerning the sovereignty over the Taba (q.v.) area (27 ILM 1421 (1988)); the arbitration of 1990 between France and New Zealand concerning the return of the French citizens accused of destroying the Greenpeace ship, the *Rainbow Warrior*; and the 1992 arbitration award in the dispute between the US and Chile concerning responsibility for the death of Letelier and Noffitt (31 ILM 1 (1992)). The dispute between Argentina and Chile over the determination of their maritime boundary in the Beagle Channel (q.v.) went through several stages. It was first decided in 1977 by an arbitral award of the Queen of England (17 ILM 631 (1978)) as nominal arbitrator, the actual tribunal consisting of five judges of the ICJ. However, Argentina rejected it as null and void (17 ILM 738 (1978)), a rare instance of a party repudiating an arbitral award. Subsequently, in 1979, the two countries agreed to mediation by the Pope (18 ILM 1 (1979)) whose proposals eventually led to an agreement between Argentina and Chile resolving the dispute in 1984 (24 ILM 10 (1985)).

The development of arbitration dealing with economic disputes between states and foreign private enterprises has been a significant trend in international arbitration. The cases of *Abu Dhabi* (q.v.), *ARAMCO* (q.v.), and three cases against Libya: *British Petroleum* (q.v.), *LIAMCO* (q.v.) and *TOPCO & CAOC* (q.v.) are examples of such arbitrations, as are the decisions within the framework of the International Centre for Settlement of Investment Disputes (q.v.). The Iran-US Claims Tribunal (q.v.) also belongs to this category of dispute settlement. By far most widely used are various arbitration institutes operating within the concept of international commercial arbitration (q.v.) such as the International Chamber of Commerce (ICC) Court of Arbitration (q.v.), the American Arbitration Association (AAA) (q.v.), and numerous other national arbitral institutions offering their services in settling international commercial disputes. Because of its flexibility and less formal nature, arbitration has become an increasingly popular method of resolving international investment and commercial disputes.

Argentina-Chile Frontier Dispute: Arbitration Award of Queen Elizabeth II, 1966. This arbitration (q.v.) involved an old territorial dispute between Argentina and Chile over certain sectors of their common border in the Andes, unsettled since an earlier arbitration by King Edward VII in 1902. The controversy centered on difficulties over exact delimitation of the boundary, caused by an apparent error of the demarcation commission which wrongly identified the course of the river Encuentro in 1903.

Under a *compromis* (q.v.) drawn up by Great Britain, a court of arbitration made up of three members, including two geographers, was requested to determine the course of the boundary in the contested sector of some 260 square miles. Formally, the award was made by Queen Elizabeth II on 9 December 1966 on the basis of the report of the court of arbitrators (16 UNRIAA 109). In an attempt to determine the real intention of the arbitrator in the 1902 award, the court of arbitrators ruled that the Eastern channel of the river Encuentro was the major channel determining the boundary as far as to the point where it began to deviate from the direction of the peak Cerro de Virgen named as a boundary mark in the award of 1902. The final boundary delimitation according to the award of 1966 left 71 percent of the disputed area to Argentina. It is noteworthy that the award was carried out without undue delay, unlike a subsequent award by Queen Elizabeth II in another arbitration which concerned the Argentina-Chile Beagle Channel (q.v.) dispute eventually settled through Papal mediation.

Asylum (Colombia/Peru) and Haya de la Torre (Colombia v. Peru), ICJ 1949-1951. This case before the ICJ (q.v.) is of special interest to Latin America where rules of international regional law allow in certain cases asylum in diplomatic premises of a foreign country. The case produced three judgments: (1) *Asylum (Colombia/Peru)* (1950); (2) *Request for Interpretation of the Judgment of 20 November 1950 in the Asylum Case (Colombia/Peru)* (1950); and (3) *Haya de la Torre (Colombia v. Peru)* (1951).

Haya de la Torre, a Peruvian national and a leader of an unsuccessful military rebellion in Peru, after three months in hiding was granted asylum in the Colombian embassy in Lima on 3 January 1949. Colombia sought a safe conduct from the government of Peru to allow the fugitive out of Peru. The Peruvian government, however, sought surrender of Haya de la Torre as a common criminal and contested Colombia's claim to unilaterally determine the nature of his offense as a political offense producing Colombia's right to grant the fugitive diplomatic asylum under the Havana Convention on Asylum of 1928 (22 *AJIL Suppl.* 158 (1928)) and Latin American regional international law in general.

The two countries agreed to bring the dispute before the ICJ which in its judgment of 20 November 1950 (1950 ICJ Rep. 266), by a vote of nine to six, ruled against Colombia on the ground that Colombia had no right to unilaterally qualify the offense in question. The Court found that no such right existed under the Havana Convention or any other convention, including the Montevideo Convention of 1933 on Political Asylum which, while recognizing the right of unilateral qualification, was not ratified by Colombia. Furthermore, as held by the Court, Colombia failed to prove the existence of a constant and uniform rule of customary law in Latin America, allowing unilateral qualification by the state granting diplomatic asylum to a fugitive. The Court also found that Peru was under no obligation to grant Haya de la Torre a safe conduct to leave Peru. Concerning Peru's counterclaim, it was ruled by the Court that, while the offense in question, a military rebellion, was political in nature, justifying the grant of asylum in urgent cases according the Havana Convention, there was no urgency present in the Haya de la Torre situation, and therefore the grant of asylum was not in compliance with the Convention.

Immediately following the delivery of the judgment of 20 November 1950, Colombia requested an interpretation of it, specifically asking the Court to clarify the question whether it should surrender Haya de la Torre to Peru. In response to this request, in its second judgment, delivered on 27 November 1950 (1950 ICJ Rep. 395), the ICJ, by a unanimous vote, refused to clarify the issues raised by Colombia's request on the ground that they were new issues requiring institution of new proceedings.

Consequently, Colombia filed an application requesting the Court's judgment concerning the question whether or not it was obliged to surrender Haya de la Torre to Peru. In its (third) judgment, 13 June 1951, in this new case, *Haya de la Torre* (*Colombia v. Peru*) (1951 ICJ Rep. 71) the Court held, by 13 votes to one, that under the Havana Convention Colombia was under no obligation to surrender political offenders. On the other hand, the Court ruled unanimously that the asylum in question should be terminated immediately. The ICJ found no contradiction in its position, suggesting that the asylum could be terminated by methods other than surrender. In reality Haya de la Torre did not leave the Colombian embassy in Lima and the territory of Peru until 1954.

The *Asylum* and *Haya de la Torre* cases are of special interest to Latin America where, unlike under general international law, regional rules allow, in certain situations, the right of asylum to political offenders in premises of a Latin American diplomatic representation.

The Court's first judgment reconfirms the principle of general international law that a country invoking the existence of a customary rule of international law must prove that by virtue of a constant and uniform usage accepted as law such rule is also binding on the other party. However, it can be argued that where a general or universal customary rule of law is invoked, a lower standard of proof is required than in the case of proving the existence of an alleged regional customary rule of international law.

Austro-German Property Arbitral Tribunal, 1961-1973. An arbitral tribunal set up under the Austro-German Property Treaty of 15 June 1957 concerning transfer to German nationals (individuals) of their former property in Austria and the question of debts connected with such property. The tribunal's function was to deliver, at the request of a domestic court, opinions interpreting the Treaty, which were then binding for the national courts. The Tribunal consisted of four judges: two from the Federal Republic of Germany and two from Austria. Its decisions were made unanimously, but in the case of disagreement the two states appointed a neutral chairman as the fifth member. In hardship cases the Tribunal was competent to reduce the debtor's debt on grounds of equity (*see* **Ex Aequo et Bono and Equity**). As a rule, however, it decided on the basis of international law and principles common to Austria and the Federal Republic. During its existence the Tribunal dealt with 107 cases.

Automatic (Self-Judging) Reservation. A reservation to acceptance by a state of the compulsory jurisdiction (q.v.) of the ICJ (q.v.) under the optional clause (q.v.) of the ICJ Statute whereby the accepting state unilaterally claims the right to determine the scope of this reservation, for example the reservation exempting from the Court's jurisdiction all matters of domestic jurisdiction. The history of the automatic or self-judging reservation in the ICJ dates back to 1946 when the US qualified its acceptance of the optional clause by excluding from the ICJ jurisdiction "disputes with regard to matters essentially within the domestic jurisdiction of the United States," and--what is expressive of the reservation--adding the phrase "as determined by the United States of America" (1 UNTS 9). Since the initiative in this respect originated with Senator Thomas Connally from Texas, the automatic reservation became popularly known as "Connally reservation" or "Connally amendment." As far as the US is concerned, the self-judging reservation is of historical interest only, in view of the fact that after 40 years, in 1986, the US terminated its acceptance of the optional clause as a whole, for reasons related to the ICJ case concerning *Military and Paramilitary Activities in and against Nicaragua* (q.v.). However, the self-judging (automatic) reservation as such is still retained by Liberia, Malawi, Mexico, the Philippines, and the Sudan.

The self-judging reservation operates automatically, enabling a state to determine subjectively and unilaterally whether or not a case brought against it falls within the scope of its acceptance of the ICJ contentious jurisdiction (q.v.) under art. 36(2) of the Court's Statute, that is, under the optional clause. Hence it has the potential for limiting the Court's optional system of compulsory jurisdiction inasmuch as by virtue of reciprocity a reservation filed by a state party to a dispute can be invoked by the other party or parties, thus depriving the Court of jurisdiction in the case. For example, in 1957 Norway, against which France had instituted proceedings before the ICJ in the case of *Certain Norwegian Loans* (q.v.), invoked the self-judging domestic jurisdiction reservation of the French optional clause declaration, as a result of which the ICJ declined jurisdiction without considering the validity of the reservation on which Norway so successfully relied. Similarly, in the *Aerial Incident of 27 July 1955* case (US v. Bulgaria) (*see* ANNEX V) the defendant state Bulgaria invoked the US Connally reservation whereupon the US withdrew its suit before the ICJ ruled on its jurisdiction.

The ICJ has so far refrained from pronouncing on the legal status of the automatic reservation. However, some ICJ judges in their individual opinions (q.v.) and numerous publicists in their writings have questioned the legality of the reservation, arguing that it contradicts the power of the Court under art. 36(6) of the

Statute to determine its own jurisdiction in the event of a dispute on this matter. Some judges, including Lauterpacht (q.v.) and Spender, have expressed the opinion that since a reservation cannot be detached from the remaining body of the acceptance of compulsory jurisdiction, the entire optional clause declaration must be null and void. In another view, only the automatic reservation is invalid while the other parts of the declaration remain unaffected.

The application of the principle of reciprocity as well as judicial and doctrinal criticism of the automatic reservation has led some countries, which had previously included such reservations in their respective optional clause declarations (France, India, Pakistan, the UK), to abandon them in accepting the ICJ jurisdiction under the optional clause.

B

Badawi, Abd-Al-Hamid (1887-1965). Egyptian national. Lawyer, diplomat and statesman. Member of the ICJ (q.v.), 1946-1965, and its Vice-President, 1955-1958. Minister of Finance, 1940-1942; member of Senate, 1942-1946; Minister of Foreign Affairs, 1945-1946. Delegate at San Francisco Conference, 1945.

Barcelona Traction, Light and Power Company, Limited (Belgium v. Spain), ICJ 1958-1961 and (New Application) 1962-1970. This important case concerned the complex question of the right of diplomatic protection of corporations and shareholders and some other issues related to the status of transnational ("multinational") corporations in international law. A corporation incorporated in Canada, named Barcelona Traction, whose business was to produce and distribute electricity in Spain, was owned by a Canadian corporation which was in turn owned, as much as 90 percent, by Belgian shareholders, both individuals and juridical persons. As a result of certain measures taken by the Spanish government against Barcelona Traction, its shareholders, including Belgian nationals, suffered losses. After litigation before Spanish courts had failed to produce a satisfactory outcome, in 1958 Belgium initiated proceedings against Spain before the ICJ (q.v.) with the object of obtaining reparation for alleged damage caused to Barcelona Traction by the actions of Spain. In 1961 the proceedings were discontinued at Belgium's request, but after unsuccessful attempts at out-of-court settlement they were resumed by a new application of Belgium in 1962. Spain raised four preliminary objections (q.v.) against the Belgian application. In its judgment of 24 July 1964 (1964 ICJ Rep. 6), the ICJ, by 12 votes to four, rejected two of these (which were of jurisdictional nature) and joined to the merits the other two which alleged inadmissibility of the Belgian claim and failure to exhaust local remedies (q.v.) respectively.

The second phase of the proceedings concluded with the Court's judgment on the merits delivered on 5 February 1970 (1970 ICJ Rep. 3). The Court held, by 14 votes to one, that Belgium had no standing to bring the case before the ICJ on behalf of a company incorporated in Canada even though that company was largely controlled by Belgian nationals. Only if the company had gone into liquidation could Belgium, the state of the shareholders' nationality, make a claim in respect of the losses suffered by them as a result of damage inflicted upon the company.

In the *Barcelona Traction* case the ICJ declined to pierce the corporate veil, rejecting any analogy with the *Nottebohm* (q.v.) case and its genuine link concept applied for purposes of the diplomatic protection of individuals. However, with one judge, the Belgian *ad hoc* judge (q.v.), dissenting and nine writing individual opinions (q.v.), the Court failed to exhaustively clarify and reach full consensus on the controversial issues of the nationality of corporations raised in the *Barcelona Traction* proceedings.

Baxter, Richard R. (1921-1980). US national. Judge of the ICJ (q.v.), 1979-1980. Also member of the PCA (q.v.), 1968-1975. A graduate of Brown University, Baxter received his law degree from Harvard Law School and Master of Law degree from Georgetown University. He also studied international law at Cambridge University. After joining the Faculty of Harvard Law School in 1954 he eventually became Manley O. Hudson Professor of Law. He served on the US State Department's Advisory Committee on the Law of the Sea, 1973-1978, and the Advisory Panel on International Law, 1970-1975. He served as Editor-in-Chief of the *AJIL* in the years 1970-1978. Baxter published numerous works on international law.

Beagle Channel Arbitration, 1977. This arbitration (q.v.) concerned a protracted dispute between Argentina and Chile over which of them had, under their 1881 boundary treaty (189 CTS 45), title to three little islands at the eastern entrance to the Beagle Channel at the southern tip of South America. Finally, the two countries agreed in 1971 to submit their dispute to arbitration by the British government, pursuant to the arbitration treaty of 28 May 1902. The *compromis* (q.v.) to this effect, signed by the two parties and the UK (10 ILM 1182 (1971)), provided for a British-appointed

arbitration tribunal of five members, all judges of the ICJ (q.v.),
with Queen Elizabeth II only accepting or rejecting their award.

Interpreting the 1881 boundary treaty in favor of Chile, the
tribunal, in its award of 22 April 1977, approved by the Queen (17
AJIL 632 (1978)), unanimously awarded the three contested
islands to Chile. However, Argentina rejected the award in its
Note of 25 January 1978 (17 ILM 738 (1978)), declaring it null
and void on the ground of alleged excess of jurisdiction by the
tribunal. This was one of the rare cases in history of rejecting an
award by a state party to an arbitration agreement.

The relations between Argentina and Chile deteriorated sharply
to the brink of an armed conflict. Eventually, however, they
accepted mediation by Pope John Paul II (18 ILM 1 (1979)) which
led to a diplomatic resolution of the dispute in 1984 (24 ILM 10
(1985)) whereby Argentina agreed to Chile's sovereignty over the
three islands in return for Chile's concessions relative to waters on
the Atlantic side of Cape Horn.

Behring Sea Arbitration, 1893. This was an important arbitration
(q.v.) between Great Britain and the US concerning their dispute
over the rights of seal fishing and exercising protective jurisdiction
over seals in the Behring Sea beyond the three-mile territorial sea
limit. As a successor of Russia from which it had acquired Alaska
under the treaty of cession of March 1867 (134 CTS 331), the US
claimed, over British protests, an exclusive right to sealing outside
of the territorial waters of Alaska. In the exercise of this claim, it
seized a number of British vessels on the ground of alleged illegal
catching of seals. The US argued that under the treaty of cession
of 1867 the sealing jurisdiction in the Behring Sea had passed to
it from Russia whose jurisdiction in the matter had been
recognized by both the US and Great Britain.

The protracted dispute generated by the US claim was
submitted by the two countries to arbitration under a *compromis*
(q.v.) signed in 1892. In its award of 15 August 1893 (179 CTS 97)
the tribunal ("Joint Commission") of seven arbitrators (two British
subjects, two Americans, a Frenchman, an Italian, and a
Norwegian) decided in favor of Great Britain, holding that Russia
had never asserted sealing jurisdiction in the Behring Sea beyond
the territorial sea; that Great Britain had never conceded such

jurisdiction; and that the US had no rights of protection of or property in seals, wild or domesticated, found beyond the limits of the territorial sea. The tribunal also formulated binding regulations for the protection of pelagic seals and referred the question of damages claimed by Great Britain to a mixed commission of two commissioners.

In historical perspective, the Behring Sea arbitration is regarded as an important step in the development of international legal rules for the protection and conservation of marine mammals and the living resources of the sea in general.

Belgian "Linguistic" Case, ECHR 1968. In this *Case Relating to Certain Aspects of the Law on the Use of Languages in Education in Belgium*, the ECHR (q.v.) delivered judgment on 23 July 1968 ([1968] ECHR. Ser. A, no. 4, reprinted in 8 ILM 825 (1969)) concerning alleged breaches by Belgium of the provisions of the European Convention for the Protection of Human Rights and Fundamental Freedoms of 4 November 1950 (213 UNTS 221) and Protocol No. 1 of 20 March 1952 (213 UNTS 262), guaranteeing the right to eduction to all without discrimination on the ground, *inter alia*, of language.

The proceedings in this case originated in a complaint lodged by the residents of five communes, in the Dutch-speaking part of Belgium and some residents from the French-speaking commune of Kraainem, with the European Commission of Human Rights, alleging that the Belgian state was failing to provide adequately for the education of their children in French. They claimed that this failure was in breach of art. 14 of the European Convention which guaranteed enjoyment of the rights protected by the Convention, especially those listed in articles 8-10, without discrimination on any ground, and of art. 2 of Protocol No. 1 guaranteeing the right to education. The matter was referred by the Commission to the ECHR.

For purposes of determining the language of instruction in state and state-supported schools, Belgium is divided into unilingual, Dutch, French, and German areas, and bilingual areas with special bilingual arrangements depending on the child's maternal or usual language. In the six applicant communes, all belonging to the latter areas, Dutch is the normal language of instruction but, at the request of 16 family heads in a commune, children may receive kindergarten and primary, but not secondary, education in French provided that the family head resides in one of the communes.

The judgment of the ECHR of 23 July 1968 held partly for the Belgian state and partly for the applicant communes. By eight votes to seven the Court ruled that the Belgian state was in breach of the Convention and Protocol No. 1 only insofar as the linguistic arrangements prevented certain children, solely on the basis of their parents' residence, from having access to the French-language schools in the six communes. On the other hand, as held by the Court, the right to education did not necessarily oblige the government to educate everybody in a particular language; the principle of the quality of treatment could be departed from if it had an objective and reasonable justification. This was the case if it was pursuing a legitimate aim such as efficient instruction, and the means employed to achieve it were in reasonable relationship of proportionality to such aim. In one commune, this aim could be achieved by making other arrangements that placed a lesser burden upon the children of the French-speaking minority.

Benelux Economic Union College of Arbitrators. An arbitral body set up under the Treaty of 3 February 1958 (5 *EYb* 167 (1957)) establishing the Benelux Economic Union, whose function is to settle disputes between the members of the Union, that is Belgium, Luxemburg and the Netherlands, which could not be resolved by the Union's Committee of Ministers. A Statute of the Committee lays down the rules governing the structure and functions of the College.

The College has not been very active since disputes between members of the Union are usually settled at the level of the Council of Ministers.

Benelux Economic Union Court of Justice (Benelux-EUCJ). A judicial body of the Benelux Economic Union, established by treaty in 1965 (13 *EYb* 237 (1965)), whose main function is to interpret the law of the Union. The Court consists of nine judges and six deputy judges elected in equal numbers by each member country from among the Supreme Court justices of each of them.

There are also three advocates-general and three registrars.

The Court has the competence to interpret, through preliminary review of legal questions referred to it by courts, not the entire body of Benelux law but only expressly designated legal rules, namely specific treaties and decisions of the Committee of Ministers not only in the economic sphere but also in other areas going beyond the economic competences of the Union. The Court can also deliver advisory opinions (q.v.) at the request of a member government and serves as an administrative tribunal (q.v.) for the staff of the Benelux Secretariat and two other Benelux agencies.

British Petroleum Arbitration, 1973 and 1974. This was one of the three major arbitrations (q.v.) resulting from nationalization by Libya of foreign oil companies, in this case the assets of British Petroleum (BP), taken over by Libya in 1971 contrary to the concession agreement of 1957 which provided, *inter alia*, that the concession agreement could be altered only by mutual consent of the parties. The agreement contained an arbitration clause, but Libya refused to appoint an arbitrator and participate in the arbitration, whereupon BP, pursuant to the agreement, requested the President of the ICJ (q.v.) to appoint a sole arbitrator. A Swedish jurist was duly appointed and, sitting in Copenhagen, delivered the award on 10 October 1973 (53 ILR 297).

The sole arbitrator found for the claimant company, ruling that the nationalization of the BP assets was arbitrary and discriminatory in character. However, he found that restitution in kind would not be appropriate and awarded damages instead, the approach followed by the sole arbitrator in the *LIAMCO* arbitration in 1977 (q.v.) but not in the *TOPCO & CAOC* arbitration, 1977 (q.v.).

In the arbitration procedure the arbitrator followed the Danish law. Pursuant to the concession agreement, the merits of his award were governed by those principles of the Libyan law which were consistent with international law complemented, if needed, by general principles of law.

In another award, on 1 August 1974 the sole arbitrator rejected the claimant's request to reopen the proceedings on the grounds of alleged errors and incompleteness of the award. However, the parties reached an out-of-court settlement on 20 November 1974 whereby Libya paid BP a sum of £17.4 million in compensation for the expropriation. Along with such cases as *ARAMCO* (q.v.), *LIAMCO* (q.v.), and *TOPCO & CAOC* (q.v.), the BP arbitration is significant as an example of arbitration between a state and a private company in which principles of international law and general principles of law were found applicable to the decisions on the substance of the disputes concerned.

Bustamante y Rivero, José Luis (1894-1975). Peruvian national. Member of the ICJ (q.v.) in the years 1961-1970. Bustamante y Rivero was professor of law at the University of Arequipa and author of numerous works on international law and organization.

Bustamante y Sirvén, Antonio Sánchez de (1865-1951). Cuban national. Bustamante y Sirvén was one of the most renowned Latin American publicists of the pre-World War II era. He was expert in both public and private international law and authored some very well known works in these areas, of which his Code of private international law, the "Bustamante Code," and a five-volume treatise on public international law are standard works in the Latin American literature. What is most noteworthy, however, is that Bustamante y Sirvén was judge of the PCIJ (q.v.) throughout most of the Court's existence, 1921-1939.

C

Canada-United States Free Trade Agreement: Dispute Settlement.
The Canada-US Free Trade Agreement of 22 December 1987 and
2 January 1988 (27 ILM 281 (1988)), designed to remove trade
barriers between the two countries, envisages two arrangements
for settling international disputes: one for general category
disputes and another for the special category of cases involving
anti-dumping and countervailing duty cases, both arrangements
conceived as a substitute for judicial review of unfair trade
practices in Canada-US relations.

Disputes belonging to the general category which could not be
resolved through consultation within 30 days are referred to a
Canada-US Trade Commission. If within 30 days the Commission
is unable to resolve the matter, it then may refer it to a binational
panel of experts which, by consensus, prepares a report for the
Commission or for a binational arbitration panel of five members
chosen from a roster of potential panelists maintained by the
Commission. The decision of the arbitration panel is binding upon
the parties.

The resolution of disputes involving a review of final orders
concerning US and Canadian anti-dumping and countervailing
duties follows a special procedure before a binational panel of five
members selected from a special roster, which is bound to issue
a final decision within 300 to 315 days. The panel may either
uphold the decision of the national agency concerned or remand
it to the agency for action. The panel's decision is final and
binding upon the parties and the Canadian and US agencies
concerned, but for extraordinary reasons, similar to those
recognized in international arbitration (q.v.), a decision may be
reviewed in an extraordinary challenge procedure by a Canada-US
committee made up of three members. They are selected from a
ten-person roster of judges or former judges of a US federal court
or a court of superior jurisdiction in Canada. The decision of the
challenge committee, to be made typically within 30 days of its

establishment, is final and binding on both Canada and the US.

Canevaro Arbitration, 1912. This arbitration (q.v.) between Peru and Italy, set up within the framework of the PCA (q.v.), concerned the claim of three Canevaro brothers, arising out of default on bond debt owed them by the Peruvian government. Claiming to be Italian nationals, the Canevaro brothers asked Italy to espouse their claims against Peru. While the Italian nationality of two of them was not disputed by Peru, Peru contended that the third one, Raphael, was in fact a Peruvian national. The two countries submitted the issue to arbitration, asking the tribunal whether Peru was bound to pay the debt and--the more important issue associated with the Canevaro case--whether Canevaro could be considered an Italian national for purposes of diplomatic protection by Italy.

In its award of 3 May 1912 (11 UNRIAA 405) the tribunal held that Peru had the right to deny Canevaro's status as an Italian claimant. In the tribunal's opinion he was a dual citizen: Italian as a son of an Italian national and Peruvian by birth in Peru. However, his conduct in Peru as a Peruvian citizen, namely running for the Senate and accepting the Peruvian government's authorization to act as the Netherlands' consul general, entitled Peru to consider him a Peruvian national and deny him the status of an Italian claimant.

The *Canevaro* arbitration is usually invoked in cases of dual nationality and was followed by a number of other cases, including the *Salem* case arbitration between Egypt and the US (1932) (2 UNRIAA 1161); the *Mergé* Claim (1955) (14 UNRIAA 236) and the *Flegenheimer* Claim (1958) (14 UNRIAA 327) before a conciliation commission under the Peace Treaty with Italy (1947) (q.v.); and in the substantively different *Nottebohm* case (q.v.) before the ICJ (q.v.).

Casablanca Arbitration, 1909. This arbitration (q.v.) between France and Germany concerned events unfolding within the context of a semi-colonial situation in Morocco in the early 20th century when French troops were occupying this still formally independent country. The arbitration is of interest as one of the first within the framework of the PCA (q.v.) and as a successful attempt at a peaceful resolution of an international dispute in the tense atmosphere of the pre-World War I era. The case concerned a French-German dispute caused by forcible removal from a German vessel moored in Casablanca of four deserters from the Foreign Legion, including two German subjects. This French action, carried out against the German consul's protests, frustrated German attempts to remove the deserters from Morocco. The incident precipitated a serious crisis in the relations between France and Germany. The award of 22 May 1909 (11 UNRIAA 119) eased tensions by its compromise approach to the legal problems arising from the conflict of jurisdiction between the French occupying forces and the German consul in the semi-colonial Morocco.

Cassin, René (1887-1976). French national. Professor of law at the Universities of Lille and Paris. France's delegate to the League of Nations, 1924-1930. With De Gaulle's Free French in World War II. Member and President of the UN Commission on Human Rights. In the years 1959-1976, judge of the ECHR (q.v.) and its President, 1965-1968.

Central American Common Market Arbitration Tribunal. An arbitration (q.v.) tribunal envisaged by the General Treaty of Central American Economic Integration of 1960 (Treaty of Managua). The tribunal was to function on an *ad hoc* basis, consisting of the Supreme Court justices of the five member states of the CACM: Costa Rica, El Salvador, Guatemala, Honduras, and Nicaragua. Its awards concerning the interpretation and application of the Treaty of Managua were to be binding for all members of the CACM. In practice the tribunal was never used as disputes between members were submitted to the executive organ of the CACM which, moribund since the late 1970s, proved to be unsuccessful in its task of economic integration of Central America.

Central American Court of Justice (CACJ). The first ever permanent international court of justice, set up on a regional basis by the Convention of Washington of 20 December 1902 by the countries of Central America, namely Costa Rica, El Salvador, Guatemala,

Honduras, and Nicaragua. The CACJ, whose seat was in Costa Rica, was made up of five judges, one from each republic, who were elected for five years by the respective country's legislature. The Court's jurisdiction was very broad, including not only disputes between states but also between private individuals, nationals of one republic, on the one hand, and any of the other state party. The CACJ decided cases on the basis of international law and its decisions were final.

The CACJ had a very meager record and soon proved to be a failure. It was involved in ten cases during its short existence (1908-1918). Five of them were brought by individuals, but none were found admissible. Two cases involving civil strife in Nicaragua between rebels and the government never reached actual judicial proceedings. The best known is the case before the CACJ concerning the legal status of the Gulf of Fonseca brought by Costa Rica and El Salvador against Nicaragua. The Court rendered two decisions, in 1916 and 1917 respectively, declaring a treaty made by Nicaragua with the US for a concession to construct an inter-oceanic canal across Nicaragua ending in the Gulf of Fonseca a violation of the rights of Costa Rica and El Salvador (11 *AJIL* 181, 674 (1917)). Nicaragua refused to accept the Court's decision, which led to the expiration of the CACJ in 1918 after ten years of existence.

In the history of international judiciary the CACJ was a significant development since it was the first permanent international tribunal, preceding the PCIJ (q.v.) by 14 years. Granting individuals standing before the CACJ was also an innovation in international adjudication.

Certain Expenses of the United Nations (Article 17, Paragraph 2, of the Charter), ICJ Adv. Op. 1961-1962. This advisory opinion (q.v.) of the ICJ (q.v.) concerned the question, put to the Court by the UN General Assembly, whether the expenses incurred by the UN on the peacekeeping forces in the Suez area (UN Emergency Force I) and in the former Belgian Congo, now Zaïre, (ONUC-Organisation des Nations Unies au Congo), which the UN General Assembly had included in the budget in separate accounts but as expenses of the Organization, were "expenses" in the meaning of art. 17(2) of the UN Charter. This paragraph provides that "The expenses of the Organization shall be borne by the Members as apportioned by the General Assembly." A number of countries, including the USSR and France, refused to contribute to the peace-keeping expenses, claiming that they had not been authorized by the competent organ of the UN, namely the Security Council.

In its advisory opinion of 20 July 1962 the ICJ, by nine votes to five, answered the General Assembly's question in the affirmative (1962 ICJ Rep. 151), holding that the expenses in question were "expenses of the Organization" under art. 17(2), that is amounts paid to defray the costs of carrying out the purposes of the Organization. The Court also declared that the fact that the peace keeping actions were initiated by the General Assembly did not necessarily mean that they were not expenses of the UN.

The ICJ opinion represented one aspect of the UN financial crisis of the early 1960s when the US and its allies threatened to invoke against the defaulting states, and especially the USSR, art. 19 of the UN Charter which deprives a defaulting state of the right to vote in the General Assembly "if the amount of its arrears equals or exceeds the amount of the contribution due from it for the preceding two full years." One of the states in question, the USSR, even threatened to leave the UN if the article were applied, as it legally should have been. However, the US gave way and agreed not to invoke art. 19. At the 1964 session of the General Assembly a compromise solution was found for the voting by resorting to the consensus device as the method for adopting the Assembly's decisions. In return, the USSR promised to make voluntary contributions toward the controversial expenses.

Certain German Interests in Polish Upper Silesia (Germany v. Poland),PCIJ 1925-1928. The five judgments of the PCIJ (q.v.) in this complex dispute between Germany and Poland (*see* the judgements listed in ANNEX I (8-12)) concerned the interpretation of the German-Polish Convention on Upper Silesia of 15 May 1922 (9 LNTS 466) with regard to liquidation by Poland of state-owned property left by Germany in that part of Upper Silesia which was ceded to Poland as a result of World War I. The liquidation proceeded on the basis of the Polish Liquidation Law of 1920 which transferred all German state assets to the Polish treasury, as otherwise recognized by well established rules of international law governing state succession. At issue were: 1. a number of large land estates; and 2.--of interest here--a nitrate factory in the Upper Silesian town of Chorzów, part of Upper Silesia transferred to Poland. The problem was that a few months before, in 1919, the factory had been conveyed by the German government to a private German company and--as claimed by Germany--could not, as private property, be taken over by Poland as part of the liquidation of German state-owned property. Poland argued that the German transaction was not in good faith, and took over the assets of the Chorzów factory.

The case was brought before the PCIJ by Germany, which espoused the claim of the Chorzów factory, by virtue of art. 23 of the 1922 Convention. Despite Polish objections that the dispute was still pending before the German-Polish Mixed Arbitral Tribunal (*see* **Mixed Arbitral Tribunals**), the PCIJ ruled in its judgment of 25 August 1925 that it had jurisdiction.

Subsequently, in its merits judgment of 25 May 1926,the PCIJ held that the Polish Liquidation Law of 1920 was in conflict with the 1922 Convention. It ruled that the factory was indeed private property since the German government had the right to dispose of its property in Upper Silesia as long as sovereignty over this region was not formally transferred to Poland. In the Court's opinion, Poland had not proved that the German government had not acted in good faith when conveying the factory to a German private company in 1919.

In its third judgment, *Factory at Chorzów*, of 26 July 1927, the PCIJ affirmed, against Polish objections, its jurisdiction to assess the amount of indemnity due for the factory, but in the order of 21 November 1927 rejected the German request to indicate provisional measures (q.v.).

In its fourth judgment, 16 December 1927, the PCIJ interpreted its two previous judgments, holding that the German company had acquired the right of ownership of the Chorzów factory notwithstanding any contrary rulings that might be made by a Polish court.

The fifth judgment (merits) of the Court of 13 September 1928 held that Poland was under an obligation to pay indemnity to the German company, but reserved the determination of the actual amount for a future judgment, which did not take place as the two countries resolved the dispute by diplomatic means.

The *Factory at Chorzów* case is of major interest from the point of view of the rules of international law governing responsibility for injury to aliens, respect for vested rights, expropriation of foreign property, and the amount of compensation for such expropriation. For this reason the judgments of the PCIJ in the matter of *Certain German Interests* and the *Factory at Chorzów* have been relied upon in subsequent judgments and arbitral awards dealing with these problems. A number of opinions expressed by the PCIJ in the five judgments has been frequently referred to by commentators and codifiers of international law, especially those who, following the traditional view, advocate an international standard of justice of adequate, prompt and effective compensation for expropriation of foreign property. The opinion of the Court that "it is a principle of international law, and even a general conception of law, that violation of an engagement involves an obligation to make reparation" has become a classical maxim found in many textbooks of international law.

Certain Norwegian Loans (France v. Norway), ICJ 1955-1957. In this case France espoused the claims of French holders of bonds floated by Norway on foreign markets in the period between 1885 and 1909, claiming--against Norway's position--that the repayment or redemption of the bonds should be effected at their value in gold at the time of the redemption or repayment. In 1955 France referred the dispute to the ICJ (q.v.) on the basis of the optional clause (q.v.) declarations filed by itself and Norway.

In its judgment of 6 July 1957 (1957 ICJ Rep. 9) the ICJ, upholding Norway's preliminary objection, by 12 votes to three declined jurisdiction (q.v.) to adjudicate the case. It held that the international law principle of reciprocity, as expressed in art. 38(2) of the ICJ Statute, allowed Norway, which had accepted the Court's jurisdiction under the optional clause without reservations, to invoke France's reservation to the acceptance of this jurisdiction excluding disputes relating to matters which were essentially within national jurisdiction as understood by France. Since France was entitled to exclude such disputes from the compulsory jurisdiction of the ICJ, Norway could do likewise and by invoking France's automatic or self-judging reservation (q.v.) could bar the Court's jurisdiction.

The *Certain Norwegian Loans* case is usually quoted to illustrate the principle that the jurisdiction of the ICJ under the optional clause applies only to the extent to which the optional clause declarations coincide in conferring such jurisdiction. In the case in question the ICJ did not pronounce on the validity of the French automatic reservation as such, but in an individual opinion (q.v.) Judge Lauterpacht (q.v.) held it to be invalid as contrary to legal thinking and art. 36(6) of the Statute of the ICJ according to which the Court itself settles disputes concerning its jurisdiction.

Chambers. As a general rule, the number and composition of permanent international tribunals do not depend on the parties. As an exception to this rule, statutes of international tribunals provide for the possibility of forming a chamber to deal with a particular case or categories of cases. The Statute of the ICJ (q.v.) distinguishes three categories of chamber. Chambers are not used in the advisory procedure (q.v.).

First, (ICJ Statute, art. 29) with a view to a speedy despatch of business, the Court annually forms a Chamber composed of five judges, with President and Vice-President always members *ex officio* (ICJ Rules, art. 15), which, at the request of the parties, may hear and determine cases by summary procedure. The Court also selects two judges for this Chamber of Summary Procedure for the purpose of replacing judges who find it impossible to sit. The Chamber of Summary Procedure has never as yet been called to meet in the ICJ, but the PCIJ (q.v.) did use summary procedure in its judgments in 1924 and 1925 respectively in a dispute between Belgium and Greece concerning the interpretation of the Treaty of Neuilly (*see* ANNEX I: JUDGMENTS OF THE PCIJ).

Second, the Court may from time to time form one or more chambers of three or more judges, as the Court may determine, for dealing with particular categories of cases, for example labor cases and cases relating to transit and communications. Cases are heard and determined by these chambers only if the parties so request (ICJ Statute, art. 26(1)). The ICJ has not yet had occasion to use such chambers. While it has considered the matter of possible formation of a chamber to deal with environmental disputes, it took the view that a special chamber, as discussed below, could deal with such cases.

The third category of chamber, specified in art. 26(2) of the Statute, is the only one to have been used by the ICJ. The Statute provides that the Court may form a chamber for dealing with a particular case, the number of judges constituting such a chamber being determined by the Court with the approval of the parties. Normally five judges, including where appropriate *ad hoc* judges (q.v.), form a chamber. Cases are heard and determined by such a chamber only if the parties so request. In the ICJ the chamber procedure pursuant to art. 26(2) of the ICJ Statute has been used to deal with four cases: *Delimitation of the Maritime Boundary in the Gulf of Maine (Canada/US)* (q.v.); *Frontier Dispute (Burkina Faso/Mali)* (q.v.); *Elettronica Sicula (US v. Italy)* (q.v.); and *Land, Island and Maritime Frontier Dispute (El Salvador/Honduras)* (q.v.).

The institution of chambers is also known in other tribunals. For example the Sea-Bed Disputes Chamber of the projected International Tribunal for the Law of the Sea (q.v.) is designed to form *ad hoc* chambers of three members to deal with a particular dispute. Unlike in the ICJ where the judges of a chamber are selected by the Court, the composition of a chamber will be determined by the Sea-Bed Disputes Chamber with the approval of the parties.

Chamizal Arbitration, 1911. The background of this arbitration (q.v.) between Mexico and the US by an International Boundary Commission of three arbitrators was as follows. Under the Treaty of Guadelupe Hidalgo of 1848 between the US and Mexico (102 CTS 29) and the Gadsden Treaty of 1853 (111 CTS 235) the Rio Grande was made, in part of its course, the boundary between the two countries. Because the Rio Grande (like the Colorado) constantly shifted its channel, the US and Mexico agreed in 1884 (164 CTS 337) that the border would follow the central and normal channel of the river (the so called *Thalweg*) notwithstanding any alterations in the banks or the course of the river, provided that they were brought about by imperceptible and gradual processes of erosion and accretion. On the other hand, changes produced by avulsion, that is a sudden and violent abandonment of an existing river bed and opening a new one (like through a flood in 1864) were to have no effect upon the boundary line which should continue to follow the former main channel of the deserted river.

In 1895 a dispute arose concerning a tract of land near El Paso of about 600 acres, the Chamizal Tract, between the old and the new bed of the Rio Grande which, mostly as a result of the flood of 1864, was left on the US side of the border. Having failed to reach agreement on the boundary line, the two countries agreed in 1910 (211 CTS 259) to submit their dispute to arbitration by the Boundary Commission with a coopted neutral President.

The Commission decided (11 UNRIAA 309) in accordance with international law that the part of the Tract which had resulted from accretion belonged to the US but that the remainder, a major part of the disputed territory, which had been produced by avulsion in the great flood of 1864, belonged to Mexico. In view of constant protests by Mexico and the existence of a dispute (q.v.) between the two countries, the Commissioners rejected the US argument that it had acquired the Tract on the basis of prescription (statute of limitations) through peaceful and uninterrupted possession. The US Commissioner dissented from the award and the US rejected it--one of the rare instances of rejection in the history of arbitration (*see also* **Beagle Channel Arbitration, 1977**)--on the ground that the Commissioners had exceeded their powers.

The US-Mexican dispute over the Chamizal Tract continued to simmer for more than 50 years until 29 August 1963 when a Convention (505 UNTS 185) divided the disputed territory, with Mexico obtaining 630.3 and the US 193.2 acres.

The *Chamizal* arbitration is of interest because it illustrates the principles of international law applicable to the delimitation of international river boundaries and provides a rare instance of rejection of an arbitration award by a party to the dispute.

Chorzów Factory *see* **Certain German Interests in Polish Upper Silesia (Germany v. Poland), PCIJ 1925-1928**

Clipperton Island Arbitration, 1931. This arbitration (q.v.) concerned a dispute between France and Mexico over an uninhabited coral reef atoll in the Pacific Ocean. Discovered in 1705 by Clipperton, a British subject, but not claimed by Great Britain, the island was shortly thereafter visited by French sailors, but not claimed by France until some 150 years later when in 1858 a French naval officer made a landing and proclaimed French sovereignty over the island. He subsequently reported his action to the French consul in Honolulu and to the government of Hawaii. Some 40 years later, in 1897, when a Mexican warship claimed Clipperton Island for Mexico and hoisted its flag, a dispute arose between France and Mexico over sovereignty with regard to the island.

Eventually the two countries agreed to submit the issue to arbitration, with the King of Italy as sole arbitrator. His award of 28 January 1931 (2 UNRIAA 1104) rejected the Mexican claim on the ground that prior to 1858 Mexico had never effectively occupied the island which therefore at the time of the French taking possession, that is in 1858, was *terra nullius*, that is, territory under no state's sovereignty. The arbitrator emphasized that, while actual taking possession of territory was required for an effective occupation and title to territory, the exact nature of the acts of sovereignty needed for a valid title depended on the particular circumstances, including the nature of the territory concerned. The uninhabited and desolate nature of Clipperton Island and the weakness of the Mexican acts relative to the competing French actions were sufficient to establish French sovereignty over the island.

Like the *Palmas* arbitration (q.v.) and the case of *Eastern Greenland* (q.v.) before the ICJ (q.v.), the *Clipperton* case illustrates the principle of international law that effective exercise of control over a territory as an essential requirement for acquiring sovereignty may vary in its intensity depending on the nature of the territory involved.

Commercial Arbitration *see* **International Commercial Arbitration**

Competence of the General Assembly for the Admission of a State to the United Nations, ICJ Adv. Op. 1949-1950. As part of the early Cold War dispute over admission of states to the UN, which had already produced the first advisory opinion of the ICJ (*see*

Conditions of Admission of a State to Membership in the United Nations (Article 4 of Charter), ICJ Adv. Op. 1947-1948), the General Assembly asked the ICJ (q.v.) to interpret art. 4(2) of the UN Charter which provides that "the admission... to membership... will be effected by a decision of the General Assembly upon the recommendation of the Security Council." Repeated Soviet vetoes in the Security Council, blocking admission to the UN of non-communist states, made a Western UN member propose in the General Assembly that the word "recommendation" in art. 4(2) need not necessarily be construed as a positive recommendation.

The General Assembly requested the ICJ to give an advisory opinion (q.v.) on the question whether admission to UN membership can be effected by a decision of the General Assembly when the Security Council has made no recommendation either because of failure to obtain the required majority or by reason of the negative vote ("veto") of a permanent member. In its opinion of 3 March 1950 (1950 ICJ Rep. 4) the ICJ, by ten votes to two, answered this question in the negative, ruling that a positive vote of the Security Council was necessary before the admission could be effected.

Compromis. An international, normally written, agreement whereby states undertake to submit a dispute to arbitration (q.v.) or an international court. A *compromis* may refer to an *ad hoc* agreement whereby the parties submit a particular, already existing, dispute to an *ad hoc* or an institutionalized tribunal (such as, for example, the "special agreement" to submit a dispute to the ICJ) (q.v.). Or it may be a general *compromis* or "compromissory" clause in a treaty whereby they refer to arbitration or judicial settlement all, or a class of, disputes which may arise in the future, as specified in a general arbitration treaty or by a compromissory clause of a treaty dealing with any other matter. A further *compromis* or protocol of submission of a specific dispute to arbitration is then normally concluded, implementing the already existing general protocol or the compromissory clause of the relevant treaty.

A *compromis* contains the major points of reference of the proceedings, defining the subject of the dispute, specifying the manner of appointing the arbitrators and the law to be applied by them, the venue, language, and other rules of procedure, and any other matters that the parties consider appropriate to include in the *compromis*. It is natural that if a dispute is to be submitted to an already existing tribunal, the contents of the *compromis* are less detailed.

Compromissory Clause *see Compromis*

Conciliation. This is a procedure of third-party diplomatic peaceful settlement of disputes between states whereby the dispute is referred to a commission of the parties' choice whose task is impartially to elucidate the facts and issue a report with a concrete proposal for a settlement of the dispute. However, the parties are under no legal obligation to accept the proposal. Hence conciliation does not belong to arbitral or judicial methods of settling disputes; a conciliation commission is neither an arbitral tribunal nor a court.

In international practice the distinction between conciliation and arbitration (q.v.) is sometimes not strictly observed and the terminology used in diplomatic instruments may be confusing, as some international agreements refer to conciliation commissions that are expected to make legally binding decisions. Such conciliation commissions are in fact arbitral tribunals, as was the case of the conciliation commissions under the Peace Treaty with Italy (1947) (q.v.).

Conciliation Commissions under the Peace Treaty with Italy, 1947. Although named "conciliation" (q.v.) commissions, these were in reality bilateral arbitral tribunals established under art. 83 of the Peace Treaty with Italy of 10 February 1947 (49 and 50 UNTS). They adjudicated claims of nationals of allied powers resulting from property and other losses suffered by them as a result of Italy's participation in the Second World War. Conciliation commissions of this kind were established by France, Greece, the Netherlands, the UK and the US. Each commission was made up of one representative of the state concerned and one representative of Italy, with a third member to be added if no agreement could be reached in three months of deliberations.

The awards of the commissions were rendered on the basis of

the Treaty within the framework of general international law and general principles of law recognized by the parties. The commissions under the Peace Treaty with Italy dealt with numerous cases of which those involving claims by persons of dual nationality, such as the *Mergé* and *Flegenheimer* claims, are well known cases in international law (see **Canevaro Arbitration**).

Conditions of Admission of a State to Membership in the United Nations (Article 4 of Charter), ICJ Adv. Op. 1947-1948. This first advisory opinion (q.v.) of the ICJ (q.v.), given on 28 May 1948 (1947-1948 ICJ Rep. 53), was requested by the UN General Assembly in the environment of the early Cold War years in 1948. It interpreted art. 4(1) of the UN Charter which lays down the substantive conditions for admission of states to the UN ("peace-loving states which accept the obligations contained in the... Charter and, in the judgment of the Organization, are able and willing to carry out these obligations.").

The USSR had repeatedly vetoed applications of non-communist states in the Security Council, being ready to end its opposition to their admission only on the condition that the four communist states in Europe which were not yet UN members, namely Albania, Bulgaria, Hungary, and Romania, be admitted simultaneously.

The question addressed to the ICJ was whether a UN member (such as the USSR) was juridically entitled to make its consent to the admission of a state dependent on conditions not expressly provided for in art. 4(1) of the Charter, and in particular, the additional condition that other states be admitted together with that state. The Court answered this question in the negative. By a majority of nine votes to six, it declared that the conditions of art. 4(1) were exhaustive and no further conditions could be imposed by UN members.

Although the General Assembly recommended that the UN members act in accordance with the Court's opinion, political considerations eventually led to the "package deal" of 1955 whereby 16 countries were admitted *en bloc* to the UN, including the four communist applicants and 12 non-communist states, both Western and from the Third World.

Connally Amendment *see* **Automatic (Self-Judging) Reservation**

Constitution of the Maritime Safety Committee of the Inter-Governmental Maritime Consultative Organization, ICJ Adv. Op. 1960. Under art. 28(a) of the Convention of 6 March 1948 (289 CTS 48) establishing the Inter-Governmental Maritime Consultative Organization (IMCO), now International Maritime Organization (IMO), its Maritime Safety Committee consists of 14 member states elected by the Organization's Assembly from the members of the Organization having an important interest in maritime safety "of which not less than eight shall be the largest ship-owning nations." In 1959, in its first election of the Committee, the IMCO Assembly elected neither Liberia nor Panama although these two states were among such eight members according to Lloyd's Register of Shipping. Liberia and Panama were not elected because most members of the Assembly, the traditional maritime nations of Europe, did not consider the two countries to be in fact maritime nations as their ships were in reality owned and operated by foreign interests which registered their ships under the "flags of convenience" of Liberia and Panama in order to avoid taxes and high operating costs.

The IMCO Assembly requested the ICJ (q.v.) to give an advisory opinion (q.v.) whether the Maritime Safety Committee was constituted in accordance with the Convention establishing the IMCO. In its advisory opinion of 8 June 1960 (1960 ICJ Rep. 150) the Court ruled, by nine votes to five, that the Committee was not constituted in accordance with the Convention. It upheld the view that, like in other maritime conventions, the phrase "ship-owning nations" referred solely to registered tonnage as the criterion of comparative size irrespective of ownership.

The advisory opinion of the Court concerning the IMCO indirectly upheld the traditional rule of international law that states have the right to fix the conditions for the grant of nationality to ships and registration of ships in their respective territory.

Contentious Jurisdiction of the ICJ. The competence of the ICJ (q.v.) to render a legally binding decision in disputes submitted to it on the basis of consent by states in adversary proceedings before the Court (*see also* **Jurisdiction of International Tribunals**). Existence of a genuine international dispute (q.v.) is a necessary prerequisite for the exercise of contentious jurisdiction by the Court. Only a state may be a party to contentious proceedings before the ICJ. International organizations or private persons have no "standing" in such proceedings. In this respect the ICJ differs from the ITLOS (q.v.) and some regional courts such as the CJEC (q.v.) where organs of the EC may institute proceedings against a member state and *vice versa*, and even individuals may pursue their alleged rights before that Court. Contentious jurisdiction of the ICJ must be distinguished from its jurisdiction to give advisory opinions (q.v.).

Unless a case is settled by the parties at any stage of the contentious proceedings or discontinued by the applicant state with subsequent removal of the case from the Court's List by an order of the Court or--in cases of discontinuance--of the Court's President, the proceedings are brought to a conclusion by the Court's judgment.

As far as the states entitled to be parties to a case before the ICJ are concerned (jurisdiction *ratione personae*), the contentious jurisdiction of the ICJ covers: (1) members of the UN; they are automatically parties to the Court's Statute which is an integral part of the UN Charter; (2) non-member states which have become parties to the Statute only, on conditions determined in each case by the UN General Assembly upon recommendation of the Security Council. Switzerland and Nauru are such states. Liechtenstein and San Marino which once belonged to this category are now UN members; and (3) any other state which has deposited a declaration with the ICJ Registry accepting the Court's jurisdiction and undertaking to comply with its decisions.

However, it must be strongly emphasized that the mere fact of a state being a party to the UN Charter with the ICJ Statute as an integral part or to the Statute (like Switzerland and Nauru) does not necessarily mean that that state is *ipso facto* subject to the Court's jurisdiction. Unlike the case of the CJEC (q.v.), the jurisdiction of the ICJ is not automatically compulsory. It is optional and based on the fundamental principle of the parties' consent, either express or implied.

In general, express consent can be manifested in one of the

following three ways. First, under art. 36(1) of the Court's Statute, the parties may, by a special *ad hoc* agreement ("special agreement") (*see Compromis*) bring an already existing dispute before the ICJ. In such cases of the notification of the special agreement to the Court there is formally neither an applicant nor a respondent state, and in the official designation of the case brought to the Court by such notification the names of the parties are separated not by "v." (*versus*) but by an oblique stroke, for example Burkina Faso/Mali or Canada/United States of America.

Second, and a majority of cases have been brought on this basis, the ICJ has jurisdiction over a dispute if the parties are bound by a "compromissory clause" (*see Compromis*) of a prior treaty providing for reference to the ICJ of a category of dispute which includes the dispute that has arisen between them. Formally, proceedings can be instituted either through the notification to the ICJ of the special agreement implementing, in the specific case of the dispute, the compromissory clause of the treaty in question, or by a written application addressed to the Registrar of the Court. In the latter case the name of the applicant state is listed first in the official designation of the case and is separated from the name of the respondent state by the abbreviation "v." (*versus*), for example United States of America v. Italy. Compromissory clauses referring matters to the ICJ can be found both in treaties dealing specifically with the problem of peaceful settlement of disputes and--much more frequently--in treaties dealing with all kinds of matters of interest to the parties, which contain a provision on reference to the ICJ of any dispute between the parties relating to the interpretation or application of the treaty. Clauses in the treaties which conferred jurisdiction upon the PCIJ (q.v.) remain in effect provided such a treaty is still in force and the states concerned are parties to the ICJ Statute. There are more than 250 treaties signed since 1933 which confer jurisdiction upon the ICJ (four of them before 1945) by their respective compromissory clauses (ICJ Yb 1989-1990, 98-115). However, although the ICJ Statute in its art. 36(1) refers to "all matters specially provided for in the Charter of the United Nations" as a basis for the Court's jurisdiction, it is generally accepted that no such matters exist since recommendations of the Security Council--unlike its decisions--are not legally binding. This apparent contradiction can be accounted for by the fact that the relevant Statute provision was drafted at a time when it was expected that the UN Charter would provide for compulsory jurisdiction of the ICJ.

The third method whereby a contentious case may be brought under the jurisdiction of the ICJ through the parties' consent is through the "optional clause" (q.v.) of art. 36(2) of the Court's Statute, historically a compromise between the countries advocating and those opposing the principle of compulsory jurisdiction. Briefly, under this provision a state may unilaterally declare that it accepts in advance, in relation to any other state accepting the same obligation, the compulsory jurisdiction of the ICJ in all legal disputes concerning any question of international law, the interpretation of a treaty, the existence of a breach of an international obligation, or the nature or extent of the reparation for the breach. However, the effectiveness of the optional clause is limited by reservations to acceptance of compulsory jurisdiction (q.v.) under art. 36(2) of which the automatic (self-judging) reservation (q.v.) is the most notorious. In cases where art. 36(2) provides the basis of consent, the proceedings can be instituted either through the notification to the Court of the special agreement or by a written application to the Court's Registrar.

The contentious jurisdiction of the ICJ pursuant to an *ad hoc* agreement or a treaty stipulation is not limited in terms of the scope and nature of the dispute involved. Hence it may also include political disputes. However, since under art. 38(1) of the Statute the Court's function is to decide disputes "in accordance with international law," a political dispute would have to be decided *ex aequo et bono* (*see* **Ex Aequo et Bono** and **Equity**) rather than according to the legal rules in force, but only if the parties agree to it. Contentious jurisdiction under the optional clause is expressly limited to "legal disputes," however. What criteria should govern the distinction between "justiciable" legal disputes and "non-justiciable" political disputes is a controversial issue (*see* **Justiciability of International Disputes**).

The ICJ has incidental jurisdiction, that is, authority to decide, in the event of a dispute over this question, whether it has jurisdiction with respect of a particular case. It also has the competence to allow intervention in the proceedings (q.v.); to indicate provisional measures (q.v.); and to construe a judgment at the request of a party. Under a few treaties it has what might be called appellate jurisdiction (*see* **International Court of Justice**). The ICJ may also admit proceedings in revision at the request of a party to a past dispute.

It is important to bear in mind that consent of a state to the Court's jurisdiction need not be express. It may also be inferred from its conduct, for example when a state responds on the merits without raising an objection to jurisdiction (*see* ***Forum Prorogatum***).

Continental Shelf (Libyan Arab Jamahiriya/Malta), ICJ 1984-1985. In response to the ICJ's (q.v.) refusal to permit Malta to intervene in the *Continental Shelf* case between Tunisia and Libya (q.v.), Libya and Malta agreed in 1984 in a special agreement to ask the ICJ to decide what principles and rules of international law are applicable to the delimitation of the continental shelf between the two states and how these principles and rules can be applied in practice in order to achieve an equitable solution.

Having previously refused Italy's application for permission to intervene (*see* **Intervention in Proceedings**) by the judgment of 21 March 1984 (1984 ICJ Rep. 3), the Court in its judgment of 3 June 1985, by 14 votes to three, (1985 ICJ Rep. 13), set forth the requested principles and rules as well as the circumstances and factors to be taken into consideration in order to achieve an equitable delimitation. They included, in particular, the general configuration of the coasts, oppositeness and their relationship to each other within the general geographical context; the disparity of the lengths of the coasts and the distance between them; and the need to avoid any excessive disproportion between the extent of the shelf area appertaining to the coast state and the length of the relevant part of its coast. The Court then proceeded to lay down the line of demarcation, starting with drawing the initial median line every point of which was equidistant from the coast of Malta and the relevant coast of Libya. The resulting line ran closer to Malta than Libya. Subsequently the Court carried out adjustments in the light of the above-mentioned circumstances and factors. The final line was drawn more to the north, that is, closer to Malta.

Continental Shelf (Tunisia/Libyan Arab Jamahiriya), ICJ 1981-1982. By a special agreement (*see Compromis*), in 1981 Tunisia and Libya asked the ICJ (q.v.)to determine what principles and rules of international law were applicable to the delimitation of the respective areas of the continental shelf of the two countries. Malta's application for permission to intervene (*see* **Intervention in Proceedings**) on the ground of an alleged interest of a legal nature which might be affected by the decision in the case (art. 62 of the ICJ Statute) was rejected by the Court in its judgment of 14 April 1981 (1981 ICJ Rep. 3).

In its judgment on the merits of 24 February 1982 (1982 ICJ Rep. 18) the Court decided on the basis of customary (general) international law that the delimitation should be effected in accordance with equitable principles and taking account of all relevant circumstances such as the necessity of ensuring a reasonable degree of proportionality between the areas allotted and the lengths of the coastlines concerned. The equidistance method was found not to lead to an equitable result in the particular circumstances of the case and was therefore rejected by the Court.

The judgment in the Tunisia/Libya case was the second one in a series of ICJ judgments dealing with the delimitation of the continental shelf between opposite and adjacent states (*see* **Continental Shelf (Libya/Malta); North Sea Continental Shelf** among others). The judgment in the Tunisia/Libya case was subsequently interpreted by the ICJ in another ICJ judgment in 1985 (*see* **Application for Revision and Interpretation of the Judgment of 24 February 1982 in the Case Concerning the Continental Shelf (Tunisia/Libyan Arab Jamahiriya) (Tunisia v. Libyan Arab Jamahiriya)**).

Corfu Channel (United Kingdom v. Albania), ICJ 1947-1949. This first contentious (q.v.) case before the ICJ (q.v.), which gave rise to three judgments and three orders of the Court, originated in the heavy mine damage and loss of life suffered in 1946 by two British destroyers proceeding, in the exercise of the right of innocent passage, in Albanian territorial waters north through the Corfu Channel, in the belief that the waters were free of mines. Three weeks later British minesweepers, disregarding Albanian protests, swept the Channel and found 22 moored mines of the same type as the mines that had damaged the two British ships. The United Kingdom accused Albania of having laid the mines or having allowed laying them by a third party. Albania denied any responsibility and the dispute was brought before the Security Council which recommended referral of the case to the ICJ, the resolution accepted by both parties to the dispute. However, after the United Kingdom had unilaterally instituted proceedings against Albania under art. 40(1) of the ICJ Statute, Albania raised a preliminary objection (q.v.) to the Court's jurisdiction (q.v.), contending that in the absence of a treaty providing for compulsory jurisdiction, only a special agreement between the parties could confer jurisdiction upon the Court. Nevertheless, in a letter to the ICJ, Albania agreed to accept the Court's jurisdiction for the case. However in the ensuing proceedings it again contested the Court's jurisdiction.

In its first judgment of 25 March 1948 (1947-1948 ICJ Rep. 15), the Court, by 15 votes to one, rejected Albania's preliminary objection, ruling that that country was precluded from objecting to the ICJ jurisdiction after having accepted it in an official letter following the initiation of the proceedings by the United Kingdom. This ruling by the ICJ is usually quoted as evidence for the possibility of *forum prorogatum* (q.v.) as a basis for the Court's jurisdiction.

The second, merits, phase of the proceedings took place on the basis of the parties' agreement (*compromis*) (q.v.) of 25 March 1948 whereby they asked the Court to decide: (1) whether Albania was responsible for the Corfu Channel incident and, if so, whether it was under the duty to pay compensation to the United Kingdom; and (2) whether the UK had violated Albania's sovereignty by its unilateral action of mine-sweeping operations in the Albanian territorial sea.

In its judgment of 9 April 1949 (1949 ICJ Rep. 4) the ICJ, by a vote of 11 to five, held that Albania was responsible for the explosions. Even if it had not laid the mines itself, it was aware of their existence but failed to warn shipping of the mines danger in its waters. By ten votes to six the Court reserved the assessment of the compensation due from Albania for further consideration. In the context of its judgment the ICJ reaffirmed, in a widely quoted pronouncement, the right of innocent passage, without previous authorization of the coastal state, of foreign warships through straits used in international navigation. In addition, by a vote of 14 to two the Court held that the passage of the British destroyers on 22 October 1946 had not violated Albania's sovereignty. On the other hand, the Court decided unanimously (including the vote of the British judge McNair (q.v.)) that the British mine-sweeping operation had violated that sovereignty and that the Court's declaration to this effect constituted appropriate satisfaction for Albania.

In its third judgment, of 15 December 1949 (1949 ICJ Rep. 244), the Court assessed the amount of compensation due by Albania to the United Kingdom at a total sum of £844,000. Albania refused to take part in this phase of the proceedings and did not pay the compensation. A few years later the United Kingdom made an attempt to collect the amount within the context of the case before the ICJ concerning *Monetary Gold Removed from Rome in 1943 (Italy v. France, United Kingdom, and US)* (1953-1954) (q.v.). However, the long dispute over the Corfu Channel incident involving the compensation due from Albania could not be finally resolved until after the fall of the communist regime in Albania in 1991.

The *Costa Rica Packet* Arbitration, 1897. This arbitration (q.v.) by a Russian international law professor, F. de Martens, acting on behalf of the Czar, concerned the arrest by the Netherlands' authorities in the Dutch East Indies of the master of the British whaling vessel, the *Costa Rica Packet*, on charges of having appropriated the contents of a derelict native boat off the Dutch East Indies three years before. The boat was adrift allegedly in the Dutch territorial waters. After it had turned out that the incident had occurred on the high seas, the master of the British vessel was released from Dutch custody. Following the Netherlands' rejection of Great Britain's claim for damages for the losses suffered by its nationals, the dispute was submitted to arbitration in a *compromis* (q.v.) signed in 1895. The sole arbitrator's award was in favor of Great Britain (184 CTS 240). It ruled that, as the alleged appropriation had taken place on the high seas, it was subject exclusively to the law of the *Costa Rica Packet's* flag state, that is

Great Britain; and that by arresting her master the Dutch authorities had violated the law of the sea irrespective of whether or not the arrest was lawful under Dutch law. In determining the amount of damages, the arbitrator took into account not only the financial losses suffered by the master and the owner of the vessel, but also the profits lost by them, minus an amount which took account of the claimant's failure to take reasonable measures designed to limit the damage, subsequent to the master's arrest by the Dutch authorities.

Court of Arbitration for Sport (CAS). This non-governmental organization is an arbitration (q.v.) tribunal founded by the International Olympic Committee in 1984, whose function is to deliver binding judgments in non-technical disputes of a private nature arising out of activities pertaining to sports whose settlement is not otherwise provided for in the Olympic Charter, such as for example questions of suspension for drug abuse, breach of contract in coaching and broadcasting, and contracts for sale of sport equipment. The CAS also functions as the final appeal court from decisions of a number of international sports federations. The CAS is made up of 60 potential arbitrators appointed for four years, 15 each by the International Olympic Committee, the International Sports Federations, the Association of National Olympic Committees, and the President of the International Olympic Committee.

Any person with the capacity to compromise, including sports federations, olympic committees, International Olympic Committee, etc. can bring a case before the CAS provided that the parties first agree in writing to the Court's jurisdiction and a Requests Panel declares the request admissible. Unless the parties select the applicable system of domestic law, general principles of law, international sports law, or other body of law, the Court will apply Swiss law as its headquarters is in Lausanne. Like in international commercial arbitration (q.v.), the awards of the CAS are recognized and enforced by domestic courts, mainly according to the rules of the New York Convention (1958) (q.v.) on the Recognition and Enforcement of Foreign Arbitral Awards.

The CAS may give, and has already given, formal advisory opinions (q.v.) at the request of the Executive Board of the

International Olympic Committee and advised international sports federations and other sports organizations. The CAS has resolved several important disputes and has the potential of becoming a truly global international sport tribunal, especially if its membership, now mostly European, acquires a wider geographical basis.

Court of Arbitration of the French Community. An independent court established in 1959 by the French Community, whose function is to adjudicate disputes concerning the interpretation or application of the rules of law binding the member states of the Community and those regarding the appointment of members of the Community's Senate. The Court also renders opinions at the request of the President of the Community. The Court is made up of seven judges appointed, for a renewable term of six years, by the President from different states of the Community. The decisions are taken by a majority of at least five judges; they are final and enforceable throughout the states of the Community.

In practice, the Court of Arbitration of the French Community has been virtually inactive and, like the other organs of the Community, has fallen into disuse.

Court of First Instance of the European Communities. A court of first instance, attached to the CJEC (q.v.), set up in 1989 by the EC Council of Ministers pursuant to the Treaty of Rome (1957), as amended by the Single European Act of 1986 (art. 168 (a)). The Court of First Instance was created at the request of the CJEC to help ease its workload by taking over jurisdiction (q.v.) in some of the routine and time-consuming work of the CJEC, namely the EC staff disputes, competition policy and steel quotas and tariff cases. Appeal to the CJEC on points of law is possible, however. The Court of First Instance does not have jurisdiction to deal with actions brought by EC institutions or member states and requests for preliminary rulings submitted by national courts. Jurisdiction in these matters is expressly reserved to the CJEC. The structure and procedure of the Court of First Instance in general follow the pattern of the CJEC.

Court of Justice of the African Economic Community (CJAEC). The judicial organ of the African Economic Community established by the Organization of African Unity under the Treaty of Abuja of 3 June 1991 (30 ILM 1241 (1991)). The function of this Court is to ensure the adherence to law in the interpretation and application of the Treaty establishing the Community and to decide disputes submitted to it by member states of the Community Assembly on grounds of the violation of the Treaty's provisions or a decision or regulation of the Community or on grounds of lack of competence or abuse of power by an organ, an authority or a member state. The Court also gives advisory opinions at the request of the Community's Assembly or Council. Details concerning the procedure and other matters relating to the Court are included in a special Protocol. The Court has not yet been active.

Court of Justice of the Cartagena Agreement (CJCA). The judicial body and integral part of the Andean Pact (Andean Common Market) founded by the Cartagena (Colombia) Agreement of 26 May 1969 (8 ILM 910(1969)), which was established by the Treaty of 28 May 1979 (18 ILM 1203 (1979)) and whose main function is to interpret the law created by the Cartagena Agreement. The members of the Andean Common Market are Bolivia, Colombia, Ecuador, Peru and Venezuela.

Located in Quito (Ecuador), the Court (*Tribunal de Justicia del Acuerdo de Cartagena*) is made up of five judges selected for six years on a staggered, 3-3, schedule from a list supplied by the individual member states. The jurisdiction of the CJCA encompasses three areas. First, it may nullify decisions of the Commission of the Andean Pact, a quasi-legislative organ of the Andean Common Market, which it finds in conflict with the legal system of the Cartagena Agreement. Second, the Andean Court may rule upon a member country's or the Junta's (a three-member organ supervising the implementation of the Cartagena Agreement) complaint that a member state is not complying with the Agreement. Third, the CJCA may render binding advisory opinions (q.v.) interpreting the law of the Andean Pact at the request of national judges in pending trials. The major objective is to ensure uniform interpretation of the law of the Andean Common Market. It is important that the decisions of the CJCA are directly applicable within the member states without the need of further transformation into domestic law.

Court of Justice of the Economic Community of Central African States (CJECCAS). The judicial body of the Economic Community of Central African States, created under the Treaty of 19 October 1983 (23 ILM 945 (1984)) establishing the Community and signed by 11 countries of the region. The function of the CJECCAS is to decide disputes between members of the Community. The Court has the power of overall supervision of the legality of the decisions, directives and regulations of the Community institutions and decides on appeals lodged by member states of the Conference of Heads of State and Governments of the Community (its supreme organ) on grounds of lack of jurisdiction and breach of the provisions of the 1983 Treaty. The Court may also make interlocutory decisions, that is decisions pronounced during the course of proceedings, on the interpretation of the Treaty and the effectiveness of the decisions, directives and regulations formulated by the Community. Like the ICJ (q.v.), the Court also renders advisory opinions (q.v.) at the request of the Conference or the Council of Ministers. The CJECCAS does not seem to have been very active in settling disputes of the Central African region.

Court of Justice of the European Communities (CJEC). Along with the Council of Ministers, the Commission, and the European Parliament, a principal institution and the judicial body of the European Community established by the Treaty of Rome in 1957. However the CJEC had been in existence since 1952 as an institution of the European Coal and Steel Community created in 1951. After the foundation of the European Economic Community (EEC) on 25 March 1957 and the European Atomic Energy Agency (Euratom) on the same day, the Court became the common judicial organ of the three Communities.

The CJEC, or briefly European Court of Justice, functions on the legal basis of the three original Community treaties and the Statute and Rules annexed to each Treaty. The Court has its seat in Luxembourg. It must not be confused with the European Court of Human Rights (q.v.) in Strasbourg.

In 1993 the European Community (EC) consisted of 12 member countries and its Court was made up of 13 judges: in practice one from each country plus one more, a national of one of the four largest members, to keep the total number uneven. The CJEC is assisted by six so-called advocates general who are court officials modeled after French procedure, whose role is to assist the Court by making, in open court, non-binding "reasoned submissions" on cases before the Court. Such submissions are often followed by the Court.

The CJEC normally sits in plenary sessions but it may also form small chambers (q.v.) of three or five judges. There are five such chambers. However, cases brought by a member state or an EC institution must be heard in plenary session. Unlike in the ICJ (q.v.), no individual opinions (q.v.), dissenting or separate, are allowed in the CJEC. A Registrar is in charge of the Court's administration.

In its decisions, the CJEC applies the "primary legislation" which includes the Community's constitutive treaties; the "secondary legislation" consisting of the law created by the Community institutions pursuant to the constitutive treaties; "regulations" (directly binding legislative measures enacted by the Commission or the Council); "directives" (binding orders); "decisions" (binding designated states or persons); and international agreements of the Community. In addition, the CJEC resorts to non-written sources: general principles of law, customary law, and--as a supplementary source--general rules of international law. In certain situations, for example for purposes of enforcement, the Court applies the national law of member states. Like the ICJ (q.v.), the CJEC does not follow the doctrine of *stare decisis* known in the common law countries; still in many cases it follows precedent while citing its past cases only sparingly.

One fundamental principle established by the CJEC is that Community law prevails over national law and is directly applicable in disputes between private parties and national authorities. This supremacy of the Community law, otherwise nowhere stipulated in the EC written law, is illustrated in such landmark cases as *Van Gend en Loos v. Nederlandse Administratie der Belastingen* (1963) (q.v.) and *Amministrazione delle Finanze dello Stato v. Simmenthal S.p.A.* (1978) (q.v.).

The jurisdiction of the CJEC is broad and complex. The main task of the Court is to ensure observance of the law in the interpretation and application of the constitutive treaties. Under the EEC Treaty, no other international court has jurisdiction in these matters.

In general, the CJEC delivers judgments and--on rare occasions--opinions. The judgments may either originate in direct actions in the Court resulting in a final judgment or may be preliminary rulings requested by a national court which must then decide in accordance with the CJEC interpretation of the law.

Apart from a less important category of direct actions where jurisdiction (q.v.) is conferred upon the CJEC by consent of the parties, the most important categories of direct actions are those in which the Court's jurisdiction is anchored directly in the Community law providing for action in the Court against the Community or a member state. Actions against a Community institution include, first, actions for judicial review instituted either to annul a Community act or appeals to oblige a Community institution (Council or Commission) to take action which it has failed to take. Proceedings in all such cases can be brought by a member state, another Community institution (a rare occurrence in practice), or by a private person if a decision is of direct concern to that person.

Another kind of direct actions where the CJEC has jurisdiction, the so-called plenary jurisdiction, goes beyond the power of judicial review. Here belong actions for non-contractual liability, that is tort, resulting from damage caused by a Community institution or its officials; appeals by individuals against penalties for violation of the EC law; and staff cases in which the CJEC functions as an international administrative tribunal of an international organization (q.v.) adjudicating disputes brought by staff members against the Community.

Finally there are the so-called enforcement actions which may be brought by a member state or--the usual case--the EC Commission against a member state for an alleged failure to fulfill an obligation under the EC Treaty. Proceedings in such cases are preceded by a preliminary stage in which the defendant member state submits its observations and the Commission delivers a reasoned opinion. If the state in question fails to abide by it,

Court proceedings are instituted.

The preliminary rulings, which the CJEC has the jurisdiction to deliver, concern the interpretation of the Treaty and the validity and interpretation of acts of the Community institutions. The Court delivers its rulings at the request of a national court, but if no judicial remedy is anymore available, the national court is obliged to bring the case before the CJEC.

The preliminary rulings of the CJEC have been very important in the process of European integration in that they have contributed to the furthering of uniform application of the Community law and establishing the doctrine of supremacy of this law over the laws of the member states.

Unlike the ICJ, the CJEC does not have a general advisory jurisdiction (q.v.), but in special circumstances provided for by any of the three Community Treaties it may deliver opinions at the request of the Community or a member state. Thus under the EEC Treaty, the Court may give opinions on the compatibility with the Treaty of an international agreement proposed by the Community or a member state. For example on 14 December 1991, at the request of the EC Commission, the CJEC gave its opinion regarding the compatibility of the judicial system proposed in the Draft Agreement between the EC and the European Free Trade Association relating to the creation of the European Economic Area (31 ILM 442 (1992)). The Court found that system incompatible with the EC law.

Interim or provisional measures of protection (q.v.), preliminary objections (q.v.) and intervention in proceedings (q.v.) are possible in the CJEC, as they are in the ICJ. Enforcement of judgments against private persons is governed by the rules obtaining in the state where the enforcement takes place. There are no express provisions in the EC Treaty on enforcing the CJEC judgments against defaulting member states, but such a state may be forced into compliance by political or economic pressures of the Community. In addition, national laws in conflict with the Community law are practically unenforceable. In practice, there have been no cases of persistent refusal by states to comply with decisions of the CJEC.

The CJEC is the most active standing (permanent) international tribunal. Compared with the still modest though growing case load of the ICJ, its docket of cases has always been full. Whereas in 1974 110 cases were brought before the CJEC which delivered 62 judgments, in 1990 the Court heard 380 cases and rendered 225 judgments. Because of its workload, mainly preliminary rulings, the average time that it takes for a ruling amounts to two years. The recently created Court of First Instance of the European Community (q.v.) is expected to relieve the CJEC of part of its workload in certain routine cases.

The decisions of the CJEC have covered a wide variety of matters relating to the law of economic integration, and especially in the area of trade law, taxation, freedom of movement and establishment, treatment of aliens, labor law, and social security including discrimination on grounds of sex or age.

CSCE Court of Conciliation and Arbitration. A court established within the CSCE by the Convention on Conciliation and Arbitration of 15 December 1992 (32 ILM 555 (1993)), whose purpose is to settle, by means of conciliation (q.v.) and arbitration (q.v.), international disputes (q.v.) submitted to it by the parties to the Convention. Twenty-nine countries signed the Convention when it was opened for signature in 1992.

The CSCE Court provides a framework within which conciliation commissions or arbitral tribunals respectively, set up for each dispute, undertake the task of settling disputes between parties to the Convention (or between parties and non-parties). The administrative structure of the Court is constituted by a Bureau consisting of a President, a Vice-President, three other members, and a Registrar with the necessary staff. The seat of the Court is in Geneva. Each state party to the Convention appoints one arbitrator and one alternate to the Court's roster, nationals of any CSCE participating state, who must possess the qualifications required in their respective countries for appointment to the highest judicial office or must be recognized jurisconsults in international law. The appointment is for a six-year once renewable term.

Without prejudice to the jurisdiction of other international courts or tribunals, requests for the constitution of an arbitral tribunal can be brought to the Court either by agreement (*see Compromis*) of the parties or by means of an application. The

Court's jurisdiction is compulsory if it is based on a declaration analogous to the optional clause (q.v.) of the ICJ (q.v.), whereby states parties may declare in a notice addressed to the depositary state of the Convention (Sweden) that they recognize as compulsory, *ipso facto* and without special agreement, the jurisdiction of an arbitral tribunal, subject to reciprocity. Such a declaration may be made for an unlimited period or for a specific time and it may cover all disputes or exclude disputes concerning a state's territorial integrity, national defense, title over land territory, or competing claims with regard to jurisdiction over other areas, for example maritime jurisdiction. A request for arbitration against a state which has filed the optional clause declaration for purpose of the CSCE Court may be made by means of an application to the Court only after a period of 30 days following transmitting to the Court of the report of the conciliation commission which has dealt with the dispute (and which has not been accepted by the parties). The Court has the authority to impose interim measures of protection (q.v.) at the request of a party or on its own initiative.

An arbitral tribunal is composed of the arbitrators appointed by the parties, who are its *ex officio* members, and members appointed by the Court's Bureau from the arbitrators on the Court's roster, in such a number that the members appointed by it total at least one more than the *ex officio* members. In addition, a judge *ad hoc* (q.v) may be appointed from the Court's roster or from other qualified nationals of a CSCE participating state by a state which is a party to a dispute submitted to an arbitration tribunal but which is not a party to the 1992 Convention. Intervention in the proceedings (q.v.) is allowed.

The proceedings of the tribunal consist of a written part and an oral stage, but hearings are held *in camera* unless the tribunal declares otherwise. Like the ICJ, the CSCE tribunal decides disputes in accordance with international law, but it may decide a case *ex aequo et bono* (q.v.) if the parties agree. Awards are taken by a majority of the members participating in the vote. The reasons for the award must be stated. Individual (separate or dissenting) opinions (q.v.) are allowed. Like a judgment of the ICJ, an award of a CSCE arbitration tribunal has binding force only between the parties to the dispute and in respect of the case to which it relates. The awards are final and non-appealable, but a request for interpretation and an application for revision on the basis of newly discovered decisive facts are possible. Detailed rules governing the procedure of the CSCE arbitration tribunals will be spelled out in the Rules to be adopted by the CSCE.

Customs Régime between Germany and Austria, PCIJ Adv. Op. 1931. This famous advisory opinion (q.v.) of the PCIJ (q.v.) concerned the proposed customs union between Austria and Germany which precipitated a serious crisis in European diplomacy in 1931. In art. 88 of the Treaty of Peace of Saint-Germain of 10 September 1919 (226 CTS 8) Austria had undertaken to abstain from any act which might by any means whatever compromise its independence. Furthermore, under Protocol No. 1 for the Restoration of Austria of 4 October 1922 (12 LNTS 368), it obliged itself not to negotiate any economic or financial engagement calculated to compromise its independence.

The Council of the League of Nations asked the PCIJ whether the customs union planned by Austria and Germany in their protocol of 1931 would violate the provisions of the Treaty of Saint-Germain and the Protocol of 1922. In its opinion of 5 September 1931 (PCIJ, Series C, No. 53) the Court, by eight votes to seven, advised that the union would be incompatible with the Protocol because it would threaten Austria's economic independence. Seven judges in the majority also found that the proposed customs régime would endanger the independence of Austria and thus be contrary to art. 88 of the Treaty of Saint-Germain.

The advisory opinion on the *Customs Régime*, and especially the individual (separate) opinion (q.v.) of Judge Anzilotti (q.v.), is well known for the Court's analysis of the nature of independence and the sovereignty of states.

D

De Visscher, Charles (1884-1972). Belgian national. An eminent scholar in international law and professor at the Universities of Leuven (Louvain) and Ghent. Member of the PCA (q.v.), 1923; member of the PCIJ (q.v.), 1937; member of the ICJ (q.v.), 1946-1952. Author of numerous works on international law, including lectures in *RCADI*.

Declaration *see* **Individual Opinion**

Defrenne v. Sabena, CJEC 1976. This case before the CJEC (q.v.) originated in the action of an air hostess, Defrenne, against her employer, Sabena S.A., over compensation claimed by her on the ground that she had suffered sex discrimination in terms of pay as compared with male colleagues doing the same work. Defrenne brought her claim to the Labor Court in Brussels which referred two questions to the CJEC with regard to the effect and implementation of art. 119 of the Treaty of Rome of 25 March 1957 which created the EEC. Art. 119 obligates each member state to ensure "during the first stage" of the transitional period and subsequently maintain the application of the principle of equal pay for equal work. The first question was whether art. 119 introduced this principle into the national law of each member state directly and independently of any national provision. If the answer was affirmative, the second question inquired as of what date the effect of art. 119 must be recognized. In its judgment of 8 April 1976 (Case 43/75 [1976] ECR 455), the CJEC answered the first question in the affirmative and--on the second question-- ruled when the application of art. 119 was to be fully secured.

The *Defrenne v. Sabena* case is an important decision of the CJEC, upholding the principle of direct applicability of the Community law by all organs of the member states, including the legislative and judicial bodies. Other related cases of the CJEC include *Amministrazione delle Finanze dello Stato v. Simmenthal*

S.p.A. (q.v.) and *Van Gend en Loos v. Nederlandse Administratie der Belastingen* (q.v.).

Delimitation of the Continental Shelf Arbitration between the UK and France, 1977, 1978. This important arbitration (q.v.) by an *ad hoc* tribunal, actually called court, set up under a *compromis* (q.v.) of 10 July 1975 and made up of five professors of international law, concerned a dispute between France and the UK over delimitation of the boundary of portions of the continental shelf in the area of the Channel Islands and in the Atlantic.

As parties to the Geneva Convention on the Continental Shelf of 29 April 1958 (499 UNTS 311), both countries accepted the median equidistance line which under art. 6 of the Convention governs delimitation in the absence of agreement and unless some other boundary line is justified by "special circumstances," except that France attached certain reservations to art. 6 which were objected to by the UK.

In its award of 30 June 1977 (18 ILM 397 (1979)) the court ruled that art. 6 was binding upon the two parties only to the extent that it was not modified by the French reservations. As a result, the delimitation was to be governed in part by art. 6 and partly by customary law. However, unlike the ICJ (q.v.) decision in the *North Sea Continental Shelf* cases (q.v.), the arbitrators did not find much difference between art. 6 and the corresponding rule of customary law as under both standards the delimitation had to be effected in accordance with equitable principles. The tribunal took into account the "special circumstance" of the geographical location of the Channel Islands close to the French coast, which warranted a delimitation method other than the equidistance median line proposed by the UK; otherwise the French continental shelf share would be substantially reduced, creating an inequity for France. The Scilly Islands were given only "half-effect" in the delimitation of the Atlantic region because their projection into the Atlantic extended twice as far from the UK southwestern coast as does the Island of Ushant from the French mainland.

At the request of the UK, the tribunal clarified certain technical aspects of the meaning and scope of its decision in a second award delivered on 14 March 1978 (18 ILM 462 (1979)).

The Anglo-French continental shelf award of 1977 was an important contribution to clarifying the principles of international law governing delimitation of maritime spaces. It is frequently quoted along with the decisions of the ICJ dealing with similar delimitation problems, such as the *North Sea Continental Shelf (Federal Republic of Germany/Denmark; Federal Republic of Germany/Netherlands)* (q.v.), *Continental Shelf (Tunisia/Libya)* (q.v.), and *Continental Shelf (Libya/Malta)* (q.v.).

Delimitation of the Maritime Boundary in the Gulf of Maine (Canada/United States of America), ICJ 1981-1984. This case in the ICJ (q.v.) concerned disagreement between Canada and the US over the delimitation of their maritime boundary dividing the fishery zones and the continental shelf in the Gulf of Maine, after the two countries had extended their respective fishery jurisdictions to 200 (nautical) miles in 1976 and 1977 respectively. The disputed waters included the Georges Bank, one of the richest fishing grounds in the oceans.

The case is also of interest in that it was for the first time that, at the request of the parties, the case was considered by an *ad hoc* chamber (*see* **Chambers**) of five judges formed pursuant to art. 26(2) of the ICJ Statute which provides that the Court may form a chamber for dealing with a particular case, the number of judges constituting such a chamber being determined by the Court with the approval of the parties. The Court formed such a chamber by an order of 20 January 1982 (1982 ICJ Rep. 3).

In its judgment of 12 October 1984 (1984 ICJ Rep. 246) the Chamber of the Court, by four votes to one, awarded the US approximately two thirds of the Gulf, including three fourths of the Georges Bank fishing grounds.

The judgment is important in that it reaffirmed the principle of the law of the sea (forming part of public international law) that maritime delimitation must not be effected unilaterally but by agreement between the parties. Furthermore, the ICJ, following its other delimitation decisions (*see* **North Sea Continental Shelf; Continental Shelf (Tunisia/Libyan Arab Jamahiriya)**), ruled that "delimitation is to be effected by the application of equitable criteria and by the use of practical methods of ensuring with regard to the geographic configuration of the area and other relevant circumstances, an equitable result." In its complex decision, the Court combined the initial criterion of the equal division of the areas of convergence and overlapping with other appropriate criteria such as the conduct of the parties in the disputed area, existing fishing patterns, and the maintenance of optimum conservation and management of living resources.

Since each party got only part of what it had claimed, the ICJ decision left many US and Canadian fishermen unhappy, as demonstrated by difficulties encountered in the enforcement of the maritime boundary in the Gulf of Maine.

Dillard, Hardy C. (1902-1982). US national. Born in New Orleans and educated at the University of Virginia where he received a law degree in 1927. On the Faculty of the University of Virginia Law School, 1927-1929, 1931-1970; Dean 1963-1968. Judge of the ICJ (q.v.), 1970-1979. President of the American Society of International Law, 1962-1963. Author of numerous publications on international law, including lectures in *RCADI*.

Dispute *see* **International Dispute**

Dissenting Opinion *see* **Individual Opinion**

Dudgeon Case, ECHR 1981. This case before the ECHR (q.v.) concerned the application of Jeffrey Dudgeon, a 35-year-old homosexual and UK citizen residing in Belfast, Northern Ireland. In 1976, while searching, with warrant, his flat for illegal drugs, the police seized Dudgeon's diaries indicating his homosexuality. He was taken to a police station and for several hours there he was grilled about his sex life under Northern Ireland's 19th century laws which made homosexual acts between consenting males a criminal offense. However, the Director of Public Prosecution decided not to prosecute Dudgeon and his papers were returned to him.

Claiming that the Northern Ireland law on homosexuality constituted an unjustified interference with his right to respect for his private life, in breach of art. 8 of the European Convention for the Protection of Human Rights and Fundamental Freedoms of 4 November 1950 (213 UNTS 221), and that he had suffered discrimination within the meaning of art. 14 of the Convention on grounds of sex, sexuality, and residence, Dudgeon lodged an application with the European Commission of Human Rights. He also claimed compensation.

The Commission expressed the opinion that legal prohibition of homosexual acts between male persons over 21 breached art. 8 and referred the case to the ECHR. In its judgment of 22 October 1981, [1981] ECHR. Ser. A, no. 45, the Court held, by 15 votes to four, that there had been a breach of art. 8 and, by 14 votes to five, that it was not necessary to examine the case under art. 14. Dudgeon applied for just satisfaction, whereupon the Court granted him an amount for certain costs and expenses but denied his claim for compensation, ruling that in view of the changes in 1982 in the law of Northern Ireland on homosexuality to bring it in line with the remainder of the UK law, the judgment of the Court constituted an adequate just compensation.

The *Dudgeon* case is important not only because it contributed to the repeal of the 19th century law on homosexuality in Northern Ireland which it found not necessary in a democratic society for the protection of morals in the meaning of art. 8 of the Convention, but also because it recognized that the right to personality was part of the right to privacy in the meaning of this article of the European Human Rights Convention.

E

East African Community Court of Appeal for East Africa and Common Market Tribunal. Of historical interest, the Court and the Tribunal were the judicial organs of the now defunct East African Community which, for all practical purposes, ceased to function ten years after the establishment of the Community by a treaty in 1967 (6 ILM 932 (1967)).

Eastern Carelia *see* **Status of Eastern Carelia, PCIJ Adv. Op. 1923**

Eastern Greenland *see* **Legal Status of Eastern Greenland (Denmark v. Norway), PCIJ 1933**

Economic Community of West African States Tribunal. The judicial organ of the ECOWAS proposed in art. 11 of the Treaty of Lagos of 28 May 1975 establishing an economic Community of 16 West African states (14 ILM 1200 (1975)). Under the Treaty of Lagos the function of the Tribunal is to ensure the observance of law and justice in the interpretation of the Treaty and to settle disputes referred to it by members of the ECOWAS. The jurisdiction of the Tribunal is not compulsory. Its decisions are final. The Authority, which is the principal organ of the ECOWAS, was charged with determining the composition, jurisdiction and other matters relating to the Tribunal. So far this judicial body has not been activated.

Elettronica Sicula S.p.A. (ELSI) (United States of America v. Italy), ICJ 1987-1989. This case was brought before the ICJ (q.v.) by the US against Italy in respect of a dispute arising out of the requisition by Italy of the plant and related assets in Palermo of Elettronica Sicula S.p.A. (ELSI), a subsidiary company wholly owned by two US corporations; the Raytheon Co. and Machlett Laboratories, Inc. The US alleged that Italy's actions with respect to ELSI had violated certain provisions of the Treaty of

Friendship, Commerce and Navigation signed by the two countries on 2 February 1948 (79 UNTS 171) as well as the supplementary Agreement of 26 September 1951 to that Treaty (404 UNTS 326). The US founded the jurisdiction (q.v.) of the ICJ upon the compromissory clause (q.v.) in art. XXVI of the Treaty.

At the request of the US, adhered to by Italy, the case was decided by a special chamber (*see* **Chambers**) of five judges constituted by the Court's unanimous order of 2 March 1987 (1987 ICJ Rep. 3). This was the third time that the special chamber procedure was adopted by the ICJ (*see* **Delimitation of the Maritime Boundary in the Gulf of Maine Area (Canada/United States of America); Frontier Dispute (Burkina Faso/Mali)**).

In its judgment of 20 July 1989 (1989 ICJ Rep. 15) the Chamber of the Court unanimously rejected an Italian objection to the admissibility of the US application because of an alleged failure of the two companies to exhaust local remedies (*see* **Exhaustion of Local Remedies**). On the other hand, the Chamber, by a vote of four to one (the US judge), decided in favor of Italy that the seizure of ELSI did not constitute an illegal, arbitrary or discriminatory taking of property in violation of the Treaty of 1948 and the supplementary Agreement of 1951. Consequently the Chamber also rejected the US claim for reparation.

Like the *Barcelona Traction* case (q.v.), the decision in *Elettronica Sicula* is of interest in that it considers important questions related to the treatment of transnational corporations and the issue of expropriation in international law.

European Court of Human Rights (ECHR). The judicial body established within the framework of the Council of Europe pursuant to the European Convention for the Protection of Human Rights and Fundamental Freedoms of 4 November 1950 (213 UNTS 221) whose general task is to supervise, along with the European Commission of Human Rights, the observance of the rights and freedoms listed in the Convention. The ECHR, effectively set up in 1959, is the most active court of human rights. Headquartered in Strasbourg, it functions within the framework of the Council of Europe (an organization not to be confused with the European Community) which, set up on 5 May 1949 (87 UNTS 103) by the original ten Western European members, has now expanded to include almost all the European countries, including former communist states such as the Czech Republic, Slovakia, Hungary, and Poland.

The ECHR is made up of judges elected by the Consultative Assembly of the Council of Europe from national lists for a nine-year renewable term, on a staggered schedule and in a number equal to that of the members of the Council of Europe. No two judges may be nationals of the same state. The institution of the *ad hoc* judges (q.v.) of the ICJ (q.v.) system is also known in the ECHR. The judges of the ECHR serve in their individual capacity; they may not concurrently hold a government office that might interfere with their independence. They receive compensation for each day of duty.

The jurisdiction of the ECHR encompasses all cases concerning the interpretation and application of the Convention which the states parties or the Commission refer to it, but only as regards those states which have expressly recognized the jurisdiction (q.v.) of the Court by a declaration analogous in its nature to the optional clause (q.v.) declaration under the Statute of the ICJ. The declaration may be made on condition of reciprocity and for a specified period. A great majority of the states parties to the 1950 Convention have accepted the compulsory jurisdiction of the ECHR, most of them for a specified renewable period. However, *ad hoc* consent may also provide a basis for the Court's jurisdiction.

Generally speaking, two fundamental principles govern the jurisdiction of the ECHR. First, only the states parties to the 1950 Convention and the European Commission of Human Rights, a quasi-judicial crucial organ of the European human rights system, have the right to bring a case before the Court. Second, the Court may deal with a case only after the Commission has found a claim admissible, has established the facts of the case, and has acknowledged the failure of efforts at a friendly settlement, and only if the case has been referred to the Court within three months following the Commission's report on the complaint sent to the Committee of Ministers.

While, owing to the nature of the rights protected by the 1950 Convention, disputes normally originate with private individuals who can petition the Commission, complaining of alleged

violations of the Convention by--usually--their own respective
country, private petitioners have no right to be parties to litigation
before the ECHR. In addition, complaints will be considered by
the Commission only if the state involved has recognized, in a
declaration, the competence of the Commission to consider the
petition and if the individual concerned has met the requirement
of the exhaustion of local remedies (q.v.). However, since 1983
individuals have been able to appear in the Court and plead their
case through their own attorneys (advocates), once the case has
been brought before the Court by: 1. the Commission; or 2. the
state whose national is alleged to be a victim; or 3. the state
against which the complaint has been lodged; or 4. a state which
referred the case to the Commission. The case of *Ireland v. United
Kingdom* (q.v.) of 8 January 1978 (Ser. A/no. 25) was one of the
very rare cases in which a state instituted proceedings against
another state. In this case the ECHR ruled that the British
interrogation techniques in Northern Ireland constituted inhuman
and degrading treatment violating art. 3 of the 1950 Convention.

The ECHR functions according to its own rules and determines
its own jurisdiction. In its judgments it may not only decide that
the Convention has been violated but also award damages to the
victim. The Court's judgments are final. All states parties to a case
(which, of course, have consented to the Court's jurisdiction) must
abide by the Court's decision. While execution of the Court's
decisions is in the hands of the Committee of Ministers of the
Council of Europe, the Convention implies voluntary compliance
which, with very few exceptions, has indeed been the case. The
state ruled in violation of the Convention must usually pay
damages to the victim and/or amend its law, as was, for example,
done by the UK (the most frequent respondent before the
ECHR) in the *Dudgeon* (q.v.) and *Sunday Times* (q.v.) cases.

Since its first, celebrated, *Lawless* (q.v.) case in 1961 the ECHR
has decided some 150 cases and its docket has been growing
rapidly, with the Court increasingly willing to find states in breach
of the human rights guarantees of the 1950 Convention. Among
the rights upheld by the Court have been: the right to liberty and
fair public trial without unreasonable delay (*Lawless* (q.v.) and
Neumeister (q.v.) cases); the right to freedom of expression
(*Sunday Times* (q.v.) case); the right to association without

discrimination (*Swedish Engine Drivers' Union* case; *Belgian "Linguistic"* (q.v.) case); the right to privacy (*Dudgeon* (q.v.) case); and the right to education (*Belgian "Linguistic"* case). In general, the ECHR has emerged as the most progressive judicial institution for the protection of human rights on the international level and became a model for the Inter-American Court of Human Rights (q.v.). At the same time, the rapidly growing workload of the Commission and the Court raised the question of reforming the European Human Rights enforcement system, for example by merging the two institutions and making the Court a full-time permanent judicial body.

Under Protocol No. 2 of 1963 to the Convention of 1950 the ECHR may give advisory opinions (q.v.) at the request of the Committee of Ministers of the Council of Europe, but so far not much use has been made of this provision.

It may be added that the judges of the ECHR provide the bench for the European Tribunal in Matters of State Immunity (q.v.) which does not possess its own members.

European Nuclear Energy Tribunal. The judicial body of the OECD Nuclear Energy Agency, a constituent operational arm of the Organization for Economic Cooperation and Development not to be confused with the European Atomic Energy Community (Euratom). The OECD Nuclear Energy Agency was established in 1957 by the Council of the OECD (at that time Organization for European Economic Cooperation, OEEC) and the Tribunal itself was created pursuant to the Convention of 1957 on the Establishment of a Security Control in the Field of Nuclear Energy, in order to adjudicate disputes of state parties and private enterprises with the Nuclear Energy Agency. The Tribunal does not seem to have been called upon to deal with any cases.

European Road Transport Agreement Case, CJEC 1971. This is the leading case before the CJEC (q.v.) on the powers of the European Community in the field of foreign relations. In a confrontation between two organs of the Community, the Commission initiated action against the Council, seeking annulment of the Council's Resolution of 20 March 1970 to the effect that the individual members of the EC would negotiate and be parties to the revised European Road Transport Agreement (ERTA) open for signature as of 1 July 1970. The Commission contended that the Council's resolution violated the rules of the Treaty of Rome providing for a common transport policy (art. 75) and the power of the Commission to negotiate agreements with states and international organizations (art. 228). The Council, for its part, alleged that there was no question of the legality of the resolution involved in the case and that no provision of the Treaty authorized the Community to enter into international transport agreements.

In its judgment of 31 March 1971 (Case 22/70 [1970] ECR 263) the CJEC held that the Community's power to conclude treaties with non-member states was not only based on express provisions of the Treaty of Rome, but might equally flow from other Treaty provisions or measures adopted by the Community institutions even in the absence of an express provision in that respect. Such implied Community powers in the field of foreign relations were, in the Court's view, exclusive and existed whenever the Community held the respective internal competence in the area involved and the agreement with a non-member state was necessary for the attainment of any objective recognized by the EC law (compare the reasoning of the ICJ (q.v.) in its advisory opinion (q.v.) on **Reparation for Injuries Suffered in the Service of the United Nations (q.v.)**).

Having reaffirmed the principle of the Community's express and implied powers in the field of foreign relations, the Court rejected the Commission's application on the merits, however, because at the advanced stage of the ERTA negotiations it was disfunctional to suggest to foreign partners that the individual Community members had no right to act as parties, especially as both the Council and the members had acted in the interest of the whole Community.

The ERTA judgment is regarded as the landmark decision recognizing the Community's implied powers in its external relations and the "ERTA doctrine" has been reaffirmed in subsequent decisions of the CJEC.

European Tribunal in Matters of State Immunity. This Tribunal was established pursuant to the Additional Protocol to the European

Convention on State Immunity adopted under the auspices of the Council of Europe on 16 May 1972 (11 ILM 470, 485 (1972)). The function of the Tribunal is to adjudicate disputes between states parties to the Protocol over the interpretation and application of the 1972 Convention. The Tribunal does not have its own judges but consists of the members of the ECHR (q.v.) and, in respect of a non-member state of the Council of Europe which is party to the Protocol, of a person with equal qualifications designated for nine years by such state, with the agreement of the Committee of Ministers of the Council of Europe. As a rule, the Tribunal is to sit in a seven-member chamber and only in serious cases the Chamber may, at any time, relinquish jurisdiction in favor of the Tribunal meeting in plenary session.

The Protocol of 1972 entered into effect in 1985 and the jurisprudence of the Tribunal is expected to contribute to the work of harmonization of national rules governing state immunity, that is immunity of one state and its property from the jurisdiction of the courts in another state.

Ex *Aequo et Bono* and Equity. In international law and adjudication *ex aequo et bono* and equity are related but different concepts. *Ex aequo et bono* is a Latin phrase derived from civil (Roman) law, meaning "on the basis of what is equitable and good" or "according to what is equitable and good." In international law it refers to the power of an international court or arbitration tribunal to decide a case, at the request of the parties, not on the basis of the law but according to what, under the circumstances, is equitable, just and good irrespective of whether or not it departs from existing legal rules and principles. Art. 38(2) of the Statute of the ICJ (q.v.) confers upon the Court the power to decide a case *ex aequo et bono* if the parties agree thereto but so far there has never been a case before the ICJ in which the parties made use of this provision. On the other hand, in international arbitration (q.v.) tribunals have occasionally been authorized by the parties to decide in this way. For example in the 1930s two boundary disputes in Latin America were decided *ex aequo et bono*. As a matter of fact, it was not until the early 20th century that international law was added to justice and equity as bases for arbitral decisions.

Although occasionally in international acts, for example in the General Act of 1928 (q.v.) and in some arbitration agreements, the meaning of *ex aequo et bono* is confused with that of equity, the two concepts must be differentiated. In international law equity means fairness and reasonableness within the confines of the existing law, especially when interpreting or filling gaps in the law. In this sense equity is part of customary international law, as pointed out by the PCIJ (q.v.) in the case of *Diversion of Waters from the Meuse* (*Belgium/Netherlands*) in 1937 (*see* ANNEX I: JUDGMENTS OF THE PCIJ). It does not involve elements of compromise that override or conflict with rules of law. Equity, equitable principles and equitable solution are concepts referred to by the ICJ in a number of cases as an important factor in the Court's decision making, especially in disputes involving delimitation of maritime zones and boundaries, for example in such cases as *North Sea Continental Shelf* (q.v.), *Fisheries Jurisdiction* (q.v.), *Continental Shelf* (q.v.) and *Frontier Dispute* (q.v.).

The concepts of *ex aequo et bono* and equity in international law must be distinguished from equity in English law where equity has a more technical meaning of a special system of law.

Exhaustion of Local Remedies. This is a rule of international law governing admissibility of claims before international arbitration (q.v.) tribunals and international courts, including the ICJ (q.v.), whereby an injured person (an individual or company) must first exhaust the legal remedies available in the respondent state, that is the state in which the injury occurred, before the state of the injured person's nationality can exercise its right of active diplomatic protection and bring an international claim before an international tribunal on behalf of its national, that is "espouse" the national's claim. The rule of exhaustion of local remedies does not apply to disputes between states in which an injury was inflicted not on a private person but on a state itself which, in such cases, directly protects its own sovereign rights. The rule may also not apply in some exceptional cases involving private claims. Thus it was agreed between the states parties that the rule of exhaustion of local remedies would not apply to claims before the Mexican Claims Commission, one of the mixed claims commissions (q.v.) between the US and Latin American countries.

The notion of local remedy includes judicial protection which an injured alien person can obtain in the respondent state, but no remedies need be exhausted if resort to them would obviously be futile and justice would be denied.

The rule of exhaustion of local remedies has been applied by the ICJ in the case of *Interhandel* (q.v.) in which Switzerland's claim against the US was rejected because of non-observance of this rule. In this case the ICJ referred to the rule as "a well established principle of customary international law." As far as arbitral tribunals are concerned, the *Ambatielos* arbitration of 1956 between Greece and the UK, which followed the ICJ judgment in the *Ambatielos* case (Greece v. UK) (q.v.) in 1953, is usually quoted to illustrate the principle of exhaustion of local remedies. In this case the arbitrators held that Ambatielos had failed to exhaust local remedies because he had not called a vital witness and had not appealed from the Court of Appeal to the House of Lords.

F

Factory at Chorzów *see* **Certain German Interests in Polish Upper Silesia (Germany v. Poland), PCIJ 1925-1928**

Fisheries (United Kingdom v. Norway), ICJ 1949-1951. This important case before the ICJ (q.v.) concerned the Anglo-Norwegian dispute over the delimitation by Norway of the baselines from which the breadth of its territorial sea should be measured along its coastline characterized by deep indentations and a fringe of innumerable islands, islets and rocks in the immediate vicinity of the coast (the so-called *skjaergaard*). Because of this configuration of the coast, a Norwegian decree of 1935 delimited Norway's fishery zone (which at that time did not extend beyond the limits of the territorial sea) by adopting, as the baseline for measuring the breadth of the territorial sea, not the line following the outlines of the coast but straight baselines drawn between 48 base points on headlands, islands, islets and rocks in the sea. By moving seawards the territorial sea base, this method helped Norway extend its sovereignty in the marine area of much of its coast. The United Kingdom protested, maintaining that the use of straight baselines was contrary to international law and that in any case the length of a baseline should not exceed ten (nautical) miles (one nautical mile = 1,852 meters). No agreement could be reached and in 1949 the UK brought the case before the ICJ by an application based on the optional clause (q.v.).

In its judgment of 18 December 1951 the Court, by a vote of ten to two, rejected the British claim, ruling that the specific Norwegian coastline warranted the application of straight baselines along the *skjaergaard* and that international law did not limit to ten miles the length of such lines. On the other hand, the Court established certain criteria for drawing the straight baselines, namely that they must not depart appreciably from the general direction of the coast and, in general, that the coastal state must take into account international, including economic, aspects of the delimitation.

The principles enunciated by the ICJ in the Anglo-Norwegian *Fisheries* case and even the Court's very language had a great impact upon the rules of the law of the sea concerning the delimitation of the baselines for measuring the breadth of the territorial sea. The concept of the straight baselines and the criteria for tracing them were adopted in the Geneva Convention of 1958 on the Territorial Sea and the Contiguous Zone and the UN Convention on the Law of the Sea of 1982.

Fisheries Jurisdiction (United Kingdom v. Iceland) and Fisheries Jurisdiction (Federal Republic of Germany v. Iceland), ICJ 1972-1974. The proceedings in these two parallel cases were unfolding against the background of Iceland's unilateral decision to extend its exclusive fishery zone and the resulting conflict with other countries whose fishermen were fishing off Iceland's coasts, especially fishermen from West Germany and the UK.

The origin of the disputes can be traced back to the year 1958 when Iceland extended its exclusive fishery zone to 12 (nautical) miles, a unilateral act which caused British and West German protests and resulted in the first "cod war." Eventually, in 1961, an agreement was reached between the disputing countries, but ten years later, in 1971, Iceland again extended, as from 1972, its exclusive fishery zone, this time to as much as 50 miles. In response, the UK and West Germany, relying on the jurisdictional provisions of the 1961 agreement, submitted the dispute to the ICJ (q.v.). Iceland contested the Court's jurisdiction and virtually ignored the proceedings, thus initiating the defendant states' practice of non-appearing before the Court which was to be followed by a number of states in future cases.

At the request of the two applicant states, the Court, in two parallel orders of 17 August 1972 (1972 ICJ Rep. 12, 30), adopted by 14 votes to one, indicated interim measures of protection (provisional measures) (q.v.) which ordered Iceland to desist from enforcing, beyond 12 miles, its 50-mile fishery regulations against British and West German vessels. At the same time, however, the Court placed some ceilings upon the respective annual catches of the two applicant countries pending the delivery of the final judgments in the two cases. Subsequent failure of Iceland to comply with the orders resulted in a series of incidents involving Icelandic patrol boats and British and West German warships and popularly known as the "second cod war." This "war"--as far as the British, but not West German, boats were concerned--terminated with an agreement in November 1973.

In the meantime, despite Iceland's continued boycott of the ICJ, the proceedings at The Hague continued, with two parallel judgments of 2 February 1973 (1973 ICJ Rep. 3, 49), adopted by 14 votes to one, confirming the Court's jurisdiction. Two parallel interim protection orders of 12 July 1973 (1973 ICJ Rep. 302, 313) followed, and on 25 July 1974 the ICJ handed down the judgments on the merits (1974 ICJ Rep. 3, 175) by a majority of ten to four. These decisions were rather ambiguous. They did not declare the Icelandic 50-mile fishery zone illegal; the Icelandic regulations were held only to be not "opposable" to the countries whose fishermen had traditionally fished in the disputed waters. Hence Iceland was not entitled to exclude their vessels from the area between 12 and 50 miles. On the other hand, the ICJ ruled that the parties had the obligation to negotiate in good faith, taking account of the preferential share of Iceland to the extent of its special dependence on the fishing industry and the established fishing rights of other states.

Iceland disregarded the judgments of 1974, but the issue soon became moot due to the emergence of a generally recognized rule of the law of the sea permitting not just 50 miles for the exclusive fishery jurisdiction of the coastal state, but a 200-mile zone, the so-called exclusive economic zone (EEZ), a development codified in art. 57 of the UN Convention of 1982 on the Law of the Sea. However, echoes of the ICJ decisions in the *Fisheries Jurisdiction* cases can be found in art. 62 of this Convention which stipulates the coastal state's duty to share the utilization of the surplus living resources of the exclusive economic zone with other, especially developing and landlocked, states.

Fitzmaurice, Sir Gerald Gray (1901-1982). British national. Member of the ICJ (q.v.), 1960-1973. Educated at Cambridge University, barrister, Queen's Counsel. Chief Legal Adviser to the Foreign Office. Legal adviser to the UK delegation at numerous international conferences, including, as Assistant Legal Adviser, the San Francisco United Nations Conference on International Organization (1945) and the Paris (1947) and Japanese (1951) Peace Conferences. Member of the International Law Commission, elected Chairman in 1959 and General Rapporteur in 1957, 1958, and 1960. Judge of the ECHR (q.v.), 1974-1980. Author of numerous publications on international law, including lectures in *RCADI*.

Forum Prorogatum. A doctrine or principle, relied upon in practice by international tribunals, including the ICJ (q.v.), whereby the tribunal founds the consent of a state to its jurisdiction not on an express declaration but on that state's tacit consent inferred from the whole of its conduct in arguing the case on its merits subsequent to the initiation of the proceedings, without raising the question of jurisdiction (q.v.).

The principle of *forum prorogatum* was introduced into the practice of the PCIJ (q.v.) and the ICJ (q.v.) because ultimately the exercise of the Court's contentious jurisdiction (q.v.) depends on the parties' consent and the ICJ Statute and the Rules of the Court do not contain any specific mandatory rules concerning the form in which such consent can be expressed.

The doctrine of *forum prorogatum* was first relied upon by the PCIJ in the case of *Mavrommatis Jerusalem Concessions* (*Greece v. UK*) (1925) (*see* ANNEX I: JUDGMENTS OF THE PCIJ). In this case, the UK reply in its written argument to an issue raised by Greece that was not within the Court's jurisdiction, was found to be sufficient to confer jurisdiction upon the Court in respect of that issue. Similarly in the case of *Rights of Minorities in Upper Silesia* (*Minority Schools*) (*Germany v. Poland*) (1928) (*see* ANNEX I: JUDGMENTS OF THE PCIJ) the PCIJ ruled that submissions by Poland of arguments on the merits, without any objections with regard to the question of jurisdiction, must be regarded as an indication of recognizing the Court's jurisdiction in the case. The ICJ also relied on the doctrine of *forum prorogatum*. Thus in the case of *Corfu Channel, Preliminary Objection* (*UK v. Albania*) (1948) (q.v.), the ICJ inferred Albania's consent to its jurisdiction from a letter that Albania (which denied the UK right to bring the case to the Court) had sent to the Court, following the initiation of proceedings, in which it stated that it was prepared to appear before the ICJ.

In its interpretation of the principle of *forum prorogatum* the ICJ has been careful to emphasize that assent, if inferred, must be clearly present; otherwise the Court will not accept jurisdiction and the case must be removed from its List.

Frontier Dispute (Burkina Faso/Republic of Mali), ICJ 1983-1986. The proceedings in this case were initiated in 1983 by a special agreement between Burkina Faso and Mali requesting the ICJ to delimit a disputed part of their common frontier. This was the second case before the ICJ in which, at the request of the parties, their dispute was decided by a chamber (*see* **Chambers**) of the Court of five judges, including two *ad hoc* judges (q.v.), unanimously constituted by an order of the Court of 5 April 1985 (1985 ICJ Rep. 10), under art. 26(2) of the Court's Statute (*see* **International Court of Justice; Delimitation of the Maritime Boundary in the Gulf of Maine Area**).

On 10 January 1986 the ICJ Chamber's order (1986 ICJ Rep. 3) unanimously indicated provisional measures (q.v.) requiring both governments to withdraw their armed forces to such lines as might be determined by agreement between them; to continue to observe the ceasefire; not to modify the situation regarding the administration of the disputed area; and to avoid any act likely to aggravate or extend the dispute.

A unanimous judgment of the Chamber was delivered on 22 December 1986 (1986 ICJ Rep. 554). It is notable that, in indicating the line of the frontier in question, the ICJ upheld the principle of intangibility of frontiers inherited from the colonial era, as an application of the international law principle of *uti possidetis* in post-colonial Africa.

G

General Act for the Pacific Settlement of International Disputes, 1923 (Revised in 1949). An abortive multilateral treaty adopted on 26 September 1928 by the Assembly of the League of Nations which consolidated the rules and procedures governing the peaceful settlement of disputes between states. The Act represented a major but unsuccessful attempt to introduce a legal obligation to settle international disputes exclusively by peaceful means. A revised text of the General Act of 1928 was approved by the UN General Assembly on 28 April 1949 (71 UNTS 101).

The General Act made a distinction (*see* **Justiciability of International Disputes**) between legal disputes which, if conciliation (q.v.) failed, were to be compulsorily decided by arbitration (q.v.) or the PCIJ (q.v.) and non-legal or political disputes to be settled by conciliation or arbitration, with the possibility of deciding a dispute *ex aequo et bono* (q.v.).

Although the General Act of 1928 seems to have outlived the League of Nations and in its revised form was signed by seven states, the validity of the 1928 text is a disputed issue. It became a matter of controversy between the parties in some cases before the ICJ (q.v.), such as the *Aegean Sea Continental Shelf* (q.v.), *Nuclear Tests* (q.v.), and the *Trial of Pakistani Prisoners of War* case (1973) which was removed from the Court's List without judgment (*see* ANNEX V). However, the ICJ preferred not to get involved in determining the legal status of the General Act of 1928.

German Interests in Polish Upper Silesia *see* **Certain German Interests in Polish Upper Silesia (Germany v. Poland), PCIJ 1925-1928.**

Golder Case, ECHR 1975. In this case before the ECHR (q.v.) the applicant, a UK national, while serving a prison term in England, was accused by a prison guard of having assaulted him during a disturbance in the prison, as a result of which he was moved to solitary confinement. However, later the guard conceded that he might have been mistaken in identifying the assailant, and another guard gave evidence to the effect that the applicant had not even taken part in the disturbance. Golder was returned to his cell after 12 days in solitary confinement, and subsequently requested permission to consult a solicitor in order to take civil action for libel against the guard who had wrongly accused him of assault in his first statement which--as he believed--still remained on his record. However, Golder was denied communicating with a solicitor under the prison rules which prohibited such communication except with the permission of the Home Secretary. Golder lodged a complaint with the European Commission of Human Rights.

The Commission found that the conduct of the prison authorities (the Home Secretary) had violated the prisoner's right of access to the courts or tribunals under art. 6(1) of the European Convention for the Protection of Human Rights and Fundamental Freedoms of 4 November 1950 (213 UNTS 221), and that art. 8 of the Convention guaranteeing, *inter alia*, the right to respect for private life and correspondence also applied to the case.

The case was referred to the ECHR by the UK. In its judgment of 21 February 1975, [1975] ECHR Ser. A, no. 18, the Court ruled that the right to a fair and public hearing before an independent and impartial tribunal under art. 6 of the Convention necessarily entailed the right of a prisoner to have free communication with, and access to, legal advisers in order to institute legal proceedings before such a tribunal. In response to this judgment the UK amended its Prison Rules in 1976.

H

Hackworth, Green Haywood (1883-1973). US national. One of the most eminent American international lawyers. Attorney at Department of State, 1916-1918. Assistant Solicitor, 1918-1925; Solicitor, 1925-1931. Legal Adviser, 1931-1946. Member of the PCA (q.v.), 1937-1946. US adviser at San Francisco Conference, 1945, and many other international conferences. Member of the ICJ (q.v.), 1946-1961, and its President, 1955-1958. Author of numerous works on international law. Best known as editor of the 8-volume *Digest of International Law*, 1940-1944 *(see* BIBLIOGRAPHY 2 E(1)).

Hague Convention of 1899 for the Pacific Settlement of International Disputes (Revised in 1907). A multilateral convention, signed on 29 July 1899 (32 Stat. 779, TS No. 392) at the First Hague Peace Conference, which codified peaceful methods of settling international disputes and is of particular interest because it established the Permanent Court of Arbitration (q.v.). The Convention of 1899 was revised at the Second Hague Peace Conference on 18 October 1907 (36 Stat. 2199, TS No. 536).

The Hague Convention was ratified by all the great powers and many other states. Currently some 80 states are parties to the Convention in its 1899 or 1907 wording.

Hostages Case *see* **United States Diplomatic and Consular Staff in Tehran (United States v. Iran), ICJ 1979-1981.**

Huber, Max (1874-1960). Swiss national. Most eminent Swiss international lawyer. Delegate at the Second Hague Peace Conference, 1907; Professor, University of Zurich, 1902-1921; Legal Adviser to the Federal Council, 1918-1922. Member of the PCIJ (q.v.), 1928-1930, and its President, 1925-1927 and Vice-President, 1928-1930. Member of the PCA (q.v.), 1923-1940. Sole Arbitrator in the Island of *Palmas* case (q.v.), 1928. Member of the International Committee of the Red Cross, 1923-1947; its President, 1928-1944 and Acting President, 1945-1947. Author of numerous works, primarily in German, on international law.

Hudson, Manley Ottmer (1886-1960). US national. Most eminent international lawyer in the US of his time. Educated at Harvard Law School (LLB and SJD). Professor, University of Missouri, 1911-1916, Harvard Law School, 1916-1960. Legal adviser of US delegation at Versailles Peace Conference. Champion of US joining the PCIJ (q.v.) Statute. Member of the PCIJ, 1935-1939. Promoter of the idea of codifying international law; Director of Harvard Research in International Law. Worked with the UN Committee on the Progressive Development of International Law and Its Codification. Member of the International Law Commission; its Chairman, 1948-1953. President of American Society of International Law. Awarded by the Society the Manley O. Hudson Medal, created in his honor in 1955. Author of many works on the PCIJ and ICJ (q.v.), including annual reports in *AJIL* on their work.

Hurst, Sir Cecil James Barrington (1870-1963). British national. International lawyer and diplomat. Legal Adviser in the Foreign Office, 1918-1929. For 17 years member of the PCIJ (q.v.), 1927-1946, and its President, 1934-1938. Author of numerous publications on international law.

I

The *I'm Alone* Arbitration, 1933, 1935. This arbitration between Great Britain and the US resulted from their dispute over the sinking in 1929 by the US Coast Guard on the high seas off the US coast of a British-flag but American-owned schooner, the *I'm Alone*, on suspicion of smuggling liquor in violation of the Prohibition rules then in force in the US. The *I'm Alone* had first been discovered by the US Coast Guard, anchored with a cargo of liquor on the high seas but less than six-and-a-half miles off the Louisiana coast. Ignoring signals to heave to she fled, pursued by one, then two US Coast Guard vessels which caught up with her some 200 miles off the US coast. After she had refused to heave to, she was fired upon and sunk with the loss of one crew member and her cargo.

Great Britain demanded compensation, claiming that the US action constituted an unnecessary and unreasonable exercise by the US of the rights under the British-US Liquor Convention of 23 January 1924 (27 LNTS 182). On the other hand, the US contended, first, that the *I'm Alone* was owned by US nationals who abused the British flag for purposes of smuggling and, second, that the sinking was an outcome of a legitimate hot pursuit under the rules of the law of the sea. The Convention of 1924 allowed US authorities to board British-flag private vessels on the high seas, but only within a distance from the US coast which could be traversed by a suspected vessel in one hour.

In their award, the commissioners, appointed under the 1924 Convention, declared (3 UNRIAA 1609) the sinking of the *I'm Alone* to be illegal under the Convention of 1924 and under general international law. Although no sum was claimed by Great Britain, it (the Canadian government) was awarded $25,000 as a material amend for the indignity suffered by her flag. Certain sums were also awarded to innocent crew members but no compensation was awarded for the loss of the American-owned vessel.

The *I'm Alone* case is frequently quoted in international law commentaries in defining the parameters of the right of hot pursuit at sea. It is also significant in that the arbitrators followed the criterion of real ownership in refusing to grant compensation for the vessel which was *de facto* owned and controlled by US nationals who used it for illegal purposes.

Individual Opinion. This is an opinion that an individual judge of an international court may attach to a Court's judgment, order, or advisory opinion, in which he states and explains his position in regard to certain points in the Court's decision. Usually associated with the ICJ (q.v.), individual opinions may also be given by judges in other international tribunals, such as the ECHR (q.v.), and I-ACHR (q.v.), but not the CJEC (q.v.).

In the ICJ, an individual opinion can take the form of a dissenting opinion, a separate opinion, or a declaration. A dissenting opinion is one given by a judge who disagrees with the decision of the majority. It states the reasons for the disagreement in one or more points with the Court's decision and why in consequence the judge voted against the majority. A separate opinion is one given by a judge who, while voting in favor of the Court's decision, disagrees with some or all of its reasoning, which means that a separate opinion may be given even if the Court's decision is unanimous. This happened in the case of *Minquiers and Ecrehos* (q.v.) in 1953. Two or more judges may write a joint dissenting or separate opinion. A declaration is a brief indication by the declaring judge recording concurrence or dissent without stating the reasons.

Until the entry into force of the revised Rules of the ICJ on 1 July 1978, the Court's decisions provided only the number of judges voting for and against each point of the operative sections of the decision, but did not reveal who voted which way. Under the new Rules each decision indicates the names of the judges constituting the majority. The number of individual opinions attached to the decisions of the ICJ is relatively high: on an average there are seven individual opinions for a decision.

The right to attach individual opinions is not known in the European continental judicial systems, but is frequently used in the common law (Anglo-American) jurisdictions. Within the ICJ system, it has been a controversial issue, however. In one view this right could weaken the authority and cohesion of the Court, but in another view the judges' right to express their opinions freely is an essential safeguard of their independence in the interest of international justice. Moreover, many individual, including dissenting, opinions have been frequently quoted because of the prestige of their authors. In this sense individual opinions occupy the position midway between judicial decisions and the teaching of publicists, that is, scholars in international law.

Inter-American Commercial Arbitration Commission. The principal international commercial arbitration (q.v.) commission of the member states of the OAS, established at the Inter-American specialized conference on private international law under the Inter-American Convention on International Commercial Arbitration in Panama City on 30 January 1975 (14 ILM 336 (1975)). Twelve Latin American states were parties to the Convention in 1990. The US joined in 1990.

The function of the Commission is to settle any differences that may arise or have arisen between parties to the 1975 Convention with respect to a commercial transaction. Arbitrators are appointed as agreed by the parties and may be of any nationality.

Inter-American Court of Human Rights (I-ACHR). The judicial body established under the American Convention on Human Rights signed in San José, Costa Rica, on 22 November 1969 (9 ILM 673 (1970), in force 18 July 1978. The general function of the I-ACHR is to supervise, along with the Inter-American Commission of Human Rights, the observance of the rights and freedoms listed in the Convention. In 1991, 22 countries were parties to the Convention. The US, which signed it in 1977, had not ratified it and was not a party as of 1992.

The inter-American treaty system for the protection of human rights is closely modeled on the European system (*see* **European Court of Human Rights**). The I-ACHR was effectively set up in 1979. It operates on the legal basis of the Convention of 1969 and the Statute of the Court drawn up by the Court and approved by the OAS General Assembly in 1979. The Court adopted its Rules of Procedure in 1980.

The I-ACHR is made up seven judges, nationals of OAS states, elected by ballot by the state parties to the Convention for six-year once renewable terms from a panel of candidates proposed by these states. To preserve a quorum (five judges),one or more so called interim judges are appointed by the parties to the Convention to serve until replaced by elected judges. In 1991, the I-ACHR included judges from Mexico, Venezuela (President), US (Vice-President), Colombia, Honduras, Costa Rica and Argentina. *Ad hoc* judges (q.v.) may be designated.

The I-ACHR has contentious (q.v.) and advisory (q.v.) jurisdiction. Only states parties and the Commission have the right to submit cases; although individuals activate proceedings, they do not have access to the Court.

Like in the ICJ (q.v.) and the ECHR (q.v.), the jurisdiction of the I-ACHR is based on the parties' consent, which means that the Court has no power to deal with a contentious case unless the states concerned have accepted the Court's jurisdiction either in general by a declaration recognizing as binding the jurisdiction of the Court on all matters relating to the interpretation and application of the Convention (an instrument analogous to the optional clause (q.v.) declaration for purposes of the ICJ) or for a specific case. As of 1991, out of the 22 parties to the Convention, 12 states (Argentina, Colombia, Costa Rica, Chile, Ecuador, Guatemala, Honduras, Panama, Peru, Suriname, Uruguay, and Venezuela) had recognized as binding the jurisdiction of the I-ACHR.

Like in the European system, the I-ACHR may not hear a case unless it has first been investigated by the Commission, as illustrated by the *Gallardo* case (*see* below). Otherwise, the Commission appears before the Court in all cases. The judgments of the Court are final and not subject to appeal. They must be accompanied by reasons. Individual (dissenting and separate) opinions (q.v.) are allowed. Provisional (interim) measures (q.v.) can be granted.

The states parties to the Convention must comply with the judgment in any case in which they are parties. While the Convention refers to the possibility of executing a judgment's clauses stipulating compensatory damages in the country concerned and in accordance with the domestic procedure, the very small number of contentious cases before the I-ACHR has so far not allowed to test the execution possibilities in actual practice.

Like the ICJ (q.v.) and the ECHR (q.v.), the I-ACHR can deliver advisory opinions (q.v.), but its advisory jurisdiction is much more extensive than in those two courts. Not only an OAS organ but also any OAS state may consult the Court regarding the interpretation of the American Human Rights Convention of 1969 or other treaties concerning the protection of human rights in the American states. In addition, any OAS member state may seek an advisory opinion on the compatibility of its law with the Convention or any such treaties. As of mid-1992, the I-ACHR had delivered seven advisory opinions: three at the request of the Inter-American Commission of Human Rights, two requested by Costa Rica, one by Peru, and one by Colombia.

Compared with the ECHR, the achievements of the I-ACHR have been extremely modest. The Court has decided only two contentious cases. In the *Viviana Gallardo et al.* case (1981) (20 ILM 1424 (1981)) it refused to take jurisdiction in a case involving the death of a Costa Rican national in a Costa Rican prison because the matter had not been first submitted to the Commission. In the *Velásquez Rodríguez* case (1988) (28 ILM 291 (1989)) and another identical case in 1989, referred to the Court by the Commission, the Court found Honduras responsible for forced disappearance and death of its nationals in violation of the American Convention on Human Rights. These decisions were an important development in the history of the American system of protecting human rights.

Interhandel (Switzerland v. United States), ICJ 1957-1959. The background of this case was as follows: During the Second World War the United States seized 90 percent of the shares of the General Aniline and Film Corporation, a US-incorporated company, on the grounds that they were enemy property, being owned by Interhandel, a Swiss company which--as claimed by the US--belonged to or was controlled by the German company IG Farben. After nine years of unsuccessful litigation in US courts to recover the assets, Interhandel petitioned the US Supreme Court for *certiorari*. While the petition was pending before the Court, Switzerland brought the case, under the optional clause (q.v.), against the US before the ICJ (q.v.) in 1957. It asked the ICJ to declare that the US was under an obligation to restore the Interhandel's seized assets or alternatively to submit the dispute to arbitration (q.v.) under the 1946 Washington Accord between the US, the UK, France and Switzerland which provided for the seizure and liquidation of German property in Switzerland and unblocking of Swiss assets in the US, or for any other method of settlement under the US-Switzerland Treaty of 1931 on Arbitration and Conciliation. In addition, Switzerland requested the ICJ to indicate provisional measures (q.v.) designed to protect its claimed assets in the US.

The US raised an objection to the ICJ jurisdiction on the ground that the disposition of shares of a US-incorporated company was a matter of domestic jurisdiction, and as such it fell under the automatic reservation (q.v.) of the US acceptance of the optional clause (q.v.). Shortly thereafter, while the case was pending before the ICJ, the US Supreme Court ordered a new trial for Interhandel, remanding the case to the District Court. Thus the case found itself pending both in the US court system and before an international tribunal.

In its order of 24 October 1957 (1957 ICJ Rep. 105), the ICJ refused to indicate provisional measures (interim measures of protection) on the ground that the Interhandel assets in the US were in no danger of being sold while the case was still pending before a US court.

Subsequently, in its judgment of 21 March 1959 (1959 ICJ Rep. 6), the ICJ, by nine votes to six, found Switzerland's claim inadmissible on the ground of non-exhaustion of local remedies (*see* **Exhaustion of Local Remedies**), the circumstance otherwise invoked by the US in its preliminary objection. However, the ICJ rejected the other objection of the US: it did not find it necessary to consider the US objection relying on its automatic reservation (q.v.).

The *Interhandel* case is a classical illustration of the well established rule of customary international law of exhaustion of local remedies (q.v.).

Interim Measures of Protection *see* **Provisional Measures**

International Arbitration *see* **Arbitration**

International Centre for Settlement of Investment Disputes (ICSID).
The ICSID is an international arbitration (q.v.) institution closely associated with the World Bank and created by the Washington Convention of 18 March 1965 on the Settlement of Investment Disputes between States and Nationals of Other States (575 UNTS 159). Its function is to provide facilities for conciliation (q.v.) and arbitration of legal investment disputes between states and foreign investors. The ICSID was established to encourage, by the services of a neutral institution, a climate of mutual confidence between private investors and governments of developing countries and thus promote the latter's economic development.

The ICSID operates through standing panels of qualified conciliators and arbitrators, some of whom are appointed, for five years, by the states parties and others are chosen for this term by the President of the World Bank. Arbitrators may be appointed either from an ICSID panel or from outside. In practice, more arbitrators are appointed by the Chairman of the Administrative Council of the ICSID at the request of the parties.

The services of the arbitrators are available to states and their nationals after a state has joined the ICSID Convention which, as of June 1991, was ratified by 95 states. Consent to submit a dispute to the ICSID must be given in writing, whereupon the state of the national involved waives its right of diplomatic protection in respect of the dispute.

An ICSID arbitral tribunal is constituted either by a sole arbitrator or any uneven number, as agreed by the parties. It applies such rules of law as may be agreed upon by them, but in the absence of agreement the tribunal applies the law of the host state, party to the dispute, and relevant rules of international law. In practice, both systems of law, domestic and international, are applied. An agreement between a host state and a foreign investor, whereby international law is to govern the case, is sometimes referred to as an "internationalized" agreement.

Awards of ICSID arbitral tribunals are made by majority vote. At the request of either party the tribunal can interpret the award. Revision is possible on the ground of discovery of fresh decisive evidence. An award can be annulled on the usual grounds recognized in international arbitration such as corruption, departure from a fundamental rule of procedure, or failure to state the reasons.

The ICSID awards are binding on the parties, and each state is obliged to recognize them and enforce the pecuniary obligations imposed by an award within its territory as if it were a final judgment of a court of that state. A party seeking recognition and enforcement of an award simply furnishes to a competent court or other authority a certified copy of the award. A recognized award becomes an executory title enforceable against an investor or its assets.

States enjoy the so-called sovereign or state immunity under international law but the exact scope of such immunity is not a settled issue. Hence enforcement and execution against a state which is the losing party depends on the extent of such immunity obtaining in the state in which execution is sought. The ICSID Convention only confirms the existence of state immunity, but does not address the question of immunity from execution. A clause stipulating prior waiver of such immunity in a contract with a state is recommended by ICSID to remedy the situation. In the US the Foreign Sovereign Immunities Act of 1976, as amended in 1978 (28 USC Sec. 1605 (a)), removes immunity of a foreign state in actions for enforcement of an arbitral agreement, including that under the ICSID Convention, and declares as not immune from execution property of a foreign state used in commercial activity (*jure gestionis*) in the US.

By June 1991 at least 26 cases had been decided by ICSID arbitration. While this is a rather modest amount, ICSID decisions are becoming an important source of practice in international economic law.

International Chamber of Commerce (ICC) Court of Arbitration. The ICC Court of Arbitration is the best known private international commercial arbitration (q.v.) body, operating within the framework and according to the rules of the ICC in Paris. The latest Rules were adopted in 1989 (28 ILM 233 (1989)).

Established in 1922, the ICC Court of Arbitration has handed down more international commercial arbitration decisions than any other similar organization. In 1990, 365 requests for arbitration were filed with the ICC.

Despite its name, the ICC Court is not a judicial institution in the traditional sense. It does not, itself, settle disputes, but for a fee provides an administrative structure for plaintiffs and defendants within which *ad hoc* arbitration tribunals deal with specific disputes of parties which, by contract, agree to employ the ICC. ICC rules are usually applied, but can be modified by the parties. Arbitrators, or a sole arbitrator, are appointed by the ICC Court from among persons nominated by the parties, but under the circumstances and according to procedures spelled out in the Rules the Court appoints the arbitrators if the parties cannot reach agreement. The parties can be represented by counsel. Arbitration is held at the place fixed by the Court unless otherwise agreed upon by the parties. In practice, in about half of the arbitration cases before the ICC, the parties take advantage of the ICC Rules.

If the parties do not determine the law applicable to the merits of the dispute, the arbitrator chooses the law which he deems appropriate. With the parties' consent, he can also assume the powers of an *aimable compositeur* in an effort to reach a compromise between the parties.

In general, proceedings before the ICC arbitration courts are less formal than those before ordinary courts. Awards must be made within six months following the signing of the terms of reference drawn by the arbitrator before the actual proceedings, but the Court may, at the arbitrator's (or arbitrators') request or at its own initiative, extend this time limit. If there are three arbitrators, the award is given by a majority decision. The decision also deals with the allocation of the costs. Before signature, all awards must be scrutinized by the Court which may modify the form of the award and, without prejudice to the arbitrators' liberty of decisions, draw their attention to points of substance. A major concern of the Court is to see to it that the award meets the requirements needed for enforcement in general jurisdiction legal proceedings. The award is final and must be carried out by the parties without delay.

In general, the ICC arbitration structure has been a successful international commercial arbitration institution except that because of its Western origins dating back to the past colonial era and associations with transnational corporations it has not been favored much by developing countries.

International Commercial Arbitration. This is a legally binding settlement of private-law international commercial disputes by an impartial arbitrator or arbitrators deciding the dispute on the basis of the parties' agreement which normally determines the choice of arbitrators, the venue, applicable law, language, and rules of the arbitration procedure. By agreeing to submit their dispute to commercial arbitration, the parties waive their right to bring it before a national court. The private-law character of international commercial arbitration distinguishes it from arbitration (q.v.) between states governed by public international law.

A number of private or state-sponsored permanent arbitral institutes exist to offer their services for payment of a fee to clients preferring arbitration to adjudication by a national court. These institutes primarily provide their organizational and administrative structure within which arbitral courts are set up for specific disputes. The International Chamber of Commerce (ICC) (q.v.) is perhaps the best known private international commercial arbitral institute and the International Centre for Settlement of Investment Disputes (ICSID)(q.v.) of the World Bank is the most important state-sponsored arbitral body. On the national level there exist arbitral institutes in many countries, such as the American Arbitration Association (AAA) (q.v.) in the US and the London Court of Arbitration in the UK. In addition to general purpose arbitral institutes there are also specialized arbitration bodies to deal with disputes in specific trade areas such as, for example, maritime and various commodity disputes. Finally, to retain control over the choice of arbitral procedure, parties may choose an *ad hoc* arbitration instead of resorting to a body of institutionalized arbitration where their dispute is normally subject to the rules governing the chosen arbitral institution.

It is in the nature of international commercial arbitration to produce legal effects in more than one national jurisdiction and potential problems in the area of recognition and enforcement of awards. The New York Convention on the Recognition and Enforcement of Foreign Arbitral Awards of 1958 (q.v.) (superseding for the signatory states the Geneva Convention of

1927) sets forth relevant rules to remedy such problems. The European Convention on International Commercial Arbitration of 21 April 1961 (484 UNTS 364) and the Inter-American Convention on International Commercial Arbitration of 30 January 1975 (14 ILM 336 (1975)) deal with similar matters but are in force for a limited number of countries.

In commercial arbitration, awards against the losing party are enforced by national courts at the request of the winner. Under certain circumstances envisaged by the New York Convention, such as invalidity of the arbitration agreement, irregular appointment of arbitrators, or error in procedure, the state of forum may refuse recognition and enforcement of an award. Enforcement of awards in disputes between states and private foreign investors is largely covered by the Convention of 18 March 1965 on the Settlement of Investment Disputes between States and Nationals of Other States (575 UNTS 159) which created the ICSID.

Commercial arbitration offers a number of advantages to business enterprises. Apart from a relatively low cost and a chance of a more speedy settlement, it allows them more flexibility as against litigation in a court. It also offers them a possibility to have their dispute decided by a tribunal potentially more impartial than a national court of either party. The possibility of choosing arbitrators who are not lawyers but experts in the required area may also encourage resort to commercial arbitration.

International Court of Justice (ICJ). One of the six principal organs of the United Nations and its principal judicial organ. A successor in fact of the Permanent Court of International Justice (PCIJ) (q.v.), the ICJ, popularly known as the "World Court," functions on the basis of Chapter XIV of the UN Charter and the ICJ Statute which forms an integral part of the Charter. The Statute is supplemented by the Rules of Court of 1946, largely based (like most other provisions) on the Rules of the PCIJ, which were amended in 1972 and thoroughly revised in 1978 (17 ILM 1286 (1978)) in order to simplify the proceedings and enhance their flexibility. In addition, the Court adopted a resolution concerning its non-binding Internal Judicial Practice, revised in 1976 (7 ILM 1305 (1968); 15 ILM 950 (1976)).

All members of the UN are *ipso facto* parties to the Statute, but non-member states may become parties on conditions to be determined in each case by the General Assembly upon the recommendation of the Security Council. With Liechtenstein and San Marino now members of the UN, today only Switzerland (since 1946, 17 UNTS 111) and more recently, since 1987, Nauru are parties to the Statute on this basis. Any other state may appear as a party before the ICJ after depositing with the Court's Registry a declaration accepting the Court's jurisdiction (*see* **Contentious Jurisdiction of the ICJ**) and undertaking to comply with its decisions in respect of all or a particular class of decisions, a provision largely outdated today considering the almost universal membership of the United Nations.

The ICJ is composed of 15 independent judges elected for a nine-year term with the possibility of re-election, with five judges elected every three years, at separate meetings, by the General Assembly and--without the right of veto--the Security Council. The judges are elected from a list of persons nominated by the "national groups" in the Permanent Court of Arbitration (PCA) (q.v.) or, if the state concerned is not represented in the PCA, by national groups appointed for this purpose by the government. Complex rules, providing for a joint conference made up of three members appointed by the Security Council and three by the General Assembly, govern situations where seats on the Court remain unfilled after a third meeting of the two UN organs. A judge replacing another whose term of office has not expired holds office only for the remainder of his predecessor's term. The judges are elected as individuals regardless of nationality, but no two of them can be nationals of the same state. A judge can be dismissed only by a unanimous decision of the other members of the ICJ.

In its composition the ICJ must as a whole assure the representation of the main forms of civilization and of the principal legal systems of the world. The permanent members of the Security Council, that is, China, France, Russia, the UK, and the US, normally have judges elected to the ICJ, but China did not have any national elected a judge in the period 1960-1984. Prior to 1960, a judge from the nationalist Republic of China in Taiwan had been sitting on the Court. In 1984 the first judge from communist China was elected to the ICJ and took office in 1985.

The Court elects its President and Vice-President for three years, with a possibility of re-election.

As of 1 June 1993, the composition of the ICJ was as follows: President: Jennings (UK), Vice-President: Oda (Japan). Judges Ago (Italy); Schwebel (US); Bedjaoui (Algeria); Ni (China); Evensen (Norway); Tarassov (Russia); Guillaume (France); Shahabuddeen (Guyana); Aguilar Mawdsley (Venezuela); Weeramantry (Sri Lanka); Ranjeva (Madagascar); Ajibola (Nigeria); and Herczegh (Hungary).

Judges of the nationality of each of the parties ("national judges") retain the right to sit in the case. Moreover, if a party before the Court does not have a judge of its nationality on the Court, it may appoint a judge *ad hoc* (q.v.).

The ICJ has its seat at The Hague in the Peace Palace funded by Andrew Carnegie before the First World War, but it may exercise its functions wherever it considers desirable. A Registry, headed by a Registrar, is the administrative organ of the Court.

As a rule, decisions are made by the full Court, with a quorum of nine sufficing to constitute the Court. However, at the request of the parties, a case may be heard and determined by a chamber (*see* **Chambers**) whose judgment is considered as rendered by the Court. As of 1 June 1993, the chamber proceedings had been used five times.

Only states may be parties in contentious cases before the ICJ. The contentious jurisdiction of the ICJ (q.v.), that is, jurisdiction to adjudicate disputes, is governed by the fundamental principle that no state can be brought before the Court without its consent, express (*ad hoc* submission, on the basis of a treaty, under the optional clause(q.v.)) or implied (for example through *forum prorogatum* (q.v.)). The principle of compulsory jurisdiction, favored by numerous small states at the 1945 San Francisco United Nations Conference on International Organization, was rejected by the great powers.

It may be added that, in a sense, the ICJ also has appellate jurisdiction resulting from provisions in a limited number of conventions providing for such jurisdiction. For example, the Convention of 1944 on International Civil Aviation (15 UNTS 295) envisages appeals to the ICJ from decisions of the ICAO Council. This happened in the ICJ case concerning *Appeal Relating to the*

Jurisdiction of the ICAO Council (India v. Pakistan) 1971-1972 (q.v.).

Pursuant to art. 96 of the UN Charter the ICJ may give advisory opinions (q.v.) on any legal question at the request of the UN General Assembly, the Security Council or a specialized agency so authorized by the General Assembly.

As a judicial body, under art. 38 of its Statute the ICJ decides disputes in accordance with international law, applying as sources of this law treaties, international custom as evidence of a general practice accepted as law, and the general principles of law recognized by civilized nations, generally meaning principles common to most or all national systems of law and general principles of international law. Furthermore, the ICJ applies judicial decisions and the teachings of the most highly qualified publicists, that is, writers in international law, as "subsidiary means for the determination of rules of law."

However, it must be emphasized that under an express provision of its Statute (art. 59) the decision of the Court has no binding force except between the parties and in respect of that particular case. This means that, unlike the courts in the countries of the common-law system, the ICJ and other international tribunals for that matter are not obliged to follow the doctrine of *stare decisis*, that is, the duty to follow its own previous decisions and--generally speaking of all international tribunals--decisions of the court concerned and those of other tribunals of equal or greater authority. Yet, despite the absence of the principle of *stare decisis* in international law, the World Court has always had a strong tendency to rely upon its prior (PCIJ and ICJ) judgments and advisory opinions. Because of its high prestige, other international courts have also occasionally referred to the World Court's pronouncements, including *obiter dicta*, that is, lesser propositions of law not connected with the principal issue, stated by the Court or by individual judges in their separate or even dissenting individual opinions (q.v.).

With the parties' consent, the ICJ has the power to decide a case *ex aequo et bono* (*see* **Ex Aequo et Bono** and **Equity**), that is, on grounds of justice and other extra-legal considerations. So far the ICJ has not decided any case on this basis.

The proceedings before the ICJ can be conducted in English or

French and are initiated either by the notification of the "special agreement" (*compromis*) (q.v.) of the parties or by a written application (*see* **Contentious Jurisdiction of the ICJ**). Intervention by other states in the proceedings is possible (*see* **Intervention in Proceedings**). To preserve the respective rights of either party the Court may indicate provisional measures (q.v.). The parties may be, and normally are, represented by agents and assisted by counsel and advocates. The proceedings consist of written pleadings (memorials, counter-memorials, and--if authorized by the Court--replies and rejoinders) and oral hearings which are public unless the Court decides otherwise or unless the parties demand a closed session. All questions are decided by a majority of the judges present; in the event of an equality of votes the President has a casting vote, as happened in the *South West Africa* (q.v.) case in 1962. The judgment must state the reasons on which it is based and must contain the names of the judges voting for and against the majority. Any judge is entitled to attach an individual opinion (q.v.), separate or dissenting, or a declaration. Proceedings before the ICJ are very frequently affected by "preliminary objections" (q.v.) raising questions of admissibility of claim and/or jurisdiction (q.v.) of the Court.

The ICJ judgment is final and without appeal, but in the event of a dispute as to the meaning or scope of the judgment the Court construes it upon the request of any party. In case of the discovery of new evidence of decisive importance an application for revision of a judgment is possible within ten years following the date of the judgment. In 1984, for the first and only time in the history of the World Court, the Court was requested to revise its judgment and, for the second time, to interpret it, when such requests came from Tunisia concerning the judgment in the *Continental Shelf (Tunisia/Libyan Arab Jamahiriya)* case (q.v.) (*see also* the ICJ judgment in **Application for Revision and Interpretation of the Judgment of 24 February 1982**).

The UN Charter provides in art. 94(1) that parties must comply with the ICJ decision. While the ICJ itself has no procedures for enforcing its decisions, according to this article failure to perform the obligations incumbent upon a party under a judgment authorizes the other party to have recourse to the Security Council which may make recommendations or decide upon measures to be taken to give effect to the judgment. These provisions of the Charter have never been effectively implemented. While the UK did have recourse to the Security Council to enforce the provisional measures (q.v.) indicated by the ICJ in 1951 in the *Anglo-Iranian Oil Co.* (q.v.) case, the obligation incumbent upon Iran was decreed by the Court not in a judgment but in an order, and it is not clear whether provisional measures indicated in an ICJ order are enforceable by the Security Council. Besides, in the *Anglo-Iranian Oil Co.* case the ICJ subsequently ruled that it lacked jurisdiction in the case. In another instance, a draft resolution of the Security Council calling for compliance with the ICJ judgment of 1986 in the case of *Military and Paramilitary Activities in and against Nicaragua (Nicaragua v. US)* (q.v.) was vetoed by the US (25 ILM 1352 (1986)).

In general, the judgments of the ICJ have been complied with. Among the few exceptions have been: Communist Albania's refusal to pay the UK compensation in the *Corfu Channel* (q.v.) case and Iran's failure to comply with the Court's judgment in the *United States Diplomatic and Consular Staff in Tehran* (q.v.) case.

A disturbing phenomenon in cases before the ICJ (especially in the 1970s and 1980s) has been non-appearance of respondent states against which proceedings were instituted by applications (*see* **Contentious Jurisdiction of the ICJ**). Such conduct, unknown in the PCIJ, has occurred ten times in the ICJ. In this respect, even some Western, ostensibly law abiding, countries refused to appear before the Court: France in the *Nuclear Tests* (q.v.) cases; Iceland in the *Fisheries Jurisdiction* (q.v.) cases; and even the US, which refused to participate in the merits phase of the case concerning *Military and Paramilitary Activities in and against Nicaragua*. Under the ICJ rules non-appearance of a party or failure to defend its case is no impediment for the Court's deciding in favor of the other party provided the Court is satisfied that it has jurisdiction and the claim is well founded in fact and law.

By 15 July 1993, that is in more than 47 years of the ICJ's existence, 67 contentious cases had been brought before this Court and placed on its General List (*see* ANNEXES III-V). This figure includes parallel proceedings in identical disputes, such as the *Nuclear Tests* and the two Lockerbie-related cases concerning the application and interpretation of the 1971 Montreal Convention, brought by Libya against the UK and US respectively in 1992 (*see* ANNEX IV: CASES PENDING BEFORE THE ICJ AS OF 15 JULY 1993), but counts the *Asylum* and *Haya de la Torre* (q.v.) proceedings as one case. Cases of interpretation of a prior judgment are treated as forming part of the original case. The figure 67 includes the proceedings instituted by Iran against the US; by Bosnia and Herzegovina against Yugoslavia; and the case between Slovakia and Hungary (*see* ANNEX IV: CASES PENDING BEFORE THE ICJ AS OF 15 JULY 1993). Out of the 67 disputes placed on the Court's List, 17 were removed from the List without any judgment (*see* ANNEX V: CONTENTIOUS CASES BEFORE THE ICJ FILED BUT REMOVED FROM THE LIST WITHOUT ANY JUDGMENT). The ICJ delivered 56 judgments, out of which 27 were on the merits. The remaining judgments dealt primarily with preliminary objections (q.v.); a few ruled the applicant as lacking standing or declared the case as moot.

As of 15 July 1993, 11 cases were pending before the ICJ, a record number in the history of the Court. This indicated a renewed interest in the World Court, especially among the non-Western countries (*see* ANNEX IV: CASES PENDING BEFORE THE ICJ AS OF 15 JULY 1993). In addition to judgments, the ICJ rendered 20 advisory opinions (q.v.) (*see* ANNEX VI: ADVISORY OPINIONS OF THE ICJ). The Court also issued about 220 orders, mostly of procedural nature.

The record of the ICJ has been mixed. While it has played a minor role in maintaining international peace and most of the disputes submitted to it have been of peripheral nature, its judgments and advisory opinions have made a significant contribution to the clarification and even development of international law. In the early 1990s the prospects for the ICJ seemed brighter as, in the post-Cold War era, more countries were willing to accept the jurisdiction of the Court and the interest in the ICJ of non-Western countries was on the rise. At the same time, a debate continued among international law scholars over various ideas concerning the reform of the World Court, such as for example allowing international organizations and individuals standing before the Court, the use of Chambers in advisory jurisdiction, and--last but not least--strengthening the Court's potential for compulsory jurisdiction.

International Criminal Courts. At present there exists no international criminal court, that is, an international tribunal designed to try offenses against international law, although numerous proposals have been put forward to establish such a tribunal and the matter has been on the agenda of the UN for some time. There seems to be consensus on the desirability of creating an international criminal court. On the other hand, governments are not very enthusiastic on this idea, being reluctant to relinquish their sovereignty and submit their citizens and perhaps even themselves to an international criminal jurisdiction in uncertain future cases where such jurisdiction might not suit their perceived interests and might turn against them.

Beginning with piracy, the first international crime, that is, a crime punishable under the law of nations (international law), some other acts have eventually been recognized as crimes committed not just in violation of domestic (national or "municipal") law but against the law of nations. Here belong: war crimes in the strict sense of the term, that is, violations of the law and custom of war, that is, breaches of the so-called international humanitarian law; and--according to the Nuremberg Tribunal--crimes against humanity (genocide) and against peace, that is, aggression. Already before the Second World War, in 1937, terrorist acts generated a draft convention for an international court to try terrorists--whatever this subjective term may mean--and more recently terrorist activities have emerged as a major category of international crime.

While currently there exists no international criminal court, two such courts were established as a sequel to the Second World War: the International Military Tribunal at Nuremberg (q.v.), popularly known as the Nuremberg Tribunal, and the International Military Tribunal for the Far East (q.v.), known as the Tokyo Tribunal. Almost a half century later, on 22 February 1993, in response to atrocities committed in the armed conflict raging in the former Yugoslav state, especially in Bosnia-Herzegovina, the UN Security Council, in its Resolution 808, unanimously voted to set up an international criminal tribunal to prosecute the individuals accused of violating international humanitarian law in the Yugoslav conflict.

International Dispute. For purposes of adjudication by international tribunals the concept of dispute has no precise connotation. As defined by the PCIJ (q.v.) in the case of *Mavrommatis Palestine Concessions (Greece v. Great Britain)* (Judgment No. 2, 1924 PCIJ, Series A, No. 2), a dispute, as a prerequisite for resorting to an international tribunal, means "disagreement on a point of law or fact, a conflict of legal views or of interests between two persons." For the ICJ (q.v.) to be seised of a case, a dispute must genuinely exist between the states concerned. As held by the PCIJ in the case *Interpretation of Judgments 7 and 8 (Factory at Chorzów) (Germany v. Poland)* (Judgment No. 11, 1927 PCIJ, Series A, No. 13), while the dispute need not necessarily be manifested by diplomatic negotiations it would be desirable for a state filing an application to the Court to make it quite clear that a difference of view existed with another state which could not be otherwise overcome. Consequently, in some cases, for example in *Electricity Company of Sofia and Bulgaria (Belgium/Bulgaria)* (Judgment, 1939 PCIJ, Series A/B, No. 77, 64), the PCIJ rejected a claim on the ground that the applicant state had not established the existence of a dispute.

What is meant by an "international" dispute is a difficult question to which no general answer can be given. Under international law, as stipulated in art. 2(3) of the UN Charter and other treaties, only "international" disputes must be settled by peaceful means. This principle is a peremptory rule (*jus cogens*) of general international law, that is, "a norm accepted and recognized by the international community of States as a whole as a norm from which no derogation is permitted and which can be modified only by a subsequent norm of general international law having the same character" (art. 53 of the Vienna Convention of 23 May 1969 on the Law of Treaties, 8 ILM 679 (1969)). Non-international disputes are disputes whose subject matter is essentially within the domestic jurisdiction of a state; under international law they need not, in principle, be settled by peaceful means. The reservation to acceptance of compulsory jurisdiction (q.v.) of the ICJ concerning domestic jurisdiction, including the automatic (self-judging) reservation (q.v.), has been a device whereby states exclude from the ICJ jurisdiction disputes which potential adversary states would otherwise like to raise to the level of international disputes, thereby subjecting them to the Court's jurisdiction.

No clear definition of the "international" element of a dispute is possible, but--as held by the PCIJ in its advisory opinion (q.v.) on *Nationality Decrees Issued in Tunis and Morocco* (1923 PCIJ, Series B, No. 4)--the scope of a state's domestic jurisdiction is essentially relative and depends upon the development of international law. The continued trend toward expanding international versus domestic jurisdiction in such matters as human rights, protection of environment, and even promoting a democratic system of national government, is likely to be reflected in the widening scope of the concept of "international" dispute before international courts and tribunals.

International Military Tribunal (IMT) at Nuremberg, 1945-1946. This most famous of all the international criminal tribunals (q.v.) was set up on an *ad hoc* basis under the London Agreement of 8 August 1945 between the US. UK, USSR, and France (later acceded to by 19 states) for the Prosecution and Punishment of the Major War Criminals of the European Axis, with an annexed Charter which provided the basis of the Tribunal's jurisdiction (82 UNTS 279).

The Tribunal consisted of four members, each with an alternate, appointed by the individual original signatory powers. The Charter empowered the Tribunal to try and punish persons who, acting in the interests of the European Axis countries, whether as individuals or as members of organizations, had committed: 1. crimes against peace; 2. war crimes; or 3. crimes against humanity; or had conspired to commit any of the foregoing categories of crime. Neither the official position nor the plea of superior orders was considered as freeing the defendants from responsibility, but the plea of superior orders might be considered in mitigation of punishment. The Tribunal was also given the jurisdiction to declare a group or organization criminal.

The Tribunal sat at Nuremberg from 20 November 1945 until 31 August 1946 and delivered its judgment on 30 September-1

October 1946. Of the 22 major war criminals, 12 (including Bormann in absentia) were sentenced to death; three to life imprisonment; two to 20 years; one to 15 years; and one to 10 years. Three defendants were acquitted. Of the six organizations indicted, three were declared criminal: the Gestapo, the SS, and the German General Staff.

The Nuremberg Tribunal has been criticized as a quasi-international tribunal set up by the victorious powers, without any judge from a neutral country, to try the crimes of the vanquished. Its international character was questioned by arguments that it was a domestic court set up in Germany by the governments then exercising joint sovereign rights in occupied Germany.

There has also been a controversy concerning the retroactive effect of some rules of international law applied by the Tribunal. On the one hand, there is general agreement that the Tribunal's judgment regarding the traditional war crimes was well founded in international law under the established rules providing for individual liability in such cases. On the other hand, the qualification of the crimes against peace defined in the Tribunal's Charter as planning, preparing, initiating or waging a war of aggression or in violation of treaties, has been criticized by some commentators as contrary to the prohibition of retroactive force of law. Most defendants at Nuremberg were found guilty of this crime and only one was found guilty under that head alone, and sentenced to life imprisonment. It has been argued that although a war of aggression was illegal under the General Treaty Providing for the Renunciation of War as an Instrument of National Policy of 27 August 1928 (94 LNTS 57) (otherwise known as the Kellogg-Briand Pact or Pact of Paris) of which Germany was a party, that treaty did not declare aggression a crime and did not impose obligations on the individuals responsible for aggression, that is, the aggressor state's leadership. One can argue, however, that already prior to World War II a number of League of Nations resolutions and international pacts and treaties , as quoted by the Tribunal, reflected the rule of customary international law declaring aggression a crime.

The criticism of the Nuremberg judgment has been especially pronounced with regard to the category of crimes called "crimes against humanity" by the IMT at Nuremberg. Prohibition of such crimes was not part of international law before World War II. Two of the accused major war criminals were found by the IMT guilty of crimes against humanity alone. Under the Nuremberg Charter criminal acts constituted a crime against humanity only if committed in execution of or in connection with a crime against peace or a war crime. In this sense the scope of the crimes against humanity under the Nuremberg law was narrower than that of the crime of genocide under the Genocide Convention adopted after the war on 9 December 1948 (78 UNTS 277).

It can be argued against the charges of retroactive legislation that no general rule of international law prohibited the IMT at Nuremberg from applying such laws. Moreover, in view of the nature and magnitude of the crimes committed by the Nuremberg defendants, especially the crimes against humanity, it would be unreasonable to argue that failure to follow the principle of *nullum crimen sine lege* (no crime without the law prohibiting it) constituted injustice inflicted upon the major Nazi criminals who must have been aware of the criminal nature of their actions.

The law of the Nuremberg Tribunal established a most important precedent for the international law governing the use of force by states and responsibility of individuals for the crimes specified in the Nuremberg Charter. The Nuremberg principles were affirmed by the UN General Assembly in 1946 and by the International Law Commission in 1950. They have been universally recognized as part of the fundamental principles of contemporary general (customary) international law.

International Military Tribunal (IMT) for the Far East. This international criminal tribunal (q.v.) was set up on an *ad hoc* basis by a Special Proclamation on 19 January 1946 of General MacArthur as Supreme Commander for the Allied Powers in the Pacific in order to try major Japanese war criminals. The Charter of the Tribunal (14 *Dept. St. Bull.* 61 (1946)) closely resembled that of the IMT at Nuremberg (q.v.) except that it did not provide for declaring organizations criminal and did not expressly exclude the right of appeal.

Composed of 11 judges representing the states at war with Japan, the Tokyo Tribunal tried 28 individuals between June 1946 and April 1948. All the defendants were found guilty, and seven of them, all of whom in addition to other crimes were found guilty of war crimes, were sentenced to death. Most of the defendants who were sentenced to terms of imprisonment were found guilty of crimes against peace only.

It is noteworthy that the US Supreme Court ruled that the Tokyo Tribunal was not a court of the US, having been set up by General MacArthur acting as the agent of the powers at war with Japan. For that reason the Supreme Court held that it had no power to review or set aside the judgments of the Tokyo Tribunal.

The criticism of the Tokyo Tribunal's judgments focused on the same legal points as were raised with regard to the IMT at Nuremberg (*see* **International Military Tribunal (IMT) at Nuremberg, 1945-1946**).

International Prize Court. An abortive international tribunal proposed at the Second Hague Peace Conference in 1907 in the Convention on International Prize Court which was conceived as a court of appeal from decisions of national prize courts, that is, courts established by belligerent states to adjudicate according to international law the lawfulness of captured enemy and neutral vessels suspected of carrying contraband or running a blockade.

The Convention was not ratified by any state and never entered into effect, mainly because of the opposition of the major maritime powers, including the UK and US. In historical perspective, the Convention is significant because it was the first international treaty to stipulate the creation of a permanent international tribunal. Incidentally, the Convention granted individuals, nationals of neutral and enemy countries, the right of access to the proposed International Prize Court.

International Tribunal for the Law of the Sea (ITLOS). The UN Convention on the Law of the Sea, signed at Montego Bay, Jamaica, on 10 December 1982 (21 ILM 1261 (1982)) provides in art. 287 for the establishment of an International Tribunal for the Law of the Sea in accordance with Annex VI of the Convention containing its Statute. The ITLOS is conceived as a permanent judicial body with its seat, Registrar and other offices in Hamburg, Germany. It is to be composed of 21 members with President and Vice-President. They are to be elected by ballot by the parties to the 1982 Convention, for nine years on a staggered schedule, with a possibility of re-election, and so as to ensure the representation of the principal legal systems and equitable geographical distribution. The first election will be held within six months of the date of entry into force of the Convention. Under art. 308(1), the Convention is to enter into force 12 months after the deposit of the 60th instrument of ratification or accession, which deposit took place in November 1993. A quorum of 11 members is required to constitute the Tribunal, but there is also a possibility of special chambers (q.v.) organized very much like in the ICJ (q.v.) except that the composition of the chamber is determined with the approval of the parties.

A special Sea-Bed Disputes Chamber of the ITLOS of 11 members, selected every three years, is to be established to deal with disputes concerning activities in the sea-bed and ocean floor and subsoil beyond the limits of national jurisdiction (the so called "Area" to be managed by a UN agency known as the International Sea-Bed Authority (ISA)), that is, in most general terms and depending on the geological data, beyond the outer edge of the continental margin or beyond 200 nautical miles from the coastal baseline. The quorum in the Sea-Bed Disputes Chamber is seven members but the Chamber itself may operate through three-member *ad hoc* chambers. Not only states and their enterprises but also the ISA, and nationals (companies and individuals) of the states parties can have standing before the Chamber. The Chamber can also give advisory opinions (q.v.) at the request of the Assembly or the Council of the ISA.

The ITLOS is open to states and--under the rules governing its Sea-Bed Disputes Chamber--entities other than states and even individuals. Furthermore, with the agreement of all the parties to a case, the Tribunal is open to entities other than states also in cases which are outside the competence of the Sea-Bed Disputes Chamber. Like in the ICJ, the procedure of the ITLOS provides, *inter alia*, for prescribing provisional measures (q.v.) and intervention in proceedings (q.v.). The judgments of the ITLOS are final and are binding only between the parties and in respect of the particular dispute before the Tribunal.

The ITLOS is one of the four categories of judicial and arbitral bodies envisaged by the 1982 Convention (art. 287), which states are free to choose in order to resolve disputes not resolved by negotiation, mediation, conciliation (q.v.) or other procedures, including regional tribunals such as the CJEC (q.v.) to which the EC members must submit their fishery disputes. The choice of one or more methods of resolving disputes is made by means of a written revocable declaration deposited with the UN.

The other three categories of judicial and arbitral bodies are: the ICJ; arbitral tribunals under Annex VII of the Convention (q.v.); and special arbitral tribunals under Annex VIII of the Convention (q.v.). All these bodies apply international law, but the disputing parties may agree to request a decision *ex aequo et bono* (*see Ex Aequo et Bono* and Equity). If a state has not selected any of the available fora, it is deemed to have accepted arbitration under Annex VII.

The Convention of 1982 lays down general rules governing the competence and procedure of the judicial and arbitral bodies settling disputes arising from the interpretation and application of the Convention. However, for reasons related to sensitivity with regard to vital national interests and sovereign rights, certain categories of disputes, such as those concerning fisheries in the exclusive economic zone (EEZ), that is a zone up to 200 nautical miles from the coastline, and marine scientific research, are excluded from compulsory settlement procedures under the circumstances spelled out in detail in art. 297 of the Convention. States also have the option of not accepting the judicial or arbitral procedures under the Convention, in respect of any or all of three categories of disputes: disputes concerning military activities; disputes being considered by the UN Security Council; and delimitation disputes, as spelled out in detail in art. 298 of the Convention.

Intervention in Proceedings. An institution in the procedure of international tribunals whereby in certain circumstances and with the permission of the tribunal a state may intervene in a case between other states before that tribunal. Historically, the first instance of the possibility of intervention by third parties is a provision among the rules of the Hague Convention of 1899 for the Pacific Settlement of International Disputes (q.v.), revised in 1907, relating to arbitration (q.v.) procedure, which allowed intervention by third states, parties to a convention the interpretation of which was in question in the proceedings. The institution of intervention was further enlarged and developed within the framework of the PCIJ (q.v.) and the ICJ (q.v.). In addition, intervention is admissible in some other international tribunals, such as the CJEC (q.v.) where (except in proceedings for preliminary rulings) it is available automatically (*ipso jure*) to member states and institutions of the EC and even--under certain conditions--to private persons.

According to the Statute of the ICJ, a state may intervene in a case between other states in two kinds of situation. First, under art. 62, a state which considers that "it has an interest of a legal nature which may be affected by the decision in the case, may submit a request to the Court to be permitted to intervene." The other situation exists when, under art. 63, a state requesting intervention is a party to a convention the construction of which is before the Court. All such states are notified of this situation by the Court's Registrar and have the right to intervene, but if they use this right, the construction given by the judgment will be equally binding upon them.

The World Court has been rather restrained in granting the right to intervene. In the PCIJ, intervention by Poland in the *Wimbledon* (q.v.) case was the only instance of intervention. It concerned interpretation of the Peace Treaty of Versailles (1919) and was based on art. 63 of the Statute although the initial application had invoked art. 62. The ICJ allowed Nicaragua intervention under art. 62 of the Statute in the case of *Land, Island and Maritime Frontier Dispute* (*El Salvador/Honduras*), 1986-1992 (q.v.). In the *Nuclear Tests* (q.v.) cases Fiji's application lapsed when the cases became moot. The Court rejected the application of Malta to intervene in the *Continental Shelf* (*Tunisia/Libyan Arab Jamahiriya*) (q.v.) case and of Italy to intervene in the case of *Continental Shelf* (*Libyan Arab Jamahiriya/Malta*) (q.v.). As far as intervention under art. 63 is concerned, Cuba intervened in the *Haya de la Torre* (*Colombia v. Peru*) case which involved the construction of the Havana Convention of 1928 on Asylum (*see* **Asylum (Colombia/Peru) and Haya de la Torre (Colombia v. Peru), ICJ 1949-1951)**. However, in the case concerning *Military and Paramilitary Activities in and* *against Nicaragua* (*Nicaragua v. United States of America*) (q.v.) the ICJ rejected El Salvador's declaration of intervention under art. 63 on the ground that it addressed the merits of the case and therefore was inadmissible at the preliminary stage of the proceedings.

Iran-United States Claims Tribunal (I-USCT). The I-USCT is a major and very active arbitration tribunal set up under the so-called Algiers Accords of 19 January 1981 (20 ILM 223(1981)) which, through Algeria's good offices, stipulated measures designed to settle the US-Iran dispute arising from detention by Iran of 52 US nationals as hostages in Iran in 1979 (*see* **United States Diplomatic and Consular Staff in Tehran (United States v. Iran), ICJ 1979-1981**). The Algiers Accords consist of: 1. Declaration of Algeria; 2. Undertakings of the US and Iran with respect to the Declaration of Algeria; 3. Declaration of Algeria concerning the Settlement of Claims by the US and Iran, which set up the I-USCT. In addition, an escrow agreement for Iranian property tied to the release of US nationals by Iran was signed by the US, the Federal Reserve Bank of New York as fiscal agent of the US, Bank Markazi Iran, and the Central Bank of Algeria acting as escrow agent.

The I-USCT has its seat at The Hague. It has jurisdiction over private claims of US nationals against Iran and nationals of Iran against the US, and over official claims of the two governments against each other concerning purchase and sale of goods and services. The Tribunal also decides disputes as to the interpretation and performance of the Algiers Accords. The I-USCT may not decide claims of the US and its nationals arising out of the seizure of the US embassy and hostages in Tehran and out of the US counteraction to these events, as well as claims arising under a contract specifically providing for the sole jurisdiction of Iranian courts. Claims had to be filed with the Tribunal between 20 October 1981 and 19 January 1982. The US filed 1,000 large and 2,795 small claims on behalf of its nationals. Iran also filed a large claim arising from undelivered American-made military equipment. Iranian nationals also filed claims against the US. Under the Declaration of Algeria concerning the Settlement of Claims, claims are presented either by claimants themselves or, in the case of claims of less than $250,000, by the national's government.

The I-USCT consists of nine members of whom three are chosen by the US, three by Iran, and three are selected by the six so chosen. The appointment of the arbitrators and the procedure are governed by the arbitration rules of the UN Commission on International Trade Law (UNCITRAL) (*see* **UNCITRAL Rules**). Under these rules the Secretary General of the Permanent Court of Arbitration (PCA) (q.v.) designated the President of the Supreme Court of the Netherlands as the appointing authority after the US and Iran had failed to agree on any of the arbitrators to be selected jointly. In two cases appointments were made by the designated appointing authority; this included the appointment of the President of the Tribunal in 1985.

Claims before the I-USCT are decided by the full tribunal of nine or by a panel of three determined by the President. The decisions are final and binding and are enforceable against either government in courts of any nation in accordance with its laws. Awards to US nationals are enforceable out of a $1 billion security fund established in the Central Bank of the Netherlands from the US-located frozen Iranian assets and replenished periodically by Iran from the accumulated interest, if it falls below $500 million. Two additional accounts totalling $5 billion were established in the Bank of England to cover bank loans. The awards of the I-USCT may, however, also be enforced under the New York Convention, 1958 (q.v.).

The Tribunal decides on the basis of respect for law, applying such choice of law rules and principles of commercial international law as it deems applicable, taking into account relevant usages of trade, contract provisions, and changed circumstances.

By June 1990 the I-USCT had delivered over 300 awards on US large (over $200,000) claims and 2,450 on small claims, all totalling $2 billion. The Iranian claims amounted to 110, totalling $130 million.

The I-USCT, still active in 1993, delivered numerous important awards and orders developing the international law of state responsibility for injury to aliens. For example it ruled that under international law aliens are entitled to just compensation for injury, defined as "the full equivalent of the property taken."

(*Phelps Dodge Corp. v. Islamic Republic of Iran*, 25 ILM 619, 626-627 (1986)).

Ireland v. UK, ECHR 1978. In this unique inter-state case Ireland filed two applications against the UK before the ECHR (q.v.), arising out of the political violence in Northern Ireland. The first application, in 1971, was declared admissible and the second, of 1972, was withdrawn by the applicant state. Ireland accused the UK of unlawful detention and of using, in Northern Ireland, interrogation techniques (the "five techniques" of wall standing, hooding, subjecting to noise, deprivation of sleep, and of food and drink) almost exclusively against members of the Irish Republican Army (IRA), which--as charged by Ireland--amounted to a practice of inhuman and degrading as well as discriminatory treatment in violation of a number of provisions of the European Convention for the Protection of Human Rights and Fundamental Freedoms of 4 November 1950 (213 UNTS 221), and especially art. 3 prohibiting torture or inhuman or degrading treatment or punishment.

The Court, sitting in plenary, ruled in its judgment of 8 January 1978 ([1978] ECHR. Ser. A, no. 25) that the use by the UK of the five interrogation techniques was inhuman and degrading treatment in breach of art. 3 but did not constitute torture in the meaning of this article. Concerning charges of unlawful detention, the Court held that the deprivations of liberty by the British authorities in Northern Ireland had been within the limits required by the public emergency there and did not constitute a breach of art. 15 of the Convention delimiting a state's right to take measures derogating from the obligations under the Convention. Here the ECHR followed its reasoning in the case of *Lawless* (q.v.), decided in 1961.

Island of Palmas *see* **Palmas, Island of, Arbitration, 1928.**

J

Jay Treaty, 1794. The Treaty of Amity, Commerce and Navigation, signed in London on 19 November 1794 (52 CTS 243) between Great Britain and the US, named after Chief Justice and former Secretary of Foreign Affairs, John Jay, who was the US plenipotentiary at the negotiations. The purpose of the Treaty was to resolve the outstanding issues between the two countries in the aftermath of the American War of Independence. However, of special interest for the history of international arbitration (q.v.) are the Jay Treaty provisions concerning the setting up of three mixed claims commissions (q.v.): one to settle the US-British border dispute and two to examine the war claims of British subjects and US citizens respectively. Some 536 claims relating to maritime seizures were settled by these two mixed claims commissions.

By reviving the institution of arbitration, the Jay Treaty represents a major landmark in its modern history. It initiated a trend which eventually led to the foundation of a true international judiciary in the 20 century.

Jennings, Sir Robert Yewdall (1913-). UK national. Member of the ICJ (q.v.) since 1982 and its President since 1991. Whewell Professor of International Law, University of Cambridge. Queen's Counsel since 1969. Counsel of the UK in a number of arbitrations (q.v.). Member of the PCA (q.v.). Editor of the *BYIL* 1974-1982. President (1981) and Honorary Member of the Institute of International law (1985). Author of various books and articles on international law, including lectures in *RCADI*.

Jessup, Philip E. (1897-1986). US national. Member of the ICJ (q.v.), 1961-1970. Professor of Law at Columbia University, 1925-1961. Diplomat; US representative at various international conferences, including the International Monetary Fund and World Bank. US representative at sessions of the UN General Assembly and

Security Council, 1948-1953. Author of numerous works on international law, including lectures in *RCADI*.

Jiménez de Aréchaga, Eduardo (1918-). Uruguayan national. Member of the ICJ (q.v.), 1970-1979, and its President, 1976-1979. Professor of International Law at the University of Montevideo, 1946-1969. Member of the International Law Commission, 1961-1969, its Chairman, 1963. Uruguayan delegate to the UN Conference on the Law of Treaties and Rapporteur of the Committee of the Whole, Vienna, 1968-1969. Counsel for Spain in the *Barcelona Traction* case (q.v.) before the ICJ. Judge *ad hoc* (q.v.) in the *Continental Shelf (Tunisia/Libya)* case (q.v.) before the ICJ. In the Uruguayan government, 1952-1955. Author of numerous publications on international law, including lectures in *RCADI*.

Judge *Ad Hoc*. A judge whom a state party before an international tribunal, such as the ICJ (q.v.), but not the CJEC (q.v.), may choose when it does not have a judge of its nationality on the bench.

Under the Statute of the ICJ (ICJ Statute, art. 31) a judge *ad hoc* may be appointed by either of the parties if the Court includes no judge of their nationality. When there are several parties to a dispute, the parties acting in the same interest may choose only one judge *ad hoc*. If one of the parties already has a judge of its nationality on the bench, it is not entitled to appoint an *ad hoc* judge. An *ad hoc* judge need not be of the same nationality as the appointing country and may have the nationality of an elected member of the Court. An *ad hoc* judge may also be appointed in cases where the ICJ sits not as a full court but in a chamber (q.v.) formed at the Court's initiative or at the request of the parties. Judges *ad hoc* participate in the case in which they sit on terms of complete equality with the other judges on the bench. They take precedence after the elected members of the Court in order of seniority of age.

In the ICJ system a judge *ad hoc* may be appointed also in cases of advisory jurisdiction. Specifically, if an advisory opinion (q.v.) is requested upon a legal question pending between two or more states, each such state may, at the Court's discretion, be allowed to appoint an *ad hoc* judge (ICJ Rules, art. 102). Whereas the PCIJ (q.v.) agreed to such appointment in six advisory cases, only two requests of this kind have been received by the ICJ (q.v.). In the case concerning the *Legal Consequences for States of the Continued Presence of South Africa in Namibia* (*South West Africa*) *Notwithstanding Security Council Resolution 276* (*1970*) (1971) (*see* ANNEX VI) the ICJ turned down the request and in the *Western Sahara* case (q.v.) accepted Morocco's request but rejected that of Mauritania.

The institution of the judge *ad hoc* in the ICJ system has been criticized as detracting from the international and impartial nature of an international tribunal. And indeed, as a rule, but not always, judges *ad hoc* have voted in favor of the country appointing them, in most cases the country of their nationality. No judge *ad hoc* has ever dissented from a majority decision favoring the appointing country, and typically judges *ad hoc* have appended individual (dissenting) opinions (q.v.) if the majority on the bench decided against their vote.

In defense of the institution of the judge *ad hoc* it has been pointed out that the decisions of the "World Court" (that is, the PCIJ and ICJ) would have been the same even without national or *ad hoc* judges. It has also been contended that this institution, a survival of the institution of national arbitrators of *ad hoc* arbitration (q.v.) tribunals, is, at the early stage in the development of international tribunals, a concession to the political context in which such tribunals operate and to the theory that the national judge, whether elected or *ad hoc*, should, as it were, "represent" the party on the bench. Furthermore it has been noted that it is useful for such a tribunal as the ICJ to have on the bench a person more familiar with the views of a party than the elected members of the Court.

Jurisdiction of International Tribunals. In general terms, jurisdiction of an international tribunal refers to its legal competence to deal, in accordance with its governing instrument ("Statute") and/or the parties' agreement ("*compromis*") (q.v.), with--as a rule-- international disputes (q.v.) brought before it by the parties.

Whereas jurisdiction of the domestic ("municipal") courts is compulsory, that is, the applicant (plaintiff) party need not obtain the respondent's (defendant's) consent to seise the court, jurisdiction of international courts and tribunals normally depends on such consent. Thus the fact that a country is a signatory to a treaty establishing an international tribunal (for example the UN Charter with the annexed Statute of the ICJ) (q.v.) does not automatically entail the tribunal's compulsory jurisdiction but requires an additional act of the parties, expressive of their acceptance of the tribunal's jurisdiction (*see* **Contentious Jurisdiction of the ICJ** as a typical example of this rule). The parties' consent may be either express, such as for example a *compromis*, or implied, as through *forum prorogatum* (q.v.). The so called "optional clause" (q.v.) is a major means expressing a state's consent to a tribunal's compulsory jurisdiction.

Only in exceptional cases, such as the CJEC (q.v.), the projected ITLOS (q.v.) Sea-Bed Disputes Chamber, and some special competence permanent arbitral tribunals, mostly of historical interest, such as the London Agreement on German External Debt (1953) Arbitral Tribunal and Mixed Commission (q.v.) is jurisdiction compulsory for the parties to the treaty concerned.

The two major dimensions of jurisdiction of international tribunals are competence with respect to persons (*ratione personae*), that is access to or standing before a tribunal, and competence with respect to subject matter (*ratione materiae*). In addition, in procedural terms a distinction must be made between procedure in contentious jurisdiction (q.v.) and that in advisory jurisdiction (q.v.).

As a general rule, access to international tribunals is limited to states, as in the typical case of the ICJ. In exceptional cases, such as the short-lived CACJ (q.v.), private persons also had standing before the tribunal. Mixed claims commissions (q.v.) and mixed arbitral tribunals (q.v.) set up under the peace treaties following World War I allowed them access as well. More recently, in the CJEC (q.v.), organs of the European Community, individuals and companies may appear as parties before the Court. The same rule applies in the projected Sea-Bed Disputes Chamber of the ITLOS. In the ECHR (q.v.) and the I-ACHR (q.v.) individuals are not, in formal terms, parties before the Court as they submit their petitions to the Human Rights Commission of the respective system, but in the ECHR individuals may appear in the Court and plead their cases through their attorneys.

The scope of the competence of the international tribunals with respect to subject matter is determined by the parties' consent. In addition, the existence of a genuine international dispute (q.v.) is a prerequisite for the tribunal's assuming jurisdiction. Historically, states have been reluctant to assume comprehensive obligations to submit their disputes to arbitration or judicial settlement proper, as illustrated by the restrictive (vital interests, honor and the like) clauses in arbitration (q.v.) agreements and reservations to acceptance of compulsory jurisdiction of the ICJ under the optional clause (q.v.), including the automatic (self-judging) reservation (q.v.), all of which, due to reciprocity, reduce the jurisdiction of the ICJ. Finally, there is the general problem of "justiciability" of international disputes (q.v.) implying that international courts and tribunals can deal only with "legal," but not "political," disputes because they decide cases on the basis of international law.

An international tribunal must, on its own initiative, establish its jurisdiction with respect to the subject matter of each specific case. Furthermore, it must give any party, and especially the respondent, adequate opportunity to challenge its jurisdiction. Many "preliminary objections" (q.v.) in the ICJ have dealt with the issue of the Court's jurisdiction. But it is a rule of international law that international courts and tribunals have themselves the power to decide any dispute as to their jurisdiction in a particular case.

Justiciability of International Disputes. The quality of an international dispute (q.v.) to be suitable for submission, under international law, to arbitration (q.v.) or judicial settlement in the strict sense of the term. Although states are obliged to settle their disputes by peaceful means, they are under no obligation to submit them to arbitral or judicial settlement unless they are bound to do so by virtue of a prior obligation, normally contracted under an international instrument such as a bilateral or multilateral treaty.

International practice has long made a distinction between "justiciable" or "legal" disputes which lend themselves to legal settlement and "non-justiciable" or "political" disputes which can be settled only by non-judicial, diplomatic means (negotiation, good offices, mediation, conciliation, possibly aided by impartial inquiry). Thus in the pre-World War I arbitration treaties disputes perceived by a party to concern vital interests, honor, independence, or interests of a third state were excluded from arbitration. After World War I the Covenant of the League of Nations (art. 13(2)) assumed that only some international disputes were suitable for submission to arbitration or judicial settlement. Among them the Covenant listed "disputes as to the interpretation of a treaty, as to any question of international law, as to existence of any fact which, if established, would constitute a breach of any international obligation, or as to the extent and nature of the reparation to be made for any such breach." This list was subsequently adopted in the optional clause (q.v.) of art. 36(2) of the Statute of the PCIJ (q.v.) and then the ICJ (q.v.). Other treaties, following the Hague Convention of 1899 for the Pacific Settlement of International Disputes(q.v.), as revised in 1907, also referred to legal disputes, including among them questions of interpretation or application of treaties. The General Act for the Pacific Settlement of International Disputes of 1928, revised in 1949 (q.v.), made a distinction between legal and non-legal disputes, and the UN Charter itself distinguishes, in art. 36(3), "legal" disputes which should "as a general rule" be referred to the ICJ, the implication being that there are other, "non-legal" disputes, to be settled, as a rule, by diplomatic methods. In more general terms of not just "disputes" but "questions," the ICJ, in its Advisory Opinion on *Western Sahara* (q.v.) (ICJ Rep. 1975, p. 12), made an attempt to elucidate the nature of "legal questions," defining them as questions that are by their very nature susceptible of a reply based on law. At the regional level, under the European Convention of 1957 on Peaceful Settlement of Disputes, all international legal disputes are susceptible to judicial settlement.

As a body deciding "in accordance with international law" (art. 38(1) of the Statute), the ICJ may hear only disputes that are essentially legal. However, as held by the Court in such cases as *Military and Paramilitary Activities in and against Nicaragua* (q.v.), *Nuclear Tests* (q.v.) and *United States Diplomatic and Consular Staff in Tehran* (q.v.), the fact that a legal dispute has a political context or is only one aspect of a political dispute does not deprive it of a legal character, that is, it does not make it non-justiciable, even if at the same time it is an object of a diplomatic attempt at solution within a political organ such as the UN Security Council.

Furthermore, while the cases brought to the ICJ under the optional clause (q.v.) of art. 36(2) of the Court's Statute are limited to "legal disputes," under art. 36(1) "all cases" are submissible to the Court. This means that a political dispute can also be "justiciable," but in such a case the ICJ in effect would decide not according to international law but *ex aequo et bono* (*see Ex Aequo et Bono* and **Equity**).

The issue of justiciability of international disputes has long preoccupied the doctrine of international law, but what criteria should govern the distinction between justiciable and non-justiciable disputes is a controversial matter. In the most common view which adopts a less vague criterion than the other approaches, a dispute is legal and justiciable if it concerns an existing legal right, the parties accepting the current legal norms governing their mutual relations as the basis for a settlement of the dispute. If, on the other hand, a state party to a dispute seeks a change of the existing law, normally a treaty, the dispute is political and non-justiciable. One could argue, however, that justiciability is determined by the parties' attitude toward the dispute and any international dispute is justiciable regardless of its subject matter.

L

Lachs, Manfred (1914-1993). Polish national. Longest serving member of the ICJ (q.v.), 1967-1993, and its President, 1973-1976. Member of the PCA (q.v.) 1956-1983. Member of the International Law Commission, 1962-1966, Rapporteur, 1962, Vice-Chairman, 1966. Chairman, 1949, 1951, 1955, and Vice-Chairman, 1952, of the Sixth Committee of the UN General Assembly. Professor of International Law at the University of Warsaw since 1952. Director of the Legal and Treaties Department of the Polish Ministry of Foreign Affairs, 1947-1960, Legal Adviser to the Minister of Foreign Affairs, 1960-1966. Member of the Polish delegation to the UN General Assembly, 1946-1952, 1955-1960, 1962-1964, and its representative in the UN Disarmament Committee, 1962-1964. Author of numerous publications on international law, including lectures in *RCADI*.

Lake Lanoux Arbitration, 1957. This arbitration (q.v.) between France and Spain concerned a dispute generated by French plans since 1917 to divert towards the Atlantic, for purposes of hydroelectric power, the waters of Lake Lanoux, a high altitude lake in the French Pyrenees which flows into the river Carol entering Spain and then, through the river Sègre, flows into the Mediterranean. Spain protested, claiming that the projected diversion was detrimental to its interests and violated the Treaty and Additional Act of Bayonne of 26 May 1866 (133 CTS 359) which defined the Franco-Spanish border and guaranteed Spain's right to the natural flow of water into the Carol. In its negotiations with Spain, France offered, in a number of ways, to take into account the interests of Spain as the downstream country, but Spain maintained its opposition to the French diversion plans. Subsequently, on the basis of their arbitration Treaty of 10 July 1929 (148 LNTS 369) the two countries signed a *compromis* (q.v.) in 1956, submitting their dispute to arbitration by a five-member tribunal which was asked to decide whether the diversion of waters of the lake without Spain's prior consent violated the Treaty of 1866.

In its award of 16 November 1957 (12 UNRIAA 281) the Tribunal found no violation of the Treaty of 1866 because Spain could not show that the diversion was detrimental to its interests. It held that, acting in good faith, France had offered to restore the original quality of water to the Carol river. While being obliged under the Treaty of 1866 to consult with Spain and take reasonable account of the interests of the co-riparian, France was under no obligation to obtain Spain's agreement before undertaking the diversion work.

The *Lake Lanoux* award is an important decision clarifying the use and utilization by riparian states of international rivers and other inland waters.

Land, Island and Maritime Frontier Dispute (El Salvador/Honduras), ICJ 1986-1992. This territorial dispute between El Salvador and Honduras was decided by a Chamber (q.v.) of the ICJ (q.v.) composed of five judges, including two judges *ad hoc* (q.v.). The dispute dated back to the mid-19th century, starting shortly after the two countries became independent states following the disintegration of the Federal Republic of Central America in 1839. In 1969 a border war (the "soccer war") was fought by them because of the dispute. The General Treaty of Peace of 30 October 1980 did not delimit the entire frontier between the two countries. Finally in 1986 El Salvador and Honduras submitted their dispute to the ICJ on the basis of a special agreement of 24 May 1986 requesting the Chamber of the Court to delineate the frontier line in the areas or sections which were not described in art. 16 of the Peace Treaty of 1980, and to determine the legal situation of the islands in the Gulf of Fonseca and maritime spaces.

Nicaragua, whose territory in part borders on the Gulf of Fonseca, asked the Court for permission to intervene (*see* **Intervention in Proceedings**). In its judgment of 13 September 1990, the Court's Chamber unanimously acceded to this application, but solely in respect of the question of the status of the Gulf of Fonseca.

The Chamber delivered its judgment, in this most complicated case ever handled by the ICJ, on 11 September 1992 (1992 ICJ Rep. -). Concerning the boundary line in the disputed six land sectors, the Chamber, by a unanimous vote on four sectors and a majority of four to one on two sectors, adjudicated roughly two thirds of the disputed 168 square miles to Honduras. In determining the frontier, the Chamber thoroughly investigated the history of the area back to the time of the Spanish colonial empire, taking account of the principle of *uti possidetis juris*, that is, the respect for the territorial boundaries at the time of gaining independence. The Chamber also stressed the evidence of the so-called *effectivités*, that is "the conduct of the administrative authorities as proof of the effective exercise of territorial jurisdiction in the colonial period."

Reviewing all the relevant circumstances concerning the legal status of the disputed islands and especially the evidence of effective possession and control of an island by one party without protests by the other, the Chamber unanimously decided that Honduras had succeeded to Spanish sovereignty over El Tigre and El Salvador to Meanguera, and by four votes to one adjudicated the island of Meanguerita to El Salvador.

The determination of the legal status of the Gulf of Fonseca, at one time on the agenda of the CACJ (q.v.), proved to be the most complex task of the Chamber. The decision on this matter was made by four votes to one. Referring largely to the decision of the CACJ of 1917, the Chamber found the Gulf to be a pluri-state historic bay subject to a special kind of threefold sovereignty of El Salvador, Honduras, and Nicaragua, the successors of the single sovereignty of the Federal Republic of Central America (1821-1839) and prior to that of Spain. However, a three-mile (one marine league) belt along the littoral of each of the three coastal states will be under the exclusive sovereignty of the state concerned. Concerning the waters outside the Gulf, the Chamber ruled that the closing line of the Gulf constituted the baseline of the territorial sea as well as of the exclusive economic zone (EEZ) and the continental shelf of the three countries, all of these zones to be held in joint entitlement by the three countries in the same way as the Gulf itself. The Chamber's view was that El Salvador, Honduras, and Nicaragua could effect a delimitation of all these maritime areas by agreement on the basis of international law.

The Chamber also observed that the binding force of the judgment did not extend to Nicaragua as intervener.

The judgment in the El Salvador/Honduras case dealt with important issues of international law governing delimitation of boundaries within the context of transition from colonial to post-colonial administration. Of special interest, however, is the Chamber's legal analysis of the concept of historical bays which will provide a good deal of material for commentators on the international law of the sea.

Lauterpacht, Sir Hersch (1897-1960). Born in Galicia (then Austro-Hungarian Empire). Studied law at the University of Lwów (then in Poland), Vienna, and London School of Economics. Became British citizen. Taught at the London School of Economics and became Professor of International Law at Cambridge University, 1938-1955. Member of the International Law Commission, 1951-1955. Member of PCA (q.v.), 1957-1960. Judge of the ICJ (q.v.), 1955-1960. Editor of *International Law Reports* (formerly *Annual Digest of Public International Law Cases*) and *BYIL*. Highly renowned author of numerous works on international law, including lectures in *RCADI*. Best known for editing and revising the fifth, sixth, seventh, and eighth editions of the classic *International Law* treatise of Oppenheim (*see* **Bibliography,** 2 G).

Law of the Sea Tribunal *see* **International Tribunal for the Law of the Sea.**

Lawless Case, ECHR 1960-1961. This first case to come before the ECHR (q.v.) concerned a complaint of Lawless, an Irish citizen, against the Republic of Ireland for arrest under the Irish Offences against the State Act of 1939 and detention without trial for five months in 1957 during a period of domestic unrest in Ireland, related to the activities of the Irish Republican Army. The applicant alleged violation by Ireland of art. 5(1)(c) of the European Convention for the Protection of Human Rights and Fundamental Freedoms of 4 November 1950 (213 UNTS 221) prohibiting unlawful arrest or detention.

In its first judgment, 1 November 1960,([1960] ECHR. Ser. A, no. 1), dealing with procedural questions, the Court ruled that the applicant had the right to receive a copy of the report of the Human Rights Commission (*see* **European Court of Human Rights**) and, even though he was not a party to the proceedings, to present his point of view through delegates of the Commission, in the Commission's Report, or as a witness.

In the judgment on the merits, 1 July 1961 ([1961] ECHR. Ser. A, no. 3) the Court ruled that, while Ireland's action in the case was, as such, contrary to art. 5(1)(c) of the Convention, the detention of Lawless without trial was justified by a public emergency threatening the life of Ireland within the meaning of art. 15 of the Convention which allows extraordinary measures derogating in time of public emergency from the rules protecting human rights, except that no derogation can be made from the right to life and the guarantees against torture, slavery and *ex post* criminal law. The Court also ruled that the emergency measures had been duly notified by Ireland under art. 15(3) of the Convention to the Secretary-General of the Council of Europe.

The Court's reasoning on the legality of derogation by states from their obligations under the Convention in time of public emergency was followed in the case of *Ireland v. UK* (q.v.) in 1978.

Legal Status of Eastern Greenland (Denmark v. Norway), PCIJ 1933. The judgment of the PCIJ (q.v.) in this important case resolved a dispute between Denmark and Norway concerning sovereignty over parts of Eastern Greenland. After Norway had proclaimed its sovereignty over the contested area on 10 July 1931, alleging that it was *terra nullius*, that is, territory under no state's sovereignty, Denmark, which claimed sovereignty over the whole of Greenland, applied to the PCIJ for a judgment declaring the invalidity of the Norwegian proclamation.

In its judgment of 5 April 1933 (1933 PCIJ, Series A/B No. 53, p. 22) the Court decided in favor of Denmark, ruling that by the critical date, that is 10 July 1931, Denmark had established a valid title to sovereignty over the whole of Greenland even though the area in question had not been colonized by it. The Court arrived at this conclusion after reviewing the history of the island throughout the centuries when the Danish-Norwegian Crown had exercised uncontested sovereignty over Greenland irrespective of the extent of colonization of the area. In 1814, under the Treaty of Kiel, the Danish King had ceded Norway to Sweden, but Greenland was expressly excluded and remained under the Danish Crown which had since continued its peaceful and continuous exercise of authority warranting a valid title to sovereignty over the whole of Greenland. Furthermore, as found by the PCIJ, in the century following the Treaty of Kiel the Danish domestic law and treaties had applied to Greenland as a whole, which was evidence of Denmark's will and intention to exercise sovereignty. In addition, Denmark had granted concessions applying to the disputed territory. In more recent years, it had taken steps to have its status as the sovereign of the whole of Greenland recognized by other countries.

Concerning the extent of effective exercise of authority necessary to establish a valid title to territory, the Court stressed the relative nature of this test in the inhospitable polar areas where very little in the way of actual exercise of sovereign rights was needed to assert sovereignty in the absence of superior claims by other states. Such Norwegian actions as the wintering of expeditions and the construction of a wireless station in Eastern Greenland, against which Denmark had lodged a protest, could not prevail against Denmark's superior claim.

The Court also ruled that the oral declaration by the Norwegian Foreign Minister in 1919, made to the envoy of Denmark, that the Norwegian government would not make any difficulty concerning the Danish claim, was binding upon Norway.

Following the PCIJ judgment, Denmark and Norway terminated their dispute over Eastern Greenland as well as another territorial dispute which concerned some areas in Southeastern Greenland. The PCIJ terminated the procedure in the latter case in an order of 11 May 1933.

The *Eastern Greenland* judgment is of considerable significance for the area of international law governing acquisition of sovereignty over territory, especially in the Arctic region and the Antarctic continent.

LIAMCO Arbitration, 1977. This was one of the three major arbitrations (q.v.), before three different tribunals, resulting from nationalization by Libya of foreign oil companies (*see also* **British Petroleum Arbitration, 1973 and 1974; TOPCO & CAOC**

Arbitration, 1977).

After Libya had nationalized the assets of the Libyan American Oil Company (LIAMCO) in 1973, the company instituted arbitral proceedings against Libya in accordance with the concession agreement of 1955, demanding either restitution of the assets or payment of damages. Like in the other two cases, Libya refused to appoint an arbitrator, and, in accordance with the concession agreement, the President of the ICJ (q.v.) appointed a sole arbitrator. The arbitrator, a Lebanese jurist, sitting in Geneva, rendered the award on 12 April 1977 (20 ILM 1 (1981)). Libya did not participate in the proceedings.

The sole arbitrator ruled that, although the principle of *pacta sunt servanda* (agreements ought to be observed) applied also to contracts between states and private persons, Libya was allowed to nationalize foreign property, subject to non-discriminatory treatment and the duty to compensate. Considering restitution in kind as practically impossible and violating Libya's sovereignty, the arbitrator awarded a sum of $80 million as compensation to LIAMCO which had demanded $200 million. The dispute was eventually settled by an agreement between the parties in 1981.

For the procedure, the tribunal applied the UNCITRAL Rules (q.v.) and for the merits, the Libyan and Islamic law consistent with international law, complemented by general principles of law.

The *LIAMCO* arbitration is significant in that it reaffirmed the right of private persons to confront states as parties before international arbitration tribunals and upheld the principle of the sanctity of contracts between such parties. It also made a contribution to the question of compensation for nationalized foreign property.

Local Remedies *see* **Exhaustion of Local Remedies**

London Agreement on German External Debts (1953) Arbitral Tribunal and Mixed Commission. An arbitral tribunal and a mixed commission set up under the London Agreement of 27 February 1953 on German External Debts (333 UNTS 2), dealing with the Federal Republic's liability for Germany's pre-war debts and for post-war debts resulting from economic aid. The two tribunals have the function to settle intergovernmental disputes regarding the interpretation and application of the London Agreement. The Arbitral Tribunal can also render non-binding advisory opinions (q.v.). An Annex to the Agreement separates the jurisdictional competences of the two bodies. In general, the Tribunal serves as a court of appeal from the decisions of the Mixed Commission which, however, has exclusive jurisdiction under Annex IV. There are also four private arbitral bodies for private parties, performing functions assigned to them by the Agreement.

The Arbitral Tribunal of the London Agreement is made up of eight members, with three appointed by Germany and three by France, the UK, and US respectively, complemented by the President and Vice-President appointed jointly by the four governments or--if no agreement can be reached--by the President of the ICJ (q.v.). The institution of judges *ad hoc* (q.v.) is also provided for. The eight permanent members of the Tribunal also serve as members of the Mixed Commission. Both the Tribunal and the Commission apply rules of international law.

Since their establishment in 1953 the Tribunal and the Mixed Commission have dealt with a limited number of cases. They are of interest in the history of international arbitration (q.v.) in that the Mixed Commission continued the trend, which started with the mixed arbitral tribunals (q.v.) of the post-World War I era, of granting individuals access to international judicial bodies, and also because the London Agreement provided for appeals from a national court to a special court of arbitration and eventually to the Mixed Commission.

"Lotus" (France v. Turkey), PCIJ 1928. This celebrated case before the PCIJ (q.v.) resulted from the collision on the high seas in the Aegean of the French merchant vessel *Lotus* with the Turkish vessel *Boz-Kourt*. The accident occurred due to alleged criminal negligence of Lieutenant Demons, the officer of the watch of the *Lotus*. As a result of the collision the Turkish ship sank with the loss of eight lives. Upon arrival of the *Lotus* in Istanbul, Demons was tried by a Turkish court and sentenced to 80 days of imprisonment and a fine of £22. The master of the Turkish vessel received a light penalty.

France challenged the trial of Demons by Turkey as contrary to international law, claiming that only the French court, as the court of the *Lotus'* flag, had jurisdiction (q.v.) in the case. Following negotiations, the two countries asked the PCIJ in a special agreement (*compromis*) (q.v.) to rule whether by trying the French lieutenant Turkey had violated art. 15 of the Convention of Lausanne of 24 July 1923 respecting conditions of residence and jurisdiction (28 LNTS 152) whereby jurisdictional questions between the signatory states should be decided according to international law; and if the answer was affirmative, what compensation was due to Demons.

In its judgment of 7 September 1927 (PCIJ, Series A, No. 10) the PCIJ held, by a slim margin of seven to six (by the President's casting vote), that by trying Demons Turkey had not acted in conflict with principles of international law. The Court reasoned that Demons could be tried not only by his flag state France but also by Turkey, not because of the nationality of the victims (a question which the Court declined to examine) but because the effects of his acting which originated aboard the French ship made themselves felt on the Turkish vessel, a place which the Court assimilated to Turkish territory. This approach of the PCIJ applied the so-called objective territorial principle of jurisdiction to collisions on the high seas. The Court rejected the French position that there was a rule of international law imposing a duty upon Turkey not to try Demons. It held that there was no rule prohibiting Turkey's exercise of jurisdiction in the case since "restrictions upon the freedom of States cannot ... be presumed." International law permitted anything that it did not forbid; there was a permissive rule of international law allowing Turkey to try the French lieutenant. If, in the past, states in Turkey's position had refrained from prosecuting, they had done so not out of the sense of legal obligation but for other reasons, such as expedience, comity, and the like.

The PCIJ judgment in the *Lotus* case was very much criticized, especially in seafaring circles, and the rule which it adopted in the matter of jurisdiction in cases of collision on the high seas, otherwise binding only in the *Lotus* case, was eventually reversed by the Brussels Convention of 10 May 1952 for the Unification of Certain Rules relating to Penal Jurisdiction in Matters of Collision or Other Incidents of Navigation (439 UNTS 233), and subsequently by art. 11 of the Geneva Convention on the High Seas of 29 April 1958 (450 UNTS 11) and art. 97 of the UN Convention on the Law of the Sea of 10 December 1982 (21 ILM 1245 (1982)) (not yet in force). Under all these treaties, penal and disciplinary proceedings in cases of collision or other navigational incidents on the high seas (beyond the territorial sea) are reserved to the state of the flag or (if it is different) to the state of the defendant's nationality.

Despite the Court's long outdated position, the *Lotus* decision belongs to the most widely cited decisions of international tribunals because in its reasons the PCIJ (and individual opinions) (q.v.) analyzed some of the most fundamental problems of international law, such as the nature of this law, its relationship to domestic ("municipal") law, the nature of customary international law, interpretation of treaties, and jurisdiction under the law of the flag.

M

McNair, Arnold Duncan, Lord (1885-1973). British national. Jurist and Professor of International Law at the University of Cambridge, 1919-1926, 1929-1939, and London School of Economics, 1926-1929. Vice-Chancellor of the University of Liverpool, 1937-1945. Member of the ICJ (q.v.), 1946-1955. Member of the ECHR (q.v.), 1959-1965. Author of numerous works on international law and editor of the fourth edition (1928) of the classic Oppenheim's *International Law* (*see* **Bibliography,** 2 G).

Military and Paramilitary Activities in and against Nicaragua (Nicaragua v. United States of America), ICJ 1984-1992. This much discussed case before the ICJ (q.v.) was a reflection of the Cold War in the Central American region, and specifically the civil war in Nicaragua in which the communist Sandinista government confronted the anti-communist Contras supported by the US.

The legal dimension of the conflict dated back to 6 April 1984 when the US, anticipating (rather belatedly) Nicaragua's action against the US before the ICJ, announced that, with immediate effect and for a period of four years, its 1946 declaration accepting the ICJ jurisdiction under the optional clause (q.v.) would not apply to disputes with any Central American state or arising out of or related to events in that region. This US announcement added a third reservation to the acceptance of compulsory jurisdiction of the ICJ (q.v.) by the US in 1946, the other two being the automatic (self-judging) reservation (q.v.) under the so-called Connally reservation or amendment and the so-called Vandenberg Amendment excluding from the ICJ jurisdiction any disputes arising under a multilateral treaty and requiring that all the parties to the treaty (UN Charter, OAS Charter and two other multilateral treaties invoked by Nicaragua in the case) affected by the ICJ decision also be parties before the Court.

Ignoring the US declaration of 6 April 1984 and immediately

following the US veto on 7 April 1984 of a UN Security Council draft resolution denouncing the US for its support of the Contras, including mining Nicaragua's harbors, on 9 April 1984 Nicaragua instituted proceedings against the US, alleging that the US was using military force against it in violation of Nicaragua's sovereignty and international law. As to the ICJ jurisdiction, Nicaragua based its application on the claim that both countries had accepted the compulsory jurisdiction of the ICJ under the optional clause of art. 36 of the Court's Statute. Nicaragua also invoked the compromissory clause (*see Compromis*) of the bilateral Treaty of Friendship, Commerce and Navigation of 21 January 1956.

Nicaragua asked the Court to adjudge and declare that by its actions the US had violated conventional, that is, treaty law and general international law and was obligated to pay Nicaragua reparations in a sum to be determined by the Court. At the same time Nicaragua requested the ICJ to indicate provisional measures (q.v.) ordering the US to cease its support of the Contras and desist from any military or paramilitary activity against Nicaragua.

The US asked the Court to remove the case from its List, contending that the Court lacked jurisdiction in view of the US declaration of 6 April 1984 and on the ground that Nicaragua's acceptance of the optional clause dating back to 1929 had never acquired legal validity because the instrument of ratification of the Statute of the PCIJ (q.v.) had never been received by the League of Nations; hence Nicaragua had never ratified the Protocol of Signature of the PCIJ Statute.

In its order of 10 May 1984 (1984 ICJ Rep. 169) the ICJ unanimously ruled that at that stage of the proceedings it did not have to determine the validity of the Nicaraguan declaration of 1929 and found that that declaration as well as the US 1946 optional clause declaration appeared to afford a sufficient basis for the Court's jurisdiction. The Court also unanimously indicated provisional measures against US blocking and mining Nicaraguan ports and called upon the parties not to aggravate the dispute or take any action which might prejudice the rights of the other party. Furthermore, by 14 votes to one (the US judge), the Court ordered that Nicaragua's right to sovereignty and political independence should be fully respected and not jeopardized by military and paramilitary activities and intervention prohibited by international law.

In a further stage of the proceedings, the Court, by nine votes to six, decided by the order of 4 October 1984 (1984 ICJ Rep. 215) not to hold a hearing on the declaration of intervention (*see* **Intervention in Proceedings**) of El Salvador, and by 14 votes to one found that country's declaration of intervention inadmissible at that stage of the proceedings because it addressed the substance of the dispute.

The ICJ judgment on its jurisdiction and the question of the admissibility of Nicaragua's application was delivered on 26 November 1984 (1984 ICJ Rep. 392). By 11 votes to five, the Court upheld its jurisdiction to entertain Nicaragua's application on the basis of art. 36 (2) (optional clause) and art. 36(5) (Nicaragua's acceptance of the optional clause under the Statute of the PCIJ) of the ICJ Statute; by 14 votes to two, it ruled that it had jurisdiction under the compromissory clause of the above-mentioned US-Nicaragua Treaty of 1956; by 15 votes to one it found that it had jurisdiction to entertain the case; and it unanimously ruled that Nicaragua's application was admissible.

The Court's reasoning was briefly as follows: Analyzing Nicaragua's declaration of 1929 and the relevant provision in art. 36(5) of the ICJ Statute (concerning continued validity of the declarations made under the PCIJ for the period which they still have to run and in accordance with their terms), the Court concluded that Nicaragua could be deemed to have given its consent to the transfer of the 1929 declaration to the ICJ when it signed and ratified the UN Charter of which the ICJ Statute forms an integral part. The Court also concluded that Nicaragua's position had been corroborated by the conduct of the parties in the intervening period (1929-1946).

Concerning the US declaration of 6 April 1984, the Court held that it could not, at the time, modify the US optional clause declaration of 1946 because any such modifications were subject to the six months' notice clause of the 1946 declaration and could not enter into effect immediately. Against the US contention that the US was free to disregard the six months' notice requirement since Nicaragua was not bound by any time restrictions of its declaration and hence was not accepting the same obligation, the

Court ruled that reciprocity applied not to the formal conditions of the optional clause such as its duration but to the scope of its substantive commitments.

As to the US multilateral treaty (Vandenberg) reservation, the ICJ ruled that its consideration should be joined to the proceedings on the merits; the reservation as such did not debar the Court from entertaining Nicaragua's application. The 1956 Nicaragua-US Treaty also provided a basis for jurisdiction.

On the question of the admissibility of Nicaragua's application, the Court found itself unable to declare the application inadmissible on any of the grounds advanced by the US, namely: that Nicaragua failed to bring before the Court other interested parties; that the whole dispute, as involving a threat to peace, fell within the competence of the Security Council; that the Court proceedings could have an impact upon the inherent right of self-defense under art. 51 of the UN Charter; that judicial proceedings could not deal with a situation involving an ongoing armed conflict; and that Nicaragua had not exhausted the regional processes of settlement, specifically diplomatic negotiations under the so-called Contadina process.

Dissatisfied with the Court's judgment of 26 November 1984, the US announced on 18 January 1985 that it would not participate further in the case (24 ILM 246 (1985)) and eventually, on 7 October 1985, formally denounced its 1946 declaration of acceptance of the ICJ's compulsory jurisdiction under the optional clause (24 ILM 1742 (1985)).

The Court's judgment on the merits was delivered on 27 June 1986 (1986 ICJ Rep. 14). As widely anticipated, by very substantial majorities, varying from 14 to one to 12 to three, depending on the issue, the ICJ decided that by its actions against Nicaragua the US had violated its obligations under customary international law and its bilateral Treaty of 1956 on friendship, commerce and navigation and that it was under a duty to immediately cease all such acts and make reparation to Nicaragua. By 11 votes to four the ICJ recognized, however, that it was required to apply the multilateral treaty (Vandenberg) reservation contained in the US declaration of acceptance of the optional clause. Finally, the Court unanimously recalled to both Nicaragua and the US their obligation to seek a peaceful solution of their dispute.

The Court's judgment on the merits contains important analyses of some central issues of international law, such as the definition and content of customary international law; the prohibition of the use of force; the right of collective self-defense (held by the Court to be legal only in response to an armed attack); and the principle of non-intervention. Of particular interest is the Court's view that, while the concept of "armed attack" may include sending by or on behalf of a state armed bands which carry out acts of armed force against another state, it does not entail assistance to rebels in the form of the provision of weapons or logistical or other support. Hence the supplying by Nicaragua of weapons to insurgents in El Salvador did not--in the Court's view--constitute an armed attack, and consequently did not warrant the US plea of collective self-defense.

A month following the ICJ judgment on the merits, Nicaragua instituted proceedings before the ICJ against Costa Rica and Honduras, charging them with "border and transborder" armed action against Nicaragua. While the proceedings against Costa Rica were, at the request of Nicaragua, discontinued by the Court's order of 19 August 1987 (1987 ICJ Rep. 182), those against Honduras continued. Nicaragua requested an indication of provisional measures on which the Court issued an order on 31 March 1988 (1988 ICJ Rep. 9), but Nicaragua withdrew its request. Subsequently, against Honduras' preliminary objections, the ICJ found in a unanimous judgment of 20 December 1988 that it had jurisdiction under art. XXI of the Pact of Bogota of 1948 (119 UNTS 3) and that Nicaragua's application was admissible.

In the meantime, on the main issue, that is the Nicaragua--US dispute, the proceedings on compensation to be paid by the US to Nicaragua continued despite the boycott by the US. However, the political developments in Central America in 1990 radically changed the judicial aspect of the Nicaragua-US conflict. In February 1990 the electoral defeat of the Sandinista government brought to power a new, anti-communist administration of President Violeta Barrios de Chamorro which on 12 September 1991 asked the ICJ to discontinue all the proceedings of Nicaragua against the US and remove the case from the Court's List, which the Court did on 26 September 1991 (31 ILM 103 (1992)). Nicaragua's proceedings against Honduras in the *Border and*

Transborder Armed Actions were also discontinued at the request of Nicaragua and removed from the List by the Court's order of 27 May 1992.

Minquiers and Ecrehos (France /United Kingdom), ICJ 1951-1953. This case was brought before the ICJ (q.v.) by the parties on the basis of a special agreement (*compromis*) (q.v.) even though they had also accepted the jurisdiction of the ICJ under the optional clause (q.v.). The case concerned a dispute between France and the UK over the sovereignty over two groups of islets situated between the island of Jersey and the French coast. In its judgment of 17 November 1953 (1953 ICJ Rep. 47) the ICJ ruled unanimously that the sovereignty over the islands belonged to the UK. In the reasons to its decision the Court traced the history of the title to the islands back to the 11th century. While examining medieval title deeds and treaties, the Court expressed the opinion that in appraising the relative strengths of the opposing claims the decisive weight should be given to possession and relative intensity of the actual exercise of sovereignty by specific legislative and administrative acts in more recent times, a test which decided the case in favor of the UK.

The *Minquiers and Ecrehos* case reaffirms the well established principle of effectiveness in cases of disputed sovereignty over territory, and in this respect it follows the reasoning of the *Palmas* case (q.v.) arbitrated between the Netherlands and the United States.

Mixed Arbitral Tribunals. Arbitral (*see* **Arbitration**) tribunals established in relations between the Allies and the defeated powers under the Peace Treaties ending the First World War. The function of the mixed arbitral tribunals was: to settle claims of nationals of the Allied and Associated Powers against Germany and its allies for damage caused by war measures such as confiscation and requisitioning; to settle claims between individuals resulting from pre-war obligations, largely processed through a clearing procedure; and to deal with claims of nationals of the defeated powers against the newly created states. Individuals as well as governments had standing before the mixed arbitral tribunals, that is, they could present their claims themselves.

Some 36 mixed arbitral tribunals were established under the Treaties of Versailles (1919), Saint-Germain (1919), Neuilly (1919), Trianon (1920), and Lausanne (1923). They involved 14 European countries, Japan and Siam. In addition, a German-US Mixed Claims Commission (q.v.) and a tripartite (US-Austria-Hungary) commission were set up separately in 1922 since the US was not a party to any of those peace treaties. A German-Mexican commission was also active. Individuals did not have direct access to these commissions, however.

Following the Second World War, the Conciliation Commissions under the Peace Treaty with Italy (1947) (q.v.) and the Property Commissions under the Peace Treaty with Japan (1951) (q.v.) were similar to the mixed arbitration tribunals after the First World War.

The mixed arbitral tribunals were made up of two national members appointed by the governments of the victorious and the defeated power respectively and a neutral chairman chosen by mutual agreement who, in practice, largely determined the outcome of the adjudication. The tribunals applied relevant treaty provisions and domestic law appropriate under private international law rules. Execution of awards involving debts was carried out according to the procedure of the debtor country. Judgments against states were executed under a clearing procedure or from the proceeds of confiscated enemy property.

The mixed arbitral tribunals of the post-World War I era were the busiest ever international tribunals. For instance, 20,000 claims were submitted before the Franco-German tribunal alone; some 10,000 before the Anglo-German tribunal; and about 13,000 were settled by the German-US Mixed Claims Commission. Many of these claims were disposed out of court, however. The activities of the tribunals were terminated in the early 1930s.

Despite political difficulties, such as were encountered in Franco-German relations, the mixed arbitral tribunals made a significant contribution to the development of international law, especially by the fact that they recognized the status of individuals, granting them the right to directly plead their cases before the tribunal.

Mixed Claims Commissions. A form of judicial settlement of international disputes by a body of commissioners set up by treaty in order to decide on claims between nationals of different states, between states and nationals of another state, or between states themselves. In the 19th century only states had the right to file claims before mixed claims commissions. This has changed in the 20th century when, under some treaties, individuals obtained direct access to such commissions.

A mixed claims commission normally consists of two or four commissioners appointed in equal numbers by the governments concerned, with another, the umpire, coopted by the commissioners or the governments. The institution of mixed claims commissions was initiated under the Jay Treaty (q.v.) in 1794. Sometimes known simply as mixed commissions, they became very common in the 19th century when some 80 of such commissions were established. Among them, the commissions set up to settle claims resulting from the Napoleonic wars, the US-Mexican claims commission of 1868 which settled more than 2,000 claims, the US-Venezuelan commission, and other commissions settling claims in relations between the US and major European powers on the one hand and Latin American countries on the other, are the best known bodies of this kind.

The 19th century mixed claims commissions can be viewed as antecedents of the mixed arbitration tribunals (q.v.) after the First World War. But still in the inter-war period mixed claims commissions were used in settling claims against Germany, and the two commissions set up by the US and Mexico in 1923 and 1924 became perhaps the best known bodies of this kind. They dealt with some 6,000 claims, almost all of them by US nationals who alleged all kinds of injuries suffered in the conditions of revolutionary turmoil in Mexico. The US-Mexican claims commissions contributed a significant body of case law on state responsibility for injury to aliens.

The law to be applied by the commission is usually specified in the treaty which establishes such a body. References are usually made to international law, justice and equity or a similar formula.

After World War II the use of mixed claims commissions declined, with states resorting to "lump sum settlement" agreements whereby one state agrees to pay another a lump sum in full satisfaction of the outstanding claims by the nationals of the latter against the former. The lump sum is then distributed to claimants by a national claims commission which normally also applies international law in adjudicating the claims.

Monetary Gold Removed from Rome in 1943 (Italy v. France, United Kingdom and United States), ICJ 1953-1954. This case concerned a dispute over the distribution under Part III of the Paris Reparation Agreement of 1946 of monetary gold found in Germany or other countries after the Second World War. The agreement provided that the gold should be pooled for distribution among the states entitled to receive a share in proportion to their respective share of total losses. Albania claimed a share since a large part of its gold reserves, kept in Rome, had been taken by Germans to Berlin in 1943. The UK contended that the gold in question should be delivered to it in partial satisfaction of the ICJ judgment in the *Corfu Channel* (q.v.) case. For its part, Italy claimed the gold on the ground that in January 1945 Albania had confiscated the assets of the National Bank of Albania, at that time largely owned by Italy.

France, the UK, and the US, which were charged with the implementation of the Reparation Agreement, submitted the question to arbitration (q.v.). The arbitrator named by the President of the ICJ (q.v.), ruled that the gold belonged to Albania. However, the governments of the three above-mentioned states had also agreed that in case the arbitrator decided in favor of Albania, the gold should be delivered to the UK unless within 90 days Albania or Italy applied to the ICJ requesting adjudication of their respective claims. While Albania took no action, Italy instituted proceedings before the ICJ against France, the UK, and the US. Subsequently, however, it raised the question of the Court's jurisdiction in the absence of Albania's consent. This is the only case in the history of the ICJ in which the applicant state has raised a preliminary objection (q.v.).

In its judgment of 15 June 1954 (1954 ICJ Rep. 19) the ICJ unanimously decided that it had no jurisdiction to decide on the merits of Italy's claim because to do so would first require a determination whether Albania had committed an international wrong against Italy and had the obligation to pay compensation, something that the Court was not authorized to do without Albania's consent. By a vote of 13 to one, the Court also ruled that it could not pronounce on the priority of the claims of Italy and the UK since that issue was dependent upon the decision on the Italian claim which the Court had no jurisdiction to adjudicate.

The *Monetary Gold* case is frequently quoted as reaffirming the well established principle of international law that an international tribunal cannot exercise its jurisdiction over a state without that state's consent.

Moore, John Bassett (1860-1947). American national. Eminent international lawyer. Official of the US State Department. Judge of the PCIJ (q.v.), 1921-1927. Author of the classic eight-volume *Digest of International Law* (1906) (*see* **Bibliography,** 2 E (1)).

Mosler, Hermann (1912-). German national. Member of the ICJ (q.v.),1976-1985. Professor of International Law at the Universities of Bonn, 1946-1949,and Frankfurt am Main, 1949-1951. Head of the Legal Department of the West German Ministry of Foreign Affairs, 1951-1953. Professor of International Law at the University of Heidelberg; Director of the Max Planck Institute, 1954-1976. Author and editor of numerous works on international law.

N

Naulilaa Arbitration, 1928. This arbitration (q.v.) of 1928 between Portugal and Germany by a Mixed Arbitral Tribunal (q.v.) established under the Peace Treaty of Versailles, 1919, resulted from a border incident in Portuguese Angola in October 1914 when Portugal was still neutral in the war. Because of a misunderstanding, two officers of a German party of soldiers and an official from the neighboring German Southwest Africa were killed by Portuguese soldiers in Angolan territory. In retaliation, Germany sent a military force into Angola which destroyed several frontier stations including Naulilaa, causing considerable loss of life and property. Furthermore, this German action precipitated a native uprising in Angola, causing additional damage to Portugal. Portugal demanded reparation which Germany refused, arguing that its action had been a lawful reprisal.

In its award of 31 July 1928 (2 UNRIAA 1013), the tribunal, made up of three Swiss arbitrators, ruled that the German action had been illegal, lacking the essential elements of legitimate reprisals under the then obtaining rules of international law, namely: violation of international law by the party against which reprisals are undertaken, demand for redress, and proportionality between the injury sustained and the retaliatory action. In the *Naulilaa* case the tribunal found that there had been no violation of international law by Portugal because the incident was due to a misunderstanding largely caused by the German interpreter; the German action had not been preceded by any negotiations, let alone unsatisfied demand of redress; and the German action had been out of all proportion to the injury suffered.

In its second award on 30 June 1930 (2 UNRIAA 1035) the tribunal determined the amount of damages to be paid by Germany for losses directly arising from the *Naulilaa* and some other incidents and assessed *ex aequo et bono* (*see* **Ex Aequo et Bono** and **Equity**) the damages in respect of the losses caused to Portugal by the native uprising. In a third award (1933) the

160

tribunal decided upon the method of payment by Germany of reparation due to Portugal for various claims which dated back to the time when Portugal was still neutral in World War I.

The award in the *Naulilaa* case correctly interpreted the rule of international law governing military reprisals in time of peace. However, today it is mainly of historical interest in view of the fact that in contemporary international law military reprisals are prohibited under the general principle, laid down in art. 2(4) of the UN Charter, banning the use and threat of force in international relations.

Neumeister Case, ECHR 1968. This was the first case in which the ECHR (q.v.) rendered a decision against a member state. Neumeister was an Austrian businessman accused by his government of complicity in a tax evasion scheme. He was arrested for a period of time in 1961 and again on 12 July 1962, whereupon he was kept in pre-trial detention for more than two years. His trial began in 1964 and it had not yet been completed when the ECHR rendered its judgment in 1968. The Commission (*see* **European Court of Human Rights**) ruled violation of arts. 5(3) and 6(1) of the European Convention for the Protection of Human Rights and Fundamental Freedoms of 4 November 1950 (213 UNTS 221) guaranteeing respectively trial within a reasonable time or release pending trial, and--in the determination of criminal charges--a fair and public hearing within a reasonable time.

In its judgment of 27 June 1968 ([1968] ECHR. Ser. A, no. 5) the ECHR unanimously ruled that there had been a breach of art. 5(3) but, by five votes to two held, against the Commission's findings, that there was no violation of art. 6(1). In 1974 the Court awarded Neumeister reparation as just satisfaction for injury suffered ([1974] ECHR. Ser. A, no. 17).

New York Convention, 1958. A multilateral convention of 10 June 1958 (330 UNTS 38) providing for recognition and enforcement of foreign arbitral awards and agreements to arbitrate. In 1992 more than 85 countries, including the US, were parties to this Convention which finds its primary application within the context of international commercial arbitration (q.v.).

While a great majority of arbitral awards are complied with voluntarily, enforcement proceedings against the losing party is necessary in some cases. For most states parties, the New York Convention applies to all private international arbitral agreements, but some states, including the US, apply it only if the legal relationship that gave rise to the dispute was commercial in character. Investment disputes are not excluded, however.

The Convention may be applied in cases of awards between states and foreign nationals in investment disputes, but in practice claimants use the arrangements of the International Centre for Settlement of Investment Disputes (ICSID) (q.v.) whose awards are much more easily enforced than under the New York Convention. Still, most cases of enforcement arise within the context of the latter agreement. Arbitration of inter-governmental disputes of a public international law character is not covered by the New York Convention.

Under the New York Convention a court in a state party must recognize and enforce an arbitral award against the losing party's assets, rendered in any state party as a result of a valid written agreement to arbitrate. However, under the circumstances listed in the Convention, recognition and enforcement of an award may be refused at the request of the party against which it is invoked.

North Atlantic Coast Fisheries Arbitration, 1910. This arbitration (q.v.) over fishing rights in the North Atlantic between the US and UK took place at The Hague within the framework of the PCA (q.v.) according to the procedural rules of the Hague Convention of 1899 for the Pacific Settlement of International Disputes (q.v.), pursuant to a *compromis* (q.v.) of 27 January 1909 signed under the two countries' General Treaty of Arbitration of 4 April 1908.

The dispute concerned the nature and scope of ancient fishing rights of American fishermen off the southern coast of Newfoundland (the "treaty coast"), confirmed by Great Britain as a liberty granted for ever in the Treaty of London of 1818, but subsequently an object of conflicts, negotiations, and awards by mixed arbitral commissions (q.v.).

The arbitral tribunal of five arbitrators was asked to answer seven questions, the first one being whether Great Britain had the right to regulate the fisheries of US fishermen without the US consent. The other questions concerned details of the exercise by US inhabitants of their fishery rights, including the right to use, for shelter and other purposes, the "American shore" which the tribunal was asked to determine. Since under the Treaty of 1818 the US had waived the right to fish in other waters of the British possessions in the North (off the non-treaty coast) "within three marine miles of any of the coasts, bays, creeks or harbors," the tribunal was also asked to define a bay.

The tribunal's award of 7 September 1910 (11 UNRIAA 173) was unanimous except for the question on bays. Generally speaking, the tribunal recognized Great Britain's sole right to regulate the fisheries in a reasonable way, with fairness and good faith and in accordance with the Treaty of 1818, subject to respect for the rights of American fishermen to fish in the treaty waters off Newfoundland and Labrador, including bays, creeks, and harbors. However, the tribunal failed to provide a legal definition of the bay, with one dissenting arbitrator arguing in favor of the ten-mile rule (referring to the entrance of a bay) which was eventually adopted by the parties.

The *North Atlantic Coast Fisheries* arbitration is largely of historical interest in view of the radical transformation of the international law of fisheries within the framework of the universally adopted 200-mile exclusive economic zone (EEZ). The award may be of interest, however, not only because of its discussion of bays but also because of the tribunal's opinion that the Treaty of 1818 did not create a servitude (that is, a right that is tied directly to the territory irrespective of any change in sovereignty), a legal institution of civil (Roman) law origin which even today is matter of controversy in the doctrine of international law.

North Sea Continental Shelf (Federal Republic of Germany/Denmark; Federal Republic of Germany/Netherlands), ICJ 1967-1969. This much discussed case was the first one in a series of cases before the ICJ (q.v.) involving the delimitation of competing national maritime jurisdictions. It concerned the delimitation of the boundaries of the continental shelf in the North Sea adjacent to the Federal Republic of Germany as against Denmark and the Netherlands. Following failure of negotiations the countries concerned signed a special agreement (*compromis*) (q.v.) whereby they requested the ICJ to decide on the principles and rules of international law applicable to the delimitation of the shelf. At the parties' request the Court joined the proceedings in the two cases.

Denmark and the Netherlands maintained that the delimitation should be governed by the equidistance principle set forth in art. 6(2) of the Geneva Convention of 29 April 1958 on the Continental Shelf (499 UNTS 311) to which the two countries were parties. They also contended that the exception of the "special circumstances" of the Convention was not applicable in the case. They claimed that even though Germany was not a party to the Convention, the equidistance rule had already become part of customary international law and thus Germany was in any case bound by this rule. The geographical situation did not warrant any exception from it on grounds of special circumstances.

Germany's position was that it was not bound by the equidistance method either by virtue of a treaty or by customary law and that the delimitation should be effected by agreement which ought to leave each state a just and equitable share. In the special geographical circumstances of the North Sea area concerned, Germany opposed the equidistance principle because its effect on the concave coastline of the three countries concerned would be to give Germany, which is situated in the middle, a smaller continental shelf than it might otherwise obtain.

In a single judgment of 20 February 1969 (1969 ICJ Rep. 3) the ICJ, by 11 votes to six, decided that the use of the equidistance method was not obligatory and that the delimitation was to be effected by agreement in accordance with equitable principles and taking account of all relevant circumstances in such a way as to leave as much as possible to each party those sections of the continental shelf that constituted a natural prolongation of its land territory. The Court further set forth principles to guide delimitation in case of overlap or convergence, but while ruling out the application of the equidistance method stipulated in the 1958 Convention, it did not deal with the question of special circumstances.

After protracted negotiations the three countries concerned reached a compromise agreement favorable to Germany, finalized

in two treaties of 28 January 1971 (857 UNTS 109, 155).
The *North Sea Continental Shelf* case is an important landmark
in the history of the law of the continental shelf. It has
significantly influenced states' practice in this area of the law of
the sea and its basic principles were incorporated in the relevant
parts of the UN Convention of 1982 on the Law of the Sea.
Furthermore, the relevance of the judgment in the *North Sea* case
transcends the subject of the law of the sea in so far as the
Court's considerations regarding the formation of customary
international law on the basis of a treaty are concerned.

**Northern Cameroons (Cameroon v. United Kingdom), ICJ 1961-
1963.** In 1961 Cameroon initiated proceedings against the UK
before the ICJ (q.v.), asking the Court to declare that the UK had
failed to observe certain obligations under the Trusteeship
Agreement of 1946 for the territory of the Cameroons under
British administration. Cameroon's application was based on art.
19 of the Agreement which provided for referring disputes
between the administering authority and a UN member to the
ICJ. Cameroon's special complaint was that the UK, by
administering the territory in question as an integral part of
Nigeria, was responsible for Northern Cameroon joining Nigeria,
a fact which was endorsed by a plebiscite under the auspices of
the UN and approved by the UN Resolution terminating the
Trusteeship Agreement on 1 June 1961. The UK raised a
preliminary objection (q.v.) contending that no real dispute existed
between it and Cameroon.

In its judgment of 2 December 1963 (1963 ICJ Rep. 15), the
ICJ, by a vote of ten to five, dismissed any objection to its
jurisdiction, but for reasons of judicial propriety decided not to
adjudicate on the merits since a judgment would not have any
practical consequences. It could not be effectively applied and
would be devoid of any purpose, especially considering the fact
that the UN General Assembly had definitively settled the
problem of the Cameroon trusteeship.

The case is of interest in that the ICJ judgment, including
individual (separate and dissenting) opinions (q.v.), elaborated on
the concepts of "disputes" (q.v.) and preliminary objections.

Norwegian Loans *see* Certain Norwegian Loans (France v. Norway), ICJ 1955-1957

Nottebohm (Liechtenstein v. Guatemala), ICJ 1951-1955. The facts in this celebrated and highly controversial case were as follows: Nottebohm, a German national born in Germany, emigrated to Guatemala in 1906 and continued to reside there, visiting Germany and Liechtenstein (where he had a brother) on a number of occasions. Following the outbreak of the Second World War he travelled to Liechtenstein in October 1939 where he obtained Liechtenstein nationality, simultaneously losing, according to German law, his German nationality. Having obtained a Guatemalan visa, he returned to Guatemala and resumed his former business activities there. After Guatemala had declared war on Germany in 1941, Nottebohm was arrested as an enemy alien and deported to the US for internment. His property was seized and formally expropriated after the war in 1949. He himself left the US and established residence in Liechtenstein, after Guatemala had refused to readmit him. Liechtenstein claimed the right to protect Nottebohm under international law and instituted proceedings before the ICJ, claiming restitution and compensation on the ground that Guatemala had acted towards its national in a manner contrary to international law.

The ICJ delivered two judgments in the Nottebohm case. First, in its judgment of 18 November 1953 (1953 ICJ Rep. 111), it unanimously upheld its jurisdiction under the optional clause (q.v.) against Guatemala's preliminary objection (q.v.), ruling that the expiration of Guatemala's acceptance of the compulsory jurisdiction (q.v.) of the ICJ after the Court had been seised of the case did not affect its jurisdiction.

In the second phase of the proceedings, in its judgment of 6 April 1955 (1955 ICJ Rep. 4), the ICJ ruled, by 11 votes to three, that Liechtenstein's claim on behalf of Nottebohm was inadmissible. While not denying Liechtenstein's right to grant nationality in the exercise of its domestic jurisdiction, the Court held that such right did not automatically produce the international effect of entitling a state to exercise diplomatic protection under international law. In the specific case, the Court denied Liechtenstein the right to exercise diplomatic protection on behalf of Nottebohm on the ground that there was no "genuine link" between him and Liechtenstein, his connection to that state being tenuous and not strong enough for Liechtenstein to entitle it to protect Nottebohm *vis à vis* Guatemala.

The *Nottebohm* judgment admitted, under specific circumstances, the possibility of dissociating the right of diplomatic protection from nationality. Hence it has been severely criticized by international law experts who also questioned the vague and relative concept of the genuine link, inappropriately--as they claimed--adopted from cases of dual nationality in the essentially different cases of diplomatic protection of nationals who may have links to other states. The concept of genuine link reemerged in its application to the nationality of ships in the ICJ advisory opinion of 1960 on the *Constitution of the Maritime Safety Committee of the Inter-Governmental Maritime Consultative Organization* (q.v.).

Nuclear Tests (Australia v. France) and Nuclear Tests (New Zealand v. France), ICJ 1973-1974. In 1973 Australia and New Zealand instituted, on the basis of the General Act of 1928 (q.v.) and art. 36 of the Statute of the ICJ (q.v.), including the optional clause (q.v.), proceedings before the ICJ against France, asking the Court to adjudge and declare that the French atmospheric nuclear tests in the South Pacific Ocean were not consistent with international law. Both countries also requested the Court to indicate interim measures of protection (provisional measures) (q.v.) against France, ordering it to desist from any such further tests pending the Court's judgment. By orders of 22 June 1973 (1973 ICJ Rep. 99, 135) the Court granted the applicants these measures. France contested the Court's jurisdiction and did not participate in the proceedings. Consideration of Fiji's request for intervention in the proceedings (q.v.) was deferred by the Court's orders of 12 July 1973 (1973 ICJ Rep. 320, 324).

The French tests continued in July and August 1973 and from June to September 1974. However, in July 1974 both the President of France and the French Defense Minister publicly stated that France intended to cease atmospheric nuclear tests following the conclusion of the 1974 series of tests. Thereupon, the ICJ, without dealing with jurisdiction, admissibility, or the merits of the case, decided in its judgments of 20 December 1974, adopted by nine votes to six (1974 ICJ Rep. 253, 457), that in view of the French declarations of July 1974 the dispute ceased to exist and therefore the claims of Australia and New Zealand no longer had any object. Fiji's application to intervene in the two countries' proceedings was declared to have lapsed by the Court's orders of 20 December 1974 (1974 ICJ Rep. 530, 535).

The ICJ judgments in the *Nuclear Tests* cases were based on a very weak majority. Six judges dissented and, of the nine who concurred with the dismissal of the case, four delivered separate opinions. Generally speaking, the ICJ was criticized for its decision as being afraid to grapple with the real issue at hand, that is, the legality of nuclear atmospheric tests in the ocean. The *Nuclear Tests* cases are of interest, however, because the Court's consideration of the French declarations of July 1974 reaffirmed the rule of international law that, under the principle of good faith, a state's obligation can originate from a public unilateral act.

Nuremberg Tribunal *see* **International Military Tribunal at Nuremberg**

O

Oda, Shigeru (1924-). Japanese national. Member of the ICJ (q.v.) since 1976 and its Vice-President since 1991. Law degree from the University of Tokyo, 1947, doctor of Law (SJD), Yale University. Assistant Professor as of 1952, Professor as of 1959, and Professor Emeritus as of 1985 at the University of Tohoku. Delegate of Japan to many international conferences, including the UN Conference on the Law of the Sea, 1973-1982. Counsel for the Federal Republic of Germany before the ICJ in the *North Sea Continental Shelf* case (q.v.). Editor-in-Chief of *Japanese Annual of International Law*. Member (1979) of the Institute of International Law. Author of numerous publications in Japanese and English, mainly on the law of the sea.

Optional Clause. A treaty provision governing the jurisdiction (q.v.) of an international court whereby a state party to this treaty may at any time declare that it consents to the compulsory jurisdiction of the court. The optional clause is usually associated with the clause of art. 36(2) of the Statute of the ICJ (q.v.), but similar optional clauses are found in the treaties establishing the European Court of Human Rights (q.v.) (art. 46) and the Inter-American Court of Human Rights (q.v.) (art. 62) respectively. The rules of the recently established CSCE Court of Conciliation and Arbitration (q.v.) also provide for jurisdiction under the optional clause.

In the ICJ the optional clause of art. 36(2) of its Statute provides that the parties may at any time declare that they recognize as compulsory *ipso facto* and without special agreement, in relation to any other state accepting the same obligation, the jurisdiction of the Court in all legal disputes concerning: 1. the interpretation of a treaty; 2. any question of international law; 3. the existence of a fact which, if established, would constitute a breach of an international obligation; 4. the nature or extent of the reparation to be made for the breach of an international obligation.

The acceptance of the Court's jurisdiction under the optional clause is effected by depositing a unilateral declaration with the Secretary-General of the UN which is registered under art. 102 of the UN Charter as an international agreement. Declarations made under the PCIJ (q.v.) system which are still in force are deemed to be acceptances of the compulsory jurisdiction of the ICJ for the period which they still have to run and in accordance with their terms.

The optional clause declarations may be made unconditionally or on condition of reciprocity, or for a certain time. However, in practice all acceptances of compulsory jurisdiction of the ICJ under the optional clause are governed by the principle of reciprocity, applying either expressly or by implication to such acceptances. Consequently, the Court's jurisdiction is scaled down to the lowest common denominator of the undertaking common in the declarations of the two parties. As a result, each party, normally the respondent, may invoke a reservation to acceptance of compulsory jurisdiction of the ICJ (q.v.) which is not stipulated in its own optional clause declaration but is included in the declaration of the other party, normally the applicant state. Hence, the Court's jurisdiction is limited to those categories of dispute which are not excluded by any state party to the proceedings, that is, to the extent that all two or more declarations coincide (there may be several applicants and respondents). It is important that under the general rule of art. 36(6) of the ICJ Statute, in the event of a dispute as to whether the Court has jurisdiction, the matter is settled by the decision of the Court.

Unlike the contentious jurisdiction of the ICJ (q.v.) based on an *ad hoc* agreement (*see also* **Compromis**) or on a treaty provision, both of which are not limited with regard to the nature of the dispute, the Court's jurisdiction under the optional clause is expressly limited to "legal disputes," an aspect of the ICJ jurisdiction related to the theoretical distinction between "justiciable" (legal) and "non-justiciable" (political) disputes (*see* **Justiciability of International Disputes**).

The optional clause is the outcome of a compromise achieved by the drafters of the Statute of the PCIJ between the states advocating and those opposing compulsory jurisdiction. This compromise continues in the Statute of the ICJ. The expectations that a widespread acceptance of the optional clause would eventually lead to a *de facto* compulsory jurisdiction of the "World Court" have not been fulfilled. As a matter of fact, the number of acceptances has diminished in terms relative to the number of states. Whereas during the PCIJ period 32 out of 52 signatories of the PCIJ Statute accepted the optional clause, in 1955 the 32 acceptances represented 50 percent of the 64 state parties and in 1991 the 53 declarations (including seven made under the PCIJ Statute) amounted to less than 30 percent of some 170 signatories of the Statute of the ICJ. More recently, in the post-Cold War period there have been some indications of renewed interest in the optional clause as a number of states, including some former communist ones, deposited declarations of acceptance. However, as a whole, in 1993 still fewer than a third of the 181 UN members were bound by the ICJ jurisdiction under art. 36(2).

The effectiveness of the optional clause has been further reduced by the states concerned assuming commitments of uncertain duration, terminable upon notice immediately or in six months, and--most importantly--by reservations to acceptance of compulsory jurisdiction of the ICJ. Although the automatic (self-judging) reservation (q.v.) appears to be losing ground, numerous reservations of an amazing variety have reduced the scope of compulsory jurisdiction under the optional clause, especially in view of the reciprocal effects that such reservations have upon the Court's jurisdiction, as illustrated for example in the *Certain Norwegian Loans* (q.v.) case.

The denunciation by the US in 1985 (in effect in 1986) of its optional clause declaration after 40 years (85 *Dpt.St.Bull.* 82 (1985)) brought about by American dissatisfaction with the ICJ decision in the case of *Military and Paramilitary Activities in and against Nicaragua* (q.v.) was a serious blow to the Court's jurisdiction under the optional clause. The termination of the US declaration under art. 36(2) of the ICJ Statute did not, however, affect the Court's jurisdiction under numerous bilateral and multilateral treaties (*see* **Contentious Jurisdiction of the ICJ**).

Organization of African Unity (OAU) Commission of Mediation, Conciliation and Arbitration. The OAU Charter of 25 May 1963

(479 UNTS 39) established (art. XIX) a Commission of Mediation, Conciliation (q.v.) and Arbitration (q.v.) whose composition and procedure are further developed in the Protocol of the Commission of 21 July 1964 (3 ILM 1116 (1964)). As far as arbitration is concerned, the Protocol provides (arts. XXVII-XXXI) that disputes between member states can be submitted to arbitration before an *ad hoc* tribunal made up of three arbitrators with legal qualifications, each party designating one arbitrator from among the 21 members of the Commission and the two thus designated coopting a third one to act as Chairman. None can be of the same nationality as the parties to the dispute. If no agreement can be reached on the name of the Chairman, he is appointed by the Bureau of the Commission. The tribunals decide according to international law, but--at the request of the parties--may decide *ex aequo et bono* (*see Ex Aequo et Bono* and Equity). The decisions are legally binding.

The activity of the OAU arbitration commission has been too insignificant to allow any judgment on its effectiveness.

Organization of Arab Petroleum Exporting Countries (OAPEC) Judicial Board. The standing tribunal of the OAPEC, an organization founded on 9 January 1968 (781 UNTS 235) with its seat in Kuwait. The composition, jurisdiction, and procedure of the Judicial Board are further set forth in the Protocol of 9 May 1978. The Board is made up of an uneven number of seven to 11 judges elected on a staggered schedule for a term of six years from different member countries by the OAPEC Council of Ministers. The President and Vice-President of the Board are elected by the judges for a three-year term.

The OAPEC Judicial Board has both contentious (q.v.) and advisory (q.v.) jurisdiction (q.v.). Within compulsory jurisdiction of the Board are: disputes involving member states, the Organization, or a company set up within the framework of the Organization, and relating to the interpretation and application of the founding instrument of 1968; inter-state disputes over petroleum operations; and disputes for which the Council of Ministers has found the Board to be competent. The Board has optional jurisdiction over: disputes between a member state and a non-member state oil company active in its territory; disputes between a member state and an oil company of another member state; and disputes between member states which are not within the mandatory jurisdiction of the Board.

The advisory jurisdiction of the Board is exercised with the approval of the OAPEC Council of Ministers. The opinions have no binding force.

The decisions of the Board are taken by a qualified majority of five, seven, or nine members, depending on the number of judges. The list of the sources of law to be applied by the OAPEC Judicial Board in general follows the sources listed in art. 38 of the Statute of the ICJ (q.v.), but Islamic law is an additional source. In cases involving its compulsory jurisdiction, the Board applies both international law and Islamic law, but in addition to treaties, customary law, and general principles of law, the Board is to resort to "common principles in the legal systems of the member states." The subsidiary means for the determination of rules of law are limited to judicial decisions and teaching of publicists of public law in the member states only. Resort to Islamic law may result in conflicts between this system of law and general international law. Thus under Islamic law natural resources are to be shared by the entire Islamic community; hence it may prove difficult to reconcile this principle with the sovereignty–oriented rules of contemporary international law. Since the activities of the OAPEC Judicial Board have so far been insignificant, no conclusions can as yet be drawn as to its contribution to peaceful settlement of disputes between the member states of the OAPEC.

P

Palmas, Island of, Arbitration, 1928. This famous arbitration (q.v.) within the framework of the PCA (q.v.) involved the dispute between the US and the Netherlands over Palmas (or Miangas), a little island in the Pacific Ocean between the Philippines and the Dutch East Indies (today Indonesia). The facts of this case were as follows: By the Treaty of Paris of 10 December 1898 (187 CTS 100) Spain ceded the Philippine Islands to the US, with the Island of Palmas described as forming part of the archipelago. However, in 1906, when a US official arrived in Palmas, to his surprise he found the Dutch flag flying there, and a dispute arose between the US and the Netherlands over sovereignty with regard to the island. Eventually, by a *compromis* (q.v.) of 23 January 1925, the two countries agreed to refer the issue to arbitration.

In his well reasoned award of 4 April 1928 (2 UNRIAA 829) the sole arbitrator, Max Huber (q.v.), a Swiss international lawyer and President of the PCIJ (q.v.), assessed the relative strengths of the competing Dutch and US claims and decided for the Netherlands. His view was that even if Spain had originally acquired sovereignty over Palmas, the Netherlands could prove a much greater degree of effective control over the island by continuous and peaceful display of its authority since at least 1700, so that by the critical date, that is 1898, it had supplanted Spain as the sovereign over the island. As a successor to Spain, the US could not acquire more rights under the Peace Treaty of 1898 than Spain itself possessed on the date.

In his reasoning the arbitrator applied the rule of the so-called intertemporal law providing the answer to the question of which period's rules should govern the validity of title to territory. Drawing a distinction between the creation of rights and their existence, the arbitrator held that even if Spain had acquired sovereignty over Palmas in the 16th century when--in European law of nations--mere discovery was sufficient for a valid title, eventually, and certainly by 1898, the requirements of this law had

174

become more exacting, necessitating the inchoate title of discovery to be completed by an effective control of the discovered territory. Spain had failed to exercise such control needed to keep up with the evolving rules of international law. On the other hand, the Netherlands had become the sovereign of the island through continuous and peaceful exercise of its authority. The arbitrator also rejected the US argument of contiguity whereby islands outside of the territorial sea should belong to a state merely because that state occupied the nearest continent or an island of considerable size.

The award in the *Palmas* case is of major importance in the law of acquisition of title to territory because of its thorough and cogent treatment of such issues as the nature of sovereignty over territory, the impact of effective control, contiguity, and the application of intertemporal law to acquisition of sovereignty. The *Palmas* award has been invoked in other arbitral decisions, for example the *Rann of Kutch* (q.v.), and in judgments of the PCIJ (*Legal Status of Eastern Greenland*) (q.v.) and the ICJ (q.v.) (*Minquiers and Ecrehos*) (q.v.), and in the advisory opinion (q.v.) of the ICJ in the case of *Western Sahara* (q.v.).

Permanent Court of Arbitration (PCA). An official panel of international jurists, established at The Hague under the Hague Convention of 1899 (revised in 1907) for the Pacific Settlement of International Disputes (q.v.), from among whom states can select arbitrators for an *ad hoc* tribunal which could adjudicate a dispute between them. The name "Permanent Court of Arbitration" is somewhat misleading since in reality, apart from the PCA permanent International Bureau with a Secretary General and the Permanent Administrative Council at The Hague, the Convention did not create a Court but rather a machinery for setting up arbitral tribunals when the need should arise. Each state party to the Convention nominates up to four persons ("members of the PCA") to serve as potential arbitrators for a renewable period of six years.

States which agree to refer a dispute to the PCA enter into a *compromis* (q.v.) and, if they cannot agree on the composition of the Tribunal, follow the selection procedures stipulated by the Convention. Briefly, each party appoints two arbitrators from the

PCA panel, who then select an umpire. If the votes are evenly divided, a third state selected by the parties chooses the umpire. If the parties cannot agree on the third state, each party chooses a different state and the choice of the umpire is made by those two states. If within two months no agreement is reached on selecting the umpire, each of the two third states presents two potential arbitrators from the PCA list, but not nationals of the parties or members selected by the parties. Drawing lots determines who shall be the umpire.

In practice, the tribunals constituted within the framework of the PCA consisted of a sole arbitrator (for instance in the *Island of Palmas* case (q.v.)), five members (for instance in the *Casablanca* case (q.v.)), or--as a rule--three arbitrators. If several arbitrators are selected, each party may not choose more than one of its nationals.

Unless otherwise provided for by the parties' *compromis*, the provisions on arbitration procedure of the Hague Convention become operative. This has happened in all the 25 cases adjudicated within the framework of the PCA. Awards are handed down on the basis of respect for law, but they can also be based on equity (*see Ex Aequo et Bono* and **Equity**).

The machinery of the PCA has proved useful in several important cases, including the *Casablanca* (1909) (q.v.), the *North Atlantic Coast Fisheries* (1910) (q.v.), and the *Island of Palmas* case (1928) (q.v.). Overall, however, states have been reluctant to submit their disputes to arbitration (q.v.) and altogether only 25 cases (of which 14 were before World War I and two after World War II) have been decided by tribunals under the PCA. The PCA is still in existence, with some 90 states parties to the 1899 or 1907 Convention. Recently, the PCA adopted optional rules for arbitrating disputes between states, effective 20 October 1992 (32 ILM 572 (1993)). The Rules are based on UNCITRAL Rules (q.v.) adapted to the public international law character of disputes between states.

The existence of the PCA inspired various plans and proposals for the creation of a permanent international tribunal. A plan for a Court of Arbitral Justice proposed at the Second Hague Peace Conference in 1907 never materialized but the trend eventually culminated in the establishment of the PCIJ (q.v.) and the ICJ (q.v.). In a way, the existence of a permanent World Court has overshadowed the basically 19th century machinery of the PCA.

Permanent Court of International Justice (PCIJ). The predecessor of the ICJ (q.v.) and the first permanently constituted international global tribunal of general, but not compulsory, jurisdiction, created pursuant to art. 14 of the Covenant of the League of Nations in order to settle disputes between states and give advisory opinions (q.v.) on "any dispute or question" referred to it by the Council or the Assembly of the League.

In accordance with art. 14 of the Covenant of the League of Nations, an Advisory Commission of Jurists drafted a Statute for the PCIJ which, following minor amendments, was approved by the League's Council and its Assembly in the Protocol of Signature of 16 December 1920. The Statute, which in legal terms was a treaty, entered into effect on 2 September 1921 and the first session of the Court was held at the Court's headquarters at The Hague in 1922. A protocol of 1929, effective in 1936, revised the Statute, the major amendments dealing with inclusion of an article on advisory opinions. The PCIJ also adopted its Rules of Procedure. At one time as many as 50 states were parties to the Statute, but the number declined as 13 states withdrew from participation. Although the US signed the Protocols of 1920 and 1929, it never acceded to the PCIJ Statute because of the Senate's refusal to ratify them. The USSR never joined the Statute.

In the years 1922 through 1940 the PCIJ delivered 32 judgments in 21 cases (*see* ANNEX I: JUDGMENTS OF THE PCIJ), the first being the judgment in the *Wimbledon* case (q.v.) in 1923. It ordered seven cases to be removed from the Court's List. The PCIJ also gave 26 advisory opinions (*see* ANNEX II: ADVISORY OPINIONS OF THE PCIJ), perhaps the best known being the opinion on the *Customs Régime between Germany and Austria* (1931) (q.v.), but refused to give an opinion in the *Eastern Carelia* (q.v.) case in 1923. The PCIJ also issued some 200 orders.

Most (18) of the advisory opinions and 11 judgments dealt with disputes related to the Versailles Peace Treaty (1919) and other post-World War I settlements. The *Eastern Greenland* (q.v.) case effected the settlement of a boundary dispute.

The activities of the PCIJ were interrupted by the German

invasion of the Netherlands in May 1940. Following the war, the PCIJ was dissolved by the last meeting of the League of Nations Assembly in 1946. The functions of the PCIJ were taken over by the ICJ which, while not being its legal successor, has in fact continued the activities of the inter-war World Court on the basis of legal rules which are a virtual duplication of the Statute of the PCIJ. The PCIJ differed from the present World Court in one major respect, namely whereas the ICJ is one of the (principal) organs of the UN and its Statute is an integral part of the UN Charter, the PCIJ, while commonly regarded as a League of Nations tribunal, was not an organ of the League and only those states that ratified the Protocol of Signature of 1920 were bound by the Statute.

Subject to a few minor differences, the composition, structure, procedure, jurisdiction (q.v.) as well as the law to be applied by the PCIJ and other rules, are now closely followed by the International Court of Justice and need not be elaborated upon in this entry. It is essential to note and emphasize that, like its successor, the PCIJ did not have compulsory jurisdiction over the disputes between the parties to the Statute. What was needed in each case of contentious jurisdiction (q.v.) was the parties' consent expressed either *ad hoc* or in a previous treaty referring to the jurisdiction of the Court, or through the optional clause (q.v.).

Even though the PCIJ, unlike a national court, had no compulsory jurisdiction, its creation was a turning point in the history of international tribunals and international legal institutions in general. Unlike the arbitral tribunals, whose experience otherwise contributed to its foundation, the PCIJ was a permanently constituted global judicial body with salaried judges, a Registrar, largely public proceedings, and published records of pleadings and other documentary evidence. The PCIJ developed judicial procedures, techniques and practices which eventually provided a blueprint for the ICJ. At the same time, the first "World Court" made a positive contribution to the interpretation and development of substantive international law and through its cases built up a judicial tradition which has continued in the work of its successor, the ICJ of the United Nations.

Petroleum Development Ltd. v. Sheikh of Abu Dhabi *see* **Abu Dhabi Arbitration, 1951**

Preliminary Objection. This is an objection raised in the practice of international tribunals by a party to a dispute, as a rule the respondent state, whereby that party, in order to prevent the court from dealing with the merits of the case, requests the court to examine first and render a decision upon a certain preliminary question or questions, distinct from the merits of the claim. In the PCIJ (q.v.) and the ICJ (q.v.) preliminary objections have been resorted to, mainly in cases brought before the Court by application, since the PCIJ case of *Readaptation of the Mavrommatis Jerusalem Concessions* in 1927. Preliminary objections are also possible in the CJEC (q.v.) and the ECHR (q.v.), among others.

In the ICJ (ICJ Rules art. 79(1)) preliminary objections can be: 1. to the jurisdiction (q.v.) of the Court; 2. to the admissibility of the application; or 3. can address other matters. Objections to jurisdiction may be based on the respondent state's contention that the treaty conferring jurisdiction upon the ICJ or the optional clause (q.v.) declaration is no longer in force or is null and void (for example *Temple of Preah Vihear* (q.v.); *Fisheries Jurisdiction* (q.v.)); or that a reservation to acceptance of compulsory jurisdiction of the ICJ (q.v.) excludes the dispute in question (*Certain Norwegian Loans* (q.v.); *Nuclear Tests* (q.v.); *Aegean Sea Continental Shelf* (q.v.); *Military and Paramilitary Activities in and against Nicaragua* (q.v.)). Preliminary objections relating to admissibility of the application include cases where the respondent state, without necessarily contesting the title to the Court's jurisdiction as such, alleges, in claims of the applicant state on behalf of its nationals, lack of link of nationality between the injured person and the applicant state, for example *Nottebohm* (q.v.), or non-exhaustion of local remedies (q.v.), for example *Barcelona Traction* (q.v.) and *Interhandel* (q.v.). The third category ("other objections") may, for example, be based on the allegation that there exists no dispute between the parties by reason of absence of negotiations (for example *Northern Cameroons* (q.v.)).

While a preliminary objection is normally raised by the respondent state in cases of application by the applicant state, the

ICJ Rules of 1978 provide (art. 78(1)) that a party other than a respondent state may also file an objection, something that occurred once in the history of the ICJ, namely in the case of *Monetary Gold Removed from Rome in 1943* (q.v.).

Preliminary objections have been frequently raised before the World Court. In the PCIJ they were raised 13 times; they were upheld in three and rejected in eight cases. In two cases the proceedings had been discontinued before the Court could decide on the objections. In the ICJ preliminary objections of respondent states contesting the Court's jurisdiction and, in some cases, admissibility of the application, have been a prominent feature of the proceedings. Furthermore, in cases where the respondent state, without formally filing preliminary objections, simply failed to appear before the Court while informally apprising the Court of its objections, the ICJ would, on its own initiative, suspend the proceedings on the merits and would order consideration of the jurisdictional issue at large, for example in the *Fisheries Jurisdiction* (q.v.) and *Nuclear Tests* (q.v.) cases.

The issues raised in the preliminary objections are dealt with in a distinct phase of proceedings terminating in the Court's decision in the form of a judgment by which the Court either upholds the objection, thus dismissing the case, or rejects it, or declares that the objection does not possess, in the circumstances of the case, an exclusively preliminary character. In the last two mentioned situations the Court fixes time limits for further proceedings.

While preliminary objections may be criticized as a device unduly hampering the jurisdiction of the ICJ, the Court must ensure that the preliminary objections procedure provides a safeguard for the principle of voluntary submission of disputes in the system of contentious jurisdiction of the ICJ (q.v.).

Property Commissions under the Peace Treaty with Japan, 1951. These were the commissions set up pursuant to art. 15 (1) of the Peace Treaty with Japan of 8 September 1951 (136 UNTS 45) whose function was to settle claims for compensation for property losses suffered during World War II, raised against Japan by nationals of Allied powers. Five commissions were established: US-Japan; UK-Japan; Netherlands-Japan; France-Japan; and Canada-Japan, but only the first three actually commenced operations. The US-Japan commission dealt with 18 cases and the UK-Japan with ten. The Dutch-Japanese commission considered one interesting case of a Dutch hospital ship sunk by the Japanese just off the Japanese territorial sea. The commission rejected the Dutch claim to salvage and return the ship because it was not "in Japan."

Each commission was made up of three members, with the two countries appointing one member each. A member from a neutral country (Sweden) was chairman.

Provisional Measures. These are measures which an international tribunal may order in the course of contentious proceedings in order to preserve the respective rights of the parties pending the tribunal's final decision and to prevent any aggravation or extension of the dispute.

Provisional measures, also known as interim measures of protection, are roughly equivalent to an interim injunction that a domestic court may issue pending the final determination of the case. Within the context of international tribunals, interim measures of protection were already known in the CACJ (q.v.). Currently, they are provided for in the respective constitutive instruments of a number of international courts, such as, in addition to the ICJ (q.v.), the ECHR (q.v.), the I-ACHR (q.v.), the CJEC (q.v.), and some lesser known courts as well as arbitration (q.v.) tribunals. Moreover, international tribunals are believed to possess the power to grant interim measures of protection even in the absence of an express provision granting such power to the tribunal.

Under art. 41 of its Statute the ICJ has the power to indicate, if it considers that circumstances so require, any provisional measures which ought to be taken to preserve the respective rights of either party. Such measures are normally requested by the applicant state, but the Court may indicate them (ICJ Rules art. 75) on its own initiative (*proprio motu*), which it has never done. If the case is brought to the Court by a special agreement, both parties may request provisional measures, as happened in the *Frontier Dispute* (q.v.) case between Burkina Faso and Mali.

Provisional measures are indicated only in cases of urgency when irreparable damage to the rights that are the subject of the dispute is imminent, for example damage through radioactive fallout to Australia and New Zealand which the provisional measures were designed to avert in the *Nuclear Tests* cases (q.v.). But the ICJ would not indicate any measures if the chances of winning the case on the merits were slim.

A request for the indication of provisional measures by the ICJ has priority over all other issues. It constitutes a separate phase of the case leading, in general, to a decision within three weeks which is handed down in the form of an order read by the President of the Court at a public sitting.

The urgent nature of the interim measures procedure frequently conflicts with the principle that the Court's jurisdiction must be based on the parties' consent. In this respect the ICJ has followed what is known as the "possibility test" (*Nuclear Tests* (q.v.); *Military and Paramilitary Activities in and against Nicaragua* (q.v.)) whereby, if warranted by the circumstances, the Court indicates provisional measures as soon as it has been ascertained that an instrument or instruments submitted by the party concerned appears to provide a *prima facie* basis for the Court's jurisdiction (q.v.) as to the merits of the case, without any reservations manifestly excluding such jurisdiction (the "Lauterpacht (q.v.) test").However, the order indicating interim measures in no way prejudges the question of the Court's jurisdiction on the merits and leaves unaffected the parties' right to submit arguments in respect of such jurisdiction. Interim measures can also be indicated in cases of non-appearance of a party.

Since the question of provisional measures frequently has political implications, for example in the parallel cases of *Questions of Interpretation and Application of the 1971 Montreal Convention Arising from the Aerial Incident at Lockerbie (see* ANNEX IV), the Court must give notice of the measures indicated and the related decisions not only to the parties but also to the UN Secretary-General for transmission to the Security Council.

As of 15 July 1993, the ICJ had received requests for provisional measures in 17 cases (including parallel cases). It indicated such measures in nine cases: *Anglo-Iranian Oil Co.* (q.v.); *Fisheries Jurisdiction* (two parallel cases) (q.v.); *Nuclear Tests* (two parallel cases) (q.v.); *United States Diplomatic and*

Consular Staff in Tehran (q.v.); *Military and Paramilitary Activities in and against Nicaragua* (q.v.); *Frontier Dispute* (q.v.) and *Application of the Convention on the Prevention and Punishment of the Crime of Genocide (Bosnia and Herzegovina v. Yugoslavia (Serbia and Montenegro)*. The Order of 8 April 1993 called upon Yugoslavia to take all measures to prevent genocide. The ICJ was not able, however, to indicate measures for the protection of any disputed rights which fell outside the scope of the Genocide Convention. Interim measures were denied in six cases (including in one instance two parallel cases): *Interhandel* (q.v.); *Aegean Sea Continental Shelf* (q.v.); *Arbitral Award of 31 July 1989* (q.v.); *Passage through the Great Belt* (*see* ANNEX V: CONTENTIOUS CASES BEFORE THE ICJ FILED BUT REMOVED FROM THE LIST WITHOUT ANY JUDGMENT); and *Questions of Interpretation and Application of the 1971 Montreal Convention Arising from the Aerial Incident at Lockerbie* (two parallel cases) (*see* ANNEX IV). In two cases, namely *Trial of Pakistani Prisoners of War* (*see* ANNEX V) and *Border and Transborder Armed Actions* (*see* ANNEX III, case 33), no measures were considered by the Court because of withdrawal of requests.

The ICJ Statute, in its art. 41, uses the ambiguous term "indicate" rather than "order" provisional measures. Hence it is not entirely clear whether the Court's orders "indicating" such measures are binding upon the parties. The General Act for the Pacific Settlement of International Disputes of 1928 (revised in 1949) (q.v.) expressly stipulated their binding legal force. This position is supported by the general rule of international law enjoining the parties to a pending case to abstain from any act that would nullify the result of the tribunal's final judgment. However, this view is not shared by all. In practice, most respondent states, claiming that the ICJ lacked jurisdiction in the case, refused to comply with the Court's interim measures order. Whether the Security Council has the authority to enforce such orders like judgments, under art. 94 of the UN Charter, is not clear. Nor was it settled in the *Anglo-Iranian Oil Co.* (q.v.) case when the issue was brought before the Security Council.

R

Rann of Kutch Arbitration, 1968. The arbitration (q.v.) in this case between India and Pakistan concerned sovereignty over a border area known as the Rann of Kutch, a 7,000-square-mile tract of desert and marshy terrain with occasional grazing areas (*bets*), situated in the west of the Indian subcontinent between the former British-protected Indian state of Kutch in the south and the former British-India province of Sind in the north.

Upon the partition of India in 1947, Sind became part of Pakistan and the Kutch state joined India, but the boundary between India and Pakistan in the Rann area remained controversial, leading--independently of the Kashmir-related war-- to open hostilities in 1965. However, on 30 June 1965 the two countries signed a *compromis* (q.v.) whereby they agreed to submit their dispute to an arbitral tribunal of three arbitrators.

India claimed the whole Rann on the ground that it had inherited it from the princely state of Kutch while Pakistan contended that the Rann, an area flooded for half of the year, should be divided in equal shares between the two countries.

On 19 February 1968 the tribunal (with the Indian member dissenting) decided in favor of India, awarding it some 90 percent of the disputed area (17 UNRIAA 1). In its reasons, the tribunal took account of maps and especially statements by the rulers of Kutch over the period of 70 years, which affirmed their sovereignty over the Rann and were acquiesced in and even confirmed by the British authorities. Pakistan was awarded parts of the Rann on its northern edge because it could prove exercise of effective control superior to the competing Indian claim. Two additional tracts of the Rann of Kutch were also awarded to Pakistan on grounds of equity.

It is remarkable that the award was respected by both India and Pakistan which demarcated the boundary by jointly erecting over 800 new boundary pillars in the formerly disputed areas.

Reparation for Injuries Suffered in the Service of the United Nations, ICJ Adv. Op. 1948-1949. This second advisory opinion (q.v.) of the ICJ (q.v.) is the leading exposition of the status of public international organizations in international law. The case arose out of the murder by Israeli extremists in Israeli-controlled Jerusalem in 1948 of Count Bernadotte, a Swedish national and the UN truce negotiator in the Arab-Israeli Palestine conflict. Believing that Israel had been negligent in failing to prevent the murder and then immediately to pursue the assassins, the UN wished to claim, under international law, reparation from Israel for injuries suffered as a result of the death of its servant. Since under traditional international law only states had the right to make a claim for compensation, it was not clear whether the UN also had such legal capacity. Consequently, the General Assembly requested the ICJ to give an advisory opinion on the question whether the UN as an organization had the capacity to bring an international claim against the responsible *de jure* or *de facto* government with a view to obtaining the reparation due, under international law, in respect of the damage caused (1) to the UN, and (2) to the victim.

In its advisory opinion of 11 April 1949 (1949 ICJ Rep. 174) the Court answered this question in the affirmative. First, by a unanimous vote, it ruled that the UN had the capacity to bring an international claim against a state--a member or not a member of the UN--which caused damage to the Organization, that is, more generally, that the UN had international personality which was a necessary attribute for an effective discharge of its functions. The Court further declared by a vote of 11 to four that the UN could claim reparation not only in respect of the damage caused to itself but also in respect of the damage suffered by the victim or persons entitled through him. The Court held that, while under traditional international law diplomatic protection was exercised by the state of the victim's nationality, the Organization itself had an implied power to make a claim on behalf of its agents and, in general, those powers which by implication had been conferred upon it as being essential for an effective performance of its functions. The Court noted that the Organization's agents would not serve it loyally unless they were sure of its protection; this would be especially the case if they were stateless or nationals of the state in which the injury occurred. Finally, by ten votes to five, the ICJ held that the risk of a possible competition between the rights to reparation of the Organization and the state of the victim's nationality could be resolved by common sense and good will by an agreement in an individual case or a general convention. In the case of Count Bernadotte no claim was brought by the victim's survivors. On the other hand, shortly after the ICJ had delivered its opinion, Israel was admitted to the UN and agreed to pay reparation to this Organization and in 1950 met the claim for the injury caused to the UN.

The advisory opinion of the ICJ in the *Reparation* case is an important landmark in the law of international organizations. It is usually quoted to illustrate the principle of international law to the effect that the quality of being a subject of international law need not necessarily be expressly conferred upon an international organization in its constituent treaty and that an international organization has such implied powers under international law as are necessary for an effective and efficient performance of its functions.

Reservation to Acceptance of Compulsory Jurisdiction of the ICJ. This is a reservation which a state, accepting the compulsory jurisdiction of the ICJ (q.v.) (*see also* **Contentious Jurisdiction of the ICJ**) under the optional clause (q.v.) of the ICJ Statute, attaches to its declaration of acceptance and which excludes from the Court's jurisdiction (q.v.) a specific category or specific categories of dispute.

Historically states have always been wary of submitting themselves to arbitration (q.v.) or judicial settlement in an all-inclusive fashion. Thus under the arbitration system of the Permanent Court of Arbitration (q.v.) vital interests, honor, independence or interests of other states were allowed to be excluded from the tribunal's jurisdiction. Eventually other types of reservation were added to the roster of such reservations. As far as the PCIJ (q.v.) is concerned, the Netherlands started the trend when in 1921 it excluded from the scope of its acceptance of the optional clause disputes which it had agreed to settle by other means of pacific settlement. On the whole, however, compared with the ICJ, there were not many reservations under the regime of the PCIJ. Among the reservations to acceptance of compulsory jurisdiction under art. 36(2), the so called domestic jurisdiction reservation derived from art. 15(8) of the Covenant of the League of Nations, excluding disputes which fall exclusively within the domestic jurisdiction of the accepting country, became most frequent and best known, primarily because of the automatic (self-judging) reservation (q.v.) ("Connally Amendment") attached to it in the US acceptance of the optional clause in 1946.

The Statute of the ICJ allows, in art. 36(3), two kinds of reservation: reservations relating to reciprocity and those relating to time. The former may be made on condition of reciprocity on the part of several or certain states, which means that until some other states have accepted the optional clause, the state making the reservation cannot be respondent in any proceedings before the Court. Whereas no state has ever made a reservation of reciprocity in the meaning of art. 36(3), a number of states have attached reservations relating to time, limiting the life of their respective declaration to a specific period, usually five or ten years, with the possibility of tacit renewal. Many declarations reserve the right to be terminated by a simple notice taking effect after the lapse of a specific period of time or--frequently--immediately. Even if no termination notice was included in the acceptance of the optional clause, acceptance may be withdrawn on reasonable notice, as ruled by the ICJ in the case of *Military and Paramilitary Activities in and against Nicaragua* (q.v.). However, expiry of the declaration of one of the parties subsequent to the Court's being seised of a case does not deprive the Court of jurisdiction. Nor is the Court's jurisdiction over a pending case affected by the withdrawal of acceptance by the state against which proceedings are taking place.

Apart from the categories of reservation explicitly allowed by the Statute of the ICJ, numerous other reservations have been made by most states which accepted the optional clause, the number of reservations reaching 11 in the case of India. These reservations have been recognized as valid by the ICJ, subject to the condition that they should not conflict with the Statute. The automatic (self-judging) reservation is one possible exception in such conflict.

The most common is the reservation which excludes disputes

that the parties are committed to submit to other means of peaceful settlement. Another fairly common reservation concerns disputes relating to matters that are "exclusively" or "essentially" within the domestic jurisdiction of the declaring state, as determined by international law (in the majority of the declarations) or--for the automatic (self-judging) reservation--as determined by the state depositing the declaration itself (Liberia, Malawi, Mexico, Philippines, and Sudan). Other reservations concern: disputes arising prior to a specific date; disputes relating to situations originating in armed conflict, collective security actions and similar conflict situations; disputes for the specific purpose of which the other party appears to have made its declaration of acceptance of the optional clause; disputes relating to certain aspects of the law of the sea; disputes between members of the British Commonwealth; and other exclusions, including the multilateral treaty reservation, in the US popularly known as the Vandenberg Amendment, which requires that all the treaty parties affected by an ICJ decision also be parties before the Court. This reservation was invoked by the US in the case of *Military and Paramilitary Activities in and against Nicaragua*. The US reservation concerning exclusion of Central American disputes was another legal basis invoked by the US to contest the Court's jurisdiction in the same case.

The reservations to acceptance of compulsory jurisdiction of the ICJ have considerably diminished the scope of the Court's contentious jurisdiction (q.v.). Moreover, their adverse effect is magnified by the condition of reciprocity which applies to all declarations and has the potential of reducing the Court's jurisdiction to the minimum common denominator of the acceptances. A reservation made by any party to a dispute can be invoked against it by the other party or parties which, by invoking the applicant state's reservation can deprive the ICJ of jurisdiction, as demonstrated by the case of *Certain Norwegian Loans* (q.v.). Similarly, the US had to withdraw its suit against Bulgaria in the case of *Aerial Incident of 27 July 1955* (1957-1960) (1960 ICJ Rep. 146) (*see* ANNEX V: CONTENTIOUS CASES BEFORE THE ICJ FILED BUT REMOVED FROM THE LIST WITHOUT ANY JUDGMENT), after Bulgaria, taking advantage of the principle of reciprocity, had invoked the US automatic (self-judging) reservation of domestic jurisdiction even though the shooting down of a foreign (Israeli) airliner (*see* **Aerial Incident of 27 July 1955 (Israel v. Bulgaria) 1957-1959**) carrying US nationals could not in good faith be considered a matter of domestic jurisdiction.

Reservations to the Convention on the Prevention and Punishment of the Crime of Genocide, ICJ Adv. Op. 1950-1951. This advisory opinion (q.v.) of the ICJ (q.v.) dealt with three questions addressed by the UN General Assembly to the Court, concerning the legal position of a state which attached reservations to its signature of the Genocide Convention of 9 December 1948 (78 UNTS 277) if other signatories of this Convention objected to these reservations. In international law reservation is a unilateral statement by a state signing or ratifying a multilateral treaty whereby it purports to exclude or modify the legal effect of certain provisions of the treaty in their application to itself. In the case in question reservations to the Genocide Convention had been attached by the countries of the then Soviet bloc.

In its advisory opinion of 28 May 1951 (1951 ICJ Rep. 15) the ICJ, by seven votes to five, held that despite the "indisputable value" of the traditional rule of international law allowing reservations only if accepted by all the signatories, this rule protecting the integrity of treaties was not applicable to certain types of treaty. In the Court's opinion, the Genocide Convention was one such agreement where reservations were allowed. As to the consequences of reservations, the Court advised that a state which had made and maintained a reservation that had been objected to by one or more of the parties to the Convention but not by others could be regarded as being a party to the Convention if the reservation was compatible with the object and purpose of the Convention. If a party objected to a perceived incompatible reservation, it could consider the reserving state as not a party to the Convention. On the other hand, if a party perceived a reservation as compatible, it could regard the reserving state as a party. Thus according to the Court's opinion, a state making a reservation could be regarded as a party to a convention by some states, but not by others. Despite some criticism in the literature of international law, the principle established by the ICJ in the advisory opinion of 1951 was adopted in the practice of the UN Secretary General in his capacity as depositary of multilateral treaties and was eventually incorporated in articles 19-23 of the Vienna Convention of 23 May 1969 on the Law of Treaties (8 ILM 679 (1969)).

Right of Passage over Indian Territory (Portugal v. India), ICJ 1955-1960. This case involved a dispute between Portugal and India concerning Portugal's right of passage between the territory of Daman on the west coast of India and two inland enclaves. In 1954 the Portuguese rule in the enclaves was overthrown by Indian nationalist groups which installed Indian local government in these territories. Against Portuguese protests, the Indian government refused to permit Portuguese officials and soldiers transit from Daman through Indian territory to the enclaves in order to restore Portuguese control. In 1955 Portugal submitted the dispute to the ICJ (q.v.), an event which took place only three days following acceptance by Portugal of the optional clause (q.v.) which had already been accepted by India. India raised six preliminary objections (q.v.) to the Court's jurisdiction (q.v.), four of which were overruled by the Court and two joined to the adjudication of the merits, in the Court's judgment on preliminary objections of 26 November 1957 (1957 ICJ Rep. 125).

In its judgment on the merits of 12 April 1960 (1960 ICJ Rep. 6) the Court, after rejecting the two remaining preliminary objections and examining, in historical perspective, the practice concerning the passage to and from the enclaves, held by 11 votes to four, that just prior to the events of 1954 Portugal had had the right of passage in respect of non-military traffic (private persons, civil officials, and goods); ruled, by eight votes to seven, that no right of passage existed with respect of armed forces and police, arms and ammunition; and decided by nine votes to six, that, given the tensions in the region following the overthrow of Portuguese rule in the enclaves, India's refusal to permit passage to Portuguese officials was in good faith and not contrary to its obligations resulting from Portugal's right of passage with respect to non-military traffic.

On its merits, the *Right of Passage* case is interesting in that in it the Court recognized that the right of passage might be derived not only from a treaty but also from a local custom between two states, resulting from a constant and uniform practice allowing free passage accepted as law by the parties concerned. As to the alleged right of self-determination, the ICJ assumed that Portugal did not automatically lose sovereignty over the enclaves because of failure to allow the population of the enclaves to exercise this right.

Rights of Nationals of the United States of America in Morocco (France v. United States), ICJ 1950-1952. This case involved a dispute between the United States and France over certain rights of US nationals (most-favored-nation clause, US consular jurisdiction) in Morocco under a US-Morocco treaty of 1836 and the General Act of Algeciras of 1906 (201 CTS 39). As claimed by the US, France continued to be bound by these acts after it established its protectorate over Morocco in 1912. Although in fact a defendant, France preempted the US by applying to the ICJ (q.v.) under the optional clause (q.v.) for a definition of the US rights in the Protectorate of Morocco.

A whole series of questions was raised, with the ICJ judgment of 27 August 1952 (1952 ICJ Rep. 176) deciding on six issues by votes reaching from unanimity to a majority of six to five. Concerning a French decree of 1948 on the regulation of imports, which in the US view adversely affected the rights of its nationals under the 1836 treaty and the General Act of 1906, the Court unanimously ruled in favor of the US since under those international agreements no Moroccan law or regulation could apply to US nationals in Morocco without US previous consent. In the matter of consular jurisdiction, the Court also unanimously favored the US position on the right to jurisdiction in cases between US nationals and protected persons under the 1836 Treaty and, by ten votes to one, to jurisdiction under the Act of 1906. On the other hand, the Court, by six votes to five, rejected the US claims to jurisdiction over cases in which only the defendant was a US national or protected person. It also rejected, unanimously, the US claim that the application to US nationals of the laws and regulations in Morocco required the assent of the US, but the US consular courts were found not to be obliged to apply those laws and regulations that had not been assented to by the US. Finally, by a vote of six to five, the Court held that the US nationals in Morocco were not exempt from taxation and, by seven votes to four, found the Moroccan consumption tax compatible with the treaty rights of the US nationals.

It may be added that in the *Rights of Nationals* case the ICJ described Morocco as a "sovereign" state maintaining its basic personality under international law despite the fact that by the Treaty of Fez of 1912 between France and the Sultan of Morocco it became a French protectorate, remaining so until 1956. The ICJ also dealt with the now historical institution of the territorial jurisdiction of consuls over their fellow nationals to the exclusion of local courts. Incidentally, with Morocco attaining its independence in 1956, the US relinquished its extraterritorial rights in that country. Finally, in the case in question, the ICJ reiterated the principle of international law that a state (France) may not invoke its law as an excuse for failure to carry out its obligations contracted under an international agreement.

Rolin, Henri (1891-1973). Belgian national. Professor of International Law at the University of Brussels. Delegate of Belgium and Chairman of the First Committee at the San Francisco United Nations Conference on International Organization. Member of the PCA (q.v.). Judge of the ECHR (q.v.), 1957-1973, and its President, 1968-1971. Author of numerous publications on international law, including lectures in *RCADI*.

Ross, Alf (1899-1979). Danish national. Professor of International Law at Copenhagen University, 1938-1969. Judge of the ECHR (q.v.), 1959-1971. Author of numerous works on international law, including a textbook (1947).

Ruda, José María (1924-). Argentine national. Member of the ICJ (q.v.), 1973-1991, and its President, 1988-1991. Professor of International Law at the University of Buenos Aires. Officer at UN Secretariat, 1950-1955. Member of the ILC, 1964-1972, and its Chairman, 1968. Permanent Representative of Argentina at the UN, 1965-1970. Undersecretary for Foreign Affairs and Worship, 1970-1973. Argentine Representative at UN General Assembly sessions, 1959-1969, and Chairman of the Argentine delegation,

1966-1969. Delegate of Argentina at numerous international conferences. Author of numerous works on international law.

S

Schücking, Walther (1875-1935). German national. Professor of International Law at the University of Marburg. Member of the PCIJ (q.v.), 1930-1935. Author of numerous publications on international law, including one on the work of the PCA (q.v.).

Schwebel, Stephen M. (1929-). US national. Member of the ICJ (q.v.), 1981- . Attorney, 1954-1961. Assistant Professor of Law, Harvard Law School, 1959-1961. Assistant Legal Adviser, US Department of State, 1961-1966. Professor of International Law, School of Advanced International Studies, Washington, DC, 1967-1981. Deputy Legal Adviser, US Department of State, 1974-1981. Member of the ILC, 1977-1981. Executive Director of the American Society of International Law; its Honorary Vice-President, 1983- . US representative at international conferences. Author of numerous works on international law, including lectures in *RCADI*.

Sea-Bed Disputes Chamber of the International Tribunal for the Law of the Sea *see* **International Tribunal for the Law of the Sea**

Self-Judging Reservation *see* **Automatic (Self-Judging) Reservation**

Singh, Nagendra (1914-1988). Indian national. Eminent jurist, diplomat, civil servant and international legal scholar. Member of the ICJ (q.v.), 1973-1988, its Vice-President, 1976-1979, and President, 1985-1988. Author of many publications on international law, especially on the law of the sea.

Soering Case, ECHR 1989. The facts in this remarkable landmark case before the ECHR (q.v.) were as follows: Jens Soering, a German national born in 1966, was accused of murdering the parents of his girlfriend in Virginia, US, in 1985. In October 1985 Soering and his girlfriend disappeared but were subsequently arrested in England in April 1986 in connection with check fraud. During his arrest Soering confessed the murders and, after charges of murder had been brought against him in Virginia, the US requested his and his girlfriend's extradition pursuant to the UK-US Extradition Treaty of 8 June 1972 (28 UST 227, TIAS No. 8468). Unlike Soering, the girl, who proved to be his accomplice, did not contest the matter and, following her extradition, was sentenced to 90 years' imprisonment as an accessory to the murder of her parents.

After the arrest of Soering in England the UK sought assurances from the US that the death penalty, if imposed upon him, would not be carried out. The US responded with assurances that the UK position would be communicated to the judge in Virginia at the time of sentencing. After his appeals against the UK decision to extradite him had been rejected, Soering filed an appeal with the European Commission on Human Rights (*see* **European Court of Human Rights**) contending that notwithstanding the US assurances there was a real likelihood of his being sentenced to death if extradited to the US. However, Soering's complaint was not against the death penalty as such, which is not banned in the European Convention for the Protection of Human Rights and Fundamental Freedoms of 4 November 1950 (213 UNTS 221) but abolished in time of peace under Protocol 6 to the Convention, of 28 April 1983 (22 ILM 538 (1983) (which Protocol, however, was not ratified by the UK), and is not interpreted as "inhuman or degrading treatment or punishment" under art. 3 of the Convention. Soering's main argument (apart from some less important ones) was that in his particular circumstances exposing him to the "death row phenomenon" would constitute treatment contrary to art. 3. Although the warrant for the surrender of Soering to the US was signed, actual transfer was halted as a result of the interim (provisional) measures (q.v.) indicated, first by the Commission and then by the Court. The request of the Federal Republic of Germany to extradite Soering as its national so that he could be tried under German law was rejected by the UK on the ground that he could not be tried there only on the strength of admission when interviewed in prison by a German prosecutor.

In response to Soering's application, the Commission declared it admissible but in its report of 19 January 1989 decided that the extradition of Soering to the US would not constitute treatment contrary to art. 3 of the Convention because none of the specific factors constituting the death row phenomenon in Soering's case (delays in the US appeal system, actual conditions of detention on the death row, execution procedure, and Soering's age and mental condition) would attain a degree of seriousness contrary to art. 3. The argument concerning the possibility of extradition to Germany was found irrelevant by the Commission. Having issued the report, the Commission referred the case to the ECHR. The UK and Germany also made referrals to the Court.

In a unanimous and rather surprising judgment of 7 July 1989 (1989 ECHR Ser. A, no. 161, *reprinted in* 28 ILM 1063 (1989)) the ECHR reversed the opinion of the Commission, ruling that in the particular circumstances of the case the decision to extradite Soering to the US would, if implemented, give rise to a breach of art. 3 of the Convention. The Court's argument was that in their cumulative impact and effect, the factors constituting the death row phenomenon and the fact that the legitimate purpose of extradition could be achieved by extradition or deportation to Germany, constituted such a cruel and inhuman treatment that the extradition of Soering to the US would be a violation of art. 3 of the Convention.

Eventually, after the US had given the British government sufficient assurances that no capital murder charges would be brought against Soering in Virginia, he was extradited to the US and sentenced to imprisonment for life.

The *Soering* case is not only an important landmark in the jurisprudence of the ECHR but also has wider ramifications, especially for the US where the death penalty is still practiced and which might encounter difficulties in obtaining extradition of fugitives facing the death penalty in the US. The implications of the *Soering* case for the US may also negatively affect this country's ratification of international human rights treaties which impose stricter standards against cruel and inhuman treatment and punishment than those obtaining under the Eighth Amendment of the US Constitution.

Sørensen, Max (1913-1981). Danish national. Professor of

International Law and Constitutional Law at the University of Aarhus, 1947-1972. In the Danish Foreign Service, 1938-1947. Legal Adviser to Danish Foreign Ministry, 1956-1972. Member of the European Commission of Human Rights, 1955-1972; Member of the CJEC (q.v.), 1973-1979; of the ECHR (q.v.), 1980-1981. Author of numerous works on international law and editor of a popular *Manual* of international law (1968) (*see* **Bibliography**, 2 G).

South West Africa (Ethiopia v. South Africa; Liberia v. South Africa), ICJ 1960-1966. This was one of a series of proceedings before the ICJ (q.v.) involving the legal status of South West Africa, now Namibia, at the time when it still remained under the control of South Africa. The *South West Africa* case was the only contentious proceedings on this issue, the other four decisions of the ICJ on the South West Africa (Namibia) question being advisory opinions (q.v.): 1. *International Status of South West Africa*, 11 July 1950 (1950 ICJ Rep. 128); 2. *Voting Procedure on Questions Relating to Reports and Petitions Concerning the Territory of South West Africa*, 7 June 1955 (1955 ICJ Rep. 67); 3. *Admissibility of Hearings of Petitioners by the Committee on South West Africa*, 1 June 1956 (1956 ICJ Rep. 23); and 4. *Legal Consequences for States of the Continued Presence of South Africa in Namibia (South West Africa) notwithstanding Security Council Resolution 276 (1970)*, 21 June 1971 (1971 ICJ Rep. 16).

In the contentious case in question, two countries which had been members of the League of Nations, namely Ethiopia and Liberia, instituted separate proceedings against South Africa, requesting the ICJ to rule that South West Africa remained a League of Nations Mandate; that South Africa had been in breach of its obligations under the Mandate; and that as the mandatory authority it was subject to the supervision of the UN. Ethiopia and Liberia based their applications on art. 7(2) of the Mandate and art. 37 of the ICJ Statute. Generally speaking, under the terms of the Mandate disputes between the mandatory power and another member of the League of Nations were to be referred to the PCIJ (q.v.) succeeded by the ICJ.

By an order of 21 May 1961 (1961 ICJ Rep. 13) the ICJ joined the proceedings of the two applicant states while South Africa

raised a number of preliminary objections (q.v.) to the Court's
jurisdiction (q.v.) and the applicants' *locus standi*, that is their
right to initiate proceedings in the case. In its judgment of 21
December 1962 (1962 ICJ Rep. 319) the ICJ, by eight votes to
seven, rejected South Africa's preliminary objections, holding that
the Mandate conferred by the League of Nations upon South
Africa survived the dissolution of the League and that the issue
constituted a "dispute" between the parties within the meaning of
Art. 7 of the Mandate which could not be settled by negotiations.

In the second phase of the proceedings, in its judgment of 18
July 1966 (1966 ICJ Rep. 6) the ICJ rejected, by eight votes to
seven (by the President's casting vote), the claims of Ethiopia and
Liberia as, in the Court's view, these states had not established
any "legal right or interest appertaining to them in the subject
matter" of their claim.

The ICJ judgment was a very controversial decision, raising
severe criticism and indignation in world public opinion, and
especially in Third World countries. In effect, the judgment
reversed the Court's earlier position adopted in the judgment of
1962 on South Africa's preliminary objections. This happened as
a result of the changes in the composition of the Court in the
intervening period, with the judges who had been in a minority in
1962 becoming a majority in 1966.

One immediate effect of the judgment was Resolution 2145
(XXI) of the UN General Assembly of 27 October 1966 which
terminated the Mandate, placing South West Africa under the
direct responsibility of the UN. It may be added that the Court's
ruling meant that South Africa's obligations towards the
inhabitants of South West Africa were owed not to individual
members of the League of Nations but to the League itself.

Southern African Development Community (SADC) Tribunal. A
tribunal established under the treaty signed on 17 August 1992 (32
ILM 116 (1993)) by Angola, Botswana, Lesotho, Malawi,
Mozambique, Namibia, Swaziland, Tanzania, Zambia, and
Zimbabwe, which founded the Southern African Development
Community (SADC) with headquarters in Gaborone, Botswana.
To ensure adherence to and the proper interpretation of the treaty
and subsidiary instruments and to adjudicate upon disputes

between member countries, the treaty provides for the establishment of a SADC Tribunal with the authority to render final and legally binding decisions and to give advisory opinions (q.v.) on such matters as the Summit and the Council (the main organs of SADC) may refer to it. The details concerning the composition, powers, functions, procedures and other related matters governing the Tribunal are to be dealt with in a protocol to be adopted by the SADC Summit, the supreme policy-making institution of SADC.

Sovereignty over Certain Frontier Land (Belgium/Netherlands), ICJ 1957-1959. This was one of the cases before the ICJ (q.v.) submitted to the Court by a special agreement in 1957. It involved a dispute between the Netherlands and Belgium concerning the sovereignty over two small plots of land in a border area characterized by intertwined enclaves of ancient feudal origin. In its case, Belgium relied on the Boundary Treaty of 1842 and the Convention of 1843, concluded after the secession of Belgium from the Netherlands. For its part, the Netherlands contended that the Boundary Convention of 1843 recognized the *status quo* favoring the Netherlands, as determined by a minute drawn up by the two communes in question in 1841, and that the provision of the minute attributing the plots to Belgium was vitiated by a mistake. The Netherlands further maintained that its sovereignty had been corroborated by state practice since 1843.

In its judgment of 20 June 1959 (1959 ICJ Rep. 209) the Court, by ten votes to four, decided in favor of Belgium, ruling that no case of mistake had occurred and that the acts of sovereignty exercised by the Netherlands since 1843, hardly noticeable by Belgium, were insufficient to displace Belgian sovereignty established by the boundary agreements in 1842 and 1843. The Court's judgment was implemented by the two countries in 1974.

Special Arbitral Tribunals under Annex VIII of the UN Convention on the Law of the Sea of 1982. These are tribunals in one of the four categories of procedure of compulsory settlement of disputes concerning the application and interpretation of the UN Convention on the Law of the Sea of 1982 (*see* **International Tribunal for the Law of the Sea**). They are called special because under Annex VIII they can deal only with disputes concerning fisheries, protection of marine environment, marine scientific research, and navigation. A special arbitral (*see* **Arbitration**) tribunal for a specific case in one of these areas is composed of five members, with each party appointing two (only one can be a national in each group), and a president, a national of a third state, appointed jointly by the parties. Arbitrators are appointed from four lists of experts drawn up and maintained in each of the above mentioned fields respectively by the FAO, UNEP, IOC, and IMO. A special tribunal may also be used by the parties to a dispute as a commission of inquiry to establish the facts giving rise to the dispute.

Status of Eastern Carelia, PCIJ Adv. Op. 1923. In this case the PCIJ (q.v.) refused to give an advisory opinion (q.v.). The request for an opinion originated in a dispute between Finland and Soviet Russia over the status of Eastern Carelia which, under the Treaty of Peace of Dorpat (today Tartu) between the two countries of 14 October 1920 (3 LNTS 5), was incorporated into Russia as part of the autonomous territory of Eastern Carelia. Details of the autonomy were set forth in a declaration by the Soviet Russian delegation, included in the protocol of signature of the Treaty of Dorpat. However, the Soviet government claimed that the declaration did not create any legal obligation and was made for information purposes only. Relying on the legal nature of the declaration, Finland complained to the Council of the League of Nations that Russia was not respecting the autonomy of Eastern Carelia. Russia, which was not a member of the League of Nations, declined to respond to these allegations.

On 21 April 1923 the Council of the League requested the PCIJ to give an advisory opinion on the question whether the Treaty of Dorpat and the annexed declaration constituted engagements of an international character placing Russia under an obligation to Finland as to carrying out the provisions of these instruments. The Soviets refused to participate in the proceedings before the Court.

In its decision of 22 July 1923 (1923 PCIJ, Series B, No. 5) the PCIJ, by seven votes to four, declined to give an advisory opinion on the ground that the opinion did not relate to an abstract question of law but to an actually pending dispute between two states; hence, answering the Council's question would in substance be equivalent to deciding a dispute between the parties, which would be contrary to an established rule of international law that no state could, without its consent, be compelled to submit its dispute to mediation, arbitration (q.v.), or judicial proceedings (*see* **Contentious Jurisdiction of the ICJ; Jurisdiction of International Tribunals**).

The reasoning of the PCIJ was not followed by its successor, the ICJ (q.v.), which in similar circumstances proved to be less sensitive to states' sovereignty and did not hesitate to assert its competence to use its advisory jurisdiction.

Sunday Times Case, ECHR 1979. This *cause célèbre* was brought before the ECHR (q.v.) in 1974 in the aftermath of the thalidomide tragedy of the early 1960s when, beginning in 1959, deformed children were born to mothers who during pregnancy had taken thalidomide, a drug produced and sold by the Distillers, a British manufacturing company. Many parents instituted legal proceedings against this company and the thalidomide affair provoked a good deal of controversy and a national debate focusing on the role of the courts in the matter and the Distillers' responsibility for the tragedy. While litigation, along with negotiations to settle the claims, was in progress, the *Sunday Times*, in September 1977, published an article critical of the Distillers' offer and urging the company to reach a more generous out-of-court settlement with the parents of the thalidomide-affected children. The article also announced that the *Sunday Times* would publish an account of the tragedy analyzing the evidence in support of the charge of negligence against the Distillers.

In response, the Distillers, after exhaustive litigation, obtained from the highest court in the land, the House of Lords, an injunction to restrain the *Sunday Times* from publishing the article upon the ground of alleged contempt of court. Five judges unanimously held that by prejudgment on an issue in pending court proceedings and pressure upon the parents not to abandon or settle their cases, the article posed a real threat to the proper administration of justice. The injunction was eventually discharged in 1976 after virtually all the claims had been settled, but in the meantime, in 1974 the publisher and editors of the *Sunday Times* brought the case to the European Commission of Human Rights alleging that the government's injunction violated the newspaper's right to freedom of expression guaranteed by art. 10 of the European Convention for the Protection of Human Rights and Fundamental Freedoms of 4 November 1950 (213 UNTS 221). The Commission, by eight votes to five, expressed the opinion in 1977 that the injunction had indeed violated art. 10, and then referred the case to the ECHR.

In its judgment of 26 April 1979 ([1979] ECHR. Ser. A, no. 28) the Court, by 11 votes to nine, decided in favor of the *Sunday Times*, holding that art. 10 had been infringed upon because the injunction, albeit "prescribed by law" and imposed for a legitimate purpose, did not correspond to a social need (listed in art. 10(2)) sufficiently pressing to outweigh the public interest in freedom of expression within the meaning of the Convention. In another judgment, on 6 November 1980 ([1980] ECHR. Ser. A. no. 38)) the Court ruled that in just satisfaction for the *Sunday Times* the government was obliged to pay, in respect of certain expenses, the sum of £22,626.

The *Sunday Times* case is an important landmark in the development of the international law of human rights in Europe. It is also interesting as the first case before the ECHR in which the Court confronted the question whether a judgment applying a rule of common law (the judgment of the House of Lords on contempt of court) complied with a provision of the Convention of 1950. As a matter of fact, the 1981 Contempt of Court Act was enacted by Parliament partly to reconcile the UK law with the Convention.

T

Taba Arbitration, 1988. This was an arbitration (q.v.) between Egypt and Israel which settled their dispute over the Taba area, a half square mile strip of beachfront on the Sinai Peninsula at the head of the Gulf of Aqaba, with a resort hotel and related facilities. Until captured by Israel in 1967, Taba had been part of Egypt. Under the Treaty of Peace between Egypt and Israel of 26 March 1979 (18 ILM 362 (1979)) Israel withdrew by stages from the Sinai Peninsula except for the Taba area where the Joint Commission failed to agree on the location of 14 pillars demarcating the boundary between the two countries. As the dispute could not be settled by negotiations, the parties agreed to submit it to arbitration pursuant to the *compromis* (q.v.) of 11 September 1986 (26 ILM 1 (1987)).

On 29 September 1988, a tribunal, composed of five members (two nominated by each country plus a neutral member coopted by them), awarded Taba to Egypt, by four votes to one ruling that during the "critical period" of the former Mandate for Palestine the disputed area was not part of the Mandate territory. In arriving at this conclusion, the tribunal gave significant weight to a crucial border pillar (the "Parker Pillar") erected in implementation of the Agreement of 1 October 1906 between Egypt and Turkey (203 CTS 19) which fixed the administrative line between Egypt and the Ottoman Empire.

The *Taba* arbitration must be regarded as a remarkable milestone in the relations between former enemies who implemented the award in good faith when the Taba area with its resort facilities was transferred to Egypt on 15 March 1989 under an agreement between the countries concluded on 26 February 1989 (28 ILM 611 (1989)).

Taft Arbitration Treaties, 1911. Two abortive arbitration (q.v.) treaties named after US President Taft, signed in 1911 by the US, one with France and the other with Great Britain, but never ratified because of the US Senate's objections related to concerns about the Monroe Doctrine and failure of the treaties to exempt matters of vital importance from the scope of arbitration.

Despite the fact that the treaties never entered into effect they are of interest in the historical development of the pacific settlement of international disputes because of their provisions on international commissions of inquiry and emphasis on arbitration. The Taft Treaties served as a model for the so-called Bryan Treaties of the US with 27 countries of 1913-1914 which referred disputes that could not be settled by arbitration to investigation by impartial commissions of inquiry. No international tribunals were envisaged, however.

Temple of Preah Vihear (Cambodia v. Thailand), ICJ 1959-1962. This case concerned a territorial dispute between Cambodia and Thailand (formerly known as Siam) over a portion of territory including the ruins of the Temple of Preah Vihear, occupied by Thailand but claimed by Cambodia since 1954. On the basis of the optional clause (q.v.) and the General Act of 1928 (q.v.), Cambodia asked the ICJ (q.v.) to seise jurisdiction and declare that the disputed territory was part of Cambodia and that Thailand should withdraw from it, returning any artifacts removed from the Temple.

In its judgment of 26 May 1961 (1961 ICJ Rep. 17) on the preliminary objections (q.v.) of Thailand alleging that its acceptance of the optional clause was invalid in view of the ICJ decision in the case of *Aerial Incident of 27 July 1955 (Israel v. Bulgaria)* (q.v.), the Court unanimously rejected the Thai objections. Subsequently, in its judgment on the merits of 15 June 1962 (1962 ICJ Rep. 6), it decided, by nine votes to three, that the Temple was part of the Cambodian territory, and, by seven votes to five, that Thailand had the obligation to restore any objects removed from the Temple during its occupation of the disputed territory.

Thailand's claim to the Temple was based on its (Siam's) treaty of 13 February 1903 with France, then holding a protectorate over Cambodia, whereby the frontier line in the area of the Temple followed the line of the watershed, the exact border to be delimited by a mixed commission, a task which was never accomplished. In 1907 a French surveying team, at the request of Siam, drew up maps of the area, never approved by the mixed commission, in which the Temple was shown on the Cambodian side even though--as later discovered--a strict adherence to the watershed line would have placed it in Siam. The ICJ ruled that although the controversial French map which favored Cambodia had no legal binding character, Siam had accepted it by acquiescence, having for many years failed to object to it. As held by the Court, the Thai plea of error in the map could not be invoked by Thailand since that country itself had contributed to the error by its own conduct; had never protested the error; had accepted the map and even asked for more copies. Here the Court applied the principle of estoppel whereby a party that has acquiesced in a situation cannot then proceed to challenge it. The ICJ also rejected Thailand's claim that at all material times it had been in possession of the Temple. In the Court's view, most of the acts of Thai possession were by local authorities and did not override the conduct of the Thai government.

The ICJ judgment made a significant contribution to the interpretation of the principles of acquiescence and estoppel in international law. It also discussed the weight to be given to maps in interpreting treaties.

Tokyo Tribunal *see* **International Military Tribunal for the Far East**.

TOPCO & CAOC Arbitration, 1977. This was one of the three major arbitrations (q.v.) resulting from the nationalization by Libya in 1971 and 1973 of foreign oil companies, in this case (in 1973) Texaco Overseas Petroleum Co. & California Asiatic Oil Co. (TOPCO & CAOC). The concession agreements ("deeds of concession") with Libya provided that the rights created by the concession could be altered only by mutual consent of the parties and that the contracts should be governed and interpreted in accordance with the law of Libya and such rules of international law as may be relevant, but only to the extent that they were not in conflict with the law of Libya. The agreements were silent on the matter of what law should govern the arbitration procedure.

The concession agreements provided for arbitration of disputes, but Libya refused to accept arbitration and did not appoint an arbitrator, whereupon, pursuant to the provision of the agreements the two companies requested the President of the ICJ (q.v.) to appoint a sole arbitrator. Professor Dupuy of France was duly appointed and on 27 November 1975 rendered a preliminary award upholding his jurisdiction.

On 19 January 1977 the sole arbitrator delivered an award on the merits (53 ILR 398; English translation: 17 ILM 1 (1978)), ruling in favor of the two companies that the concession agreements were binding on the parties and that by nationalizing the companies' assets Libya had breached its obligations. He also ruled that Libya was bound to perform the contracts by restitution in kind, a ruling contrary to the indemnity approach adopted by the arbitrator in the *British Petroleum* arbitration, 1973 and 1974 (q.v.).

In his cogently reasoned award, the sole arbitrator held that the arbitration procedure in the case should be governed by international law which also provided the source for the validity of the contracts ("internationalization" of the contracts). Furthermore, as held by the arbitrator, both Libyan law and international law required that agreements ought to be observed, and neither the plea of acts of sovereignty nor the notion of permanent sovereignty over a nation's natural resources, proclaimed by the UN General Assembly, freed Libya from responsibility toward the companies.

Although Libya did not participate in the arbitration, the dispute soon ended in a compromise whereby Libya agreed to provide the two companies over the next 15 months with $152 million worth of crude oil while the companies agreed to terminate the arbitration proceedings.

The *TOPCO-CAOC* arbitration was significant in that it touched upon some highly controversial aspects of international economic law which reflected the conflict between the industrialized countries and the developing world. In this respect, the sole arbitrator's decision unambiguously upheld the principles of traditional international law.

Trail Smelter Arbitration, 1938, 1941. This arbitration (q.v.) between the US and Canada is a landmark case setting forth some fundamental principles governing the law of state responsibility for damage caused by transfrontier air pollution and, more generally, by hazardous activities resulting in harm in another state. The facts of this case were as follows: A Canadian company operated a smelting plant at Trail, BC, near the US border, emitting deleterious sulphur dioxide gas clouds which, carried southward, caused considerable damage to crops and other interests in the State of Washington. After negotiations, which had started in 1927, the matter was brought before the Canada-US International Joint Commission, established by the two countries by the Treaty Relating to the Boundary Waters and Questions Arising along the Boundary, of 11 January 1909 (36 Stat. 2448; TS 548). In 1931 the Commission reported that the smelter operations had caused damage in the US estimated at $350,000 by 1 January 1932. Canada had not disputed its liability and agreed to pay the amount, but the US refused to accept the Commission's decision.

The smelter continued to operate and eventually the question of damage caused after 1 January 1932 was referred to arbitration by the Convention of 15 April 1953 (162 UNTS 73). This *compromis* (q.v.) settled the question of indemnity for damage caused prior to 1932; established an arbitration tribunal of three members, assisted by technical experts and authorized to carry out investigations; and, as the applicable law, chose the law applied in similar questions in the US and international law, but directed the tribunal to reach a solution just to all parties concerned.

In answer to the question concerning the damage caused after 1931 and indemnity payable by Canada, the tribunal, in its decision of 16 April 1938 (3 UNRIAA 1911), awarded the US (which claimed about $2 million) $78,000 compensation in respect of the damage caused through 1937. In answer to two other questions, the tribunal established a temporary régime for the operation of the Trail smelter, designed to obtain data necessary for the establishment of a permanent régime of pollution control in the smelter.

In its second decision, on 11 March 1941 (3 UNRIAA 1938), the tribunal rejected, on the grounds of *res judicata* (that is, the principle that an issue decided by the court should not be re-opened) and lack of manifest error, the US request to reconsider the claim decided in the first award, and disallowed the claim with respect to any alleged damage caused after 1937. However, the tribunal ruled that the Trail smelter should be required to refrain from causing future damage to the State of Washington, and in this connection made a statement concerning responsibility for transfrontier pollution damage, for which the *Trail Smelter* arbitration has become famous, to the effect that "under the principles of international law, as well as the law of the United States, no State has the right to use or permit the use of its territory in such a manner as to cause injury by fumes in or to the territory of another." Furthermore--and this was a noteworthy development in international arbitration--the tribunal laid down a régime for the future operation of the smelter, aimed at reducing pollution to an acceptable level. Should pollution damage occur, Canada would have to pay an agreed indemnity and, if a damage of over $7,500 should occur in a year, the US would be compensated up to $7,500 a year for any necessary investigation.

Tyrer Case, ECHR 1978. This case involved Tyrer, a UK citizen residing in the Isle of Man who in 1972, when 15 years of age, was sentenced by a juvenile court to three strokes of birch for assault with bodily harm in violation of Manx law. Tyrer filed a complaint against the UK with the European Commission of Human Rights claiming that the birching was contrary to art. 3 of the European Convention for the Protection of Human Rights and Fundamental Freedoms of 4 November 1950 (213 UNTS 221) which prohibits torture or inhuman or degrading punishment. At the time in question the Convention extended to the Isle of Man (a largely self-governed territory and not a part of the UK) by virtue of a notification made by the UK under art. 63 of the Convention which provides for the extension of the Convention to any territory for whose international relations a state party is responsible, "with due regard, however, to local requirements." Although Tyrer later sought to withdraw his application, the Commission considered the case and in its report of 14 December 1976 held, by 14 votes to one, that the birching was degrading, and referred the case to the ECHR (q.v.).

The ECHR confirmed, by six votes to one, the Commission's opinion, ruling ([1978] ECHR. Ser. A, no. 26) that corporal punishment was degrading as an institutionalized use of physical violence and assault upon a person's dignity and physical integrity.

The fact that it was claimed to be an effective deterrent on the Isle of Man did not exempt birching from the prohibition of art. 3 of the Convention. As a living instrument, the Convention had to be influenced by and interpreted according to the standards of the penal policy of the member states of the Council of Europe (under whose auspices the Convention had been adopted).

It may be added that in another case against the UK, *Campbell and Cosans* ([1982] ECHR. Ser. A, no. 48), the ECHR held that corporal punishment in schools in Scotland did not constitute inhuman or degrading punishment.

U

UNCITRAL Rules. A set of recommended arbitration rules in 41 articles for international commercial arbitration (q.v.) disputes, adopted by the UN Commission on International Trade Law (UNCITRAL) on 28 April 1976 (15 ILM 701 (1976)) as an alternative to privately sponsored rules, such as those of the International Chamber of Commerce (ICC) (q.v.). Among other arbitral arrangements, the UNCITRAL Rules govern the appointment of arbitrators and the procedure of the Iran-US Claims Tribunal (q.v.). UNCITRAL has contributed to the development of international commercial arbitration, *inter alia*, by adopting on 21 June 1985 a Model Law on International Commercial Arbitration with a detailed commentary discussing the individual articles (24 ILM 1302 (1985)). The PCA (q.v.) optional rules of 1992 for arbitrating disputes between states are based on the UNCITRAL Rules.

United States Diplomatic and Consular Staff in Tehran (United States v. Iran), ICJ 1979-1981. The proceedings in this case brought the celebrated affair of the US hostages in Iran before the ICJ (q.v.). Following the capture in November 1979 of its diplomatic and consular staff in Tehran by militant fundamentalist elements, the US (apart from appealing to the UN Security Council) instituted proceedings against Iran before the ICJ, basing the Court's jurisdiction on the Vienna Convention on Diplomatic Relations of 18 April 1961 (500 UNTS 95), the Vienna Convention on Consular Relations of 24 April 1963 (596 UNTS 261), the Optional Protocols to these two conventions concerning the compulsory settlement of disputes (500 UNTS 241; 596 UNTS 487), the bilateral Treaty of Amity, Economic Relations, and Consular Rights of 15 August 1955 (284 UNTS 93), and the Convention of 14 December 1973 on the Prevention and Punishment of Crimes against Internationally Protected Persons Including Diplomatic Agents (1035 UNTS 167). The US requested the Court to adjudge and declare violation by Iran of international law; to rule that Iran immediately release the hostages and allow them and other US nationals to leave Iran safely and that it pay the US reparations and prosecute the individuals responsible for the crimes. The US also applied for interim measures of protection (provisional measures) (q.v.) ordering immediate release of the hostages and restoration of the embassy premises to the US. Iran did not appear before the ICJ but in a letter contested the Court's jurisdiction (q.v.), claiming that the hostages question was only one minor aspect of the overall problem of the long standing US interference in Iran's internal affairs. The Court rejected all these arguments and in the order of 15 December 1979 (1979 ICJ Rep. 7) unanimously indicated provisional measures as requested by the US.

The Court's interim measures were confirmed in its judgment of 24 May 1980 (1980 ICJ Rep. 3) which, by vote margins ranging from unanimity to 12 votes to three, upheld the various elements of the US claim. The judgment also reaffirmed the cardinal importance of the principle of international law governing diplomatic and consular immunity. The Court would not comment on the legality of the abortive US military action to rescue the hostages but found this operation as undermining respect for judicial process in international relations and adversely affecting the pending proceedings.

The hostages were ultimately released on 20 January 1981 as a result of the negotiated settlement between the parties, as set forth in the Declaration of Algeria of 19 January 1981. Consequently, the ICJ removed the case from its List by an order of 12 May 1981 (1981 ICJ Rep. 45). The claims resulting from the US-Iran dispute as well as other claims between the two countries have been adjudicated by a special tribunal, the Iran-United States Claims Tribunal (I-USCT) (q.v.).

Upper Silesia Arbitral Tribunal. An arbitral tribunal of historical interest established by Germany and Poland pursuant to a Convention of 15 May 1922 (9 LNTS 466) whose function was to adjudicate disputes involving claims to vested rights by members of an ethnic minority in Upper Silesia against their own and other governments. The tribunal was significant in that, like mixed arbitration commissions (q.v.), it conferred upon individuals the right to bring petitions before it, to that extent bestowing upon them the status of subjects under international law. During its existence (1922-1937) the Tribunal decided 3,726 cases.

V

Van Gend en Loos v. Nederlandse Administratie der Belastingen, CJEC 1963. This case and the case of *Amministrazione delle Finanze dello Stato v. Simmenthal S.p.A.,* 1978 (q.v.), are landmark cases before the CJEC (q.v.), dealing with the fundamental problem of the relationship between the EC law and the laws of the member states of the Community.

In September 1960 Van Gend en Loos, a Dutch company, imported a plastic product (ureaformaldehyde) from West Germany. At the time when the EEC Treaty of Rome entered into effect, that is, on 1 January 1958, the product in question was subject to a three percent duty, but in 1958 a reclassification by the Netherlands, under a Protocol signed by that country, Belgium, and Luxembourg, raised the duty to eight percent. Van Gend en Loos then complained to the Dutch Fiscal Administration (*Administratie der Belastingen*) that the levying of the higher duty violated art. 12 of the EEC Treaty of Rome which bars member states from introducing between themselves any new duties on imports or exports and from increasing existing duties. After the company's appeal had been rejected, it appealed to the Dutch fiscal court which, before deciding the case, on 16 August 1962 requested a preliminary ruling under art. 177 of the Treaty of Rome (*see* **CJEC**) from the CJEC on two questions: 1. whether art. 12 of the Treaty of Rome was directly applicable in the territory of a member state, that is, whether citizens of the member state can, on the basis of this article, enforce their individual rights which the courts should protect; and 2. if the answer were affirmative, whether the increase in the import duty was unlawful in the meaning of art. 12 or only a reasonable alteration not prohibited by this article.

In answer to the questions, the CJEC, in its decision of 5 February 1963 (Case 26/62 [1963] ECR 1) held that art. 12 of the Treaty of Rome produced direct effects and created individual rights which national courts must protect. The CJEC left the answer to the second question to be determined by the national court.

The CJEC decision in the *Van Gend en Loos* case upheld the principle that the EC law creates direct rights and obligations for individuals in member states' courts (is, so to speak, "self-executing") and that in a case of conflict between the two systems the Community law takes precedence over national law. The Court's statement that "the Community constitutes a new legal order of international law for the benefit of which the States have limited their sovereign rights, ... and the subjects of which comprise not only member States but also their nationals" helped establish the standing of private persons before the CJEC.

W

Waldock, Sir Humphrey (1904-1982). British national. Professor of International Law at Oxford University, 1947-1972. Member of the ILC, 1961-1981. Member of the PCA (q.v.), 1965-1982. Judge of the ECHR (q.v.), 1966-1974. Member of the ICJ (q.v.), and its President, 1979-1982. Author of numerous works on international law and editor of Brierly's classic *Law of Nations* (6th ed., 1963) (*see* **Bibliography, 2 G**).

Western European Union (WEU) Tribunal. An abortive judicial body of the WEU, a non-EC organization linked to NATO, proposed under the Paris Convention of 14 December 1957 which, however, never entered into force, having failed to obtain the necessary ratification of France, one of the WEU's member states. The objective of the WEU Tribunal was to be the protection of private interests against measures for the control of armaments, and for this reason the Convention of 1957 envisaged access of individuals as parties in the proceedings before the projected tribunal.

Western Sahara, ICJ Adv. Op. 1974-1975. This advisory opinion (q.v.) of the ICJ (q.v.) concerned the legal status of Western Sahara, a desert but phosphate-rich territory on the West African coast, inhabited mostly by nomadic tribes and under Spanish colonial rule since 1884. After 1966, Spain (the "administering Power" in the UN terminology) was prepared to hold a referendum on the future status of the territory which, however, was claimed by Morocco (and initially by Mauritania) by virtue of an alleged historic title predating the Spanish colonization. Following rejection by Spain of Morocco's proposal to submit the dispute to the ICJ, the UN General Assembly on 13 December 1974 requested the ICJ to give an advisory opinion on the question whether the Western Sahara (Río de Oro and Saguia el Hamra) had been, at the time just prior to colonization by Spain, a territory belonging to no one (*terra nullius*); and, if not, what were the legal ties between this territory and the Kingdom of Morocco and the Mauritanian "entity."

In its advisory opinion delivered on 16 October 1975 (1975 ICJ Rep. 12) the ICJ unanimously replied to the first question in the negative. In reply to the second question, the Court, by 14 votes to two, expressed the opinion that at the time of the Spanish colonization there existed legal ties between the Sultan of Morocco and some of the local tribes; and, by 15 votes to one, that there were legal ties and rights, including some rights relating to the land, between the Mauritanian entity and the territory of Western Sahara. However, the Court found no evidence indicating the existence or international recognition of legal ties of territorial sovereignty between Western Sahara and Morocco and the Mauritanian entity respectively. The Court did not find any legal ties of such nature as might affect the application of the UN General Assembly Resolution of 14 December 1960 containing the Declaration on the Granting of Independence to Colonial Countries and Peoples in the decolonization of Western Sahara and of the principle of self-determination through free and genuine expression of the will of the peoples of the territory.

The *Western Sahara* advisory opinion could not affect the political developments in the territory which, occupied by Morocco, became a theater of protracted warfare between the Moroccan forces (Mauritania withdrew from the territory in 1979) and the Polisario (Popular Front for the Liberation of Saguia el Hamra and Río de Oro) guerrillas. By the early 1990s, Morocco, which controlled most of the territory, had been gaining the upper hand. A UN-sponsored cease-fire as a first step in a peace plan intended to allow the inhabitants to decide their own future in a UN-supervised referendum had not yet been implemented by mid-1993.

The *Western Sahara* opinion is of interest in that it was the first case of advisory proceedings in which the ICJ allowed a judge *ad hoc* (q.v.) to join the bench. It is also important that, unlike the PCIJ (q.v.) in the *Status of Eastern Carelia* case (q.v.), the ICJ did not consider it improper to give an advisory opinion that might be regarded as circumvention of the principle that jurisdiction (q.v.) to settle a dispute (q.v.) requires the consent of the parties, in this case Spain which had refused to become a party to any contentious proceedings over the situation in Western Sahara and objected to the Court's giving an advisory opinion on the matter. The Court noted that Spain was a member of the UN and as a party to the ICJ Statute had given its consent in general to the exercise by the Court of its advisory jurisdiction. In the Court's view, it was important that the Western Sahara dispute had arisen within the framework of the UN General Assembly decolonization proceedings and that the Court's advisory opinion was addressed not to any particular state but to the General Assembly in order to aid it in the decolonization of Western Sahara.

S.S. "Wimbledon" (France, Italy, Japan, UK v. Germany), PCIJ 1923. This first contentious jurisdiction (q.v.) case before the PCIJ (q.v.) originated in 1921 when a dispute arose between the UK, France and Poland on the one hand and Germany on the other over the German government's denial of passage through the Kiel Canal, located in German territory, of the British-flag vessel, the *S.S. Wimbledon*, chartered by a French company and carrying munitions for Poland, then at war with Soviet Russia. In justification of its denial (which in fact represented indirect aid to the Soviets) Germany contended that the passage would constitute a breach of neutrality proclaimed in the German Neutrality Orders of 1920. Despite the French request to allow the *Wimbledon* to pass the Canal in accordance with art. 380 of the Peace Treaty of Versailles, Germany persisted in its denial of passage, claiming that art. 380 was no obstacle to the implementation of Germany's neutrality. Art. 380 provides that "the Canal and its approaches shall be maintained free and open to the vessels of commerce and war of all nations at peace with Germany on terms of entire equality." The *Wimbledon* was compelled to use the longer route via the Danish Straits, with consequent losses sustained by the charterer.

Following the Russo-Polish War (which ended in the defeat of the Soviets) the allied powers (France, Italy, Japan and the UK) instituted proceedings before the PCIJ against Germany on 13 January 1923 on the basis of art. 386(1) of the Peace Treaty of Versailles. Poland's request to intervene (*see* **Intervention in Proceedings**) was granted by the Court in its judgment of 28 June 1923 (PCIJ, Ser. A, No. 1) since Poland was also a party to the

Treaty of Versailles whose construction was in question for the parties concerned in the case before the Court. In its judgment on the merits on 1 August 1923 (PCIJ Ser. A, No. 1), the PCIJ, by nine votes to three, ruled against Germany, holding that art. 380 of the Treaty of Versailles prevailed over any German neutrality orders and even a passage of a belligerent warship would not have compromised German neutrality; hence Germany had wrongfully refused passage to the *Wimbledon* and was under an obligation to pay compensation for the losses sustained by the vessel and its charterers.

Winiarski, Bohdan Stefan (1884-1969). Polish national. International lawyer. Long-serving member of the ICJ (q.v.), 1946-1967, and its President, 1961-1964. Educated at Warsaw, Cracow, and Paris. Member of the Polish National Committee in Paris, 1917-1920. Legal adviser to the Polish Delegation at Paris Peace Conference. Professor of Law at the University of Poznań, 1922-1939; Dean, 1936-1939. In the inter-war period delegate of Poland to various international conferences. Member of International Oder River Commission, 1921-1930. Managed to escape from German-occupied Poland in 1940. In exile in London, teaching international law at Oxford. In 1946 he became one of the first 15 original judges of ICJ. Author of numerous works in Polish and French on international and constitutional law.

ANNEX I
Judgments of the PCIJ

1. SS "Wimbledon" (Great Britain, France, Italy and Japan (with Poland intervening) v. Germany):
    1.   Judgment No. 1, 6 June 1923 (permitting intervention by Poland) 1923, PCIJ, Series A, No. 1.
    2.   Judgment No. 1 (merits), 17 August 1923. 1923, PCIJ, Series A, No. 1.

2. Mavrommatis Palestine Concessions (Greece v. Great Britain):
    3.   Judgment No. 2, 30 August 1924 (jurisdiction). PCIJ, Series A, No. 2.

Mavrommatis Jerusalem Concessions (Greece v. Great Britain):
    4.   Judgment No. 5, 26 March 1925 (merits). PCIJ, Series A, No. 5.

Readaptation of the Mavrommatis Jerusalem Concessions:
    5.   Judgment No. 10, 10 October 1927 (jurisdiction declined). PCIJ, Series A, No. 11.

3. Treaty of Neuilly, Art. 179, Annex, Paragraph 4 (Interpretation); (Bulgaria/Greece). (The only PCIJ summary procedure).
    6.   Judgment No. 3 of 12 September 1925. PCIJ, Series A, No. 3.

Interpretation of Judgment No. 3:
    7.   Judgment No. 4 of 26 March 1925 (rejecting Greece's request for interpretation). PCIJ, Series A, No. 4.

4. Certain German Interests in Polish Upper Silesia (Germany v. Poland):
    8.   Judgment No. 6 of 25 August 1925 (jurisdiction). PCIJ, Series A, No. 6.
    9.   Judgment No. 7 of 25 May 1926 (merits). PCIJ, Series A, No. 7.

Factory at Chorzów (Germany v. Poland):
    10.   Judgment No. 8 of 26 July 1927 (jurisdiction). PCIJ,

Series A, No. 9.

Interpretation of Judgments Nos. 7 and 8 (Factory at Chorzów):

11. Judgment No. 11 of 16 December 1927. PCIJ, Series A, No. 13.

Factory at Chorzów:

12. Judgment No. 13 of 13 November 1928 (merits), PCIJ, Series A, No. 17.

5. "Lotus" (Turkey/France):

13. Judgment No. 9 of 7 September 1927. PCIJ, Series A, No. 10.

6. Rights of Minorities in Upper Silesia (Minority Schools) (Germany v. Poland):

14. Judgment No. 12 of 26 April 1928. PCIJ, Series A, No. 15.

7. Serbian Loans (France/Yugoslavia):

15. Judgment No. 14 of 12 July 1929. PCIJ, Series A, No. 20.

8. Brazilian Loans (Brazil/France):

16. Judgment No. 15 of 12 July 1929. PCIJ, Series A, No. 21.

9. Territorial Jurisdiction of the International Commission of the River Oder (Czechoslovakia, Denmark, France, Germany, Sweden, United Kingdom/Poland):

17. Judgment No. 16 of 10 September 1929. PCIJ, Series A, No. 23.

10. Free Zones of Upper Savoy and the District of Gex (France/Switzerland):

18. Judgment of 7 June 1932. PCIJ, Series A/B, No. 46, p. 96.

11. Interpretation of the Statute of the Memel territory (France, Italy, Japan, United Kingdom v. Lithuania):

19. Judgment of 24 June 1932 (Preliminary Objection). PCIJ, Series A/B, No. 47, p. 243.

20. Judgment of 11 August 1932 (Merits). PCIJ, Series A/B, No. 49, p. 294.

12. Legal Status of Eastern Greenland (Denmark v. Norway):

21. Judgment of 5 April 1933. PCIJ, Series A/B, No. 53, p. 22.

13. Appeal from a Judgment of the Hungaro/Czechoslovak Mixed
   Arbitral Tribunal (The Peter Pázmány University)
   (Czechoslovakia v. Hungary):
  22. Judgment of 15 December 1933. PCIJ, Series A/B,
    No. 61, p. 208.
14. Lighthouses Case between France and Greece (France/Greece):
  23. Judgment of 17 March 1934. PCIJ, Series A/B, No.
    62, p. 4.
   Lighthouses in Crete and Samos (France/Greece):
  24. Judgment of 8 October 1937. PCIJ, Series A/B, No.
    71, p. 94.
15. Oscar Chinn (Belgium/United Kingdom):
  25. Judgment of 12 December 1934. PCIJ, Series A/B,
    No. 63, p. 65.
16. Pajzs, Csáki, Esterházy (Hungary v. Yugoslavia):
  26. Judgment of 16 December 1936. PCIJ, Series A/B,
    No. 68, p. 30.
17. Diversion of Water from the Meuse (Netherlands v. Belgium):
  27. Judgment of 28 June 1937. PCIJ, Series A/B, No.
    70, p. 4.
18. Borchgrave (Belgium/Spain):
  28. Judgment of 6 November 1937. PCIJ, Series A/B,
    No. 72, p. 158. (Case discontinued by Order of 30
    April 1938, PCIJ, Series A/B, No. 73, p. 4.)
19. Phosphates in Morocco (Italy v. France):
  29. Judgment of 14 June 1938. PCIJ, Series A/B, No.
    74, p. 10.
20. Panevezys-Saldutiskis Railway (Estonia v. Lithuania):
  30. Judgment of 28 February 1939. PCIJ, Series A/B,
    No. 76, p. 4.
21. Electricity Company of Sofia and Bulgaria (Belgium v. Bulgaria):
  31. Judgment of 4 April 1939. PCIJ, Series A/B, No. 77,
    p. 64. (Case discontinued)
22. Société Commerciale de Belgique (Belgium v. Greece):
  32. Judgment of 15 June 1939. PCIJ, Series A/B, No.
    78, p. 160.

Note: Seven other cases were ordered to be removed from the
Court's List or otherwise failed to reach their normal conclusion.

ANNEX II
Advisory Opinions of the PCIJ

1. Designation of Workers' Delegate for the Netherlands at the Third Session of the International Labour Conference. 31 July 1922. PCIJ, Series B, No. 1.
2. Competence of the ILO in Regard to International Regulation of the Conditions of Labour of Persons Employed in Agriculture. 12 August 1922. PCIJ, Series B, No. 2.
3. Competence of the ILO to Examine Proposals for the Organization and Development of the Methods of Agricultural Production. 12 August 1922. PCIJ, Series B, No. 3.
4. Nationality Decrees Issued in Tunis and Morocco. 7 February 1923. PCIJ, Series B, No. 4.
5. Status of Eastern Carelia. 23 July 1923. PCIJ, Series B, No. 5.
6. German Settlers in Poland. 10 September 1923. PCIJ, Series B, No. 6.
7. Acquisition of Polish Nationality. 15 September 1923. PCIJ, Series B, No. 7.
8. Jaworzina. 6 December 1923. PCIJ, Series B, No. 8.
9. Monastery of Saint-Naoum. 4 September 1924. PCIJ, Series B, No. 9.
10. Exchange of Greek and Turkish Populations. 21 February 1925. PCIJ, Series B, No. 10.
11. Polish Postal Service in Danzig. 16 May 1925. PCIJ, Series B, No. 11.
12. Interpretation of Article 3, Paragraph 2 of the Treaty of Lausanne. 21 November 1925. PCIJ, Series B, No. 12.
13. Competence of the ILO to Regulate Incidentally the Personal Work of the Employer. 23 July 1926. PCIJ, Series B, No. 13.
14. Jurisdiction of the European Commission of the Danube. 8 December 1927. PCIJ, Series B, No. 14.
15. Jurisdiction of the Courts of Danzig. 3 March 1928. PCIJ, Series B, No. 15.
16. Interpretation of the Greco-Turkish Agreement of 1 December 1926 (Final Protocol, Article IV). 28 August 1928. PCIJ, Series

B, No. 16.
17. Greco-Bulgarian "Communities." 31 July 1930. PCIJ, Series B, No. 17.
18. Free City of Danzig and ILO. 26 August 1930. PCIJ, Series B, No. 18.
19. Access to German Minority Schools in Upper Silesia. 15 May 1931. PCIJ, Series A/B, No. 40, p. 4.
20. Customs Régime between Germany and Austria. 5 September 1931. PCIJ, Series A/B, No. 41, p. 37.
21. Railway Traffic between Lithuania and Poland. 15 October 1931. PCIJ, Series A/B, No. 42, p. 108.
22. Access to, or Anchorage in, the Port of Danzig, of Polish War Vessels. 11 December 1931. Series A/B, No. 43, p. 128.
23. Treatment of Polish Nationals and Other Persons of Polish Origin or Speech in the Danzig Territory. 4 February 1932. PCIJ, Series A/B, No. 44, p. 4.
24. Interpretation of the Greco-Bulgarian Agreement of 9 December 1927. 8 March 1932. PCIJ, Series A/B, No. 45, p. 68.
25. Interpretation of the Convention of 1919 concerning Employment of Women during the Night. 15 November 1932. PCIJ, Series A/B, No. 50, p. 365.
26. Minority Schools in Albania. 6 April 1935. PCIJ, Series A/B, No. 64. p. 4.
27. Consistency of Certain Danzig Legislative Decrees with the Constitution of the Free City. 4 December 1935. PCIJ, Series A/B, No. 65, p. 41.

Note: In addition, one case (Expulsion of the Oecumenical Patriarch) was removed from the List before any advisory opinion was given. PCIJ, Series C, No. 9(II).

ANNEX III
Contentious Cases and Judgments of the ICJ

1. Corfu Channel (United Kingdom v. Albania):
   1. Judgment of 25 March 1948 (Preliminary Objection). ICJ Reports 1947-1948, p. 15.
   2. Judgment of 9 April 1949 (Merits). ICJ Reports 1949, p. 4.
   3. Judgment of 15 December 1949 (Assessment of Amount of Compensation). ICJ Reports 1949, p. 244.

2. Asylum (Colombia/Peru):
   4. Judgment of 20 November 1950. ICJ Reports 1950, p. 266.

   Request for Interpretation of the Judgment of 20 November 1950 in the Asylum Case (Colombia v. Peru):
   5. Judgment of 27 November 1950 (request refused). ICJ Reports 1950, p. 395.

   Haya de la Torre (Colombia v. Peru):
   6. Judgment of 13 June 1951. ICJ Reports 1951, p. 71.

3. Fisheries (United Kingdom v. Norway):
   7. Judgment of 18 December 1951. ICJ Reports 1951, p. 116.

4. Ambatielos (Greece v. United Kingdom):
   8. Judgment of 1 July 1952 (Preliminary Objection). ICJ Reports 1952, p. 28.
   9. Judgment of 19 May 1953 (Merits). ICJ Reports 1953, p. 10.

5. Anglo-Iranian Oil Co. (United Kingdom v. Iran):
   10. Judgment of 22 July 1952 (declining jurisdiction). ICJ Reports 1952, p. 93.

6. Rights of Nationals of the United States of America in Morocco (France v. United States of America):
   11. Judgment of 27 August 1952. ICJ Reports 1952, p. 176.

7. Minquiers and Ecrehos (France/United Kingdom):

12. Judgment of 17 November 1953. ICJ Reports 1953, p. 47.

8. Nottebohm (Liechtenstein v. Guatemala):
13. Judgment of 18 November 1953 (Preliminary Objection). ICJ Reports 1953, p. 111.
14. (Second Phase) Judgment of 6 April 1955. ICJ Reports 1955, p. 4.

9. Monetary Gold Removed from Rome in 1943 (Italy v. France, United Kingdom and United States of America):
15. Judgment of 15 June 1954 (declining jurisdiction). ICJ Reports 1954, p. 19.

10. Certain Norwegian Loans (France v. Norway):
16. Judgment of 6 July 1957 (declining jurisdiction). ICJ Reports 1957, p. 9.

11. Right of Passage over Indian Territory (Portugal v. India):
17. Judgment of 26 November 1957 (Preliminary Objections). ICJ Reports 1957, p. 125.
18. Judgment of 12 April 1960 (Merits). ICJ Reports 1960, p. 6.

12. Application of the Convention of 1902 Governing the Guardianship of Infants (Netherlands v. Sweden):
19. Judgment of 28 November 1958. ICJ Reports 1958, p. 55.

13. Interhandel (Switzerland v. United States of America):
20. Judgment of 21 March 1959 (claim held inadmissible). ICJ Reports 1959, p. 6.

14. Aerial Incident of 27 July 1955 (Israel v. Bulgaria):
21. Judgment of 26 May 1959 (declining jurisdiction). ICJ Reports 1959, p. 127.

15. Sovereignty over Certain Frontier Land (Belgium/Netherlands):
22. Judgment of 20 June 1959. ICJ Reports 1959, p. 209.

16. Arbitral Award Made by the King of Spain on 23 December 1906 (Honduras v. Nicaragua):
23. Judgment of 18 November 1960. ICJ Reports 1990, p. 192.

17. Temple of Preah Vihear (Cambodia v. Thailand):
24. Judgment of 26 May 1961 (Preliminary Objections). ICJ Reports 1961, p. 17.
25. Judgment of 15 June 1962 (Merits). ICJ Reports

1962, p. 6.
18. South West Africa (Ethiopia v. South Africa; Liberia v. South Africa) (proceedings joined):
    26. Judgment of 21 December 1962 (Preliminary Objections). ICJ Reports 1962, p. 319.
    27. (Second Phase) Judgment of 18 July 1966. ICJ Reports 1966, p.6.
19. Northern Cameroons (Cameroon v. United Kingdom):
    28. Judgment of 2 December 1963. ICJ Reports 1963, p. 15.
20. Barcelona Traction, Light and Power Company, Limited (Belgium v. Spain):
    29. Judgment of 24 July 1964 (Preliminary Objections). ICJ Reports 1964, p. 6.
    30. (Second Phase) (New Application) Judgment of 5 February 1970. ICJ Reports 1970, p. 3.
21. North Sea Continental Shelf (Federal Republic of Germany/Denmark; Federal Republic of Germany/Netherlands) (proceedings joined):
    31. Judgment of 20 February 1969. ICJ Reports 1969, p. 3.
22. Appeal Relating to the Jurisdiction of the ICAO Council (India v. Pakistan):
    32. Judgment of 18 August 1972. ICJ Reports 1972, p. 46.
23. Fisheries Jurisdiction (United Kingdom v. Iceland), Jurisdiction of the Court:
    33. Judgment of 2 February 1973. ICJ Reports 1973, p. 3.
24. and: Fisheries Jurisdiction (Federal Republic of Germany v. Iceland), Jurisdiction of the Court:
    34. Judgment of 2 February 1973. ICJ Reports 1973, p. 49.
    Fisheries Jurisdiction (United Kingdom v. Iceland), Merits:
    35. Judgment of 25 July 1974. ICJ Reports 1974, p. 3.
    and: Fisheries Jurisdiction (Federal Republic of Germany v. Iceland), Merits:
    36. Judgment of 25 July 1974. ICJ Reports 1974, p. 175.
25. Nuclear Tests (Australia v. France):

37. Judgment of 20 December 1974. ICJ Reports 1974, p. 253.
26. and: Nuclear Tests (New Zealand v. France):
38. Judgment of 20 December 1974. ICJ Reports 1974, p. 457.
27. Aegean Sea Continental Shelf (Greece v. Turkey):
39. Judgment of 19 December 1978 (declining jurisdiction). ICJ Reports 1978, p. 3.
28. United States Diplomatic and Consular Staff in Tehran (United States of America v. Iran):
40. Judgment of 24 May 1980. ICJ Reports 1980, p. 3. (Case discontinued by the Court's Order of 12 May 1981). ICJ Reports 1981, p. 45.
29. Continental Shelf (Tunisia/Libyan Arab Jamahiriya):
41. Judgment of 21 March 1981 (Application for Permission to Intervene). ICJ Reports 1981, p. 3.
42. Judgment of 24 February 1982. ICJ Reports 1982, p. 18.
30. Continental Shelf (Libyan Arab Jamahiriya/Malta):
43. Judgment of 21 March 1984 (Application for Permission to Intervene). ICJ Reports 1984, p. 3.
44. Judgment of 3 June 1985. ICJ Reports 1985, p. 13.
31. Delimitation of the Maritime Boundary in the Gulf of Maine (Canada/United States of America) (Case referred to a Chamber):
45. Judgment of 12 October 1984. ICJ Reports 1984, p. 246
32. Military and Paramilitary Activities in and against Nicaragua (Nicaragua v. United States of America):
46. Judgment of 26 November 1984 (Jurisdiction and Admissibility). ICJ Reports 1984, p. 392.
47. Judgment of 27 June 1986 (Merits). ICJ Reports 1986, p. 14. (Case discontinued by Court's Order of 26 September 1991).
33. Border and Transborder Armed Actions (Nicaragua v. Honduras):
48. Judgment of 20 December 1988 (Jurisdiction and Admissibility). ICJ Reports 1988, p. -. (Case discontinued by the Court's Order of 27 May 1992).

Application for Revision and Interpretation of the Judgment of 24 February 1982 in the Case Concerning the *Continental Shelf (Tunisia/Libyan Arab Jamahiriya)* (Tunisia v. Libyan Arab Jamahiriya): (*see* Case No. *29*.)
49. Judgment of 10 December 1985. ICJ Reports 1985, p. 192.

34. Frontier Dispute (Burkina Faso/Republic of Mali) (Case referred to a Chamber):
50. Judgment of 22 December 1986. ICJ Reports 1986, p. 554.

35. Elettronica Sicula S.p.A. (ELSI) (United States of America v. Italy) (Case referred to a Chamber):
51. Judgment of 20 July 1989. ICJ Reports 1989, p. 15.

36. Land, Island and Maritime Frontier Dispute (El Salvador/ Honduras) (with Nicaragua intervening) (Case referred to a Chamber):
52. Judgment of 13 September 1990 (Application for permission to intervene). ICJ Reports 1990, p. -.
53. Judgment of 11 September 1992 (Merits). ICJ Reports 1992, p. -.

37. Arbitral Award of 31 July 1989 (Guinea-Bissau v. Senegal):
54. Judgment of 12 November 1991. ICJ Reports 1991, p. -.

38. Certain Phosphate Lands in Nauru (Nauru v. Australia):
55. Judgment of 26 June 1992 (Preliminary Objections). ICJ Reports 1992, p. -.

39. Maritime Delimitation in the Area between Greenland and Jan Mayen (Denmark v. Norway):
56. Judgment of 14 June 1993. ICJ Reports 1993, p. -.

ANNEX IV
Cases Pending before the ICJ as of 15 July 1993

1. Aerial Incident of 3 July 1988 (Iran v. United States of America). 1989---.
2. Certain Phosphate Lands in Nauru (Nauru v. Australia). 1989---. (*see* ANNEX III, Judgment 55).*
3. Territorial Dispute (Libyan Arab Jamahiriya/Chad). 1990---.
4. Certain Activities of Australia with Respect to East Timor (Portugal v. Australia). 1991---.
5. Maritime Delimitation between Guinea-Bissau and Senegal (Guinea-Bissau v. Senegal). 1991---. (Application filed by Guinea-Bissau on 12 March 1991, but the Court did not fix any time-limit for the pleadings pending the outcome of negotiations between the parties).
6. Maritime Delimitation and Territorial Questions between Qatar and Bahrain (Qatar v. Bahrain). 1991---.
7. Questions of Interpretation and Application of the 1971 Montreal Convention Arising from the Aerial Incident at Lockerbie (Libyan Arab Jamahiriya v. United Kingdom). 1992---.
8. Questions of Interpretation and Application of the 1971 Montreal Convention Arising from the Aerial Incident at Lockerbie (Libyan Arab Jamahiriya v. United States of America). 1992---.
9. Case concerning Oil Platforms (Iran v. United States of America). 1992---. (This case concerned the destruction of Iranian oil platforms by US armed forces in 1987 and 1988. Iran founded the Court's jurisdiction on art. XXI(2) of the Iran-US Treaty of Amity, Economic Relations and Consular Rights of 15 August 1955 (284 UNTS 93)).
10. Application of the Convention on Prevention and Punishment of the Crime of Genocide (Bosnia and Herzegovina v. Yugoslavia (Serbia and Montenegro)). 1993---. (Order of provisional measures issued on 8 April 1993).

---

* This case was settled out of court in August 1993.

11. Gabcikovo-Nagymaros Project (Hungary/Slovakia). 1993---. (This case concerns the dispute regarding the construction and operation by Slovakia of a barrage system on the river Danube, a project abandoned by Hungary).

ANNEX V
Contentious Cases before the ICJ Filed But
Removed from the List without Any Judgment

A. At the Request of the Parties:
1. Protection of French Nationals and Protected Persons in Egypt (France v. Egypt). 1949-1950.
2. Electricité de Beyrouth Company (France v. Lebanon). 1953-1954.
3. Aerial Incident of 27 July 1955 (United States of America v. Bulgaria) 1957-1960.
4. Aerial Incident of 27 July 1955 (United Kingdom v. Bulgaria) 1957-1959.
5. Barcelona Traction, Light and Power Company, Limited (Belgium v. Spain). 1958-1961. (But see ANNEX III, Judgments Nos. 29 and 30.)
6. Compagnie du Port, des Quais et des Entrepôts de Beyrouth and Société Radio-Orient (France v. Lebanon). 1959-1960.
7. Trial of Pakistani Prisoners of War (Pakistan v. India). 1973.
8. Border and Transborder Armed Actions (Nicaragua v. Costa Rica). 1986-1987.
9. Passage through the Great Belt (Finland v. Denmark). 1991-1992.

B. At the Court's Initiative:
1. Treatment in Hungary of Aircraft and Crew of United States of America (United States of America v. USSR). 1954.
2. Treatment in Hungary of Aircraft and Crew of United States of America (United States of America v. Hungary). 1954.
3. Aerial Incident of 10 March 1953 (United States of America v. Czechoslovakia). 1955-1956.
4. Antarctica (United Kingdom v. Argentina). 1955-1956.
5. Antarctica (United Kingdom v. Chile). 1955-1956.
6. Aerial Incident of 7 October 1952 (United States of America v. USSR). 1955-1956.
7. Aerial Incident of 4 September 1954 (United States of America v. USSR). 1958.

8. Aerial Incident of 7 November 1954 (United States of America
   v. USSR). 1959.

ANNEX VI
Advisory Opinions of the ICJ

1. Conditions of Admission of a State to Membership in the United Nations (Article 4 of the Charter), 1947-1948. 28 May 1948. ICJ Reports 1947-1948, p. 57.
2. Reparation for Injuries Suffered in the Service of the United Nations. 1948-1949. 11 April 1949. ICJ Reports 1949, p. 174.
3. Interpretation of Peace Treaties with Bulgaria, Hungary and Romania. 1949-1950. First Phase: 30 March 1950. Second Phase: 18 July 1950. ICJ Reports 1950, pp. 65 and 221.
4. Competence of the General Assembly for the Admission of a State to the United Nations. 1949-1950. 3 March 1950. ICJ Reports 1950, p. 4.
5. International Status of South West Africa. 1949-1950. 11 July 1950. ICJ Reports 1950, p. 128.
6. Reservations to the Convention on the Prevention and Punishment of the Crime of Genocide. 1950-1951. 28 May 1951. ICJ Reports 1951, p. 15.
7. Effect of Awards of Compensation Made by the United Nations Administrative Tribunal. 1953-1954. 13 July 1954. ICJ Reports 1954, p. 47.
8. Voting Procedure on Questions relating to Reports and Petitions concerning the Territory of South West Africa. 1953-1954. 7 June 1955. ICJ Reports 1955, p. 67.
9. Judgments of the Administrative Tribunal of the ILO upon Complaints Made against UNESCO. 1955-1956. 23 October 1956. ICJ Reports 1956, p. 77.
10. Admissibility of Hearings of Petitioners by the Committee of South West Africa. 1955-1956. 1 June 1956. ICJ Reports 1956, p. 23.
11. Constitution of the Maritime Safety Committee of the Intergovernmental Maritime Consultative Organization. 1959-1960. 8 June 1960. ICJ Reports 1960, p. 150.
12. Certain Expenses of the United Nations (Article 17, paragraph 2, of the Charter). 1961-1962. ICJ Reports 1962, p. 161.

13. Legal Consequences for States of the Continued Presence of South Africa in Namibia (South West Africa) notwithstanding Security Council Resolution 276 (1970). 1970-1971. 21 June 1971. ICJ Reports 1971, p. 16.
14. Application for Review of Judgment No. 158 of the United Nations Administrative Tribunal. 1972-1973. 12 July 1973. ICJ Reports 1973, p. 166.
15. Western Sahara. 1974-1975. 16 October 1975. ICJ Reports 1975, p. 12.
16. Interpretation of the Agreement of 25 March 1951 between the WHO and Egypt. 1980. 20 December 1980. ICJ Reports 1980, p. 73.
17. Application for Review of Judgment No. 273 of the United Nations Administrative Tribunal. 1981-1982. 20 July 1982. ICJ Reports 1982, p. 325.
18. Application for Review of Judgment No. 333 of the United Nations Administrative Tribunal. 1984-1987. 27 May 1987. ICJ Reports 1987, p. 18.
19. Applicability of the Obligation to Arbitrate under Section 21 of the United Nations Headquarters Agreement of 26 June 1947. 1988. 26 April 1988. ICJ Reports 1988, p. 12.
20. Applicability of Article VI, Section 22, of the Convention on the Privileges and Immunities of the United Nations. 1989. 15 December 1989. ICJ Reports 1989, p. 177.

BIBLIOGRAPHY
Table of Contents

Introduction 241

1. Abbreviations 245

2. General International Law Introduction 251
   A. Research Tools: Bibliographies, Guides, Indexes ... 251
   B. Encyclopedias and Dictionaries 252
   C. Treaty Collections and Guides 253
      (1) General 253
      (2) US 253
      (3) Europe 253
   D. Current and Most Recent Primary Source
      Documentation 254
   E. Digests 254
      (1) US 254
      (2) Other Countries 254
   F. Casebooks 255
   G. Manuals and Treatises 256

3. International Tribunals in General 259

4. Permanent Court of International Justice 268
   A. Collections of Documents 268
      (1) Official 268
      (2) Unofficial 268
   B. Literature 269
      (1) In General 269
      (2) Individual Judgments 271
      (3) Individual Advisory Opinions 273

5. International Court of Justice 275
   A. Collections of Documents 275

(1) Official 275
(2) Unofficial 275

B. Literature 276
   (1) In General 276
   (2) Advisory Jurisdiction 288
   (3) Individual Judgments 289
   (4) Individual Advisory Opinions 300

6. Administrative Tribunals of International
   Organizations 304

7. International Tribunal for the Law of the Sea 307

8. International Criminal Courts 309

9. Court of Justice of the European Communities 312

10. Court of First Instance of the European
    Communities 319

11. Benelux Economic Union Court of Justice and
    College of Arbitrators 321

12. European Court of Human Rights 322

13. Inter-American Court of Human Rights 326

14. Court of Justice of the Cartagena Agreement 328

15. Central American Court of Justice 329

16. Arbitration in General 330

17. Arbitration: Cases 340

18. International Centre for Settlement of
    Investment Disputes 347

19. Iran-United States Claims Tribunal   349

20. Canada-United States Free Trade
    Agreement: Dispute Settlement   352

21. International Commercial Arbitration   353

INTRODUCTION

This first comprehensive bibliography on international courts and tribunals encompasses selected primary and secondary materials on the various judicial bodies and related subjects discussed in this *Dictionary*. The table of contents preceding the present Introduction provides a convenient overview of the organization and contents of the following bibliography.

Conceptually and systematically international tribunals are one specialized topic within the general field of international law. Hence bibliographical research on this topic must resort to the same tools that are employed in retrieving international law documentation as a whole. But this bibliography is only on international tribunals and not on peaceful settlement of international disputes in general. Items of general international law documentation are listed in sec. 2. They can be useful either as documentation of primary sources or --casebooks and treatises--as sources of further information, especially on the legal background of cases before international tribunals. However, international law textbooks contain information only on the major international courts and tribunals.

As far as retrospective bibliographies are concerned, the most useful and detailed multi-volume works are the two publications of Harvard Law School. Its *Catalog of International Law and Relations* is especially helpful in finding older publications (up to the early 1960s), including a very rich selection of works on arbitration. The other publication, the 21-volume set of *Harvard Legal Bibliography* published annually in the years 1961-1981, lists books and articles from the world literature on all subjects of law, including, in the international law section, international tribunals. For current articles, there are *Index to Legal Periodicals* and *Index to Foreign Legal Periodicals*, but by far more inclusive and indispensable for any serious research in international law and tribunals is the semi-annual *Public International Law* bibliography of all publications in international law, including, since 1990, also books. Reviews of books in international law journals, especially *AJIL*, alert the readers to the recent publications in book form. The best source to obtain substantive information on international tribunals are the many entries on such tribunals and cases before them, included in *Encyclopedia of Public International Law* (EPIL). However, this work, whose installments I and II are most relevant for this *Dictionary*, is already about a dozen years old.

As far as primary sources are concerned, the texts of the treaties establishing international tribunals can be found either in treaty collections listed in sec. 2C or --for major tribunals-- in supplements to international casebooks (2F). *International Legal Materials* (ILM) is the standard and most useful source for most recent primary materials. Collections of courts decisions are listed in the respective sections of this bibliography. In addition, some major decisions of the most important international tribunals can be found in international law casebooks.

For the World Court, a retrospective bibliography on the PCIJ and the ICJ, covering the years 1918-1964, was published in 1966 (*see* 5A (2)). In addition, the ICJ periodically publishes a bibliography of which 41 issues have so far appeared. Information on the literature concerning the regional European international courts, can be obtained, in addition to the already mentioned bibliographies, from the works, mainly by Europeans authors, discussing the court concerned. They are listed in the respective sections of this bibliography. A number of European international legal journals (*AFDI, JDI, CDE, RIE, RTDE,* among others) periodically review the case law of the European international tribunals and refer to selected current literature. As part of its annual review of European legal problems, *Annuaire Européen-European Yearbook* (*AE*) includes a selective bibliography of periodical and pamphlet material which includes sections on the CJEC, the Court of First Instance, and the ECHR. But there exists no comprehensive bibliography on any of the regional international tribunals listed in this *Dictionary*.

The bibliography of this *Dictionary* is necessarily selective, with emphasis on more recent publications. It is multilingual, but most items are in English. About one third of the items are on the World Court, including the PCIJ. Arbitration, including international commercial arbitration, is the next largest area covered, followed by the CJEC and the ECHR. Other, less known, tribunals are also covered if any relevant literature is available. Some of the most recently established and not yet active tribunals, such as those of various African organizations, have not yet generated any literature.

This bibliography is the first attempt to fill the need for a bibliographic guide to materials on international tribunals. It cannot claim to be free of gaps, but the author hopes that scholars and other concerned readers will find it a useful tool as they proceed with further study and research in various aspects of international courts and tribunals.

1. ABBREVIATIONS

AE	Annuaire Européen-European Yearbook (Dordrecht)
AFDI	Annuaire Français de Droit International (Paris)
AJCL	American Journal of Comparative Law (Berkeley, CA)
AJICL-RADIC	African Journal of International and Comparative Law-Revue Africaine de Droit International et Comparé (London)
AJIL	American Journal of International Law (Washington)
ASIL Proc.	American Society of International Law Proceedings (Washington)
AUJIL&Pcy	American University Journal of International Law and Policy (Washington)
Australian YIL	Australian Yearbook of International Law (Canberra)
AVR	Archiv des Völkerrechts (Tübingen)
Boston Coll&CLR	Boston College International and Comparative Law Review (Newton, MA)
BUILJ	Boston University International Law Journal (Boston)
BYIL	British Yearbook of International Law (Oxford)
CalifWILJ	California Western International Law Journal (San Diego, CA)
CanBarR	Canadian Bar Review-Revue du Barreau Canadien (Ottawa)
CanYIL	Canadian Yearbook of International Law-Annuaire Canadien de Droit International (Vancouver, BC)
Case WRJIL	Case Western Reserve Journal of International Law (Cleveland, OH)

CDE	Cahiers de Droit Européen (Brussels)
Cmd.	Command Papers, 2d Series (London)
CML Rev	Common Market Law Review (London)
ColJTransnL	Columbia Journal of Transnational Law (New York)
ColLR	Columbia Law Review (New York)
ComI	Comunità Internazionale (Padua)
ConnJIL	Connecticut Journal of International Law (Hartford, CT)
ConnLR	Connecticut Law Review (West Hartford, CT)
DenJIL&Pcy	Denver Journal of International Law and Policy (Denver, CO)
Dept. St. Bull.	Department of State Bulletin (Washington)
DI	Diritto Internazionale (Naples)
DickJIL	Dickinson Journal of International Law (Atlanta, GA)
Duke LJ	Duke Law Journal (Washington)
ed.	edited, editor
eds.	editors
EJIL-JEDI	European Journal of International Law-Journal Européen de Droit International (Florence)
ELR	European Law Review (London)
Emory ILR	Emory International Law Review (Atlanta, GA)
Emory JIDisRes	Emory Journal of International Dispute Resolution (Atlanta, GA)
EPIL	Encyclopedia of Public International Law
et al.	*et alii* (and others)
EuR	Europarecht (Munich)
Fordham ILJ	Fordham International Law Journal (New York)
Foro It.	Foro Italiano (Rome)
Georgia JIL	Georgia Journal of International Law (Athens, GA)
Georgia JI&CL	Georgia Journal of International and Comparative Law (Athens, GA (formerly Georgia JIL)

GPO	Government Printing Office (Washington)
GWashJIL&Econ	George Washington Journal of International Law and Economics (Washington)
GYIL	German Yearbook of International Law (Berlin)
Harvard ILJ	Harvard International Law Journal (Cambridge, MA)
Hastings I&CLR	Hastings International and Comparative Law Review (San Francisco)
Houston JIL	Houston Journal of International Law (Houston, TX)
HYIL	Hague Yearbook of International Law (The Hague)
ICLQ	International and Comparative Law Quarterly (London)
IJIL	Indian Journal of International Law (New Delhi)
ILA Rep.	International Law Association Conference Report (London)
ILawyer	International Lawyer (Washington)
ILC	International Law Commission
ILM	International Legal Materials (Washington)
ITLJ	International Trade Law Journal (Baltimore, MD)
JBL	Journal of Business Law (London)
JDI	Journal du Droit International (Clunet) (Paris)
JIArb	Journal of International Arbitration (London)
JIR	Jahrbuch für internationales Recht (Göttingen)
JöR	Jahrbuch des öffentlichen Rechts der Gegenwart (Tübingen)
Jus G	Jus Gentium-Diritto delle Relazioni Internazionali (Rome)
LJIL	Leyden Journal of International Law (Leyden)
LNTS	League of Nations Treaty Series
LQR	Law Quarterly Review (London)

LR	Law Review
MalLR	Malaya Law Review (Singapore)
MdJIL&T	Maryland Journal of International Law and Trade (Baltimore, MD)
MichJIL	Michigan Journal of International Law (Ann Arbor, MI)
NILR	Netherlands International Law Review (Leyden)
NordJIL	Nordic Journal of International Law (Copenhagen) (formerly: NordTiR)
NordTiR	Nordisk Tidsskrift for International Ret (Copenhagen)
NTIR	Nederlands Tijdschrift voor Internationaal Recht (Leyden (now: NILR)
NYIL	Netherlands Yearbook of International Law (Dordrecht)
NYUJIL& Politics	New York University Journal of International Law and Politics (New York)
P	Press
p.	pages
PCIJ	Permanent Court of International Justice
PiP	Państwo i Prawo [State and Law] (Warsaw)
PYIL	Polish Yearbook of International Law (Warsaw)
RBDI	Revue Belge de Droit International (Brussels)
RCADI	Recueil des Cours de l'Académie de Droit International de La Haye (The Hague)
RDH	Revue des Droits de l'Homme. Droit International et Droit Comparé-Human Rights Journal. International and Comparative Law (Paris)
RDI	Rivista di Diritto Internazionale (Milan)
RDILC	Revue de Droit International et de Législation Comparée (Brussels) (-----1939)
RDIP	Revue de Droit International Privé (Paris)
REDI	Revista Española de Derecho Internacional (Madrid)
RevArb	Revue de l'Arbitrage (Paris)

Rev. ed.	Revised edition
RGDIP	Revue Générale de Droit International Public (Paris)
RHDI	Revue Hellénique de Droit International (Athens)
RIDC	Revue Internationale de Droit Comparé (Paris)
RIDU	Rivista Internazionale dei Diritti dell'Uomo (Milan)
RIE	Revista de Instituciones Europeas (Madrid)
RIW-AWD	Recht der internationalen Wirtschaft-Aussenwirtschaftsdienst des Betriebsberaters (Heidelberg)
RTDE	Revue Trimestrielle de Droit Européen (Paris)
RW	Rechtskundig Weekblad (Antwerp)
San Diego LR	San Diego Law Revue (San Diego, CA)
SchweizJIR	Schweizerisches Jahrbuch für internationales Recht-Annuaire Suisse de Droit International (Zurich)
sec(s)	section(s)
SEW	Sociaal-Economische Wetgeving (Zwolle, Netherlands)
SJ	Semaine Judiciaire (Geneva)
SovEMP	Sovetskiy ezhegodnik mezhdunarodnovo prava [Soviet Yearbook of International Law] (Moscow)
SovGP	Sovetskoe gosudarstvo i pravo [Soviet State and Law] (Moscow)
Stanford JIL	Stanford Journal of International Law (Stanford, CA)
Stat.	Statutes at Large
Suppl.	Supplement
SyrJIL&Com	Syracuse Journal of International Law and Commerce (Syracuse, NY)
TexILJ	Texas International Law Journal (Austin, TX)
TIAS	Treaties and Other International Acts Series (1945----) (single pamphlets) (formerly

	TS)
TS	Treaty Series (US treaties up to 1945)
U	University
U Miami I-ALR	University of Miami Inter-American Law Review (Coral Cables, FL)
UNCITRAL	United Nations Commission on International Trade Law
UP	University Press
VandJTransnL	Vanderbilt Journal of Transnational Law (Nashville, TN)
VirJIL	Virginia Journal of International Law (Charlottesville, VA)
vol.	volume
vols.	volumes
World Arb&MediRep	World Arbitration and Mediation Report (New York)
Yale JIL	Yale Journal of International Law (New Haven, CT)
YEL	Yearbook of European Law (Oxford)
YWA	Yearbook of World Affairs (London)
ZaöRV	Zeitschrift für ausländisches öffentliches Recht und Völkerrecht-Heidelberg Journal of International Law (Stuttgart)
ZVglRWiss	Zeitschrift für vergleichende Rechtswissenschaft. Archiv für internationales Wirtschaftsrecht (Stuttgart)

2. GENERAL INTERNATIONAL LAW
INTRODUCTION

A. Research Tools: Bibliographies, Guides, Indexes

Beyerly, Elizabeth. *Public International Law: A Guide to Information Sources*. London and New York: Munsell Publishing Ltd., 1991. 279 p.

Cambridge, University of. *The Squire Law Library. Catalogue of International Law*. 4 vols. Dobbs Ferry, NY: Oceana, 1972.

Carroll, Berenice A., Clinton F. Fink &Jane E. Mohraz. *Peace and War: A Guide to Bibliographies*. Santa Barbara, CA: ABC-CLIO, 1983. 580 p.

Delupis, Ingrid. *Bibliography of International Law*. London and New York: Bowker, 1975. 670 p.

The George Washington Journal of International Law and Economics. *Guide to International Legal Research*. Salem, NH: Butterworths Legal Publishers, 1990. 400 p.

Goedan, Juergen Christoph. *Legal Bibliographies - General and International: An Evaluation*. Translated from German by John E. Pickron. Ardsley-on-Hudson: Transnational Publishers, 1991. 350 p.

Harvard Law School Library. *Annual Legal Bibliography*. 21 annual volumes. ed. by V. Mostecky (-1969) and (1969-) M. Moody. Cambridge, MA: Harvard Law School Library, 1961-1981.

_____. *Catalog of International Law and Relations*. 20 vols. ed. by Margaret Moody. Cambridge, MA: Harvard Law School Library, 1965-1967.

Index to Legal Periodicals (monthly). New York: H. W. Wilson Co., 1928----.

Index to Foreign Legal Periodicals (quarterly). Berkeley, CA: University of California.

Merrills, J.G. *A Current Bibliography of International Law*. London: Butterworths, 1978. 277 p.

Paenson, Isaac. *Manual of the Terminology of Public International Law (Law of Peace) and International Organizations*. Brussels:

Etablissements E. Bruylant, 1983. 846 p. (English-French-Spanish-Russian).

Public International Law. A Current Bibliography of Books and Articles (semiannual). Ed. by Max Planck Institute for Comparative Public Law and International Law. Berlin and Heidelberg: Springer, 1974----. (Books included since 1990). Prior to 1974 part of *ZaöRV*.

Wiktor, Christian L. *Canadian Bibliography of International Law*. Toronto: Toronto UP, 1984. 767 p.

B. Encyclopedias and Dictionaries

Bledsoe, Robert L. & Boleslaw A. Boczek. *The International Law Dictionary*. Santa Barbara, CA, and Oxford: ABC-CLIO, 1987. 422 p. (especially Chapter 10).

Dictionnaire de la terminologie du droit international (Dictionnaire Basdevant). Paris: Editions Sirey, 1960. 755 p.

Encyclopedia of Public International Law. 12 instalments. Published under the Auspices of Max Planck Institute for Comparative Public Law and International Law under the Direction of Rudolf Bernhardt. Amsterdam: North Holland, 1981-1990. Especially: Instalment 1 - *Settlement of Disputes* (1981) and Instalment 2 - *Decisions of International Courts and Tribunals and International Arbitrations* (1981). Also: Instalment 6 - *Regional Cooperation, Organizations and Problems* (1983) and Instalment 8 - *Human Rights and the Individual in International Law. International Economic Relations* (1985). Referred to as: *EPIL*.

Fox, James. *Dictionary of International and Comparative Law*. Dobbs Ferry, NY: Oceana, 1991. 412 p.

Francescakis, P. *Répertoire de droit international*. 2 vols. Paris: Dalloz, 1968-1969.

Kuehl, Warren F. (ed.). *Bibliographical Dictionary of Internationalists*. Westport, CT, and London: Greenwood Press, 1983. 934 p.

Parry, Clive, John P. Grant, Anthony Parry & Arthur D. Watts. *Encyclopaedic Dictionary of International Law*. Dobbs Ferry, NY: Oceana, 1986. 564 p.

Strupp, Karl & Hans Jürgen Schlochauer. *Wörterbuch des Völkerrechts*. 2d ed. 3 vols. Berlin: de Gruyter, 1960-1962.

C. Treaty Collections and Guides

(1) *General:*

Consolidated Treaty Series. Ed. by Clive Parry. 231 vols. plus 10 Index volumes. Dobbs Ferry, NY: Oceana, 1969-1981. Referred to as CTS.

League of Nations Treaty Series. Treaties and International Engagements Registered with the Secretariat of the League. 205 vols. plus nine Indexes. Treaties 1920-1946. Geneva: League of Nations. Microfilm: Oceana. Referred to as LNTS.

United Nations Treaty Series. Treaties and International Agreements Registered or Filed and Recorded with the Secretariat of the United Nations. New York: UN, 1946----. Over 1370 vols. by the end of 1992. 17 Indexes. Referred to as UNTS.

World Treaty Index. 5 vols. Compiled by P. Rohn. Santa Barbara, CA: ABC-CLIO. 2d ed. 1983-1984.

(2) *US:*

Treaties and Other International Agreements of the United States of America 1776-1949. 13 vols. Compiled under the direction of Charles I. Bevans. Washington, DC: GPO, 1968-1976.

Treaties in Force. A List of Treaties and Other International Agreements of the United States in Force on January 1 ----. Annual, 1929----. Compiled by the Treaty Affairs Staff, Office of the Legal Adviser, Department of State, Washington, DC: GPO.

United States Treaties and Other International Agreements (UST). Washington, DC: GPO. Volumes published on a calendar-year basis beginning as of 1 January 1950.

Note:

TIAS = Treaties and Other International Acts Series, issued singly in pamphlets by the Department of State since 1945. Prior to that it was called Treaty Series (TS) or Executive Agreement Series (EAS).

(3) *Europe:*

European Treaty Series. Strasbourg: Council of Europe. 1950----.

European Yearbook (Annuaire Européen). Council of Europe. Dordrecht: Nijhoff, 1952----. Contains also articles and documentation reviewing all the European organizations.

D. Current and Most Recent Primary Source Documentation

International Legal Materials (bimonthly). Washington, DC: American Society of International Law, 1961----. Reproduces official documents whenever possible. Foreign-language documents in translation. Includes, among other materials, treaties and major decisions of international courts and tribunals. Referred to as ILM.

Note:

Texts of some treaties of interest to the subject of international tribunals can be found in documentary supplements to casebooks, listed below at F. *See also* Lowenfeld (Sec. 3, International Tribunal in General).

E. Digests

(1) *US:*

Digest of United States Practice in International Law. Department of State, Office of the Legal Adviser. Washington, DC: GPO. Conceived as an annual volume of current US practice and, in a way, successor to Whiteman's *Digest* (*see below*). So far 10 volumes (1973-1980) plus *Cumulative Index* have been published (in the years 1973-1989). Chapter 13, secs. 2 and 3 respectively deal with arbitration and judicial settlement of international disputes.

Hackworth, Green Haywood. *Digest of International Law.* 8 vols. Washington, DC: GPO, 1940-1944.

Moore, John Bassett. *A Digest of International Law.* 8 vols. Washington, DC: GPO, 1906.

Wharton, Francis. *A Digest of the International Law of the United States.* 3 vols. Washington, DC: GPO, 1886.

Whiteman, Marjorie M. *Digest of International Law.* 15 vols, including vol. 15, General Index. Washington, DC: GPO, 1963-1973.

(2) *Other Countries:*

A British Digest of International Law. Ed. by Clive Parry. London: Stevens & Sons, 1967. Volumes 2, 5, 6, 7, and 8 have so far appeared.

Répertoire de la Pratique Française en Matière de Droit International Public. Ed. by Alexandre Charles Kiss. 7 vols. Paris: Centre

National de la Recherche Scientifique, 1962-1972.

F. Casebooks

Carter, Barry E. & Phillip R. Trimble. *International Law*. Boston: Little, Brown, 1991. 1444 p.

_____(eds.). *International Law. Selected Documents*. Boston: Little Brown, 1991. 788 p.

Harris, D.J. *Cases and Materials on International Law*. 4th ed. London: Sweet & Maxwell, 1991. 1040 p.

Henkin, Louis, Richard Crawford Pugh, Oscar Schachter, and Hans Smit. *International Law: Cases and Materials*. 2d ed. St. Paul, MN: West Publishing Co., 1987. 1517 p.

_____(eds.). *Basic Documents Supplement to International Law: Cases and Materials*. 2d ed. St. Paul, MN: West Publishing Co., 1987. 677 p.

McDougal, Myres S. & W. Michael Reisman. *International Law in Contemporary Perspective: The Public Order of the World Community - Cases and Materials*. Mineola, NY: The Foundation Press, 1981. 1584 p.

Steiner, Henry J. & Detlev F. Vagts. *Transnational Legal Problems: Materials and Text*. 3d ed. Mineola, NY: The Foundation Press, 1986. 1128 p.

_____(eds.). *Documentary Supplement 1991 Revised Edition. For Use with Transnational Legal Problems. Materials and Text*. 3d ed. Westbury, NY: The Foundation Press, 1991. 142 p.

Sweeney, Joseph Modeste, Covey T. Oliver, and Noyes E. Leech. *Cases and Materials on The International Legal System*. 3d ed. Westbury, NY: The Foundation Press, 1988. 1505 p.

_____(eds.). *Documentary Supplement to Cases and Materials on The International Legal System*. 3d ed. Westbury, NY: The Foundation Press, 1988. 574 p.

Weston, Burns H., Richard A. Falk, and Anthony D'Amato. *International Law and World Order: A Problem-Oriented Casebook*. 2d ed. St. Paul, MN: West Publishing Co., 1990. 1335 p.

_____(eds.). *Basic Documents in International Law and World Order*. 2d ed. St. Paul, MN: West Publishing Co., 1990. 960 p.

G. Manuals and Treatises

Akehurst, Michael. *A Modern Introduction to International Law*. 6th ed. London: Allen & Unwin, 1987. 315 p.

American Law Institute. *Restatement of the Law - Third. The Foreign Relations of the United States*. 2 vols. St. Paul, MN: American Law Institute Publishers, 1987. 641 and 561 p.

Bogaert, E.R.C. Van. *Volkenrecht*. Antwerp: Kluwer, 1982. 648 p.

Brierly, J.L. *The Law of Nations: An Introduction to the International Law of Peace*. 6th ed. by Sir Humphrey Waldock. New York and Oxford: Oxford UP, 1963. 442 p.

Brownlie, Ian. *Principles of Public International Law*. 4th ed. Oxford: Clarendon Press, 1990. 748 p.

Buergenthal, Thomas & Harold G. Maier. *Public International Law in a Nutshell*. 2d ed. St. Paul, MN: West Publishing Co., 1990. 275 p.

Carreau, Dominique. *Droit International*. 2d ed. Paris: Pedone, 1988. 618 p.

Cassese, Antonio. *International Law in a Divided World*. Oxford: Clarendon Press, 1986. 429 p.

Castel, J.-G. *International Law Chiefly as Interpreted and Applied in Canada*. 3d ed. Toronto: Butterworths, 1976. 1,268 p.

Chen, Lung-chu. *An Introduction to Contemporary International Law: A Policy-Oriented Perspective*. New Haven and London: Yale UP, 1989. 500 p.

Conforti, Benedetto. *Diritto internazionale*. 3d ed. Naples: Editoriale Scientifica, 1987. 432 p.

Giuliano, Mario, Tullio Scovazzi, and Tullio Treves. *Diritto internazionale*. 2d ed. 2 vols. Milan: Giuffrè, 1983. Vol. 1, 674 p.; vol. 2, 610 p.

_____. *Diritto internazionale: Parte generale*. Milan: Giuffrè, 1991. 605 p.

Glahn, Gerhard von. *Law Among Nations: An Introduction to Public International Law*. 6th rev. ed. New York: Macmillan, 1992. 919 p.

Green, Leslie C. *International Law: A Canadian Perspective*. 2d ed. Toronto: Carswell, 1988. 409 p.

Green, N.A. Maryan. *International Law*. 3d ed. London: Pitman Publishing, 1987. 333 p.

Hyde, Charles Cheney. *International Law Chiefly as Interpreted and*

Applied by the United States. 3 vols. 2d rev. ed. Boston: Little Brown, 1947. 2,489 p.

Janis, Mark W. *An Introduction to International Law.* Boston: Little Brown, 1988. 299 p.

Jiménez de Aréchaga, Eduardo. *El Derecho internacional contemporáneo.* Madrid: Editorial Tecnos, 1980. 379 p.

Levi, Werner. *Contemporary International Law: A Concise Introduction.* 2d ed. Boulder, CO: Westview Press, 1991. 365 p.

Münch, Ingo von. in collaboration with Philip Kunig. *Völkerrecht in programmierter Form.* 2d ed. Berlin and New York: Walter de Gruyter, 1982. 484 p.

Nguyen, Quoc Dinh. *Droit international public.* Rev. and updated by Patrick Dailler and Alain Pellet. 3d ed. Paris: Librairie Générale de Droit et de Jurisprudence, 1987. 1,189 p.

Oppenheim, Lassa F.L. *International Law: A Treatise.* 2 vols. Vol. 1: *Peace* (9th ed.) in two books, ed. by Sir Robert Jennings and Sir Arthur Watts. Harlow, Essex: Longman, 1992. Vol. 2: *Disputes, War and Neutrality* (7th ed.), ed. by H. Lauterpacht. New York: McKay, 1952. 941 p.

Pastor Ridruejo, José Antonio. *Curso de derecho internacional público.* Madrid: Editorial Tecnos, 1986. 582 p.

Rousseau, Charles. *Droit international public.* Vol. 5. Paris: Editions Sirey, 1983. 504 p.

_____. *Droit international public.* 11th ed. Paris: Dalloz, 1987.

Schwarzenberger, Georg. *International Law As Applied by International Courts and Tribunals.* 3 vols. London: Stevens, 1957, 1968, 1976. Vol. 2, 881 p.; vol. 3, 680 p.

Seara Vázquez, Modesto. *Derecho internacional público.* 13th ed. Mexico: Porrúa, 1991. 733 p.

Seidl-Hohenfeldern, Ignaz. *Völkerrecht.* 6th ed. Cologne: Carl Heymann, 1987.

Sepúlveda, César. *Derecho internacional.* 16th ed. Mexico: Porrúa, 1991. 746 p.

Shaw, Malcolm N. *International Law.* 3d ed. Cambridge: Grotius Publications, 1991. 782 p.

Snyder, Frederick E. & Surakiart Sathirathai (eds.). *Third World Attitudes toward International Law: An Introduction.* Dordrecht: Nijhoff, 1987. 850 p.

Sørensen, Max (ed.). *Manual of Public International Law.* New York:

St. Martin's Press, 1968. 930 p.

Starke, J.G. *Introduction to International Law.* 9th ed. London: Butterworths, 1984. 664 p.

Thierry, Hubert *et al. Droit international public.* 3d ed. Paris: Editions Mont-Chrestien, 1981. 780 p.

Verdross, Alfred & Bruno Simma. *Universelles Völkerrecht: Theorie und Praxis.* 3d ed. Berlin: Duncker & Humblot, 1984. 956 p.

Verzijl, J.H.W. *International Law in Historical Perspective.* 11 vols. Alphen aan den Rijn: Sijthoff & Noordhoff, 1968-1990.

Wallace, Rebecca M.M. *International Law.* London: Sweet & Maxwell, 1986. 275 p.

3. INTERNATIONAL TRIBUNALS IN GENERAL

Amerasinghe, Chittharanjan F. "The Local Remedies Rule in an Appropriate Perspective," 36 *ZaöRV* 727-59 (1976).

_____. "The Rule of Exhaustion of Domestic Remedies in the Framework of International Systems for the Protection of Human Rights," 28 *ZaöRV* 257-300 (1968).

Amlund, Curtis Arthur. "Development of a Theoretical Decision-Significance Index for the International Tribunal," 11 *Liverpool Law Review* 79-88 (1989).

Anand, Ram Prakash. *International Courts and Contemporary Conflicts.* New York: Asia Publishing House, 1974. 479 p.

_____. *Studies in International Adjudication.* Dobbs Ferry, NY: Oceana, 1970.

Berlia, Georges. *Essai sur la portée de la clause de jugement en équité en droit des gens.* Paris: Sirey, 1937. 214 p.

_____. "Jurisprudence des tribunaux internationaux en ce qui concerne leur compétence," 88 *RCADI* 105-57 (1955-II).

Bernhardt, Rudolf. "Die gerichtliche Durchsetzung völkerrechtlicher Verpflichtungen," 47 *ZaöRV* 17-31 (1987).

Bierzanek, Remigiusz. "Some Remarks on the Function of International Courts in the Contemporary World," 7 *PYIL* 121-50 (1975).

Bilder, Richard B. "International Third Party Dispute Settlement," 17 *DenJIL&Pcy* 471-503 (1989).

_____. "An Overview of International Dispute Settlement," 1 *Emory JIDisRes* 1-32 (1986).

Borel, Eugène. "L'Acte général de Genève," 27 *RCADI* 497-595 (1929-II).

Bourne, C. B. "Mediation, Conciliation and Adjudication in the Settlement of International Drainage Basin Disputes," 9 *CanYIL* 114-58 (1971).

Bowett, D. W. "Contemporary Developments in Legal Techniques in the Settlement of Disputes," 179 *RCADI* 169-235(1983-I).

_____. *The Law of International Institutions.* 4th ed. New York:

Praeger, 1982.

Brierly, J. L. "The General Act of Geneva," 11 *BYIL* 119-33 (1928).

Butler, Nicholas Murray. *The International Mind: An Argument for the Judicial Settlement of Disputes.* New York: Scribner's, 1912. 121 p.

Cançado Trindade A.-A. "Exhaustion of Local Remedies in International Law and the Role of National Courts," 17 *AVR* 333-70 (1977).

Castberg, Frede. "L'excès de pouvoir dans la justice internationale," 35 *RCADI* 353-472 (1931-I).

Chappez, J. *La règle de l'épuisement des voies de recours internes.* 1972.

Cheng, Bin. *General Principles of Law As Applied by International Courts and Tribunals.* Cambridge: Grotius Publications, 1953. Reprinted in 1987. 427 p.

Choate, Joseph H. *The Two Hague Conferences.* Princeton, NJ: Princeton UP, 1913. 109 p.

Cocatre-Zilgien, A. "Justice internationale facultative et justice internationale obligatoire," 80 *RGDIP* 689-737 (1976).

Contini, P. (ed.). *A Survey of Treaty Provisions for the Pacific Settlement of International Disputes, 1949-1962.* New York; UN, 1966.

Convention for the Pacific Settlement of International Disputes, July 29, 1899, 32 Stat. 1779, TS No. 392.

Convention for the Pacific Settlement of International Disputes, Oct. 18, 1907, 36 Stat. 2199, TS No. 536.

Darby, W. Evans. *International Tribunals: A Collection of the Various Schemes Which Have Been Propounded and of Instances Since 1815.* London: Dent, 1900. 516 p.

Davis, Calvin D. *The United States and the First Hague Peace Conference.* Ithaca, NY: Cornell UP, 1962. 236 p.

Delbez, Louis. *Les principes généraux du contentieux international.* Paris: Pichon et Durand-Auzias, 1962. 339 p.

Del Vecchio, Angela. *Le Parti nel processo internazionale.* Milan: Giuffrè, 1975. 319 p.

Doehring, Karl. "Local Remedies, Exhaustion of," in Bernhardt (ed.), *EPIL* 1 (1981) 136-40.

Dumbauld, Edward. *Interim Measures of Protection in International Controversies.* The Hague, 1932. 204 p.

Economides, Constantin. "La déclaration de Manille sur le

règlement pacifique des différends internationaux," 28 *AFDI* 613-33 (1982).

Elias, Taslim Olawale (ed.). *New Horizons in International Law.* Dobbs Ferry, NY: Oceana, 1979.

Franck, Thomas M. *The Structure of Impartiality.* New York: Macmillan, 1968. 344 p.

Garner, J. W. "The Geneva Protocol for the Pacific Settlement of International Disputes," 19 *AJIL* 123-32 (1925).

Giustini, Anthony. "Compulsory Adjudication in International Law: The Past, the Present, and the Prospect for the Future," 9 *Fordham ILJ* 223-56 (1986).

Gormley, W. P. "The Procedural Status of the Individual before Supranational Judicial Tribunals," 41 *U Detroit LJ* 282-341 (1984).

Gray, Christine D. *Judicial Remedies in International Law.* New York: Oxford UP, 1987. 272 p.

Guggenheim, Paul. "Les mesures conservatoires dans la procédure arbitrale et judiciaire," 40 *RCADI* 645-764 (1932-II).

_____. "La validité et la nullité des actes internationaux," 74 *RCADI* 191-268 (1949-I).

Guyomar, G. *Le défaut des parties à un différend devant les juridictions internationales.* Paris: Pichon et Durand-Auzias, 1960. 242 p.

Habicht, Max (ed.). *Post-War Treaties for the Pacific Settlement of International Disputes.* Cambridge, MA: Harvard UP, 1931. 1,109 p.

_____. *The Power of the International Judge to Give a Decision "ex aequo et bono."* London: Constable, 1935. 88 p.

Haesler, T. *The Exhaustion of Local Remedies in the Case Law of International Courts and Tribunals.* Leyden: Sijthoff, 1968. 163 p.

Heydte, Baron Friedrich August von der, "General Act for the Pacific Settlement of International Disputes (1928 and 1949)," in Bernhardt (ed.), *EPIL* 1 (1981) 62-5.

_____. "Geneva Protocol for the Pacific Settlement of International Disputes (1924)," in Bernhardt (ed.), *EPIL* 1 (1981) 65-7.

_____. "L'individu et les tribunaux internationaux," 107 *RCADI* 287-359 (1962-III).

Holls, Frederick W. *The Peace Conference at the Hague and Its Bearing on International Law and Policy.* London: Macmillan, 1900. 572 p.

Holton, Thomas. *An International Peace Court: Design for a Move from State Crime toward World Law.* The Hague: Nijhoff, 1970. 109 p.

Hostie, J. "Différends justiciables et non justiciables," 55 *RDILC* 263-81, 568-87 (1928).

Hudson, Manley O. "The Geneva Protocol," 3 *Foreign Affairs* 226-35 (1924).

_____. *International Tribunals: Past and Future.* Washington, DC: Carnegie Endowment and Brookings Institution, 1944. 287 p.

Iaccarino, U. "Della c.d. competenza sulla competenza dei tribunali internazionali," 14 *DI* 357-425 (1960).

International Disputes: The Legal Aspects. A Report of a Study Group of the David Davies Memorial Institute of International Studies. Sir Humphrey Waldock Chairman. London: Europa Publications, 1972. 324 p.

Janis, Mark (ed.). *International Courts for the Twenty-First Century.* The Hague: Nijhoff, 1992. 272 p.

Jenks, C. Wilfred. *The Prospects of International Adjudication.* London: Stevens. Dobbs Ferry, NY: Oceana, 1964. 806 p.

Jennings, Sir Robert. "The Judicial Enforcement of International Obligation," 47 *ZaöRV* 3-16 (1987).

Jessup, Philip C. *The Price of International Justice.* New York and London: Columbia UP, 1971. 82 p.

Katz, Milton. *The Relevance of International Adjudication.* Cambridge: Harvard UP, 1968. 165 p.

Lauterpacht, Elihu. *Aspects of the Administration of International Justice.* Cambridge: Grotius Publications, 1991. 152 p.

_____. "The Development of the Law of International Organization by the Decisions of International Tribunals," 152 *RCADI* 377-478 (1976-IV).

Lauterpacht, Hersch. "La théorie des différends non justiciables en droit international," 34 *RCADI* 493-654 (1930-IV).

Lieblich, William C. "Determination by International Tribunals of the Economic Value of Expropriated Enterprises," 7 *JIArb* 37-76 (1990).

Lillich, Richard B. (ed.). *Fact-Finding before International Tribunals.* Irvington-on-Hudson: Transnational Publishers, 1992, 326 p.

Limburg, "L'autorité de chose jugée des décisions des juridictions internationales," 30 *RCADI* 519-618 (1929-V).

Lowenfeld, Andreas F. *International Litigation and Arbitration* (Casebook). St. Paul, MN: West Publishing Co., 1993. 875 p. With Supplement: *Selected Treaties, Statutes and Rules.* 275 p.

Mani, V. S. *International Adjudication: Procedural Aspects.* The Hague: Nijhoff, 1980. 456 p.

Matscher, Franz. "Standing before International Courts and Tribunals," in Bernhardt (ed.), *EPIL* 1 (1981) 191-6.

Max-Planck Institut für ausländisches öffentliches Recht und Völkerrecht. *Internationale Gerichte und Schiedsgerichte.* Cologne: Heymanns, 1961. 497 p.

McNair, Sir Arnold. *The Place of Law and Tribunals in International Relations.* Manchester: Manchester UP, 1957.

McWhinney, Edward. "Judicial Settlement of Disputes: Jurisdiction and Justiciability," 221 *RCADI* 9-194 (1990-II).

_____. *Judicial Settlement of International Disputes: Jurisdiction, Justiciability and Judicial Law-Making of the Contemporary International Court.* Dordrecht: Nijhoff, 1991. 185 p.

Mendelson, M. H. "Interim Measures of Protection in Cases of Contested Jurisdiction," 46 *BYIL* 259-322 (1972).

Merrills, J. G. *International Dispute Settlement.* Cambridge: Grotius Publications, 1991. 310 p.

Miller, David. H. *The Geneva Protocol.* New York: Macmillan, 1925. 113 p.

Morelli, Gaetano. *Nuovi studi sul processo internazionale.* Milan: Giuffrè, 1972. 173 p.

_____. "La théorie générale du procès international," 61 *RCADI* 253-373 (1937-III).

Mosler, Hermann. "Judgments of International Courts and Tribunals," in Bernhardt (ed.), *EPIL* 1 (1981) 111-18.

_____ & Rudolf Bernhardt (eds.). *Judicial Settlement of International Disputes.* An International Symposium Sponsored by Max Planck Institute for Comparative Public Law and International Law. Berlin, Heidelberg, and New York: Springer Verlag, 1974. 572 p.

Mummery, D. R. "The Content of the Duty to Exhaust Local Judicial Remedies," 58 *AJIL* 389-414 (1964).

Murty, B. S. "Settlement of Disputes," in Max Sørensen (ed.). *Manual of Public International Law.* New York: St. Martin's Press, 1968. Pp. 673-717 (secs. 11.07-11.23).

Nantwi, E. K. *The Enforcement of International Judicial Decisions and Arbitral Awards in Public International Law.* Leyden: Sijthoff, 1966. 209 p.

Niboyet, J.-P. "Le rôle de la justice internationale en droit international privé: Conflit des lois," 40 *RCADI* 153-235 (1932-II).

Noel-Baker, Philip John. *The Geneva Protocol for the Pacific Settlement of International Disputes.* London: King & Son, 1925. 228 p.

Norton, Patrick M. "A Law of the Future or a Law of the Past? Modern Tribunals and the International Law of Expropriation," 85 *AJIL* 474-505 (1991).

Nussbaum, Arthur. *A Concise History of the Law of Nations.* Rev. ed. New York: Macmillan, 1953. 376 p.

Oellers-Frahm, Karin. "Compromis," in Bernhardt (ed.), *EPIL* 1 (1981) 45-7.

_____. *Die einstweilige Anordnung in der internationalen Gerichtsbarkeit.* Berlin, Heidelberg, New York: Springer Verlag, 1975. 168 p.

_____. "Interim Measures of Protection," in Bernhardt (ed.), *EPIL* 1 (1981) 69-72.

_____. "Judicial and Arbitral Decisions: Validity and Nullity," in Bernhardt (ed.), *EPIL* 1 (1981) 118-20.

_____ & Norbert Wühler (compiled). *Dispute Settlement in Public International Law: Text and Materials.* Berlin: Springer Verlag, 1984. 913 p.

Oort, H. *Beweis voor de internationale rechter.* Leyden: Sijthoff, 1966. 279 p.

Prott, Lyndel V. *Der internationale Richter im Spannungsfeld der Rechtskulturen,* Berlin: Duncker & Humblot, 1975. 257 p.

_____. *The Latent Power of Culture and the International Judge.* Abington: Professional Books, 1979. 250 p.

Randolph, Lillian L. *Third-Party Settlement of Disputes in Theory and Practice.* Dobbs Ferry, NY: Oceana, 1973. 335 p.

Reichert, Douglas. "Provisional Remedies in International Litigation: A Comprehensive Bibliography," 19 *ILawyer* 1429-57 (1985).

Reisman, William M. "Enforcement of International Judgments," 63 *AJIL* 1-27 (1969).

_____. *Nullity and Revision: The Review of Enforcement of International Judgments and Awards.* New Haven and London:

Yale UP, 1971. 890 p.

_____. *Systems of Control in International Adjudication and Arbitration. Breakdown and Repair.* Durham, NC: Duke UP, 1992. 184 p.

Salvioli, Gabriele. "Problèmes de procédure dans la jurisprudence internationale," 91 *RCADI* 553-617 (1957-I).

_____. "La responsabilité des Etats et la fixation des dommages et intérêts par les tribunaux internationaux," 28 *RCADI* 231-89 (1929-III).

Sandifer, Durward V. *Evidence before International Tribunals.* Vol. 13 in The Procedural Aspects of International Law Series. Charlottesville, VA: UP of Virginia, rev. ed. 1975. 519 p.

Schachter, Oscar. "Enforcement of International Judicial and Arbitral Decisions," 54 *AJIL* 1-24 (1960).

Schwarzenberger, Georg. "Present-Day Relevance of the Jay Treaty Arbitrations," 53 *Notre Dame Lawyer* 715-33 (1978).

_____. "The Principles of the United Nations in International Judicial Perspective," 30 *YWA* 303-37 (1976).

_____. *William Ladd: An Examination of an American Proposal for an International Equity Tribunal.* London: Constable, 1935. 78 p.

Schwebel, Stephen M. (ed.). *The Effectiveness of International Decisions.* Leyden: Sijthoff, 1971.

Scott, James Brown (ed.). *The Hague Conventions and Declarations of 1899 and 1907.* 2d ed. New York: Oxford UP, 1915. 303 p.

_____ (ed.). *The Hague Peace Conferences of 1899 and 1907.* 2 vols. 1909. Reprinted in 1972.

Séfériadès, Stélio. "Le problème de l'accès des particuliers à des juridictions internationales," 51 *RCADI* 1-120 (1935-I).

Sereni, Angelo Piero. "Les opinions individuelles et dissidentes des juges des tribunaux internationaux," 66 *RGDIP* 819-57 (1964).

Shelton, Dina L. "Judicial Review of State Action by International Courts," 12 *Fordham ILJ* 361-98 (1989).

Shihata, Ibrahim F. I. *The Power of the International Court to Determine Its Own Jurisdiction: Compétence de la Compétence.* The Hague: Nijhoff, 1965. 400 p.

Shinkaretskaya, G. "A Changing Attitude towards International Adjudication in the Soviet Union," 3 *LJIL* 59-66 (1990).

Sohn, Louis B. "Settlement of Disputes Relating to the Interpretation and Application of Treaties," 150 *RCADI* 195-294 (1976-II).

_____ (ed.). *Systematic Survey of Treaties for the Pacific Settlement of Disputes, 1928-1948.* 1948.

Steinberger, Helmut. "Judicial Settlement of International Disputes," in Bernhardt (ed.), *EPIL* 1 (1981) 120-33.

Strupp, Karl. *Das Werk von Locarno: eine völkerrechtlich-politische Studie.* Berlin: de Gruyter, 1926. 179 p.

Summers, L. M. "The Senate and the Arbitration and Adjudication of International Disputes," 3 *ILawyer* 564-92 (1969).

Thirlway, H.W. A. "Preliminary Objections," in Bernhardt (ed.), *EPIL* 1 (1981) 179-83.

_____. "Procedure of International Courts and Tribunals," in Bernhardt (ed.), *EPIL* 1 (1981) 183-7.

_____. "Reciprocity in the Jurisdiction of the International Court," 15 *NYIL* 97-138 (1984).

Tomuschat, Christian. "International Courts and Tribunals," in Bernhardt (ed.), *EPIL* 1 (1981) 92-9.

Ullmann, W. "The Medieval Papal Court as an International Tribunal," 11 *VirJIL* 356-71 (1971).

UN Office of Legal Affairs. Codification Division. *Handbook on Peaceful Settlement of Disputes between States.* New York: UN, 1992. 229 p.

Verdross, Alfred von. "Les principes généraux de droit dans la jurisprudence internationale," 52 *RCADI* 191-251 (1935-II).

Verzijl, J. H. W. "La validité et la nullité des actes juridiques internationaux," 15 *Revue de droit international* (de La Pradelle) 284-339 (1935).

Visscher, Charles De. *De l'équité dans le règlement arbitral ou judiciaire des litiges de droit international public.* Paris: Pedone, 1973. 118 p.

_____. *Problèmes de l'interprétation judiciaire en droit international public.* Paris: Pedone, 1963. 269 p.

Wegen, Gerhard. *Vergleich und Klagerücknahme im internationalen Prozess.* Berlin: Duncker & Humblot, 1987. 484 p.

Wehberg, Hans. *Das Problem eines internationalen Staatengerichts-hofes.* Munich, Leipzig, 1912. 243 p.

_____. *The Problem of an International Court of Justice.* Translated from German by Charles G. Fenwick. Oxford: Clarendon, 1918.

_____. "Le Protocole de Genève," 7 *RCADI* 1-150 (1925-I).

White, Gillian M. *The Use of Experts by International Tribunals.*

Procedural Aspects of International Law Series No. 4. Syracuse, NY: Syracuse UP, 1965. 259 p.

Witenberg, Joseph C. *L'organisation judiciaire, la procédure et les sentences internationales.* Paris: Pedone, 1937. 436 p.

———. "La recevabilité des réclamations devant les juridictions internationales," 41 *RCADI* 1-136 (1932-III).

———. "La théorie des preuves devant les juridictions internationales," 56 *RCADI* 1-105 (1936-II).

4. PERMANENT COURT OF INTERNATIONAL JUSTICE

A. Collections of Documents

(1) *Official:*
Series A. Collection of Judgments - Recueil des arrêts (Nos. 1-25) (through 1930).
Series B. Collection of Advisory Opinions - Recueil des avis consultatifs (Nos. 1-18) (through 1930).
Series A/B. Judgments, Orders and Advisory Opinions - Arrêts, ordonnances et avis consultatifs (Nos. 40-80) (starting in 1931).
Series C. Acts and Documents Relating to Judgments and Advisory Opinions - Actes et documents relatifs aux arrêts et avis (Nos. 1-19) (through 1930).
Series C. Pleadings, Oral Statements and Documents - Plaidoiries, exposés oraux et documents (Nos. 52-88) (starting in 1931).
Series D. Acts and Documents Concerning the Organization of the Court - Actes et documents relatifs à l'organisation de la Cour (Nos. 1-6).
Series E. Annual Reports - Rapports annuels (Nos. 1-16).
Series F. General Indexes - Index généraux (Nos. 1-4).

(2) *Unofficial:*
Fontes Iuris Gentium. Series A, Sec. I:
Handbuch der Entscheidungen des Ständigen Internationalen Gerichtshofs - Répertoire des Décisions de la Cour Permanente de Justice Internationale - Digest of the Decisions of the Permanent Court of International Justice. Victor Bruns (ed.). Vol. 1, *1922-1930* (1931); Vol. 2, *1931-1934* (1935); Vol. 4, *1935-1940* (1964).
Guggenheim, Paul (ed.). *Répertoire des décisions et des documents de la procédure écrite et orale de la Cour permanente de Justice internationale et de la Cour internationale de Justice 1922-1945.* Serie 1, *Cour permanente de Justice internationale:* Vol. 1, *Droit international et droit interne;* Vol. 2, *Les sources du droit*

international; Vol. 3, *Les sujets du droit international.* Geneva: Librairie Droz, 1961, 1967, 1973.

Hambro, Edvard (ed.). *The Case Law of the International Court - A Répertoire of the Judgments, Advisory Opinions and Orders of the Permanent Court of International Justice and of the International Court of Justice.* Vol. 1. *1923-1952.* 1952.

Hudson, Manley O. (ed.). *World Court Reports - A Collection of the Judgments, Orders and Opinions of the Permanent Court of International Justice 1922-1942.* 4 vols. Vol. 1, *1922-1926* (1934); Vol. 2, *1927-1932* (1935); Vol. 3, *1932-1935* (1938); Vol. 4, *1936-1942* (1943). New York: Carnegie Endowment, 1934-1943 (reprinted by Oceana).

Marek, Krystyna (ed.). *Précis de la jurisprudence de la Cour Internationale - A Digest of the Decisions of the International Court.* Vol. 1, *Cour permanente de Justice Internationale - Permanent Court of International Justice.* The Hague: Nijhoff, 1974. 1,193 p.

Verzijl, J. H. W. *The Jurisprudence of the World Court: A Case by Case Commentary.* Vol. 1, *The Permanent Court of International Justice, 1922-1940.* Leyden: Sijthoff, 1965. 600 p.

B. Literature

(1) *In General:*

Baker, P. J. "The Obligatory Jurisdiction of the Permanent Court of International Justice," 6 *BYIL* 68-102 (1925).

Beuve-Méry, M. *La compétence consultative de la Cour permanente de Justice internationale.* Paris: Pedone, 1926. 158 p.

Bonvalot, C. *Les avis consultatifs de la Cour permanente de Justice internationale.* Paris: University of Paris, Thesis, 1925.

Bruns, Victor. "La Cour permanente de Justice internationale, son organisation et sa compétence," 62 *RCADI* 547-671 (1937-IV).

Bustamante y Sirvén, Antonio Sánchez. *The World Court* (translated from Spanish by Elizabeth F. Read). New York: Macmillan, 1922. 379 p.

Coloyanni, Mégalos. "L'organisation de la Cour permanente de Justice et son avenir," 38 *RCADI* 651-786 (1931-IV).

Dauvergne, C. *La fonction consultative de la Cour permanente de Justice internationale.* Montpellier: University of Montpellier, Thesis, 1925.

Dunne, Michael. *The United States and the World Court, 1920-1935.* New York: St. Martin's Press, 1988. 306 p.

Fachiri, A. P. *The Permanent Court of International Justice: Its Constitution, Procedure and Work.* 2d ed. London: Oxford UP, 1932. 416 p.

Feinberg, Nathan. "La juridiction et la jurisprudence de la Cour permanente de Justice internationale en matière de mandats et de minorités," 59 *RCADI* 587-708 (1937-I).

Goodrich, M. "The Nature of the Advisory Opinions of the Permanent Court of International Justice," 32 *AJIL* 738-58 (1938).

Habicht, Max. "Le pouvoir du juge international de statuer ex aequo et bono," 49 *RCADI* 277-371 (1934-III).

Hudson, Manley O. "Les avis consultatifs de la Cour permanente de Justice internationale," 8 *RCADI* 341-412 (1925-II).

_____. *The Permanent Court of International Justice, 1920-1942: A Treatise.* New York: Macmillan, rev. ed. 1943. Reprinted: New York: Garland, 1972. 807 p.

Jessup, Philip C. "The United States and the Permanent Court of International Justice. The Acceptance of the Senate Reservation," *International Conciliation,* No. 273 (1931) 591-670.

Lloyd, Lorna. "A Springboard for the Future: A Historical Examination of Britain's Role in Shaping the Optional Clause of the Permanent Court of International Justice," 79 *AJIL* 28-51 (1985).

Négulesco, Démètre. "L'évolution de la procédure des avis consultatifs de la Cour permanente de Justice internationale," 57 *RCADI* 1-96 (1936-III).

Niemeyer, Hans Gerd. *Einstweilige Verfügungen des Weltgerichtshofes, ihr Wesen und ihre Grenzen.* Leipzig: Noske, 1932. 108 p.

Permanent Court of International Justice. *Bibliographical List of Official and Unofficial Publications Concerning the Permanent Court of International Justice.* Series E, No. 12 (1936) 237-330.

Pessoa, Epitácio. *Côrte Permanente de Justiça Internacional.* Rio de Janeiro, 1960. 276 p.

Rundstein, Simon. "La Cour permanente de Justice internationale comme instance de recours," 43 *RCADI* 1-113 (1933-I).

Salvioli, Gabriele. *La Corte permanente di giustizia internazionale.* Rome: Associazione italiana per la Società delle Nazioni, 1928. 55 p.

_____. "La jurisprudence de la Cour permanente de Justice internationale," 12 *RCADI* 1-114 (1926-II).

Scerni, Mario. "La procédure de la Cour permanente de Justice internationale," 65 *RCADI* 561-681 (1938-III).

Schlochauer, Hans-Jürgen, "Permanent Court of International Justice," in Bernhardt (ed.), *EPIL* 1 (1981) 163-79.

Scott, James Brown. *The Project of a Permanent Court of International Justice and Resolutions of the Advisory Committee of Jurists.* Washington, DC: The Endowment, 1920. 235 p.

Strupp, Karl. "Le droit du juge international de statuer selon l'équité," 33 *RCADI* 351-481 (1930-III).

Thèvenaz, H. *Les compromis d'arbitrage devant la Cour permanente de Justice internationale.* Neuchâtel, 1938. 110 p.

Visscher, Charles De. "Les avis consultatifs de la Cour permanente de Justice internationale," 26 *RCADI* 1-76 (1929-I).

(2) *Individual Judgments:*
Baxter, Richard R. "Passage of Ships through International Waterways in Time of War," 31 *BYIL* 187-216 (1954).

Berge, G. W. "The Case of the S.S. Lotus," 26 *Michigan Law Review* 362-82 (1928).

Brierly, J.L. "The Lotus Case," 44 *LQR* 154-63 (1928).

Bülck, Hartwig. "Société Commerciale de Belgique Case," in Bernhardt (ed.), *EPIL* 2 (1981) 258-60.

Doehring, Karl. "Mavrommatis Concessions Cases," in Bernhardt (ed.), *EPIL* 2 (1981) 182-5.

Dolzer, Rudolf. "Chinn case," in Bernhardt (ed.), *EPIL* 2 (1981) 52-3.

Fachiri, A. P. "The Case of the S.S. Lotus," 9 *BYIL* 131-44 (1932).

Götz, Volkmar. "Serbian Loans Case," in Bernhardt (ed.), *EPIL* 2 (1981) 256-7.

Herndl, Kurt. "Borchgrave Case," in Bernhardt (ed.), *EPIL* 2 (1981) 37-9.

_____. "The Lotus," in Bernhardt (ed.), *EPIL* 2 (1981) 173-77.

_____. "Meuse, Diversion of Water Case," in Bernhardt (ed.), *EPIL* 2 (1981) 187-9.

_____. "Pajzs, Czáky, Esterházy Case," in Bernhardt (ed.), *EPIL* 2 (1981) 221-3.

Hofmann, Rainer, "Appeals from Judgments of the Hungaro-Czechoslovak Mixed Arbitral Tribunal (Cases)," in Bernhardt (ed.), *EPIL* 2 (1981) 18-9.

_____. "Electricity Company of Sofia Case," in Bernhardt (ed.), *EPIL* 2 (1981) 86-8.

Hyde, Charles Cheney. "The Case Concerning the Legal Status of Greenland," 27 *AJIL* 732-8 (1933).

Katte, Christoph von. "Brazilian Loans Case," in Bernhardt (ed.), *EPIL* 2 (1981) 39-40.

Lamers, Karl. "Interpretation of Memel Territory Statute Case," in Bernhardt (ed.), *EPIL* 2 (1981) 147-8.

_____. "Jurisdiction of the International Commission of the Oder Case," in Bernhardt (ed.), *EPIL* 2 (1981) 163-4.

_____. "Losinger Dispute (Orders)," in Bernhardt (ed.), *EPIL* 2 (1981) 172-3.

_____. "Neuilly Peace Treaty Cases," in Bernhardt (ed.), *EPIL* 2 (1981) 200-1.

_____. "Prince von Pless Administration (Orders)," in Bernhardt (ed.), *EPIL* 2 (1981) 236-7.

Martens, Ernst K. "Sovereignty over Certain Frontier Land Case (Belgium/Netherlands)," in Bernhardt (ed.), *EPIL* 2 (1981) 270-1.

Mikos, S. *Wolne Miasto Gdańsk i Liga Narodów* [Free City of Danzig and the League of Nations]. Warsaw, 1959.

Münch, Ingo von. "Eastern Greenland Case," in Bernhardt (ed.), *EPIL* 2 (1981) 81-4.

_____. "The Wimbledon," in Bernhardt (ed.), *EPIL* 2 (1981) 293-6.

Portail, R. *L'affaire de Lotus*. Paris: University of Paris, Thesis, 1928.

Prudhomme, A. "Les emprunts des Etats brésilien et serbe devant la Cour permanente de Justice internationale de La Haye," 56 *JDI* 837-95 (1929).

Riedel, Eibe H. "Lighthouses Cases," in Bernhardt (ed.), *EPIL* 2 (1981) 171-2.

_____. "Panevezys Saldutiskis Railway Case," in Bernhardt (ed.), *EPIL* 2 (1981) 224-5.

Schulte-Braucks, Antonella, "Phosphates in Morocco Case," in Bernhardt (ed.), *EPIL* 2 (1981) 225-7.

Seidl-Hohenveldern, Ignaz. "German Interests in Polish Upper Silesia Cases," in Bernhardt (ed.), *EPIL* 2 (1981) 111-4.

Svarlien, Oscar. *The Eastern Greenland Case in Historical Perspective*. Gainesville: U of Florida P, 1964. 74 p.

Verzijl, J. H. W. "L'affaire du Lotus devant la Cour permanente de Justice internationale," 55 *RDILC* 1-32 (1928).

Weber, Ludwig. "Free Zones of Upper Savoy and Gex Case," in Bernhardt (ed.), *EPIL* 2 (1981) 104-6.

Weil, Christof. "German Minorities in Poland, Cases Concerning the,"in Bernhardt (ed.), *EPIL* 2 (1981) 114-6.

_____. "Polish Agrarian Reform (Orders)," in Bernhardt (ed.), *EPIL* 2 (1981) 230-1.

(3) *Individual Advisory Opinions:*

Benedek, Wolfgang. "Exchange of Greek and Turkish Populations (Advisory Opinion)," in Bernhardt (ed.), *EPIL* 2 (1981) 91-2.

_____. "Nationality Decrees in Tunis and Morocco (Advisory Opinion)," in Bernhardt (ed.), *EPIL* 2 (1981) 197-8.

Beyerlin, Ulrich. "Railway Traffic between Lithuania and Poland (Advisory Opinion)," in Bernhardt (ed.), *EPIL* 2 (1981) 239-40.

Bruha, Thomas. "Competence of ILO Concerning Personal Work of the Employer (Advisory Opinion)," in Bernhardt (ed.), *EPIL* 2 (1981) 55-7.

_____. "Danzig and ILO (Advisory Opinion)," in Bernhardt (ed.), *EPIL* 2 (1981) 71-2.

_____. "Designation of Workers' Delegate at ILO Conference (Advisory Opinion)," in Bernhardt (ed.), *EPIL* 2 (1981) 76-7.

Gregory, C. N. "An Important Decision by the Permanent Court of International Justice," 17 *AJIL* 298-307 (1923) (On Nationality decrees in Tunis and Morocco).

Hajnal, H. "La Commission européenne du Danube et le dernier avis consultatif de la Cour," 55 *RDILC* 588-645 (1928).

Herndl, Kurt. "Eastern Carelia (Request for Advisory Opinion)," in Bernhardt (ed.), *EPIL* 2 (1981) 79-81.

Hilf, Meinhard. "Interpretation of Convention Concerning Employment of Women during the Night (Advisory Opinion)," in Bernhardt (ed.), *EPIL* 2 (1981) 144-6.

Kalijarvi, T. "The Question of East Carelia," 18 *AJIL* 93-8 (1924).

Katte, Christoph von. "Greco-Bugarian Communities (Advisory Opinion)," in Bernhardt (ed.), *EPIL* 2 (1981) 122-3.

_____. "Interpretation of Greco-Bulgarian Agreement of 1927 (Advisory Opinion)," in Bernhardt (ed.), *EPIL* 2 (1981) 146.

_____. "Interpretation of Greco-Turkish Agreement of 1926

(Advisory Opinion)," in Bernhardt (ed.), *EPIL* 2 (1981) 146.

Kopelmanas, Lazare. "Compatibilité de certains décrets-lois dantzikois avec la Constitution de la ville libre," 43 *RGDIP* 437-83 (1936).

La Pradelle, Paul de Geouffre de. "Les décrets du 8 novembre 1921 sur la nationalité d'origine en Tunisie et en Maroc (zone française) devant la Cour permanente de Justice internationale," 18 *RDIP* 1-287 (1922-23).

Le Fur, Louis Erasme. "Le litige sur la compétence des tribunaux dantsikois," 35 *RGDIP* 268-84 (1928).

Schweisfurth, Theodor. "Jurisdiction of the Courts of Danzig (Advisory Opinion)," in Bernhardt (ed.), *EPIL* 2 (1981) 159-60.

_____. "Polish Nationals in Danzig (Advisory Opinion)," in Bernhardt (ed.), *EPIL* 2 (1981) 231-2.

_____. "Polish Postal Service in Danzig (Advisory Opinion)," in Bernhardt (ed.), *EPIL* 2 (1981) 232-3.

_____. "Polish War Vessels in the Port of Danzig (Advisory Opinion)," in Bernhardt (ed.), *EPIL* 2 (1981) 233-4.

Vierheilig, Monika. "Customs Régime between Germany and Austria (Advisory Opinion)," in Bernhardt (ed.), *EPIL* 2 (1981) 69-71.

Weil, Christof. "Acquisition of Polish Nationality (Advisory Opinion)," in Bernhardt (ed.), *EPIL* 2 (1981) 2.

_____. "German Settlers in Poland (Advisory Opinion)," in Bernhardt (ed.), *EPIL* 2 (1981) 118.

_____. "Minorities in Upper Silesia (Advisory Opinion)," in Bernhardt (ed.), *EPIL* 2 (1981) 189-91.

Wühler, Norbert. "Jurisdiction of the European Commission of the Danube (Advisory Opinion)," in Bernhardt (ed.), *EPIL* 2 (1981) 160-1.

5. INTERNATIONAL COURT OF JUSTICE

A. Collections of Documents

(1) *Official:*

Reports of Judgments, Advisory Opinions and Orders - Recueil des arrêts, avis consultatifs et ordonnances. 1947/48 -----.

Pleadings, Oral Arguments, Documents - Mémoires, plaidoiries et documents. 1948 -----.

Acts and Documents Concerning the Organization of the Court - Actes et documents relatifs à l'organisation de la Cour: Charter of the United Nations, Statute and Rules of Court and Other Documents. Nos. 1-4. 1947-1978.

(2) *Unofficial:*

Fontes Iuris Gentium. Series A, Sec. I, Vols. 5-7.

Digest of the Decisions of the International Court of Justice - Répertoire des Décisions de la Cour internationale de Justice-Handbuch der Entscheidungen des Internationalen Gerichtshofs. Rudolf Bernhardt et al. (eds.), Max Planck Institute for Comparative Public Law and International Law. Vol. 5, *1947-1958* (1961); Vol. 6, *1959-1975* (1978); Vol. 7, *1976-1985* (1990). Berlin, Heidelberg, and New York: Springer Verlag.

Hambro, Edvard (ed.). *The Case Law of the International Court - A Répertoire of the Judgments, Advisory Opinions and Orders of the International Court of Justice.* Vol. 1 (incl. the PCIJ) *1923-1952* (1952); Vol. 2 *1952-1958* (1960); Vol. 3, *Individual and Dissenting Opinions 1947-1958* (in 2 parts, 1963); Vol. 4, *1959-1963* (in 2 parts, 1966). Vols. 5-8 edited by Edvard Hambro & Arthur W. Rovine: Vol. 5, *1964-1966* (in 2 parts, 1968); vol. 6, *1967-1970* (in 2 parts, 1972); Vol. 7. *1971-1972* (in 2 parts, 1974); Vol. 8, *1973-1974* (1976). Vols. 4-8 include dissenting and separate opinions. Vol. 4 has also Part 3 (C) which includes J. Douma, *Bibliography of the International Court of Justice Including the Permanent Court, 1918-1964. (See* 5B (1)). All volumes published in Leyden: Sijthoff,

1952-1976.

Marek, Krystyna. *A Digest of Decisions of the International Court/Précis de la Jurisprudence de la Cour internationale.* Dordrecht: Nijhoff, 1978. 2d vol. (Parts 1 & 2) 716 & 1423 p.

Rosenne, Shabtai. *Documents on the International Court of Justice.* Leyden: Sijthoff, 2d ed. 1979.

Syatauw, J. J. G. *Decisions of the International Court of Justice: A Digest.* Leyden: Sijthoff, 2d ed. 1969.

Verzijl, J. H. W. *The Jurisprudence of the World Court: A Case by Case Commentary.* Vol. 2: *The International Court of Justice 1947-1965.* Leyden: Sijthoff, 1967. 594 p. (Includes Index to vols. 1 and 2.)

B. Literature

(1) *In General*

Abi-Saab, Georges. *Les Exceptions préliminaires dans la procédure de la Cour Internationale. Etude des notions fondamentales de procédure et des moyens de leur mise en oeuvre.* Paris: Pedone, 1967. 280 p.

Anand, Ram Prakash. *Compulsory Jurisdiction of the International Court of Justice.* New York: Asia Publishing House, 1962. 342 p.

Arend, Anthony Clark (ed.). *The United States and the Compulsory Jurisdiction of the International Court of Justice.* Lanham, MD: UP of America, 1986. 250 p.

Audéoud, Olivier. "La Cour internationale de justice et le règlement des différends au sein des organisations internationales," 81 *RGDIP* 945-1006 (1977).

Bastid, Suzanne. "Les problèmes territoriaux dans la jurisprudence de la Cour Internationale de Justice," 107 *RCADI* 361-495 (1962-III).

Bloed, Arie & P. van Dijk (eds.). *Forty Years International Court of Justice: Jurisdiction, Equity and Equality.* Utrecht: Europa Instituut, 1988. 177 p.

Bosco, Giorgio. *La soluzione delle controversie giuridiche internazionali nel quadro delle Nazioni Unite.* Padova: Cedam, 1989. 163 p.

Briggs, Herbert. "Reservations to the Acceptance of Compulsory Jurisdiction of the International Court of Justice," 93 *RCADI* 223-367 (1958-I).

Brown, Colton. "Enforcement of ICJ Decisions in United States Courts," 11 *MdJIL&T* 73-92 (1987).

Casado Raigón, Rafael. *La jurisdicción contenciosa de la Corte Internacional de Justicia: estudio de las reglas de competencia.* Córdoba: Servicio de Publ. de la Universidad de Córdoba, 1987. 190 p.

Cellamare, Giovanni. *Le forme di intervento nel processo dinanzi alla Corte Internazionale di Giustizia.* Bari: Cacucci Editore, 1991. 316 p.

Charney, Jonathan I. "Compromissory Clauses and the Jurisdiction of the International Court of Justice," 81 *AJIL* 855-87 (1987).

Chinkin, C. M. "Third-Party Intervention before the International Court of Justice," 80 *AJIL* 495-531 (1986).

Crawford, J. "The Legal Effect of Automatic Reservations to the Jurisdiction of the International Court," 50 *BYIL* 63-86 (1979).

Crockett, G. H. "The Effects of Interim Measures of Protection in the International Court of Justice," 7 *CalifWILJ* 348-84 (1977).

D'Amato, Anthony. "The United States Should Accept, by a New Declaration, the General Compulsory Jurisdiction of the World Court," 80 *AJIL* 331-6 (1986).

Damrosch, Lori Fisler (ed.). *The International Court of Justice at a Crossroads.* Ardsley-on-Hudson: Transnational Publishers, 1987. 539 p.

Davi, Angelo. *L'intervento davanti alla Corte Internazionale di Giustizia.* Naples: Casa Editrice Jovene, 1984. 292 p.

Dillard, Hardy Cross. "The World Court: Reflections of a Professor Turned Judge," 27 *American University Law Review* 205-50 (1978).

Dolzer, Rudolf. "Connally Reservation," in Bernhardt (ed.), *EPIL* 1 (1981) 55-7.

Donner, Ruth. *International Adjudication: Using the International Court of Justice, with Special Reference to Finland.* Helsinki: Suomalainen Tiedeakatemia, 1988. 116 p.

Douma, J. *Bibliography of the International Court of Justice Including the Permanent Court, 1918-1964.* Leyden: Sijthoff, 1966. 387 p. (Vol. IV-C of Edvard Hambro (ed.) *The Case Law of the International Court*) (*see* 5A (2)).

Dubisson, M. *La Cour Internationale de Justice.* Paris: Pichon et Durand-Anzias, 1964. 470 p.

Eisemann, P. M. "Les effets de la non comparaison devant la Cour internationale de Justice," 19 *AFDI* 351-75 (1973).

_____, V. Coussirat-Coustère & P. Hur. *Petit Manuel de la Jurisprudence de la Cour Internationale de Justice.* 2d ed. Paris: Pedone, 1980.

Elias, Taslim O. *The International Court of Justice and Some Contemporary Problems: Essays on International Law.* The Hague: Nijhoff, 1983. 374 p.

_____. "The Role of the International Court of Justice in Africa," 1 *AJICL-RADIC* 1-12 (1989).

_____. *United Nations Charter and the World Court.* Lagos: Nigerian Institute of Advanced Legal Studies, 1989. 243 p.

Elkind, Jerome B. "The Duty to Appear before the International Court of Justice," 37 *ICLQ* 674-81 (1988).

_____. *Interim Protection: A Functional Approach.* The Hague: Nijhoff, 1981. 287 p.

_____. *Non-Appearance before the International Court of Justice: Functional and Comparative Analysis.* Dordrecht: Nijhoff, 1984. 233 p.

Elsen, Theodoor J. *Litispendence between the International Court of Justice and the Security Council.* The Hague: T. M. C. Asser Instituut, 1986. 125 p.

Evensen, Jens. "The International Court of Justice Main Characteristics and Its Contribution to the Development of the Modern Law of Nations," 57 *NordJIL* 3-64 (1988).

Evgeneva, E.& F. Kozhevnikov. "Rol' Mezhdunarodnovo Suda OON v mirnom uregulirovanii sporov," [The Role of the UN International Court of Justice in the pacific settlement of disputes] *SovGP* (No. 10) 108-115 (1986).

Falk, Richard. *Reviving the World Court.* Charlottesville, VA: UP of Virginia, 1986. 197 p.

Fitzmaurice, Sir Gerald. *The Law and Procedure of the International Court of Justice.* 2 vols. Cambridge: Grotius Publications, 1986. 860 p.

_____. "The Problem of the 'Non-Appearing' Defendant Government," 51 *BYIL* 89-122 (1980).

Fleming, Denna Frank. *The United States and the World Court 1920-1961.* Rev. ed. New York: Russell & Russell, 1968. 223 p.

Franck, Thomas. *Judging the World Court.* New York: Twentieth Century Fund, 1986.

Fritzemeyer, Wolfgang. *Die Intervention vor dem Internationalen Gerichtshof.* Baden-Baden: Nomos Verlagsgesellschaft, 1984. 216 p.

Gamble, John King & Dana D. Fischer. *The International Court of Justice: An Analysis of a Failure.* Lexington, MA: Lexington Books, D.C. Heath, 1976. 157 p.

_____. "The International Court of Justice: A Test of Suggested Reforms," 11 *ILawyer* 163-78 (1977).

García Arias D., Luis. *Balance y perspectivas del Tribunal Internacional de Justicia.* Madrid: Real Academia de Jurisprudencia, 1972. 93 p.

Goldie, L. F. E. "The Connally Reservation: A Shield for An Adversary," 9 *University of California Los Angeles Law Review* 277-359 (1962).

Goldsworthy, Peter J. "Interim Measures of Protection in the International Court of Justice," 68 *AJIL* 258-77 (1974).

Gordon, Edward. "Observation on the Independence and Impartiality of the Members of the International Court of Justice," 2 *ConnJIL* 397-426 (1987).

_____. "The World Court and the Interpretation of Constitutive Treaties," 59 *AJIL* 794-833 (1965).

Greig, D. W. "The Balancing of Interests and the Granting of Interim Protection by the International Court," 11 *Australian YIL* 108-40 (1991).

_____. "Third Party Rights and Intervention before the International Court," 32 *VirJIL* 285-376 (1992).

Grisel, Etienne. *Les Exceptions d'incompétence et d'irrecevabilité dans la procédure de la Cour Internationale de Justice.* Bern: Herbert Lang, 1968. 241 p.

Gross, Leo (ed.). *The Future of the International Court of Justice.* 2 vols. Dobbs Ferry, NY: Oceana, 1976. 862 p.

_____. "The International Court of Justice and the United Nations," 120 *RCADI* 313-440 (1967-I).

_____. "The International Court of Justice: Consideration of Requirements for Enhancing Its Rôle in the International Legal Order," 65 *AJIL* 253-326 (1971).

_____. "Review of the Rôle of the International Court of Justice," 66 *AJIL* 479-90 (1972).

_____. "Some Observations on the International Court of Justice," 56

AJIL 33-62 (1962).

———. "The Time Element in the Contentious Proceedings in the International Court of Justice," 63 *AJIL* 74-85 (1969).

———. "Underutilization of the International Court of Justice," 27 *Harvard ILJ* 571-97 (1986).

Guyomar, Geneviève. *Commentaire du Règlement de la Cour Internationale de Justice: Interprétation et pratique.* 2d ed. Paris: Pedone, 1983. 760 p.

Hakenberg, Michael. "Die Rechtsprechung des Internationalen Gerichtshofes in den Jahren 1985 und 1986," 30 *GYIL* 276-314 (1987).

Hambro, Edvard. "Dissenting and Individual Opinions in the International Court of Justice," 17 *ZaöRV* 229-48 (1956).

———. "The Jurisdiction of the International Court of Justice," 76 *RCADI* 121-215 (1950-I).

———. "Les opinions individuelles et dissidentes des membres de la Cour internationale de Justice," 34 *NordTIR* 181-199 (1964).

———. "Some Observations on the Compulsory Jurisdiction of the International Court of Justice," 25 *BYIL* 133-57 (1948).

Hensley, Thomas R. "Bloc Voting on the International Court of Justice," 22 *Journal of Conflict Resolution* 39-60 (1978).

Highet, Keith. "Winning and Losing: The Commitment of the United States to the International Court of Justice - What Was It, What Is It, and Where Has It Gone?" 1 *Transnational Law & Contemporary Problems* 157-200 (1991).

Hussain, Ijaz. *Dissenting and Separate Opinions of the World Court.* Dordrecht: Nijhoff, 1984. 335 p.

———. "Sir Zafrulla Khan - The Silent Judge," 23 *AVR* 478-92 (1985).

International Court of Justice, *The International Court of Justice.* 2d ed. The Hague: ICJ, 1979. 112 p.

———. *Bibliography of the International Court of Justice.* (Appears periodically. Latest No. 41, 1990.)

———. "Resolution Containing Revision of Internal Judicial Practice of the Court, 12 April 1976," *reprinted* in 15 *ILM* 950-2 (1976).

———. *Rules of Court,* in ICJ, *Acts and Documents Concerning the Organization of the Court,* No. 4 (1978). *Reprinted* in 17 *ILM* 1286-1304 (1978) and 73 *AJIL* 748-82 (1979).

———. *Summary of Judgments, Advisory Opinions and Orders of the International Court of Justice.* 1992. 227 p.

_____. *Yearbook.* Annual. Latest issue: *Yearbook 1989-1990,* No. 44. 203 p. The Hague: ICJ, 1990.

Isaïa, H. "Les opinions dissidentes des juges socialistes dans la jurisprudence de la Cour internationale de Justice," 79 *RGDIP* 657-718 (1975).

Istituto di Diritto Internazionale. *Comunicazioni e Studi.* 1-1082 (1975) (Issue devoted to the ICJ, several contributors).

Jennings, Sir Robert Y. "The Internal Judicial Practice of the International Court of Justice," 59 *BYIL* 31-47 (1988).

_____. "Recent Cases on 'Automatic' Reservations to the Optional Clause," 7 *ICLQ* 349-66 (1958).

Jessup, Philip C. "The Development of a United States Approach toward the International Court of Justice," 5 *VandJTransnL* 1-46 (1971).

Jhabvala, Farrokh. "Declarations by Judges of the International Court of Justice," 72 *AJIL* 830-55 (1978).

_____. "The Scope of Individual Opinions in the World Court," 13 *NYIL* 33-59 (1982).

Jiménez de Aréchaga, Eduardo. "The Amendments to the Rules of Procedure of the International Court of Justice," 67 *AJIL* 1-22 (1973).

_____. "The Work and the Jurisprudence of the International Court of Justice 1947-1986," 58 *BYIL* 1-38 (1987).

Kebbon, Niklas. "The World Court's Compulsory Jurisdiction under the Optional Clause - Past, Present and Future," 58 *NordJIL* 257-86 (1989).

Kelly, J. Patrick. "The Changing Process of International Law and the Role of the World Court," 11 *MichJIL* 129-66 (1989).

_____. "The International Court of Justice: Crisis and Reformation," 12 *Yale JIL* 342-74 (1987).

Kerno Ivan S. "L'organisation des Nations Unies et la Cour internationale de Justice," 78 *RCADI* 507-74 (1951-I).

Kolb, C. E. M. "The Jurisprudence of Judge Hardy Cross Dillard," 11 *VandJTransnL* 609-52 (1978).

Lachaume, J. F. "Le juge 'ad hoc'" 70 *RGDIP* 265-358 (1966).

Lachs, Manfred. "Some Reflections on the Contribution of the International Court of Justice to the Development of International Law," 10 *SyrJIL&Com* 239-78 (1983).

_____. "Thoughts on the Recent Jurisprudence of the International

Court of Justice," 4 *Emory ILR* 77-94 (1990).

Lagoni, Rainer. "Die Rechtsprechung des Internationalen Gerichtshofes in den Jahren 1981 und 1982," 25 *GYIL* 585-608 (1982).

Lamm, Vanda. "Some Remarks about Non-Appearance before the International Court of Justice," 3 *Questions of International Law* 111-31 (1986).

Larson, A. "The Facts, the Law, and the Connally Amendment," *Duke Law Journal* 74-119 (1961).

Lauterpacht, Sir Hersch. *The Development of International Law by the International Court.* Cambridge: Grotius Publications, 1960. 541 p. (reprinted in 1982).

Lawson, R. C. "The Problem of the Compulsory Jurisdiction of the World Court," 46 *AJIL* 219-38 (1952).

Leonhard, A. T. "Regional Particularism: The Views of the Latin American Judges on the International Court of Justice," 22 *University of Miami Law Review* 674-85 (1968).

Liacouras, P. J. *The International Court of Justice.* Durham, NC: Duke UP, 1962. 2 vols.

Lillich, Richard B. & G. Edward White. "The Deliberative Process of the International Court of Justice: A Preliminary Critique and Some Possible Reforms," 70 *AJIL* 28-40 (1976).

Lissitzyn, Oliver J. *The International Court of Justice: Its Role in the Maintenance of International Peace and Security.* New York: Carnegie Endowment, 1951.

Luth, Robert E II. "Perspectives on the World Court, the United States, and International Dispute Resolution in a Changing World," 25 *ILawyer* 675-711 (1991).

Mack, T. C. "Polemic in the International Court of Justice," 3 *SyrJIL&Com* 183-203 (1975).

Magiera, Siegfried. "Die Rechtsprechung des Internationalen Gerichtshofes," 19 *GYIL* 443-54 (1976).

_____. "Die Rechtsprechung des Internationalen Gerichtshofes in den Jahren 1977 und 1978," 22 *GYIL* 403-13 (1979).

Malintoppi, Antonio. *Plaidoiries davanti alla Corte internazionale di Giustizia.* Milano: Giuffrè, 1989. 413 p.

Mbaye, Keba. "L'intérêt pour agir devant la Cour internationale de Justice," 209 *RCADI* 223-346 (1988-II).

McWhinney, Edward. "Contemporary Divergences in National

Attitudes to the International Court of Justice," 27 *CanYIL* 319-28 (1989).

_____. *The International Court of Justice and the Western Tradition of International Law* (The Paul Martin Lectures in International Relations and Law). Dordrecht: Nijhoff, 1987. 158 p.

_____. "Law, Politics and 'Regionalism' in the Nomination and Election of World Court Judges," 13 *SyrJIL&Com* 1-27 (1986).

_____. "Western and Non-Western Legal Cultures and the International Court of Justice," 65 *Washington University Law Quarterly* 873-908 (1987).

_____. *The World Court and the Contemporary International Law-Making Process*. Alphen aan den Rijn: Sijthoff & Nordhoff, 1979. 219 p.

Mendelson, M. H. "Interim Measures of Protection in Cases of Contested Jurisdiction," 46 *BYIL* 259-322 (1975).

Merrills, J. G. "Interim Measures of Protection and the Substantive Jurisdiction of the International Court of Justice," 36 *CambLJ* 86-109 (1977).

_____. "The International Court of Justice and the General Act of 1928," 39 *CambLJ* 137-171 (1980).

_____. "The Optional Clause Today," 50 *BYIL* 87-116 (1979).

_____. "Sir Gerald Fitzmaurice's Contribution to the Jurisprudence of the International Court of Justice," 48 *BYIL* 183-240 (1978).

Meyer, Lukas H. "The Ad Hoc Chambers: Perspectives of the Parties and the Court," 27 *AVR* 413-41 (1989).

Morelli, Gaetano. "Accettazione incondizionata della giurisdizione della Corte internazionale di giustizia," 66 *RDI* 94-101 (1983).

Mosquera Irurita, Tito. *La Corte Internacional de Justicia*. Bogotá: Ed. Temis, 1988. 131 p.

Nafziger, James A. R. "Some Remarks on the Writing Style of the International Court of Justice," in *Contemporary Issues in International Law. Essays in Honour of Louis B. Sohn*, ed. by Thomas Buergenthal. Kehl: Engel, 1984. 325-45.

Non-Appearance before the International Court of Justice - La non-comparution devant la Cour Internationale de Justice, in 64 (Part I) Institute of International Law, Yearbook - Institut de Droit International, Annuaire. Session of Basel, 1991 - Session de Bâle, 1991. Paris: Pedone, 1991.

Nsereko, D. D. "The International Court, Impartiality and Judges Ad

Hoc," 13 *IJIL* 207-30 (1973).

Oda, Shigeru, "Reservations in the Declarations of Acceptance of the Optional Clause and the Period of Validity of Those Declarations. The Effect of the Schultz Letter," 59 BYIL 1-30 (1989).

Oellers-Frahm, Karin. "Die Verfahrensordnung des Internationalen Gerichtshofs vom 14. April 1978," 18 *AVR* 309-320 (1978/80).

Orihuela Calatayud, Esperanza. "España y la jurisdicción obligatoria del Tribunal Internacional de Justicia," 41 *REDI* 69-105 (1989).

Owen, H. J. "Compulsory Jurisdiction in the International Court of Justice," 3 *Georgia Law Review* 704-26 (1969).

Pastor Ridruejo, J. A. *La jurisprudencia del tribunal internacional de La Haya.* Madrid: RIALP, 1962. 504 p.

Patterson, D. S. "The United States and the Origins of the World Court," 91 *Political Science Quarterly* 279-95 (1976).

Pirotte, O. "La notion d'équité dans la jurisprudence récente de la Cour internationale de justice," 77 *RGDIP* 92-135 (1973).

Preuss, Lawrence. "The International Court of Justice, the Senate, and Matters of Domestic Jurisdiction," 40 *AJIL* 720-36 (1946).

Prott, L. V. "The Future of the International Court of Justice," 33 *YWA* 283-303 (1979).

———. "The Role of the Judge in the International Court of Justice," 10 *RBDI* 473-507 (1974).

Reisman, W. Michael & Eric E. Friedman. "The Plaintiff's Dilemma: Illegally Obtained Evidence and Admissibility in International Adjudication," 76 *AJIL* 737-753 (1982).

Röben, Volker. "Le précédent dans la jurisprudence de la Cour internationale," 32 *GYIL* 382-407 (1990).

Rogoff, Martin A. "International Politics and the Rule of Law: The United States and the International Court of Justice," 7 *BUILJ* 267-99 (1989).

Rosenne, Shabtai. "The Changing Role of the International Court," 20 *Israel LR* 182-205 (1985).

——— (ed.). *Documents on the International Court of Justice / Documents relatifs à la Cour internationale de Justice* (First Bilingual Edition) Dordrecht: Nijhoff, 1991. 912 p.

———. "L'Exécution et la mise en vigueur des décisions de la Cour internationale de Justice," 57 *RGDIP* 532-83 (1953).

———. "The *Forum Prorogatum* in the International Court of Justice," 6 *RHDI* 1-26 (1953).

_____. "Judge John E. Reed and the International Court of Justice," 17 *CanYIL* 3-29 (1979).

_____. *The Law and Practice of the International Court.* 2 vols. Leyden: Sijthoff, 2d ed. 1985.

_____. *Procedure in the International Court: A Commentary on the 1978 Rules of the International Court of Justice.* The Hague: Nijhoff, 1983. 305 p.

_____. "Publications of the International Court of Justice," 81 *AJIL* 681-96 (1987).

_____. "Some Reflections on the 1978 Revised Rules of the International Court of Justice," 19 *ColJTransnL* 235-53 (1981).

_____. *The Time Factor in the Jurisdiction of the International Court of Justice.* Leyden: Sijthoff, 1960. 86 p.

_____. *The World Court. What It Is and How It Works.* 4th rev. ed. With the assistance of Terry D. Gill. Dordrecht: Nijhoff, 1989. 320 p. (UN publication).

Scheffer, David J. "Non-Judicial State Remedies and the Jurisdiction of the International Court of Justice," 27 *Stanford JIL* 83-154 (1990).

Schlochauer, Hans-Jürgen. "International Court of Justice," in Bernhardt (ed.), *EPIL* 1 (1981) 72-92.

Schwarzenberger, Georg. "The Judicial Corps of the International Court of Justice," 36 *YWA* 231-67 (1982).

Schwebel, Stephen M. "Ad Hoc Chambers of the International Court of Justice," 81 *AJIL* 831-54 (1987).

_____. "Human Rights in the World Court," 24 *VandJTransnL* 945-70 (1991).

Schwelb, Egon. "The International Court of Justice and the Human Rights Clauses of the Charter," 66 *AJIL* 337-51 (1972).

_____. "The Process of Amending the Statute of the International Court of Justice," 64 *AJIL* 880-91 (1970).

Scott, Gary L. & Craig L. Carr. "The ICJ and Compulsory Jurisdiction: The Case for Closing the Clause," 81 *AJIL* 57-77 (1987).

Scott, Gary L. & Karen D. Csajko. "Compulsory Jurisdiction and Defiance in the World Court: A Comparison of the PCIJ and the ICJ," 16 *DenJIL&Pcy* 377-92 (1988).

Sharan, S. *International Court of Justice.* Calcutta: New Age Publishers, 1971. 268 p.

Shinkaretskaya, G. "The International Court of Justice and the Development of the Law of the Sea," 12 *Marine Policy* 201-10 (1988).

"Should the United States Reconsider Its Acceptance of World Court Jurisdiction?" 79 *ASIL Proc.* 95-109 (1985) (Contributions by various authors).

Singh, J. N. *International Justice: Jurisprudence of the World Courts (PCIJ & ICJ)*. New Delhi: Harnam Publications, 1991. 260 p.

Singh, Nagendra. "Codification and Progressive Development of International Law: The Role of the International Court of Justice," 18 *IJIL* 1-16 (1978).

_____. *The Role and Record of the International Court of Justice (1946 to 1988. In Celebration of the 40 Anniversary)*. Dordrecht: Nijhoff, 1989. 443 p.

Skubiszewski, Krzysztof. "Elements of Custom and the Hague Court," 31 *ZaöRV* 810-54 (1971).

Sohn, Louis B. "Suggestions for the Limited Acceptance of Compulsory Jurisdiction of the International Court of Justice by the United States," 18 *Georgia JI&CL* 1-18 (1988).

Stańczyk, Janusz. "The International Court of Justice on the Competence and Function of the Security Council," 15 *PYIL* 193-216 (1986).

Starace, Vincenzo. *La Competenza della Corte Internazionale di Giustizia in materia contenziosa.* Naples: Editore Jovene, 1970. 239 p.

Stern, Brigitte. "Chronique de jurisprudence de la Cour internationale de Justice (janvier-juillet 1984)," 113 *JDI* 771-99 (1986).

_____. "Chronique de jurisprudence de la Cour internationale de Justice," 117 *JDI* 683-703 (1989).

Stillmunkes, P. "Le 'forum prorogatum' devant la Cour permanente de Justice internationale et la Cour internationale de Justice," 68 *RGDIP* 665-86 (1964).

Stone, Julius. *The International Court and World Crisis*. New York: Carnegie Endowment, January 1962 (*International Conciliation* No. 536).

Suh, Il Ro. "Voting Behavior of National Judges in International Courts, 63 *AJIL* 224-36 (1969).

Szafarz, Renata. *Obowiązkowa jurysdykcja Międzynarodowego Trybunału Sprawiedliwości.*[Compulsory Jurisdiction of the

International Court of Justice]. Wroclaw: Zakład Narodowy imienia Ossolińskich, 1991. 208 p.

Sztucki, Jerzy. *Interim Measures in the Hague Court: An Attempt at a Scrutiny.* Deventer: Klüwer Law and Taxation Publishers, 1983. 332 p.

_____. "Intervention under Article 63 of the I.C.J. Statute in the Phase of Preliminary Proceedings: The Salvadoran Incident," 79 *AJIL* 1005-36 (1985).

Terry, G. J. "Factional Behaviour on the International Court of Justice: 1945-51 and 1961-67," 10 *Melbourne University Law Review* 59-117 (1975).

Thierry, Hubert. "Les résolutions des organes internationaux dans la jurisprudence de la Cour internationale de Justice," 167 *RCADI* 385-450 (1980-II).

Thirlway, Hugh. "The Law and Procedure of the International Court of Justice 1960-1989," Part 1: 60 *BYIL* 1-157 (1990); Part 2: 61 *BYIL* 1-133 (1991); Part 3: 62 *BYIL* 1-75 (1992).

_____. *Non-Appearance before the International Court of Justice.* Cambridge: Cambridge UP, 1985.

Toope, Stephen J. "Pragmatic Compromise or Mere Transaction? The Use of Chamber Procedure in International Adjudication," 31 *VirJIL* 53-97 (1990).

Toraldo-Serra, N. M. *Le misure provvisorie internazionali: ricerca storico-giuridica.* Rome: Bulzoni, 1973. 193 p.

US Congress. Senate Committee on Foreign Relations. *Strengthening the International Court of Justice.* Washington, DC: GPO, 1973. 293 p.

Visscher, Charles De. *Aspects récents du droit procédural de la Cour internationale de Justice.* Paris: Pedone, 1966. 219 p.

Waldock, C. H. M. "The Decline of the Optional clause," 32 *BYIL* 244-87 (1957).

_____. "The Plea of Domestic Jurisdiction before International Tribunals," 31 *BYIL* 96-142 (1954).

Wehberg, Hans & H. W. Goldschmidt. *Der Internationale Gerichtshof: Entstehungsgeschichte, Analyse, Dokumentation.* Berlin: Berlin Verlag, Arno Spitz, 1973. 115 p.

Williams, W. L. Jr. *Attitudes of the Lesser Developed Countries toward the International Court of Justice.* Washington, DC: World Association of Lawyers, 1976. 63 p.

"World Court Jurisdiction and U.S. Foreign Policy in Latin America," 78 *ASIL Proc.* 321-37 (1984) (various contributors).

Yarnold, Barbara M. *International Fugitives: A New Role for the International Court of Justice.* New York: Praeger, 1991. 142 p.

Zimmermann, Andreas. "Ad Hoc Chambers of the International Court of Justice," 8 *DickJIL* 1-32 (1989).

(2) *Advisory Jurisdiction:*

Ago, Roberto. "'Binding' Advisory Opinions of the International Court of Justice," 85 *AJIL* 439-51 (1991).

Daillier, P. "L'intervention du Sécrétaire Général des Nations Unies dans la procédure consultative devant la Cour international de Justice," 19 *AFDI* 376-410 (1973).

Elias, Taslim O. "How the International Court of Justice Deals with Requests for Advisory Opinions," in *Essays in International Law in Honour of Judge Manfred Lachs.* Ed. by Jerzy Makarczyk. The Hague: Nijhoff (1984) 355-74.

Greig, D. W. "The Advisory Jurisdiction of the International Court and the Settlement of Disputes between States," 15 *ICLQ* 325-68 (1966).

Jiménez de Aréchaga, Eduardo. "Judges *Ad Hoc* in Advisory Proceedings," 31 *ZaöRV* 697-711 (1971).

Keith, Kenneth James. *The Extent of the Advisory Jurisdiction of the International Court of Justice.* Leyden: Sijthoff, 1971. 271 p.

Mathy, D. "Un juge ad hoc en procédure consultative devant la Cour internationale de Justice," 12 *RBDI* 528-54 (1976).

Ostrihansky, Rudolf. "Advisory Opinions of the International Court of Justice As Reviews of Judgments in International Administrative Tribunals," 18 *PYIL* 101-21 (1988).

Pomerance, Michla. *The Advisory Function of the International Court in the League and U.N. Eras.* Baltimore: Johns Hopkins UP, 1973. 440 p.

Pratap, Dharma. *The Advisory Jurisdiction of the International Court.* Oxford: Oxford UP, 1972. 292 p.

Puente Egido, J. "Consideraciones sobre la naturaleza y efectos de las opiniones consultivas," 31 *ZaöRV* 730-809 (1971).

Schwebel, Stephen M. "Was the Capacity to Request an Advisory Opinion Wider in the Permanent Court of International Justice than It Is in the International Court of Justice?" 62 *BYIL* 77-118

(1992).

Suh, Il Ro. "National Judges in Advisory Proceedings of the International Court," 19 *IJIL* 20-47 (1979).

Waldock, C. H. M. *Aspects of the Advisory Jurisdiction of the International Court of Justice.* 1976.

(3) *Individual Judgments:*

Aegean Sea (Greece v. Turkey):

Elkind, Jerome B. "The Aegean Sea Case and Article 41 of the Statute of the International Court of Justice," 32 *RHDI* 285-345 (1979).

Gross, Leo. "The Dispute between Greece and Turkey concerning the Continental Shelf in the Aegean," 71 *AJIL* 31-59 (1977).

Johnson, D. H. N. "The International Court of Justice Declines Jurisdiction Again (the Aegean Sea Continental Shelf Case)," 7 *Australian YIL* 309-31 (1976-77).

Oellers-Frahm, Karin. "Aegean Sea Continental Shelf Case," in Bernhardt (ed.), *EPIL* 2 (1981) 5-7.

Robol, Richard T. "Jurisdiction. Limits of Consent. The Aegean Sea Continental Shelf Case," 18 *Harvard ILJ* 649-75 (1977).

Ambatielos (Greece v. UK):

Johnson, D. H. N. "The Ambatielos Case," 19 *Modern Law Review* 510-17 (1956).

Pinto, Roger. "La sentence Ambatielos," 84 *JDI* 540-614 (1957).

Wühler, Norbert. "Ambatielos Case," in Bernhardt (ed.), *EPIL* 2 (1981) 13-5.

Anglo-Iranian Oil Co. (UK v. Iran):

Dolzer, Rudolf. "Anglo-Iranian Oil Company Case," in Bernhardt (ed.), *EPIL* 2 (1981) 15-7.

Nakasian, S. "Anglo-Iranian Oil Case: A Problem in International Judicial Process," 41 *Georgetown Law Journal* 459-94 (1953).

O'Connell, D. P. "A Critique of the Iranian Oil Litigation," 4 *ICLQ* 267-93 (1955).

Asylum (Colombia/Peru) and *Haya de la Torre (Colombia v. Peru):*

Barcia Trelles, Camilo. "El derecho de asilo diplomático y el caso

Haya de la Torre," 3 *REDI* 753-801 (1950).

García-Mora, M. R. "The Colombian-Peruvian Asylum Case and the Doctrine of Human Rights," 37 *Virginia Law Review* 927-65 (1951).

Hailbronner, Kay. "Haya de la Torre Cases," in Bernhardt (ed.), *EPIL* 2 (1981) 128-30.

Lalive, J. F. "Asylum Case (Haya de la Torre Case)," 80 *JDI* 684-93 (1953).

Barcelona Traction (Belgium v. Spain):

Briggs, Herbert W. "Barcelona Traction: The *Jus Standi* of Belgium," 65 *AJIL* 327-345 (1971).

Caflisch, L. C. "The Protection of Corporate Investments Abroad in the Light of the Barcelona Traction Case," 31 *ZaöRV* 162-96 (1971).

García Arias, L. "El caso Barcelona Traction ante el Tribunal Internacional de Justicia," 23 *REDI* 201-30 (1970).

Miaja de la Muela, Adolfo. *Aportación de la Sentencia del Tribunal de la Haya en el Caso de la Barcelona Traction a la jurisprudencia internacional.* Valladolid: Cuadernos de la Cátedra J.B. Scott, 1970. 144 p.

"Round Table: Toward More Adequate Diplomatic Protection of Private Claims: 'Aris Gloves,' 'Barcelona Traction,' and Beyond," 65 *ASIL Proc.* 335-65 (1971).

Seidl-Hohenveldern, Ignaz. "Der Barcelona Traction-Fall," 22 *Österreichische Zeitschrift für öffentliches Recht* 255-309 (1971).

Wallace, Cynthia. "Barcelona Traction Case," in Bernhardt (ed.), *EPIL* 2 (1981) 30-3.

Continental Shelf (Libya/Malta):

Conforti, Benedetto. "L'arrêt de la Cour internationale de Justice dans l'affaire de la délimitation du plateau continental entre la Libye et Malte," 90 *RGDIP* 313-43 (1986).

Decaux, Emmanuel. "L'arrêt de la Cour internationale de Justice dans l'affaire du Plateau continental (Libye/Malte). Arrêt du 3 juin 1985," 31 *AFDI* 294-323 (1985).

McDorman, Ted L. "The Libya-Malta Case: Opposite States Confront the Court," 24 *CanYIL* 335-67 (1986).

McGinley, Gerald P. "Intervention in the International Court: the Libya/Malta Continental Shelf Case," 34 *ICLQ* 671-94 (1985).

Continental Shelf (Tunisia/Libya):

Brown, E. D. "The Tunisia-Libya Continental Shelf Case: A Missed Opportunity," 7 *Marine Policy* 142-62 (1983).

Decaux, Emmanuel. "L'arrêt de la Cour internationale de Justice dans l'affaire du Plateau continental (Tunisie/Libye), Arrêt de 24 février 1982," 28 *AFDI* 357-91 (1982).

Evensen, Jens. "The Delimitation of the Exclusive Economic Zones and Continental Shelves As Highlighted by the International Court of Justice," in Christos L. Rozakis & Constantin A. Stephanou (eds.), *The New Law of the Sea* 107-54. Amsterdam: North Holland, 1983.

Feldman, Mark B. "The Tunisia-Libya Continental Shelf Case: Geographic Justice or Judicial Compromise?" 77 *AJIL* 219-38 (1983).

Herman, L. L. "The Court Giveth and the Court Taketh Away: An Analysis of the Tunisia-Libya Continental Shelf Case," 33 *ICLQ* 825-58 (1984).

Hodgson, Douglas C. "The Tuniso-Libyan Continental Shelf Case," 16 *Case WRJIL* 1-37 (1984).

Labouz, Marie-Françoise. "L'affaire du plateau continental tuniso-libyen. L'arrêt de la Cour internationale de Justice," *Maghreb-Machrek* (No. 101) 46-65 (1982).

Corfu Channel (UK v. Albania):

Bernhardt, Rudolf. "Corfu Channel Case," in Bernhardt (ed.), *EPIL* 2 (1981) 61-4.

Chung, L. Y. *Legal Problems Involved in the Corfu Channel Incident.* Geneva: University of Geneva, Thesis, 1959.

Gardiner, L. *The Eagle Spreads Its Claws. A History of the Corfu Channel Dispute and of Albania's Relations with the West, 1945-1965.* 1966.

Waldock, C. H. M. "*Forum Prorogatum* or Acceptance of a Unilateral Summons to Appear before the International Court of Justice," 2 *International Law Quarterly* 377-91 (1948).

Elettronica Sicula (US v. Italy):

Adler, Matthew H. "The Exhaustion of the Local Remedies Rule after the International Court of Justice Decision in ELSI," 39 *ICLQ* 641-53 (1990).

Jeancolas, Catherine. "L'arrêt Elettronica Sicula S.p.A. (ELSI) du 20 juillet 1989 (Etats Unis d'Amérique c. Italie)," 94 *RGDIP* 701-42 (1990).

Murphy, Sean D. "The ELSI Case: An Investment Dispute at the International Court of Justice," 16 *Yale JIL* 391-452 (1991).

Fisheries (UK v. Norway):

Bourquin, M. "La portée générale de l'arrêt rendu le 18 décembre 1951 par la Cour internationale de Justice dans l'affaire anglo-norvégienne des pêcheries," 22 *NordTIR-Acta Scandinavica Juris Gentium* 101-32 (1952).

Evensen, Jens. "The Anglo-Norwegian Fisheries Case and Its Legal Consequences," 46 *AJIL* 609-30 (1952).

Gündling, Lothar. "Fisheries Case (U.K. v. Norway)," in Bernhardt (ed.), *EPIL* 2 (1981) 94-5.

Johnson, D. H. N. "The Anglo-Norwegian Fisheries Case," 1 *ICLQ* 145-80 (1952).

Smith, H. A. "The Anglo-Norwegian Fisheries Case," 7 *YWA* 283-307 (1953).

Waldock, C. H. M. "The Anglo-Norwegian Fisheries Case," 28 *BYIL* 114-71 (1951).

Fisheries Jurisdiction (UK v. Iceland; Fed. Rep. of Germany v. Iceland):

Bilder, R. B. "The Anglo-Icelandic Fisheries Dispute," 37 *Wisconsin Law Review* 37-132 (1973).

Churchill R. R. "The Fisheries Jurisdiction Cases: The Contribution of the International Court of Justice to the Debate on Coastal States Fisheries Rights," 24 *ICLQ* 82-105 (1975).

Goy, R. "Le règlement de l'affaire des pêcheries islandaises," 82 *RGDIP* 434-536 (1978).

Jaenicke, Günther. "Fisheries Jurisdiction Cases (U.K. v. Iceland; Federal Republic of Germany v. Iceland)," in Bernhardt (ed.), *EPIL* 2 (1981) 95-8.

Rao, S. Rama. "The ICJ Judgment in the Fisheries Jurisdiction Case - A Critique," 18 *Indian Yearbook of International Affairs* 124-59 (1980).

Young, Donald A. "Contributions to International Law and World Order by the World Court's Adjudication of the Icelandic

Fisheries Controversy," 1 *Boston Coll&CLR* 175-96 (1977).

Gulf of Maine (Canada/US):
Alexander, Lewis M.(ed.). *The Gulf of Maine Case: An International Discussion.* (Studies in Transnational Legal Policy). St. Paul, MN: West Publishing Co., 1988. 113 p.
Brauer, Robert H. "International Conflict Resolution: The ICJ Chambers and the Gulf of Maine Dispute," 23 *VirJIL* 463-86 (1982-83).
Clain, Levi E. "Gulf of Maine: A Disappointing First in the Delimitation of a Single Maritime Boundary," 25 *VirJIL* 521-620 (1985).
Costi, Alberto. "L'arrêt de la Cour internationale de Justice dans l'affaire du Golfe du Maine (Canada c. Etats-Unis d'Amérique)," 2 *Revue Québécoise de Droit International* 323-70 (1985).
Robinson, Davis R., David A. Colson & Bruce C. Rashkow. "Some Perspectives on Adjudicating before the World Court: The Gulf of Maine Case," 79 *AJIL* 539-77 (1985).
Schneider, Jan. "The Gulf of Maine Case: The Nature of an Equitable Result," 79 *AJIL* 539-77 (1985).
Terres, Nora T. "The United States/Canada Gulf of Maine Maritime Boundary Delimitation," 9 *MdJIL&T* 135-80 (1985).
Vorsey, Louis de & Megan C. de Vorsey. "The World Court Decision in the Canada-United States Gulf of Maine Seaward Boundary Dispute: A Perspective from Historical Geography," 18 *Case WRJIL* 415-42 (1986).

Interhandel (Switzerland v. US):
Briggs, Herbert W. "Interhandel: The Court's Judgment of March 21, 1959 on the Preliminary Objections of the United States," 53 *AJIL* 547-63 (1959).
Perrin, G. "L'affaire de l'Interhandel, Phase des exceptions préliminaires," 16 *SchweizJIR* 73-208 (1959).
Simmonds, K. R. "The Interhandel Case," 10 *ICLQ* 495-547 (1961).
Weber, Ludwig. "Interhandel Case," in Bernhardt (ed.), *EPIL* 2 (1981) 136-8.

Military and Paramilitary Activities (Nicaragua v. US):
Czaplinski, Wladyslaw. "Sources of International Law in the

Nicaragua Case," 38 *ICLQ* 151-66 (1989).

Eisemann, Pierre Michel. "L'arrêt de la C.I.J. du 27 juin 1986 (fond) dans l'affaire des activités militaires et paramilitaires au Nicaragua et contre celui-ci," 32 *AFDI* 153-91 (1986).

Gill, Terry D. "The Law of Armed Conflict in the Context of the Nicaragua Case," 1 *Hague YIL* 30-58 (1988).

_____. *Litigation Strategy at the International Court. A Case Study of the Nicaragua v. United States Dispute.* Dordrecht: Nijhoff, 1989. 362 p.

Greig, D. W. "Nicaragua and the United States: Confrontation over the Jurisdiction of the International Court," 62 *BYIL* 119-281 (1992).

Highet, Keith. "Evidence, the Court, and the Nicaragua Case," 81 *AJIL* 1-56 (1987).

_____. "Reflections on Jurisprudence for the 'Third World': The World Court, the 'Big Case,' and the Future," 27 *VirJIL* 287-304 (1987).

_____. "'You Can Run but You Can't Hide' - Reflections on the U.S. Position in the Nicaragua Case," 27 *VirJIL* 551-72 (1987).

Janis, Mark W. "Somber Reflections on the Compulsory Jurisdiction of the International Court of Justice," 81 *AJIL* 144-6 (1987).

"The Jurisprudence of the Court in the Nicaragua Decision," 81 *ASIL Proc* 258-77 (1987) (Various Contributors).

Kahn, Paul W. "From Nuremberg to the Hague: The United States Position in Nicaragua v. United States and the Development of International Law," 12 *Yale JIL* 1-62 (1987).

Lang, Caroline. *L'affaire Nicaragua/* (sic) *Etats-Unis devant la Cour internationale de Justice.* Paris: Librairie générale de Droit et de Jurisprudence, 1990. 301 p.

Macdonald, R.St.J. "The Nicaragua Case: New Answers to Old Questions?" 24 *CanYIL* 127-60 (1986).

Maier, Harold G. (ed.). "Appraisals of the ICJ's Decision: Nicaragua v. United States (Merits)," (16 contributors), 81 *AJIL* 77-183 (1987).

"Nicaragua v. the United States before the International Court of Justice," 148 *World Affairs* 1-70 (1985). (Special issue with several contributors).

Norton, Patrick M. "The Nicaragua Case: Political Questions before the International Court of Justice," 27 *VirJIL* 459-526 (1987).

O'Connell, Mary Ellen. "The Prospects for Enforcing Monetary Judgments of the International Court of Justice: A Study of Nicaragua's Judgment against the United States," 30 *VirJIL* 891-940 (1990)

Rowles, James P. "Nicaragua versus the United States: Issues of Law and Policy," 20 *ILawyer* 1245-88 (1986).

Tama, Noreen M. "Nicaragua v. United States: The Power of the International Court of Justice to Indicate Interim Measures in Political Disputes," 4 *DickJIL* 65-87 (1985).

Turner, Robert F. "Peace and the World Court: A Comment on the Paramilitary Activities Case," 20 *VandJTransnL* 53-79 (1987).

Minquiers and Ecrehos (France/UK):

Bishop, William W. Jr. "The Minquiers and Ecrehos Case," 48 *AJIL* 316-26 (1954).

Herndl, Kurt. "Minquiers and Ecrehos Case," in Bernhardt (ed.), *EPIL* 2 (1981) 192-4.

Hudson, Manley O. "The Minquiers and Ecrehos Case," 48 *AJIL* 6-12 (1954).

Johnson, D. H. N. "The Minquiers and Ecrehos Case," 3 *ICLQ* 189-216 (1954).

Roche, A. *The Minquiers and Ecrehos Case.* Geneva: Librairie Droz, 1959. 200 p.

North Sea Continental Shelf (Fed. Rep. of Germany v. Denmark and v. Netherlands):

Eustache, François. "L'affaire du plateau continental de la mer du Nord devant la Cour internationale de Justice," 74 *RGDIP* 590-639 (1970).

Friedmann, Wolfgang. "The North Sea Continental Shelf - A Critique," 64 *AJIL* 229-40 (1970).

Goldie, L. F. E. "The North Sea Continental Shelf Cases," 16 *New York Law Forum* 326-77 (1970).

Grisel, Etienne. "The Lateral Boundaries of the Continental Shelf and the Judgment of the International Court of Justice in the North Sea Continental Shelf Cases," 64 *AJIL* 562-93 (1970).

Jaenicke, Günther. "North Sea Continental Shelf Case," in Bernhardt (ed.), *EPIL* 2 (1981) 205-8.

Manin, P. "Le juge international et la règle générale. Réflexions à partir des arrêts rendus par la C.I.J. dans l'affaire du plateau continental de la mer du Nord (1969) et dans l'affaire des pêcheries," 80 *RGDIP* 7-54 (1976).

Merrills, J. G. "Images and Models in the World Court: the Individual Opinions in the North Sea Continental Shelf Cases," 41 *Modern Law Review* 639-59 (1978).

Rothpfeffer, Tomas. "Equity in the North Sea Continental Shelf Cases: A Case Study in the Legal Reasoning of the International Court of Justice," 42 *NordTIR* 81-137 (1972).

Schenk, D. von. "Die vertragliche Abgrenzung des Festlandsockels unter der Nordsee zwischen der Bundesrepublik Deutschland, Dänemark und den Niederlanden nach dem Urteil des Internationalen Gerichtshofes vom 20. Februar 1969," 15 *JIR* 370-98 (1970).

Nottebohm (Liechtenstein v. Guatemala):

Bastid, Suzanne. "L'affaire Nottebohm devant la Cour Internationale de Justice," 15 *Revue critique de droit international privé* 607-33 (1956).

Knapp, B. "Quelques considérations sur la jurisprudence de la Cour internationale de Justice en matière de nationalité," 17 *SchweizJIR* 147-78 (1960).

Mangoldt, Hans von. "Nottebohm Case," in Bernhardt (ed.), *EPIL* 2 (1981) 213-6.

Visscher, Charles De. "L'affaire Nottebohm," 60 *RGDIP* 238-66 (1956).

Nuclear Tests (Australia v. France; New Zealand v. France):

Berg, Axel. "Nuclear Tests Cases (Australia v. France, New Zealand v. France)," in Bernhardt (ed.), *EPIL* 2 (1981) 216-9.

Dupuy, Pierre Marie. "L'affaire des essais nucléaires français et le contentieux de la responsabilité internationale publique," 20 *GYIL* 375-405 (1977).

Falsafi, H. *L'affaire des essais nucléaires devant la Cour internationale de Justice.* Neuchâtel: University of Neuchâtel, Thesis, 1978.

Franck, Thomas M. "Word-Made Law: The Decision of the ICJ in the Nuclear Test Cases," 69 *AJIL* 612-20 (1975).

Kos, J. Stephen. "Interim Relief in the International Court: New Zealand and the Nuclear Test Cases," 14 *Victoria University of*

Wellington Law Review 357-87 (1984).

Lellouche, P. "The International Court of Justice: The Nuclear Test Cases," 16 *Harvard ILJ* 614-37 (1975).

McWhinney, Edward. "International Law-Making and the Judicial Process. The World Court and the French Nuclear Tests Case," 3 *SyrJIL&Com* 9-46 (1975).

Sur, S. "Les affaires des essais nucléaires," 79 *RGDIP* 972-1027 (1975).

Thierry, Hubert. "Les arrêts du 20 décembre 1974 et les relations de la France avec la Cour internationale de Justice," 20 *AFDI* 286-98 (1974).

Verma, Dhirendra P. "The Nuclear Tests Cases: An Inquiry into the Judicial Response of the International Court of Justice," 8 *South African Yearbook of International Law* 20-57 (1982).

Right of Passage (Portugal v. India):
Cot, J.-P. "Affaire de droit de passage sur territoire indien," 6 *AFDI* 315-37 (1960).

Visscher, Charles De. "L'affaire de droit de passage sur territoire indien devant la Cour internationale de Justice," 64 *RGDIP* 693-710 (1960).

Weber, Ludwig. "Right of Passage over Indian Territory Case," in Bernhardt (ed.), *EPIL* 2 (1981) 244-6.

Temple of Preah Vihear (Cambodia v. Thailand):
Cot, J.-P. "Affaire de temple de Préah Vihéar (Cambodge c. Thailande)," 7 *AFDI* 229-51 (1961); 8 *AFDI* 217-47 (1962).

Johnson, D. H. N. "Judgments of May 26, 1961 and June 15, 1962. The Case Concerning the Temple of Preah Vihear," 11 *ICLQ* 1183-1204 (1962).

Rustenmeyer, Ann. "Temple of Preah Vihear Case," in Bernhardt (ed.), *EPIL* 2 (1981) 273-4.

US Diplomatic and Consular Staff in Tehran (US v. Iran):
Bernhardt, J.-P. A. "The Provisional Measures Procedure of the International Court of Justice to U.S. Staff in Tehran: Fiat Justitia, Pereat Curia?" 20 *VirJIL* 557-613 (1980).

Bretton, P. "L'affaire des otages américains devant la Cour internationale de Justice," 107 *JDI* 787-828 (1980).

Gordon, Edward & Patricia J. Youngblood. "The Role of the International Court in the Hostages Case - A Rejoinder," 13 *ConnLR* 429-58 (1981).

Gross, Leo. "The Case of United States Diplomatic and Consular Staff in Tehran. Phase of Provisional Measures," 74 *AJIL* 395-410 (1980).

Janis, Mark W. "The Role of the International Court in the Hostages Case," 13 *ConnLR* 263-289 (1981).

Jeffery, Anthea. "The American Hostages in Tehran: The I.C.J. and the Legality of Rescue Missions," 30 *ICLQ* 717-29 (1981).

Morelli, Gaetano. "L'elemento della controversia nell'affare degli ostaggi americani in Iran," 64 *RDI* 5-13 (1981).

Munson, Valerie J. "The Case Concerning United States Diplomatic and Consular Staff in Tehran," 3 *CalifWILJ* 543-68 (1981).

Oellers-Frahm, Karin. "United States Diplomatic and Consular Staff in Tehran Case," in Bernhardt (ed.), *EPIL* 2 (1981) 282-6.

Röling, B. V. A. "Aspects of the Case Concerning United States Diplomatic and Consular Staff in Tehran," 11 *NYIL* 125-53 (1980).

Stein, Ted L. "Contempt, Crisis, and the Court: The World Court and the Hostage Rescue Attempt," 76 *AJIL* 499-531 (1982).

Wegen, Gerhard. "Discontinuance of International Proceedings: The Hostages Case," 76 *AJIL* 499-531 (1982).

Zoller, E. "L'affaire du personnel diplomatique et consulaire des Etats-Unis à Téhéran," 84 *RGDIP* 973-1026 (1980).

Other Cases:

Benedek, Wolfgang. "Northern Cameroon Case," in Bernhardt (ed.), *EPIL* 2 (1981) 208-10.

Berg, Axel. "Antarctica Cases (U.K. v. Argentina; U.K. v. Chile)," in Bernhardt (ed.), *EPIL* 2 (1981) 17-8.

Decaux, Emmanuel. "L'arrêt de la C.I.J. dans l'affaire des actions armées frontalières et transfrontalières (Nicaragua c. Honduras), Compétence et recevabilité, 20 décembre 1988," 34 *AFDI* 147-64 (1988).

_____. "L'arrêt de la Chambre de la Cour internationale de Justice dans l'affaire du différend frontalier (Burkina Faso/République du Mali) (Arrêt du 22 décembre 1986)," 32 *AFDI* 215-37 (1986).

Delaume, G. P. "Jurisdiction of Courts and International Loans: A Study of Lenders' Practice," 6 *AJCL* 189-214 (1957).

Gross, Leo. "Bulgaria Invokes the Connally Amendment," 56 *AJIL* 357-82 (1962).

Hailbronner, Kay. "Aerial Incident Cases (U.S. v. Hungary; U.S. v. U.S.S.R.; U.S. v. Czechoslovakia)," in Bernhardt (ed.), *EPIL* 2 (1981) 7-9.

_____. "Aerial Incident of 27 July 1955 Cases (Israel v. Bulgaria; U.S. v. Bulgaria; U.K. v. Bulgaria)," in Bernhardt (ed.), *EPIL* 2 (1981) 10-11.

_____. "Jurisdiction of the ICAO Council Case," in Bernhardt (ed.), *EPIL* 2 (1981) 161-3.

Hamrock, Kurt J. "The ELSI Case: Toward an International Definition of 'Arbitrary' Conduct," 27 *Texas ILJ* 837-64 (1992).

Hofmann, Rainer. "Electricité de Beyrouth Company Case," in Bernhardt (ed.), *EPIL* 2 (1981) 85-6.

Johnson, D. H. N. "Case Concerning the Arbitral Award Made by the King of Spain on December 23, 1906," 10 *ICLQ* 328-37 (1961).

_____. "The Case Concerning the Northern Cameroons," 13 *ICLQ* 1143-92 (1964).

Martens, Ernst K. "Norwegian Loans Case," in Bernhardt (ed.), *EPIL* 2 (1981) 210-1.

Oellers-Frahm, Karin. "Trial of Pakistani Prisoners of War Case," in Bernhardt (ed.), *EPIL* 2 (1981) 280-1.

Sánchez Rodríguez, Luis Ignacio. "*Uti possidetis:* la reactualización jurisprudencial de un viejo principio. (A propósito de la Sentencia del TIJ (Sala) en el asunto Burkina Faso/República de Mali)," 40 *REDI* 121-51 (1988).

Shachor-Landau, C. "The Judgment of the International Court of Justice in the Aerial Incident Case between Israel and Bulgaria," 8 *AVR* 277-90 (1960).

Silagi, Michael. "Guardianship of Infants Convention Case," in Bernhardt (ed.), *EPIL* 2 (1981) 125-6.

_____. "United States Nationals in Morocco Case," in Bernhardt (ed.), *EPIL* 2 (1981) 286-7.

Wühler, Norbert. "Arbitral Award of 1906 Case (Honduras v. Nicaragua)," in Bernhardt (ed.), *EPIL* 2 (1981) 22-4.

_____. "Monetary Gold Case," in Bernhardt (ed.), *EPIL* 2 (1981) 195-6.

(4) *Individual Advisory Opinions:*

Barbier, M. "L'avis consultatif de la Cour de la Haye sur le Sahara occidental," 30 *Revue juridique et politique, indépendence et coopération* 67-103 (1976).

Bernhardt, Rudolf. "Homogenität, Kontinuität, und Dissonanzen in der Rechtsprechung des Internationalen Gerichtshofs. Eine Fallstudie zum Südwestafrika/Namibia-Komplex," 33 *ZaöRV* 1-37 (1973).

Bishop, William W. "Application for Review of Judgment No. 158 of the United Nations Administrative Tribunal. Advisory Opinion of July 12, 1973," 68 *AJIL* 340-9 (1974).

Boleslaw A. Boczek. *Flags of Convenience: An International Legal Study.* Cambridge, MA: Harvard UP, 1962. 323 p.

Bothe, Michael. "Certain Expenses of the United Nations (Advisory Opinion)," in Bernhardt (ed.), *EPIL* 2 (1981) 48-51.

Bruha, Thomas. "Judgments of ILO Administrative Tribunal (Advisory Opinion)," in Bernhardt (ed.), *EPIL* 2 (1981) 157-9.

Byman, A. "The March on the Spanish Sahara: A Test of International Law," 6 *DenJIL&Pcy* 95-121 (1976).

Chappez, J. "L'avis consultatif de la Cour internationale de Justice du 16 octobre 1976 dans l'affaire du Sahara occidental," 80 *RGDIP* 1132-87 (1976).

Eagleton, Clyde. "International Organization and the Law of Responsibility," 76 *RCADI* 319-425 (1950-I).

Fitzmaurice, Gerald G. "Reservations to Multilateral Conventions," 2 *ICLQ* 1-26 (1953).

Flory, M. "L'avis de la Cour internationale de Justice sur le Sahara occidental," 21 *AFDI* 253-77 (1975).

Franck, Thomas M. "The Stealing of the Sahara," 70 *AJIL* 694-721 (1976).

García Arias, L. "El primer dictamen del Tribunal internacional de Justicia: Las condiciones de admisión de un estado como nuevo Miembro de la ONU," 2 *REDI* 145-76 (1949).

———. "El segundo dictamen del Tribunal internacional de Justicia: La reparación por daños sufridos al servicio de las Naciones Unidas," 2 *REDI* 977-1005 (1949).

Gray, Christine. "The International Court's Advisory Opinion on the WHO-Egypt Agreement of 1951," 32 *ICLQ* 534-41 (1983).

Hardy, M. J. L. "Jurisdiction of the Administrative Tribunal of the

International Labour Organisation. The Advisory Opinion of the International Court of Justice of October 23, 1956," 6 *ICLQ* 338-47 (1956).

Herndl, Kurt. "Admission of a State to Membership in United Nations (Advisory Opinion)," in Bernhardt (ed.), *EPIL* 2 (1981) 3-5.

_____. "Interpretation of Peace Treaties with Bulgaria, Hungary and Romania (Advisory Opinion)," in Bernhardt (ed.), *EPIL* 2 (1981) 148-50.

Hevener, N. "The 1971 South-West African Opinion - A New International Juridical Philosophy," 24 *ICLQ* 791-810 (1975).

Hill, Humphrey M. "IMCO Maritime Safety Committee. Constitution of (Advisory Opinion)," in Bernhardt (ed.), *EPIL* 2 (1981) 134-6.

Hockenjos, H. R. *Vorbehalte zur Genocide-Vereinbarung. Besprechung des Gutachtens des Internationalen Gerichtshofs im Haag vom 28. Mai 1951.* Basel: University of Basel, Thesis, 1956.

Jacque, J.-P. "L'avis de la Cour internationale de Justice du 21 juin 1971," 76 *RGDIP* 1046-97 (1972).

Janis, Mark W. "The International Court of Justice: Advisory Opinion on the Western Sahara," 17 *Harvard ILJ* 609-21 (1976).

Klein, Eckart. "Genocide Convention (Advisory Opinion)," in Bernhardt (ed.), *EPIL* 2 (1981) 107-9.

_____. "Reparation for Injuries Suffered in the Service of UN (Advisory Opinion)," in Bernhardt (ed.), *EPIL* 2 (1981) 242-4.

_____. "South West Africa/Namibia (Advisory Opinions and Judgments)," in Bernhardt (ed.), *EPIL* 2 (1981) 260-70.

Lissitzyn, Oliver J. "International Law and the Advisory Opinion on Namibia," 11 *ColJTransnL* 50-73 (1972).

Maluwa, Tijanjana. "Treaty Interpretation and the Exercise of Presidential Discretion by the International Court of Justice; Some Reflections on the PLO Mission Case," 37 *NILR* 330-46 (1990).

Meyers, H. *The Nationality of Ships.* The Hague: Nijhoff, 1967. 395 p.

Ndiaye, B. "Avis de la C.I.J. sur le Sahara occidental," 10 *Revue Sénégalaise de Droit* 31-53 (1976).

Oellers-Frahm, Karin. "Interpretation of Agreement of 25 March 1951 between WHO and Egypt (Advisory Opinion)," in Bernhardt (ed.), *EPIL* 2 (1981) 142-4.

_____. "Western Sahara (Advisory Opinion)," in Bernhardt (ed.),

EPIL 2 (1981) 291-3.

Okere, B. O. "The Western Sahara Case," 28 *ICLQ* 296-312 (1979).

Riedel, Eibe H. "Confrontation in Western Sahara in the Light of the Advisory Opinion of the International Court of Justice of 16 October 1975," 19 *GYIL* 405-42 (1976).

Rovine, Arthur W. "The World Court Opinion on Namibia," 11 *ColJTransnL* 203-39 (1972).

Ruda, J. M. "Reservations to Treaties," 146 *RCADI* 95-218 (1975-III).

Ruete, Mathias. "Judgment No. 158 of UN Administrative Tribunal. Application for Review of (Advisory Opinion)," in Bernhardt (ed.), *EPIL* 2 (1981) 156-7.

Shaw, Malcolm. "The Western Sahara Case," 40 BYIL 119-54 (1978).

Simmonds, K. R. "The Constitution of the Maritime Safety Committee of IMCO," 12 *ICLQ* 56-87 (1963).

Simon, Denys. "L'interprétation de l'accord du 25 mars 1951 entre l'OMS et l'Egypte (Avis Consultatif de la Cour internationale de Justice du 20 décembre 1980)," 85 *RGDIP* 793-841 (1981).

Tavernier, Paul. "L'avis consultatif de la Cour internationale de Justice du 20 juillet 1982 dans l'affaire de la demande de réformation du jugement no. 273 du Tribunal administratif des Nations Unies (Affaire Mortished)," 28 *AFDI* 392-424 (1982).

_____. "L'avis consultatif de la Cour internationale de Justice du 27 mai 1987 dans l'affaire de la demande de réformation du jugement no. 333 du Tribunal administratif des Nations Unies (Affaire Yakimetz)," 33 *AFDI* 211-38 (1987).

Verzijl, J. H. W. "Judgments of the Administrative Tribunal of the I.L.O. upon Complaints Made against the U.N.E.S.C.O." 4 *NTIR* 236-53 (1957).

Weber, Ludwig. "Awards of Compensation Made by UN Administrative Tribunal (Advisory Opinion)," in Bernhardt (ed.), *EPIL* 2 (1981) 29-30.

Wright, Quincy. "The Jural Personality of the United Nations," 43 *AJIL* 509-16 (1949).

_____. "Responsibility for Injuries to United Nations Officials," 43 *AJIL* 95-104 (1949).

Yuen-Li-Liang. "Notes on Legal Questions Concerning the United Nations. Conditions of Admission of a State to Membership in the U.N.," 43 *AJIL* 288-311 (1949).

Zuidwijk, A. "The International Court and South West Africa: Latest

Phase," 3 *Georgia JIL* 323-43 (1973).

6. ADMINISTRATIVE TRIBUNALS OF INTERNATIONAL ORGANIZATIONS

Amerasinghe, Chittaharanjan F. *Case Law of the World Bank Administrative Tribunal: An Analytical Digest.* Oxford: Clarendon Press, 1989.

_____ (ed.). *Documents on International Administrative Tribunals.* Oxford: Clarendon Press, 1989. 224 p.

_____. "The Implications of the Merode Case for International Administrative Law," 43 *ZaöRV* 1-48 (1983).

_____. *The Law of the International Civil Service As Applied by International Administrative Tribunals.* 2 vols. Oxford: Clarendon Press, 1988. Vol. 1, 664 p.; vol.2, 714 p.

_____. "The World Bank Administrative Tribunal," 31 *ICLQ* 748-64 (1982).

_____ & D. Bellinger. *Index of Decisions of International Administrative Tribunals.* 2d ed. Washington, DC: IBRD, 1985. 149 p.

_____ & D. Bellinger. *Index to Decisions of the World Bank Administrative Tribunal.* 2d ed. Washington, DC: IBRD, 1985. 32 p.

_____ & D. Bellinger. *Main Points in Decisions of the World Bank Administrative Tribunal. Vol. II (1983-1985).* Washington, DC: IBRD, 1985. 33 p.

_____ & D. Thorslund. "Claimants to Staff Membership before International Administrative Tribunals," 38 *ICLQ* 653-67 (1989).

Ballaloud, Jacques. *Le Tribunal Administratif de l'Organisation Internationale du Travail et sa Jurisprudence.* Paris: Pedone, 1967. 159 p.

Bastid, Suzanne. "Les tribunaux administratifs internationaux et leur jurisprudence," 92 *RCADI* 343-517 (1957-II).

_____. "United Nations Administrative Tribunal," in Bernhardt (ed.), *EPIL* 5 (1983) 281-7.

Gomula, Joanna. "The International Court of Justice and Administrative Tribunals of International Organizations," 13

MichJIL 83-121 (1991).

Grimes, David M. "The OAS Administrative Tribunal: Proposals for Appellate Review," 1 *Emory JIDisRes* 257-74 (1987).

Guillaume, G. "La Commission de recours de l'Organisation du Traité de l'Atlantique Nord et sa Jurisprudence," 14 *AFDI* 322-332 (1968).

ILO. *Statute and Rules of the Administrative Tribunal.* Geneva: ILO, 1954.

"International Labour Organization Administrative Tribunal (ILOAT)," (Summary reports of judgments in *UN Juridical Yearbook,* Annual).

Jiménez de Aréchaga, Eduardo. "The World Bank Administrative Tribunal," 14 *NYUJIL& Politics* 895-909 (1982).

"Jurisprudence du Tribunal Administratif des Nations Unies," (Reports in *AFDI*).

Knapp, Blaise. "Jurisprudence du Tribunal Administratif de l'Organisation internationale du Travail," (Reports in *AFDI*).

Koh, Byung Chul. *The United Nations Administrative Tribunal.* Baton Rouge: Louisiana State UP, 1966. 176 p.

Lemoine, J. "Jurisprudence du Tribunal administratif de l'Organisation internationale du Travail," (Reports in *AFDI*).

Lukyanov, V. V. "K voprosu ob administrativnoy yustitsii v organizatsii Obedinionnykh Natsii," [On the question of administrative judiciary in the United Nations] *SovEMP* 110-27 (1980).

Meron, Theodor & Betty Elder. "The New Administrative Tribunal of the World Bank," 14 *NYUJIL& Politics* 1-27 (1981).

Ostrihansky, Rudolf. "Trybunaly administracyjne organizacji miedzynarodowych," [Administrative tribunals of international organizations] 44 *PiP* (no.3) 70-7 (1989).

Priess, Hans-Hoachim. *Internationale Verwaltungsgerichte und Beschwerdeausschüsse; eine Studie zum gerichtlichen Rechtschutz für Beamte internationaler Organisationen.* Berlin: Duncker & Humblot, 1989. 325 p. (Publications of Institut für Internationales Recht an der Universität Kiel, 107).

Robert, J. "Les tribunaux administratifs dans les organisations européennes," 20 *AE* [1972] 124-52 (1974).

Ruzié, David. "Jurisprudence du Tribunal administratif de l'Organisation internationale du travail," (Reports in *AFDI*).

Schechter, Alan H. *Interpretation of Ambiguous Documents by International Administrative Tribunals.* New York; Praeger, 1964. 183 p.

Schwob, Jacques. "Tribunal administratif des Nations Unies," (Reports in *AFDI*, 1978----).

Seyersted, F. "Settlement of Internal Disputes of Intergovernmental Organizations by Internal and External Courts," 24 *ZaöRV* 1-121 (1964).

Sicault, Jean-Didier. "L'évolution récente de la jurisprudence des tribunaux administratifs des Nations Unies et de l'OIT en matière de droits acquis," 94 *RGDIP* 7-47 (1990).

Tavernier, Paul. "La fusion des Tribunaux administratifs des Nations Unies et de l'OIT: Nécessité ou utopie?" 25 *AFDI* 442-59 (1979).

Touscoz, J. "Les tribunaux administratifs internationaux," in *JurisClasseur de Droit International,* fascicules 230-311, 1969 (updated).

UN. *Judgments of the United Nations Administrative Tribunal.* New York: UN, 1991. 715 p.

Vandersanden, Georges. "Administrative Tribunals, Boards and Commissions in International Organizations," in Bernhardt (ed.), *EPIL* 1 (1981) 1-4.

Vuyst de, Bruno M. (ed.). *Statutes and Rules of Procedure of International Administrative Tribunals.* 2 vols. 2d ed. Washington, DC: World Bank Administrative Tribunal, July 1981.

_____. "The World Bank Administrative Tribunal," 16 *RBDI* 81-94 (1981-82).

7. INTERNATIONAL TRIBUNAL FOR THE LAW OF THE SEA

Adede, A.O. "Prolegomena to the Dispute Settlement Part of the Law of the Sea Convention," 10 *NYUJIL& Politics* 253-392 (1977).

_____. "Settlement of Disputes Arising under the Law of the Sea Convention," 69 *AJIL* 798-818 (1975).

_____. *The System for Settlement of Disputes under the United Nations Convention on the Law of the Sea: A Drafting History and a Commentary.* Dordrecht: Nijhoff, 1987. 285 p.

Bernaerts, Arnd. "Seegerichtshof-Tiefseebergbau," 37 *RIW/AWD* 209-18 (1991).

Bernhardt, J. P. A. "Compulsory Dispute Settlement in the Law of the Sea Negotiations: A Reassessment," 19 *VirJIL* 69-105 (1978).

Brown, E. D. "Dispute Settlement," 5 *Marine Policy* 282-5 (1981).

Caflisch, Lucius. "Le règlement judiciaire et arbitral des différends dans le nouveau droit international de la mer," in *Festschrift für Rudolf Bindschädler.* Bern (1980) 351-71.

Cannone, Andrea. *Il Tribunale internazionale del diritto del mare.* Bari: Cacucci Editore, 1991. 247 p.

Carnegie, A. R. "The Law of the Sea Tribunal," 28 *ICLQ* 669-84 (1979).

Coquia, Jorge R. "Settlement of Disputes in the UN Convention in the Law of the Sea: New Directions in the Settlement of International Disputes," 25 *IJIL* 171-90 (1985).

Erasmus, Gerhard. "Dispute Settlement in the Law of the Sea," *Acta Juridica* 15-27 (1986).

Gaertner, Marianne P. "The Dispute Settlement Provisions of the Convention on the Law of the Sea: Critique and Alternatives to the International Tribunal for the Law of the Sea," 19 *San Diego LR* 577-97 (1982).

Gamble, John King. "The 1982 Convention on the Law of the Sea: Binding Dispute Settlement?" 9 *BUILJ* 39-58 (1991).

Giorgi, M. Cristina. "Le Tribunal international du droit de la mer," *Collection espaces et ressources maritimes* (No. 2) 171-84 (1987).

Mestral, de, A. L. C. "Compulsory Dispute Settlement in the Third United Nations Conference on the Law of the Sea: A Canadian Perspective," in *Contemporary Issues in International Law-Essays in Honour of Louis B. Sohn*. Ed. by Thomas Buergenthal. Kehl: Engel, 1984, 169-88.

Noyes, John. "Compulsory Third-Party Adjudication and the 1982 United Nations Convention on the Law of the Sea," 4 *Conn JIL* 675-96 (1989).

Pierce, George A. "Dispute Settlement Mechanisms in the Draft Convention on the Law of the Sea," 10 *Den JIL&Pcy* 331-54 (1981).

Platzöder, Renate. "Sitz in Hamburg: Die Bundesrepublik Deutschland und der Internationale Seegerichtshof," 34 *Vereinte Nationen* 204-7 (1986).

Richardson, Elliot L. "Dispute Settlement under the Convention on the Law of the Sea: A Flexible and Comprehensive Extension of the Rule of the Law to Ocean Space," in *Contemporary Issues in International Law - Essays in Honour of Louis B. Sohn*. Ed. by Thomas Buergenthal. Kehl: Engel, 1984, 149-63.

Rosenne, Shabtai. "The Settlement of Disputes in the New Law of the Sea," *Revue Iranienne des Relations Internationales* 401-33 (1978).

Sohn, Louis B. "Settlement of Disputes Arising out of the Law of the Sea Convention," 12 *San Diego LR* 495-517 (1975).

Sola, Juan Vicente. *The International Tribunal for the Law of the Sea.* Geneva: Institut Universitaire de Hautes Etudes Internationales, 1986. 158 p.

Studier, Alphons. "La Cour Internationale de la Mer dans le cadre de la nouvelle Convention du Droit de la Mer," *Revue Internationale de Droit Contemporain* 49-57 (1990).

Tyagi, Yogesh K. "The System of Settlement of Disputes under the Law of the Sea Convention: An Overview," 25 *IJIL* 191-209 (1985).

UN Office for Ocean Affairs. *The Law of the Sea: A Bibliography on the Law of the Sea 1969-1988* (Chapter VI, 321-6). New York: UN, 1991. 483 p.

8. INTERNATIONAL CRIMINAL COURTS

Bassiouni, M. Cherif (ed.). *A Draft International Criminal Code and Draft Statute for an International Criminal Code.* 1987.

_____ (ed.). *International Criminal Law.* 3 vols. Ardsley-on-Hudson: Transnational Publishers, 1986.

_____. "The Time Has Come for an International Criminal Court," 1 *Indiana International & Comparative Law Journal* 1-43 (1991).

_____ & Christopher L. Blakesley. "The Need for an International Criminal Court in the New International World Order," 25 *VandJTransnL* 151-82 (1992).

Bosch, W. J. *Judgment on Nuremberg. American Attitudes toward the Major German War Crimes Trials.* Chapel Hill, NC: U of North Carolina P, 1970. 272 p.

Bridge, J. W. "The Case for an International Court of Criminal Justice and the Formulation of International Criminal Law," 13 *ICLQ* 1255-81 (1964).

Cavicchia, Joel. "The Prospects for an International Criminal Court in the 1990s," 10 *DickJIL* 223-61 (1992).

Centre de droit international de l'Institut de Sociologie de l'Université de Bruxelles. *Le procès de Nuremberg: Conséquences et actualisation.* Brussels: Editions Bruylant, Editions de l'Université de Bruxelles, 1988. 181 p.

Conot, Robert E. *Justice at Nuremberg.* New York: Harper & Row, 1983. 593 p.

Davidson, Eugene. *The Trial of the Germans, Nuremberg 1945-1946: An Account of the Twenty-Two Defendants before the International Military Tribunal at Nuremberg.* New York: Macmillan, 1967. 636 p.

Ferencz, Benjamin B. "International Criminal Court," in Bernhardt (ed.), *EPIL* 1 (1981) 99-101.

_____. "An International Criminal Code and Court: Where They Stand and Where They're Going," 30 *ColJTransnL* 375-99 (1992).

_____. *An International Criminal Court. A Step toward World Peace. A Documentary History and Analysis.* Vol. 1: *Half a Century of*

Hope. 538 p. Vol. 2: *The Beginning of Wisdom.* 674 p. London, Rome, New York: Oceana Publications, 1980.

Ginsburg, George & V. N. Kudriavtsev (eds.). *The Nuremberg Trial and International Law.* Dordrecht: Nijhoff, 1990. 304 p.

Glueck, Sheldon. *The Nuremberg Trial and Aggressive War.* New York: Knopf, 1946. 121 p.

Graefrath, Bernhard. "Universal Criminal Jurisdiction and an International Criminal Court," 1 *EJIL-JEDI* 67-88 (1990).

Heydecker, J. J. & J. Leeb. *The Nuremberg Trial.* Cleveland: World Publishing, 1962. 398 p.

Hosoya, C., N. Ando, Y. Onuma, & R. Minear (eds.). *The Tokyo War Crimes Trial: An International Symposium.* Tokyo: Kodansha International Ltd., 1986. 226 p.

International Military Tribunal, Nuremberg. *Trial of the Major War Criminals before the International Military Tribunal, Nuremberg. 14 November 1945-1 October 1946.* 42 vols. 1947-1949.

Kopelman, Elizabeth. "Ideology and International Law: The Dissent of the Indian Justice at the Tokyo War Crimes Trial," 23 *NYUJIL& Politics* 373-444 (1991).

Lewis, John (compiled and ed.). *Uncertain Judgment: A Bibliography of War Crimes Trials.* Santa Barbara, CA: ABC-CLIO, 1979. 251 p.

Lippman, Matthew. "Nuremberg: Forty Years Later," 7 *ConnJIL* 1-64 (1991).

Maugham, Viscount. *U.N.O. and War Crimes.* London: Murray, 1951. 143 p.

Neave, A. M. S. *Nuremberg: A Personal Record of the Trial of the Major Nazi War Criminals in 1945-6.* London: Hodder & Stoughton, 1978. 348 p.

Neumann, Inge S. (compiled). *European War Crimes Trials: A Bibliography.* New York: Carnegie Endowment, 1951. 113 p.

Pritchard, R. & S. Zaide. *The Tokyo War Crimes Trial.* 1981.

Saurel, L. *Le procès de Nuremberg.* Paris: Rouff, 1965. 188 p.

Scharf, Michael. "The Jury Is Still Out on the Need for an International Criminal Court," *Duke Journal of Comparative and International Law* 135-66 (1991).

Smith, Bradley F. *The American Road to Nuremberg: The Documentary Record 1944-1945.* Stanford: Hoover Institution P, 1982. 272 p.

_____. *Reaching Judgment at Nuremberg.* Meridian, NY: New American Library, 1977. 349 p.

Sottile, Antoine. *The Problem of the Creation of a Permanent International Criminal Court* (Reprint of 1951 ed.). Milwood, NY: Kraus Reprint, 1990.

Taylor, Telford. *The Anatomy of the Nuremberg Trials: A Personal Memoir.* New York: Knopf, 1992. 703 p.

Trial of Japanese War Criminals: Documents. Washington, DC: GPO, 1946. (Department of State Publication No. 2613). 104 p.

Trial of War Criminals: Documents. Washington: GPO, 1945. 89 p. (Department of State Publication No. 2420).

Tutorow, Norman E. (compiled and edited, with the special assistance of Karen Winnovich). *War Crimes, War Criminals, and War Crimes Trials: An Annotated Bibliography and Source Book.* New York: Greenwood Press, 1986. 548 p.

UN Secretary General. *Historical Survey of the Question of International Criminal Jurisdiction.* Lake Success, NY: UN, 1949. 147 p.

Woetzel, Robert K. *The Nuremberg Trials in International Law.* New York: Praeger, 1960. Rev. ed. 1962.

Wright, Quincy. "The Law of the Nuremberg Trial," 41 *AJIL* 38-72 (1947).

9. COURT OF JUSTICE OF THE EUROPEAN COMMUNITIES

Achim, André. *Beweisführung und Beweislast im Verfahren vor dem Europäischen Gerichtshof* (Kölner Schriften zum Europarecht, Vol. 6). Cologne, Berlin, Bonn, Munich: Heymanns Verlag, 1966. 252 p.

Acosta, Estévez, José B. *Proceso, procedimiento y recursos ante el Tribunal de Justicia de las Comunidades Europeas.* Barcelona: Promociones y Publicaciones Univ., 1988. 290 p.

Amphoux, Jean. "A propos de l'arrêt 26/62 rendu le 5 février 1963 par la Cour de Justice des Communautés européennes," 68 *RGDIP* 11-57 (1964).

———. "Cour de Justice des Communautés européennes. Décisions rendues du 19 août 1988 au 13 juillet 1989," 26 *CDE* 75-210 (1990).

———. "Cour de Justice des Communautés européennes et Tribunal de première instance. Décisions rendues d'août 1989 à juillet 1990," 27 *CDE* 101-242 (1991).

Arnull, Anthony, "Does the Court of Justice Have Inherent Jurisdiction?" 27 *CMLRev* 683-708 (1990).

———. "References to the European Court," 15 *ELR* 375-91 (1990).

L'Association belge pour le droit européen & l'Institut d'Etudes européennes de l'Université de Bruxelles. *La Cour de Justice des Communautés européennes et les Etats membres.* Brussels: Editions de l'Université de Bruxelles, 1981. 128 p.

Aubert, F. "La Cour de Justice des Communautés européennes," 7 *RTDE* 78-106 (1971).

Barav, Ann. "The Judicial Power of the European Economic Community," 53 *South California Law Review* 461-525 (1980).

Bartelot, Pascale. *Babylone à Luxembourg: jurilinguistique à la Cour de Justice.* Saarbrücken: Europa-Institut, 1988. 32 p.

Bebr, Gerhard. *Development of Judicial Control of European Communities.* The Hague: Nijhoff, 1981. 822 p.

———. *Judicial Control of the European Communities.* London:

Stevens, 1962. 268 p.

―――. "Preliminary Rulings of the Court of Justice: Their Authority and Temporal Effect," 18 *CMLRev* 475-507 (1981).

Bergerès, Maurice-Christian. *Contentieux Communautaire (Droit fondamental).* Paris: Presses Universitaires de France, 1989. 346 p.

Borchardt, Guus. "The Award of Interim Measures by the European Court of Justice," 22 *CMLRev* 203-36 (1985).

Borgsmidt, Kirsten. "Der Generalanwalt beim Europäischen Gerichtshof und einige vergleichbare Institutionen," 22 *EuR* 162-77 (1987).

Boulouis, Jean. "Cour de Justice des Communautés européennes," 32 *AFDI* 239-44 (1986).

―――. "La Jurisprudence de la Cour de Justice des Communautés européennes relative aux relations extérieures des Communautés," 160 *RCADI* 335-94 (1978-II).

―――. "Jurisprudence de la Cour de Justice des Communautés européennes," 14 *AFDI* 260-77 (1968).

―――― & R. M. Chevallier. *Grands arrêts de la Cour de Justice des Communautés européennes.* Vol. 1: *Caractères généraux du droit communautaire, droit institutionnel, contrôle juridictionnel.* Paris: Dalloz, 1974. 453 p. 2d ed. 1978. 511 p.

Brown, L. Neville & Francis G. Jacobs. *The Court of Justice of the European Communities.* London: Sweet & Maxwell, 1977. 254 p.

Calvet, Hugues & Franck Dintilhac. "Chronique de jurisprudence en matière de liberté d'établissement et de libre prestation de services. Cour de Justice des Communautés européennes 1er janvier 1989 - 31 décembre 1990," 27 *RTDE* 59-78 (1991).

"Chronique de jurisprudence de la Cour de justice des Communautés européennes," 116 *JDI* 389-465 (1989).

Common Market Law Reports. Ed. by Neville Hunnings. London: European Law Centre. 1951----.

Court of Justice of the European Communities. *Reports of the.* Annual.

―――. *Review of Cases Heard by.* Annual.

"Crónica de la jurisprudencia del Tribunal de justicia de las Comunidades europeas: Año 1983 (III)," 12 *RIE* 235-74 (1985).

Dashwood, A. A. "The Advocate General in the Court of Justice of the European Communities," 2 *Legal Studies* 202-16 (1982).

Donner, André M. "The Constitutional Powers of the Court of Justice of the European Communities," 11 *CMLRev* 127-40 (1974).

———. "Les rapports entre la compétence de la Cour de Justice des Communautés européennes et les tribunaux internes," 115 *RCADI* 1-61 (1965-II).

Eeckman, P. & H. Vanhees. "Overzicht van de rechtspraak van het Hof van Justitie van de Europese Gemeenschappen (september 1989-juli 1990) (Eerste deel)," 54 *RW* 22: 729-45 (1991).

Feld, Werner. *The Court of Justice of the European Communities: New Dimension in International Adjudication.* The Hague: Nijhoff, 1964. 127 p.

Freeman, Elizabeth. "Decisions of the European Court of Justice Relating to the Jurisdiction of the Court," 1 *YEL* 407-16 (1981).

Gaffin, Léon. "La jurisprudence de la Cour de justice sur les droits de la défense," 76 *CDE* 127-44 (1980).

Gijlstra, D. J., Henry G. Schermers, E. L. M. Völker, & J. A. Winter. *Leading Cases on the Law of the European Communities.* Deventer: Kluwer, 1982. 599 p.

Goletti, Giovanni Battista. "La Corte dei conti delle Comunità europee nel quadro istituzionale," 64 *Foro amministrativo* 3931-57 (1988).

Gray, Christine. "Advisory Opinions and the European Court of Justice," 8 *ELR* 24-30 (1983).

———. "Interim measures of Protection in the European Court," 4 *ELR* 80-102 (1979).

Green, Andrew Wilson. *Political Integration by Jurisprudence: The Work of the Court of Justice of the European Communities in European Political Integration.* Leyden: Sijthoff, 1969. 848 p.

Grementieri, V. & C. J. Golden Jr. "The United Kingdom and the European Court of Justice: An Encounter between Common and Civil Law Traditions," 21 *AJCL* 664-90 (1973).

Guegan, J. *Les méthodes de la Cour de Justice des Communautés européennes.* Rennes: University of Rennes, Thesis, 1979.

Gulmann, C. "Methods of Interpretation of the European Court of Justice," 24 *Scandinavian Studies in Law* 187-204 (1980).

Henrichs, Helmut. "Die Rechtsprechung des Europäischen Gerichtshofs in Personalsachen," 15 *EuR* 134-53 (1980).

Hermann-Rodeville, Jeannine. "Un exemple de contentieux économique: le recours en indemnité devant la Cour de justice des

Communautés européennes," 22 *RTDE* 1-51 (1986).

Hoffman, Rainer. "Sea Fisheries Restrictions Case (E.C. Commission v. Ireland)," in Bernhardt (ed.), *EPIL* 2 (1981) 254-56.

Houtte, Albert van. "La Cour de Justice de la Communauté européenne du Charbon et de l'Acier," 2 *AE* 183-218 (1954).

_____. "La Cour de Justice des Communautés européennes: organisation et procédure," 19 *CDE* 3-35 (1983).

Joliet, R. "Voorstelling van het Hof van justitie van de Europese Gemeenschappen," 48 *RW* 1121-44 (1984).

Kawass, I. I. "The Court of Justice of the European Communities: An Annotated Bibliography," 8 *VandJTransnL* 523-650 (1974-1975).

Klein, Eckart. "International Fruit Company Case," in Bernhardt (ed.), *EPIL* 2 (1981) 138-40.

Lagrange, M. "La Cour de Justice des Communautés européennes: Du plan Schumann à l'Union européenne," 14 *RTDE* 1-17 (1978).

_____. "The European Court of Justice and National Courts," 8 *CMLRev* 313-24 (1971).

Lasok, D. "La Cour de justice, instrument de l'intégration communautaire," 2 *Revue d'intégration européenne* 391-413 (1979).

Lecourt, R. "Le rôle de la Cour de justice dans le développement des Communautés," 24 *AE* 19-41 (1976).

Lenz, Karl Otto. "The Court of Justice of the European Communities," 14 *ELR* 127-39 (1989).

Louis, Jean-Victor. "Los efectos de las sentencias del Tribunal de Justicia de las Comunidades Europeas," 10 *RIE* 9-21 (1983).

Mackenzie, Stuart, Alexander John Lord. "Die Rolle des Gerichtshofes in der Rechtsordnung der Europäischen Gemeinschaft," 29 *Zeitschrift für Rechtsvergleichung* 202-14 (1988).

Mann, Clarence J. *The Function of Judicial Decision in European Economic Integration.* The Hague: Nijhoff, 1972. 515 p.

McMahon, J. F. "The Court of the European Communities: Judicial Interpretation and International Organisation," 37 *BYIL* 320-50 (1962).

Mertens de Wilmars, J. & J. Steenbergen. "The Court of Justice of the European Communities and Governance in an Economic Crisis," 82 *Michigan Law Review* 1377-98 (1984).

Migliazza, A. "La Corte di giustizia delle Comunità europee e il suo ambito di giurisdizione," 14 *Rivista trimestrale-diritto e procedura civile* 595-60 (1960).

Pacilio, Ombretta. *La Corte de Justicia de la Comunidad Económica Europea.* Buenos Aires: Ed. Depalma, 1989. 198 p.

Parkinson, Kimberley A. "Admissibility of Direct Actions by Natural or Legal Persons in the European Court of Justice: Judicial Distinctions between Decisions and Regulations," 24 *TexILJ* 561-621 (1989).

Pescatore, Pierre. "Aspects of the Court of Justice of the European Communities of Interest from the Point of View of International Law," 32 *ZaöRV* 239-52 (1972).

_____. "Court of Justice of the European Communities," in Bernhardt (ed.), *EPIL* 6 (1983) 92-105.

_____. "External Relations in the Case Law of the Court of Justice of the European Communities," 16 *CMLRev* 615-45 (1979).

_____. "Le recours dans la jurisprudence de la Cour de Justice des Communautés européennes à des normes déduites de la comparaison des droits des Etats modernes," 32 *RIDC* 337-59 (1980).

_____. "Rôle et chance du droit et des juges dans la construction de l'Europe,' 26 *RIDC* 5-19 (1974).

Petersmann, Ernst U. "European Road Transport Agreement Case," in Bernhardt (ed.), *EPIL* 2 (1981) 88-91.

Plender, Richard. "The European Court as an International Tribunal," 42 *CambLJ* 279-98 (1983).

Plouvier, Liliane. *Les décisions de la Cour de Justice des Communautés européennes et leurs effets juridiques.* Brussels: Etablissement Emile Bruylant, 1975. 310 p.

Reuter, Paul. "La Cour de Justice des Communautés européennes et le droit international," in *Recueil d'Etudes de Droit International Public en Hommage à Paul Guggenheim* 665-86. Geneva: Faculté de Droit de l'Université de Genève, 1968.

Riesenfeld, S. A. & R. M. Buxbaum. "A Pioneering Decision of the Court of Justice of the European Communities," 58 *AJIL* 152-9 (1964).

Roberts, Thomas B. "Judicial Review of Legislative Measures: The European Court of Justice Breathes Life into the Second Paragraph of Article 215 of the Treaty of Rome," 26 *ColJTransnL* 245-81 (1988).

Schermers, Henry G. "The European Court of Justice: Promoter of European Integration," 22 *AJCL* 444-64 (1974).

_____ & Michel Waelbroeck. *Judicial Protection in the European Communities*. 4th ed. Deventer: Kluwer, 1987.

Schlüter-Lapierre, Martine. "Van Gend en Loos Case," in Bernhardt (ed.), *EPIL* 2 (1981) 287-90.

Schroth, P. W. "Marburg and Simmenthal: Reflections on the Adoption of Decentralized Judicial Review by the Court of Justice of the European Community," 12 *Loyola of Los Angeles Law Review* 869-902 (1979).

Schulte, B. & H. F. Zacher. "Das Sozialrecht in der Rechtsprechung des Europäischen Gerichtshofs," 1 *Jahrbuch des Sozialrechts der Gegenwart* 353-90 (1979).

Schwarze, Jürgen. *The Role of the European Court of Justice (ECJ) in the Interpretation of Uniform Law among the Member States of the European Communities (EC)*. Baden-Baden: Nomos Verlag, 1988. 53 p.

Slynn, Gordon. "The Court of Justice of the European Communities," 33 *ICLQ* 409-29 (1984).

Somerville, Kurt F. "Political Integration through Jurisprudence: An Analysis of the European Court of Justice's Rulings of Freedom of Movement of Workers," 6 *Boston Coll&CLJ* 273-314 (1983).

Stein, Torsten. "Donckerwolcke Case," in Bernhardt (ed.), *EPIL* 2 (1981) 79-81.

_____. "Premiums for Reducing Dairy Production Case (E.C. Commission v. Italy)," in Bernhardt (ed.), *EPIL* 2 (1981) 235-6.

_____. "Rutili Case," in Bernhardt (ed.), *EPIL* 2 (1981) 247-8.

Stoelting, David. "The Jurisdictional Framework of the European Court of Justice," 29 *Coll/TransnL* 193-214 (1991).

Tizzano, Antonio. *La Corte di Giustizia delle Comunità Europee*. Vol. I. Naples: Eugenio Jovene, 1967. 480 p.

Tomuschat, Christian. "La contribution de la Cour de Justice des Communautés européennes au règlement des conflits entre Etats membres," 78 *RGDIP* 40-59 (1974).

Toth, A. G. "The Authority of Judgments of the European Court of Justice: Binding Force and Legal Effects," 4 *YEL* 1-77 (1984).

Tsirikas, Dimitros. *Die Wirkungen der Urteile des Europäischen Gerichtshofs im Vertragsverletzungsverfahren (Art. 169 ff. EWGV)*. Berlin: Duncker & Humblot, 1990. 227 p.

Usher, John A. *European Court Practice*. London, Rome, New York: Oceana, 1983. 357 p.

_____. "The Interpretation of Community Law by the European Court of Justice," 11 *Law Teacher* 162-77 (1977).

Valentine, D. G. *The Court of Justice of the European Coal and Steel Community.* The Hague: Nijhoff, 1954. 273 p.

_____. *The Court of Justice of the European Communities.* 2 vols. Vol. 1: *Jurisdiction and Procedure.* 601 p.; Vol. 2: *Judgments and Documents 1954-1960.* Translated and edited. 873 p. London: Stevens & Sons. South Hackensack, NJ: Rothman & Co., 1965.

Vandersanden, G. "Le rôle de la Cour de Justice des Communautés européennes dans le processus d'intégration Communautaire," 25 *Aussenwirtschaft* 403-26 (1970).

Waelbroeck, Michel. "Le rôle de la Cour de justice dans la mise en oeuvre de l'Acte unique européen," 25 *CDE* 41-62 (1989).

_____. "The Role of the Court of Justice in the Implementation of the Single European Act," 11 *MichJIL* 671-90 (1990).

Zieger, G. "Die Rechtsprechung des Europäischen Gerichtshofs," 22 *Jahrbuch des öffentlichen Rechts der Gegenwart* 293-356 (1973).

10. COURT OF FIRST INSTANCE OF THE EUROPEAN COMMUNITIES

Biancarelli, Jacques. "La création du Tribunal de première instance des Communautés européennes: un luxe ou une nécessité?" 26 *RTDE* 1025(1990).

Crossick, Stanley. "A Court of First Instance at Last in Session," 140 *New Law Journal* 524-27 (1990).

Dué, Olé. "The Court of First Instance," 8 *YEL* 1-10 (1988).

Galmot, Yves. "Le Tribunal de première instance des Communautés européennes," 5 *Revue Française de Droit Administratif* 567-78 (1989).

Ginderachter, E. van. "Le tribunal de première instance des Communautés européennes: Un nouveau-né prodige?" 25 *CDE* 63-105 (1989).

Joliet, R. & W. Vogel. "Le tribunal de première instance des Communautés européennes," *Revue du Marché Commun et de l'Union européenne* (No. 329) 423-31 (1989).

Jung, Hans. "El Tribunal de Primera Instancia de las Comunidades Europeas: Aspectos de la ampliación a dos órganos de la jurisdicción comunitaria," 16 *RIE* 339-78 (1989).

Lenaerts, Koen. "Het Gerecht van eerste aanleg van de Europese Gemeenschappen," 38 *SEW* 527-48 (1990).

_____. "Das Gericht erster Instanz der Europäischen Gemeinschaften," 25 *EuR* 228-48 (1990).

_____. "Le Tribunal de première instance des Communautés européennes: genèse et premiers pas," 109 *Journal des Tribunaux* 5553: 400-15 (1990).

Matienzo, Sonia. "En torno al Tribunal de Primera Instancia de la Comunidad Europea," *Revista de Estudios de las Comunidades Europeas* 383-98 (1989).

Millett, Timothy. *The Court of First Instance of European Communities*. London: Butterworths, 1990. 144 p.

_____. "The New European Court of First Instance," 38 *ICLQ* 811-33 (1989).

Saggio, Antonio. "Il Tribunale comunitario di primo grado," 27 *Diritto comunitario e degli Scambi internazionali* 611-29 (1988).

Schermers, Henry G. "The European Court of First Instance," 25 *CMLRev* 541-58 (1988).

Tizzano, Antonio. "L'istituzione del 'Tribunale di primo grado' delle Comunità Europee," 114 *Foro It.* 75-85 (1989).

Weidner, Neil J. "The Court of First Instance of the European Communities," 17 *SyrJIL&Com* 241-66 (1991).

11. BENELUX ECONOMIC UNION COURT OF JUSTICE AND COLLEGE OF ARBITRATORS

Binsbergen, W. C. van. "Ontwerp-Verdrag tot instelling van een Benelux-Gerechtshof," 12 *SEW* 308-18 (1964).

Demez, G. "La Cour de justice Benelux," 12 *CDE* 149-78 (1976).

Dumon, F. *La Cour de Justice Benelux.* 1980.

Kruijtbosch, E. D. J. "Benelux Economic Union, College of Arbitrators and Court of Justice," in Bernhardt (ed.), *EPIL* 6 (1983) 39-42.

Mewissen, E. Het Beneluxgerechtshof, een beknopt overzicht van zijn statuut," 35 *RW* 1329-38 (1972).

Schneider, J. W. "The Benelux Court," 4 *NYIL* 193-235 (1973).

Vreese, de, A. "Het Benelux-Gerechtshof," 30 *SEW* 563-82 (1982).

12. EUROPEAN COURT OF HUMAN RIGHTS

Berger, Vincent. *The Case Law of the European Court of Human Rights 1. 1960-1987.* Dublin: Round Hall, 1989. 478 p.

_____. *Jurisprudence de la Cour européenne des droits de l'homme.* 2d ed. Paris: Editions Sirey, 1989. 418 p.

Bonner, David. "Ireland v. United Kingdom," 27 *ICLQ* 897-907 (1978).

Boxman, Renée F. "The Road to *Soering* and Beyond: Will the United States Recognize the 'Death Row' Phenomenon?" 14 *Houston JIL* 151-82 (1991).

Cançado Trindade, A. A. "Exhaustion of Local Remedies in the Jurisprudence of the European Court of Human Rights: An Appraisal," 10 *RDH* 141-85 (1977).

Castro-Rial Garrone, Fanny. "Decisiones del Tribunal Europeo de Derechos Humanos (1989)," 18 *RIE* 283-301 (1991).

Cohen-Jonathan, Gérard. "Cour européenne des droits de l'homme (1982-1983-1984)," 22 *CDE* 203-32 (1986).

_____. "Cour européenne des droits de l'homme (Chronique 1985-1986-1987)," 24 *CDE* 438-90 (1988).

Council of Europe. (ed.). *Digest of Strasbourg Case Law Relating to the European Convention on Human Rights.* 5 vols. Cologne: Carl Heymanns Verlag. 1984-1985 Vol. 6: *General Index to Volumes 1-5.* 1985. 662 p.

_____. *Yearbook of the European Convention on Human Rights - Annuaire de la Convention européenne des Droits de l'Homme.* Serial. Vol. 29 (1986): Dordrecht, Nijhoff, 1991. 624 p.

Coussirat-Coustère, Vincent. "La jurisprudence de la Cour européenne des Droits de l'homme en 1984," 31 *AFDI* 391-417 (1985).

_____. "La jurisprudence de la Cour européenne des Droits de l'homme en 1985," 32 *AFDI* 275-303 (1986).

_____. "La jurisprudence de la Cour européenne des Droits de l'homme en 1986," 33 *AFDI* 239-63 (1987).

Eissen, Marc-André. "La Cour européenne des droits de l'homme,"

25 *Cahiers de Droit* 873-933 (1984).

_____. "La Cour européenne des droits de l'homme: de la Convention au Règlement," 5 *AFDI* 618-58 (1959).

_____. "Der Europäische Gerichtshof für Menschenrechte," 64 *Deutsche Richterzeitung* 1-12 (1986).

Ermacora, Felix. "L'accès aux mécanismes juridictionnels de protection des personnes privées dans la Convention européenne des Droits de l'Homme," 6 *RDH* 645-57 (1973).

Facchin, Roberto (ed.). *L'interpretazione giudiziaria della Convenzione europea dei diritti dell'uomo: guida alla giurisprudenza della Corte (1960-1987)*. Padua: Cedam, 1988. 560 p.

Faucett, J. E. S. *The Application of the European Convention on Human Rights*. 2d ed. New York: Oxford UP, 1987. 456 p.

Fernández Sagado, Francisco. "La libertad de expresión en la doctrina del Tribunal Europeo de Derechos Humanos," *Revista de Estudios Políticos* (No. 70) 93-124 (1990).

Frowein, Jochen A. "The European and the American Conventions on Human Rights: A Comparison," 1 *Human Rights Law Journal* 44-65 (1980).

_____. "European Convention on Human Rights," in Bernhardt (ed.), *EPIL* 8 (1985) 184-92.

Gappa, David L. "European Court of Human Rights - Extradition - Inhuman or Degrading Treatment or Punishment," 20 *Georgia JI&CL* 463-88 (1990).

Hampson, Françoise J. "The United Kingdom before the European Court of Human Rights," 9 *YEL* 121-73 (1989).

Lillich, Richard B. "The Soering Case," 85 *AJIL* 128-49 (1991).

Mahoney, P. "Developments in the Procedure of the European Court of Human Rights: The Revised Rules of Court," 3 *YEL* 127-67 (1983).

Meersch van der & W. J. Ganshof. "European Court of Human Rights," in Bernhardt (ed.), *EPIL* 8 (1985) 192-207.

Merrills, J. G. "Sir Gerald Fitzmaurice's Contribution to the Jurisprudence of the European Court of Human Rights," 53 *BYIL* 115-62 (1982).

Nadelmann, Kurt H. "Due Process of Law before the European Court of Human Rights," 66 *AJIL* 509-25 (1972).

Nørgaard, Carl Aage. "European Commission of Human Rights," in Bernhardt (ed.), *EPIL* 8 (1985) 178-84.

Pelloux, Robert. "Les arrêts rendus par la Cour européenne des Droits de l'homme en 1981," 28 *AFDI* 492-512 (1982).

_____. "Les arrêts rendus par la Cour européenne des Droits de l'homme en 1982," 29 *AFDI* 246-65 (1983).

_____. "Les arrêts rendus par la Cour européenne des Droits de l'homme en 1983," 30 *AFDI* 446-65 (1984).

Pettiti, Louis. "Le opinioni individuali dei giudici della Corte dei diritti dell'uomo: una rassegna," 1 *RIDU* 30-40 (1988).

_____. "Le opinioni separate, dissenzienti e concordanti dei giudici della Corte europea dei diritti dell'uomo," 2 *RIDU* 406-17 (1989).

Robertson, A. H. "The European Court of Human Rights," 9 *AJCL* 1-28 (1960).

_____. *Human Rights in Europe*. Dobbs Ferry, NY: Oceana, 1963. 280 p.

Rolland, Patrice & Paul Tavernier. "Chronique de jurisprudence de la Cour européenne des droits de l'homme," 112 *JDI* 185-231 (1985); 113 *JDI* 1051-91 (1986); 114 *JDI* 771-814 (1987); 116 *JDI* 793-851 (1989); 117 *JDI* 705-744 (1990).

Schermers, Henry G. "Factual Merger of the European Court and Commission of Human Rights," 11 *ELR* 350-52 (1986).

Sudre, Frédéric. "Extradition et peine de mort: Arrêt Soering de la Cour européenne des droits de l'homme, du 7 juillet 1989," 94 *RGDIP* 103-21 (1990).

Suy, Eric. "De zaak 'De Becker' voor het Europese hof der mensenrechten," 52 *Rechtskundig Tijdschrift voor België* 131-52 (1962).

Tizzano, Antonio. "Corte europea dei diritti dell'uomo (lo gennaio - 30 giugno 1988)," 114 *Foro It.* 271-88 (1989).

_____. "Corte europea dei diritti dell'uomo (lo luglio - 31 dicembre 1989)," 115 *Foro It.* 506-34 (1990).

Valticos, Nicolas. "Les recours à la Cour européenne des droits de l'homme: quelques cas récents," 112 *SJ* 209-24 (1990).

Warbrick, Colin. "Coherence and the European Court of Human Rights: The Adjudicative Background to the Soering Case," 11 *MichJIL* 1073-96 (1990).

Weil, Gordon Lee. *The European Convention on Human Rights: Background, Developments and Prospects*. Leyden: Sijthoff, 1962. 260 p.

Wong, Wing-Wah Mary. "The Sunday Times Case: Freedom of

Expression versus English Contempt-of-Court Law in the European Court of Human Rights," 17 *NYUJIL& Politics* 35-75 (1984).

13. INTER-AMERICAN COURT OF HUMAN RIGHTS

Abranches, de, C. A. Dunshee. "The Inter-American Court of Human Rights," 30 *American University Law Review* 79-125 (1980).

American Convention on Human Rights, Opened for signature in San José, 22 November 1969, entered into force 18 July 1978, in OAS, *Handbook of Existing Rules Pertaining to Human Rights in the Inter-American System,* OEA/Ser.L./V/ii.60, Document 28, at 29. Reprinted in 9 *ILM* 673 (1970).

Buergenthal, Thomas. "The Advisory Practice of the Inter-American Human Rights Court," 79 *AJIL* 1-27 (1985).

_____. "American Convention on Human Rights," in Bernhardt (ed.), *EPIL* 8 (1985) 23-7.

_____. "Inter-American Court of Human Rights," in Bernhardt (ed.), *EPIL* 8 (1985) 324-6.

_____. "The Inter-American Court of Human Rights," 76 *AJIL* 231-45 (1982).

_____ & Robert E. Norris (eds.). *Human Rights: The Inter-American System.* Binders I, II, and III. (Updated periodically). Dobbs Ferry, NY: Oceana, 1982-1983.

_____, Robert E. Norris & Dinah Shelton. *Protecting Human Rights in the Americas: Selected Problems.* 3d ed. (A publication of the International Institute of Human Rights, Strassbourg). Kehl: Engel, 1990. 562 p.

Cerna, Christina M. "La Cour interaméricaine des Droits de l'Homme-ses premières affaires," 29 *AFDI* 300-12 (1983).

_____. "La Cour interaméricaine des Droits de l'Homme: Les affaires récentes," 33 *AFDI* 351-69 (1987).

Cohen-Jonathan, Gérard. "Cour interaméricaine des droits de l'homme: L'arrêt Velásquez," 94 *RGDIP* 455-71 (1990).

Davidson, Scott. *The Inter-American Court of Human Rights.* Brookfield, VT: Dartmouth Publishing Company, 1992. 271 p.

Deodhar, Neal S. "First Contentious Cases before the International American Court of Human Rights," 3 *AUJIL&Pcy* 283-97 (1988).

Dwyer, Amy S. "The Inter-American Court of Human Rights: Towards Establishing an Effective Regional Contentious Jurisdiction," 13 *Boston Coll&CLJ* 127-66 (1990).

Farer, Tom J. "Inter-American Commission on Human Rights," in Bernhardt (ed.), *EPIL* 8 (1985) 321-4.

Gómez, Rojas A. *La Corte Interamericana de Justicia.* Bogotá: Pontificia Universidad Javeriana, 1966.

Gros Espiell, Héctor. "Contentious Proceedings before the Inter-American Court of Human Rights," 1 *Emory JIDisRes* 175-218 (1987).

_____. "La Convention américaine et la Convention européenne des droits de l'homme. Analyse comparative," 218 *RCADI* 167-412 (1989-VI).

_____. "El procedimiento contencioso ante la Corte Interamericana de Derechos Humanos," 19 *Boletín Mexicano de Derecho Comparado* 511-48 (1986).

_____. "Le système interaméricain comme régime régional de protection internationale des droits de l'homme," 145 *RCADI* 1-55 (1975-II).

I-ACHR. Annual Report of the Inter-American Court of Human Rights (annual). 1981---- Washington, DC: OAS.

Kokott, Juliane. "Der interamerikanische Gerichtshof für Menschenrechte und seine bisherige Praxis," 44 *ZaöRV* 806-39 (1984).

Méndez, Juan E. & José Miguel Vivanco. "Disappearances and the Inter-American Court: Reflections on a Litigation Experience," 13 *Hamline Law Review* 507-77 (1980).

OAS General Secretariat. *Handbook of Existing Rules Pertaining to Human Rights in the Inter-American System.* Washington, DC: OAS, 1985.

Padilla, Miguel M. "El hábeas corpus durante emergencias según la opinión de la Corte Interamericana de Derechos Humanos," 1 *Revista Jurídica de Buenos Aires* 49-67 (1990).

Pena, B. "Human Rights: The Statute of the Inter-American Court of Human Rights," 21 *Harvard ILJ* 735-42 (1980).

Ventura, Manuel E. & D. Zovatto. *La Función Consultiva de la Corte Interamericana de Derechos Humanos: Naturaleza y Principios 1982-1987.* San José & Madrid: Instituto Interamericano de Derechos Humanos/Editorial Civitas, 1989. 463 p.

14. COURT OF JUSTICE OF THE CARTAGENA AGREEMENT

Keener, E. Barlow. "The Andean Common Market Court of Justice: Its Purpose, Structure, and Future," 2 *Emory JIDisRes* 39-71 (1987).

Linares, Antonio. "El Tribunal de Justicia del Acuerdo de Cartagena," 2 *Anuario Argentino de Derecho Internacional* 53-63 (1984/86).

Lochridge, E. P. "The Role of the Andean Court in Consolidating Integration Effort," 10 *Georgia JI&CL* 351-83 (1980).

Maclean, R. "A Note on the Creation of the Andean Tribunal," 1 *Houston JIL* 143-5 (1979).

Meisel Lanner, Roberto. *El Tribunal Andino de Justicia: antecedentes, creación legal y procedimiento ante ese organismo.* Bogota: Librería del Profesional, 1988. 196 p.

Morales Molina, H. "Tribunal de justicia del Pacto Andino," *Revista Uruguaya de Derecho Procesal* 179-92 (1979).

Nikken, Pedro. "Andean Common Market Court of Justice," in Bernhardt (ed.), *EPIL* 6 (1983) 15-20.

Orrego Vicuña, F. "La creación de un Tribunal de Justicia en el Grupo andino," 15 *Revista de derecho de la integración* 31-45 (1974).

Pierola, Nicolas de. "The Andean Court of Justice," 2 *Emory JIDisRes* 11-37 (1987).

Toledano Laredo, Armando. "El abogado general en el Tribunal de Justicia Andino y en el Tribunal de Justicia de las Comunidades Europeas," 11 *RIE* 809-16 (1984).

Zalduendo de, S. C. "El Tribunal Andino de Justicia," 4 *Integración Latinoamericana* 32-37 (1979).

15. CENTRAL AMERICAN COURT OF JUSTICE

Gutiérrez, G. J. *La Corte de Justicia Centro-Americana.* San José: Ediciones Juricentro,1978 (Colección Escuela Libre de Derecho). 161 p.

Hill, Humphrey. "Central American Court of Justice," in Bernhardt (ed.), *EPIL* 1 (1981) 41-45.

Hudson, Manley O. "The Central American Court of Justice," 26 *AJIL* 759-86 (1932).

Maza y Rodríguez, E. *La Corte de Justicia Centroamericana.* San Salvador: Organización de Estados Americanos, 1966.

Pena, Velasco Cuéllar C. *La Corte de Justicia Centroamericana y las relaciones internacionales.* México: Universidad Nacional Autónoma de México, Thesis, 1963. 154 p.

16. ARBITRATION IN GENERAL

Annual Digest of Public International Cases: Vols. 1-6. *Annual Digest and Reports of Public International Law Cases:* Vols. 7-16 (1919-1942). Since 1950 appears as *International Law Reports:* vols. 17---. Edited by Hersch Lauterpacht, Elihu Lauterpacht, Arnold D. McNair *et al.* London: Longmans, Green, 1932-1937; Butterworths, 1938----.

Arbitration Commission on Property, Rights and Interests in Germany, *Decisions* - Die Schiedskommission für Güter, Rechte und Interessen in Deutschland, *Entscheidunden* - La Commission Arbitrale sur les Biens, Droits et Intérêts en Allemagne - *Décisions.* 10 vols. Coblenz: Published by Direction of the Arbitral Commission by W. Euler, member of the Commission, 1958-1969.

Balasko, A. *Causes de nullité de la sentence arbitrale en droit international public.* Paris: Pedone, 1938. 403 p.

Balch, Thomas W. *International Courts of Arbitration.* 6th ed. Philadelphia: Allen, Lane & Scott, 1915 (1st ed. 1874). 78 p.

Balladore Pallieri, I. "La natura giuridica dell'arbitrato internazionale," 21 *RDI* 328-55 (1929).

Banqué y Faliú, José. *El arbitraje en la Grecia antigua.* Barcelona, 1934.

Bemis, Samuel Flagg. *Jay's Treaty: A Study in Commerce and Diplomacy.* 2d rev. ed. New Haven: Yale UP, 1962. 526 p.

Beus, de J. G. *The Jurisprudence of the General Claims Commission United States and Mexico under the Convention of September 8, 1923.* The Hague: Nijhoff, 1938. 342 p.

Bishop, Crawford. M. *International Arbitral Procedure.* Washington, DC: Byrne & Co., 1931. 259 p.

Blakeney, M. "The Olney-Pauncefote Treaty of 1897: The Failure of Anglo-American General Arbitration," 8 *Anglo-American Law Review* 175-90 (1979).

Blüdorn, Rudolf. "Le fonctionnement et la jurisprudence des Tribunaux arbitraux mixtes créés par les traités de Paix," 41 *RCADI* 137-244 (1932-II).

Borel, Eugène. "Les voies de recours contre les sentences arbitrales," 52 *RCADI* 1-104 (1935-II).

Bos, M. "The International Law Commission's Draft Convention on Arbitral Procedure in the General Assembly of the United Nations," 3 *NTIR* 234-61 (1956).

Brown, Laura Ferris. *A Selected Bibliography of International Arbitration 1970-1976.* New York: Eastman Library of the American Arbitration Association, 1976. 26 p.

Burchard, A. "The Mixed Claims Commissions and German Property in the United States of America," 21 *AJIL* 472-80 (1927).

Carlston, Kenneth S. "Codification of International Arbitral Procedure," 47 *AJIL* 203-50 (1953).

_____. "Draft Convention on Arbitral Procedure of the International Law Commission," 48 *AJIL* 296-99 (1954).

_____. *The Process of International Arbitration.* New York: Columbia UP, 1946.

Chapal, Philippe. *L'arbitrabilité des différends internationaux.* Paris: Pedone, 1964. 294 p.

Chaudhri, Mahammed Ahsen (ed.). *The Prospects of International Arbitration.* Karachi: Pakistan Publishing House, 1966. 131 p.

Claims Commission United States-Mexico. *Opinions of the Commissioners.* 3 vols. Washington, DC: GPO, 1927, 1929, 1931.

Clarke, R. F. "A Permanent Tribunal of International Arbitration: Its Necessity and Value," 1 *AJIL* 342-408 (1907).

Coerper, Milo G. "The Foreign Claims Settlement Commission and Judicial Behavior," 50 *AJIL* 868-79 (1956).

Coing, Helmut. "London Agreement on German External Debts," in Bernhardt (ed.), *EPIL* 8 (1985) 364-67.

Copithorne, M. D. "The Permanent Court of Arbitration and the Election of Members of the International Court of Justice," 16 *CanYIL* 315-27 (1978).

Cory, Helen M. *Compulsory Arbitration of International Disputes.* New York: Columbia UP, 1932. 281 p.

Coussirat-Coustère, Vincent & Pierre Michel Eisemann (eds.). *Répertoire de la jurisprudence arbitrale internationale/Repertory of International Arbitral Jurisprudence.* Vol. 1. *1794-1918.* (1989) 546 p.; vol II. *1919-1945.* (1989) 872 p.; vol. III. 1946-1988 (1991) 1008 p. Dordrecht: Nijhoff (Kluwer Academic Publishers).

Damrosch, Lori Fisler. "Retaliation or Arbitration - or Both? The 1978 United States-France Aviation Dispute," 74 *AJIL* 785-807 (1980).

"Decisions before the Anglo-Japanese Property Commission," 6 *Japanese Annual of International Law* 107-65 (1962).

Delaume, Georges. *Contemporary Problems in International Arbitration* (J. Lew ed.), 1987.

Dennis, W. C. "Arbitration Treaties and the Senate Amendments," 6 *AJIL* 614-28 (1912).

Dolzer, Rudolf. "Mixed Claims Commissions," in Bernhardt (ed.), *EPIL* 1 (1981) 146-9.

Feller, A. H. *The Mexican Claims Commissions, 1923-1934: A Study in the Law and Procedure of International Tribunals.* New York: Macmillan, 1935. 572 p.

Finch, G. A. The Bryan Peace Treaties," 10 *AJIL* 882-90 (1916).

Fontes Iuris Gentium. Series A, Section I, vol. 3. *Handbuch der Entscheidungen des Ständigen Schiedshofs - Répertoire des Décisions de la Cour Permanente d'Arbitrage - Digest of the Decisions of the Permanent Court of Arbitration, 1902-1928.* 1931.

Fouchard, Philippe. "Où va l'arbitrage international?" 34 *McGill Law Journal* 435-53 (1989).

———. "Quand un arbitrage est-il international?" *RevArb* (no. 2) 59-77 (1970).

François, J. P. A. "La Cour permanente d'Arbitrage, son origine, sa jurisprudence, son avenir," 87 *RCADI* 457-553 (1955-I).

———. "Le développement future de la Cour Permanente d'Arbitrage," 9 *NTIR* 264-72 (1962).

Goekjian, S. V. "The Conduct of International Arbitration," 11 *Lawyer of the Americas* 409-74 (1979).

Gonsiorowski, M. "Political Arbitration under the General Act for the Pacific Settlement of International Disputes," 27 *AJIL* 469-90 (1933).

Guermanoff, D. *L'excès de pouvoir de l'arbitre.* Paris: University of Paris, Thesis, 1928.

Guyomar, G. "La Commission Arbitrale sur les Biens, Droits et Intérêts en Allemagne," 6 *AFDI* 528-70 (1960); 7 *AFDI* 279-300 (1961); 8 *AFDI* 391-6 (1962); 11 *AFDI* 308-18 (1965); 12 *AFDI* 162-8 (1966); 13 *AFDI* 239-45 (1967); 16 *AFDI* 366-75 (1970).

Hambro, Edvard. "Norwegian Attitude to International Arbitration,"

12 *AVR* 369-98 (1965).

Hudson, Manley O. "The Permanent Court of Arbitration," 27 *AJIL* 3-41 (1943).

Hunt, Bert L. *American and Panamanian General Claims Arbitration under Conventions between the United States and Panama of 1926 and 1932.* Washington, DC: Department of State Arbitration Series, No. 6, 1934.

"International Dispute Resolution: Enforcement of Awards or Agreements Resulting from Arbitration, Mediation and Conciliation," (several contributors) 10 *Loyola Los Angeles International and Comparative Law Journal.* 567-627 (1988).

Jarrosson, Charles. "L'arbitrage et la Convention européenne des droits de l'homme," 4 *RevArb* 573-607 (1989).

Johnson, D. H. N. "The Constitution of an Arbitral Tribunal," 30 *BYIL* 152-77 (1953).

_____. "International Arbitration Back in Favor?" 34 *YWA* 305-28 (1980).

La Fontaine, H. *Pasicrisie Internationale: Histoire documentaire des arbitrages internationaux.* Bern: Stämpfli, 1902. 670 p.

_____. "Histoire sommaire et chronologique des arbitrages internationaux (1794-1900)," 34 *RDILC* 349-80, 558-82, 623-48 (1902).

Lammasch, Heinrich. *Die Lehre von der Schiedsgerichtsbarkeit in ihrem ganzen Umfange.* Stuttgart: Kohlhammer, 1914. 239 p.

_____. *Die Rechtskraft internationaler Schiedsprüche.* Chistiania (Oslo) 1913. 227 p.

Langkeit, Jochen. *Staatenimmunität und Schiedsgerichtsbarkeit; verzichtet ein Staat durch Unterzeichnung einer Schiedsgerichtsvereinbarung auf seine Immunität?* Heidelberg: Verlag Recht Wirtschaft, 1989. 307 p.

La Pradelle, A. de Geouffre de. "L'excès de pouvoir de l'arbitre," 55 *RDILC* 5-64 (1928).

_____, Nicolas S. Politis & André Salomon. *Recueil des Arbitrages Internationaux.* 3 vols. 2d ed. Paris: Editions Internationales. Vol. I (*1798-1855*), 1957; vol. II (*1856-1872*), 1957; vol. III (*1872-1876*), 1954.

League of Nations. *Arbitration and Security: Systematic Survey of the Arbitrations Conventions and Treaties of Mutual Security Deposited with the League of Nations.* Geneva: League of Nations, 2d ed.

1927. 491 p.

Lieblich, William C. "Determination by International Tribunals of the Economic Value of Expropriated Enterprises," 7 *JIArb* 37-76 (1990).

Lindencrona, Gustaf & Nils Mattson. *Arbitration in Taxation.* Deventer: Kluwer, 1981. 92 p.

Makowski, Julien. "L'organisation actuelle de l'arbitrage international," 36 *RCADI* 263-384ter (1931-II).

Mangoldt, Hans von. "Mixed Commissions," in Bernhardt (ed.), *EPIL* 1 (1981) 149-52.

_____. *Die Schiedsgerichtsbarkeit als Mittel internationaler Streitschlichtung.* Berlin: Springer, 1974. 214 p.

Manning, W. R. (ed.). *Arbitration Treaties among the American Nations to the Close of the Year 1910.* New York: Oxford UP, 1924. 472 p.

Mayer, Pierre. "L'autonomie de l'arbitrage international dans l'appréciation de sa propre compétence," 217 *RCADI* 319-454 (1989-V).

Mérignac, Aléxandre Giraud J. A. *Traité théorique et pratique de l'arbitrage international.* Paris: Larose, 1895. 528 p.

Miyazaki, Shigeki. "Property Commissions Established Pursuant to Art. 15 (a) of Peace Treaty with Japan (1951)," in Bernhardt (ed.), *EPIL* 1 (1981) 187-8.

Moore, John Bassett. *History and Digest of the International Arbitrations to Which the United States Has Been a Party.* 6 vols. Washington, DC: GPO, 1898. (Referred to as *1. Arb.*)

_____ (ed.). *International Adjudications: Ancient and Modern. History and Documents.* Ancient Series, vol. II; Modern Series, vols. I, III-VI. New York, 1929-1936.

Morris, Robert C. *International Arbitration and Procedure.* New Haven, CT: Yale UP, 1911. 238 p.

_____. *Report before the United States and Venezuelan Claims Commissions Organized under the Protocol of February 17, 1903.* Washington, DC. 1904. 563 p.

Murdock, J. O. "Arbitration and Conciliation in Pan America," 23 *AJIL* 273-91 (1929).

Myers, D. P. "The Origin of the Hague Arbitral Courts," 8 *AJIL* 769-801 (1914).

Newcomb, J. T. "New Light on Jay's Treaty," 28 *AJIL* 685-92 (1934).

Nielsen, Fred K. (reporter). *American and British Claims Arbitration under Agreement of August 8, 1910.* Washington, DC: GPO, 1926 ("Nielsen Reports").

_____. *American-Turkish Claims Settlement under the Agreement of December 24, 1923.* Washington, DC: GPO, 1937.

Nippold, O. "Das Problem der obligatorischen Schiedsgerichtsbarkeit," 8 *JöR* 1-55 (1914).

Novacovitch, M. *Les compromis et les arbitrages internationaux du XIIe au XVe siècle.* Paris, 1905.

Paasivirta, Esa. *Participation of States in International Contracts and Arbitral Settlement of Disputes.* Helsinki: Lakimiesliiton Kustannus - Finnish Lawyers' Publishing Company, 1990. 357 p.

Park, William W. & Jan Paulsson. "The Binding Force of International Arbitral Awards," 23 *VirJIL* 253-85 (1983).

Permanent Court of Arbitration - Cour Permanente d'Arbitrage. *Rapport du Conseil administratif de la Cour Permanente d'Arbitrage sur les travaux de la Cour.* 1901 ---- (Annual).

Politis, Nicolas S. *La justice internationale.* Paris: Hachette, 1924. 325 p.

"President Taft on International Peace," 5 *AJIL* 718-25 (1911).

Probst, Yürg. "Die Schweiz und die internationale Schiedsgerichtsbarkeit," *SchweizJIR* 99-146 (1960).

Raeder, A. *L'arbitrage international chez les Hellènes.* Kristiania (Oslo), 1912.

Ralston, Jackson H. *International Arbitral Law and Procedure.* Boston, 1910.

_____. *International Arbitration from Athens to Locarno.* Stanford: Stanford UP, 1929. 417 p.

_____. *The Law and Procedure of International Tribunals.* Stanford: Stanford UP, 1926 (revised 1910 edition). 512 p. *Supplement,* 1936. 231 p.

_____ (ed.), assisted by W. T. Sherman Doyle. *Venezuelan Arbitrations of 1903, Including Protocols, Personnel and Rules of Commissions, Opinions and Summary of Awards.* Washington, DC: GPO, 1904.

Recueil des décisions de la Commission de Conciliation Franco-Italienne instituée en exécution de l'Article 83 du Traité de Paix avec l'Italie. 7 fascicules. vols. 1-8. Rome.

Recueil des décisions des Tribunaux Arbitraux Mixtes institués par les

Traités de Paix. (ed. by Gilbert Gidel) 10 vols. Paris: 1922-1930.

Rideau, J. *L'arbitrage international, public et commercial.* Paris: Colin, 1969. 112 p.

Root, Elihu. "The Relations between International Tribunals of Arbitration and the Jurisdiction of National Courts," 3 *AJIL* 529-36 (1909).

Sáenz de Santa María, M. Paz Andrés. *El Arbitraje internacional en la práctica convencional española (1794-1978).* Oviedo: Universidad de Oviedo, 1989. 365 p.

Scelle, Georges. *Reports on Arbitration Procedure* (UN Documents A/CN. 4/18 of 21 March 1950 and A/CN. 4/46 of 28 May 1951.) New York: UN, 1951.

Schätzel, W. "Die gemischten Schiedsgerichte der Friedensverträge," 18 *JöR* 378-455 (1930).

Schindler, Dietrich. "Les progrès de l'arbitrage obligatoire depuis la création de la Société des Nations," 25 *RCADI* 233-364 (1928-V).

_____. *Die Schiedsgerichtsbarkeit seit 1914: Entwicklung und heutiger Stand.* Stuttgart, 1938. 212 p.

Schlochauer, Hans-Jürgen. "Die Entwicklung der internationalen Schiedsgerichtsbarkeit," 10 *AVR* 1-41 (1962).

_____. "Jay Treaty, 1794," in Bernhardt (ed.), *EPIL* 1 (1981) 108-111.

_____. "Permanent Court of Arbitration," in Bernhardt (ed.), *EPIL* 1 (1981) 157-63.

_____. "Taft Arbitration Treaties (1911)," in Bernhardt (ed.), *EPIL* 1 (1981) 196-8.

Schoch, M. M. "Decisions of the Arbitral Commission on Property, Rights and Interests in Germany," 59 *AJIL* 682-5, 974-5 (1965).

Schücking, Walther. *Das Werk von Haag.* Vol. 1: *Die gerichtlichen Entscheidungen. Die Judikatur des Ständigen Schiedshofs von 1899-1913* (in three parts). Munich, 1914.

Schwarzenberger, Georg. "Present Day Relevance of the Jay Treaty Arbitration," 53 *Notre Dame Lawyer* 715-33 (1978).

Schwebel, Stephen M. *International Arbitration: Three Salient Problems.* Cambridge: Grotius Publications, 1987. 303 p.

_____ & J. Gillis Wetter. "Arbitration and the Exhaustion of Local Remedies," 60 *AJIL* 484-501 (1966).

Scott, James Brown (ed.). *The Hague Court Reports (Second Series).* 2 vols. New York: Oxford UP, 1932.

_____. *An International Court of Justice. Letter and Memorandum on January 12, 1914.* New York: Oxford UP, 1916. 108 p.

_____ (ed.). *Proceedings of Fourth National Conference, American Society for Judicial Settlement of International Disputes, December 4-6, 1913.* Washington, DC and Baltimore: Williams & Williams, 1914. 412 p.

_____. *The Project Relative to a Court of Arbitral Justice.* Washington, DC: Carnegie Endowment, 1920. 106 p.

Seidel, Katharine (ed.). *A Dictionary of Arbitration and Its Terms. Labor, Commercial, International.* Dobbs Ferry, NY: Oceana, 1970. 334 p.

_____ (ed.). *The Paul Felix Warburg Catalog of Arbitration: A Selected Bibliography and Subject Index of Peaceful Dispute Settlement Procedures.* 3 vols. Totowa, NJ: Rowman & Littlefield, 1974. 444, 462, 334 pp.

Seidl-Hohenveldern, Ignaz. *The Austrian-German Arbitral Tribunal Established by the Property Treaty of June 15, 1957.* Syracuse: Syracuse UP, 1972. 261 p.

_____. "Chronique de jurisprudence du tribunal arbitral établi par le traité austro-allemand sur les biens," 105 *JDI* 915-26 (1978).

_____. "Conciliation Commissions Established Pursuant to Art. 83 of Peace Treaty with Italy of 1947," in Bernhardt (ed.), *EPIL* 1 (1981) 51-55.

_____. "General Principles of Law As Applied by the Conciliation Commissions Established under the Peace Treaty with Italy of 1947," 53 *AJIL* 853-72 (1959).

_____. "Le Tribunal Arbitral institué par le Traité Austro-Allemand du 15 juin 1957 portant Règlement des Problèmes des Biens," 15 *AFDI* 266-75 (1969).

Simmonds, Kenneth R., Ruth Lapidoth & Hans W. Baade. "Public International Arbitration," 22 *TexILJ* 149-68 (1987).

Simpson, John L. "The Agreement on German External Debts," 6 *ICLQ* 472-86 (1957).

_____ & Hazel Fox. *International Arbitration: Law and Practice.* London: Stevens, 1959. 330 p.

Sohn, Louis B. "The Function of International Arbitration Today," 108 *RCADI* 1-113 (1969-I).

_____. "The Role of Arbitration in Recent International Multilateral Treaties," 23 *VirJIL* 171-89 (1983).

Soons, A. H. A. (ed.). *International Arbitration: Past and Prospects. A Symposium to Commemorate the Centenary of the Birth of Professor J. H. W. Verzijl (1888-1987)*. Dordrecht: Nijhoff, 1989. 221 p.

Strupp, Karl. "The Competence of the Mixed Arbitral Courts of the Treaty of Versailles," 17 *AJIL* 661-90 (1923).

Stuyt, A.M. (ed.). *Survey of International Arbitration 1794-1970*. Dobbs Ferry, NY: Oceana, 1972.

_____ (ed.). *Survey of International Arbitration: 1794-1989*. 3d updated edition. Dordrecht: Nijhoff, 1990. 658 p.

Sultan, A. "The United Nations Arbitration Convention and United States Policy," 53 *AJIL* 807-25 (1959).

Summers, L. M. & A. Fraleigh. "The United States-Japanese Property Commission," 56 *AJIL* 407-32 (1962).

Taft Arbitration Treaty: France-United States, 3 August 1911, in 5 *AJIL* Supp. 249-53 (1911); Great Britain-United States, 3 August 1911, in 5 *AJIL* Supp. 253-57 (1911).

Taube, Michel de. "Les origines de l'arbitrage international: Antiquité et Moyen Age," 42 *RCADI* 1-115 (1932-IV).

Teyssaire, J & P. de Solère. *Les tribunaux arbitraux mixtes*. Paris, 1931. 243 p.

Tod, Marcus Niebur. *International Arbitration amongst the Greeks*. Oxford: Clarendon Press, 1913. 196 p.

Toope, Stephen J. *Mixed International Arbitration*. Cambridge: Grotius Publications, 1990. 436 p.

Turner, G. *et al.* "The Question of the General Arbitration Treaties," 6 *ASIL Proc.* 87-114 (1912).

United Nations. *Reports of International Arbitral Awards - Recueil des sentences arbitrales*. (Serial) 1947----. 19 volumes through 1993.

United Nations International Law Commission. *Commentary on the Draft Convention on Arbitral Procedure by the International Law Commission at Its Fifth Session*. UN Doc. A/CN.4.92 (1955).

_____. *Model Rules on Arbitral Procedure, Draft*, in "Report of the International Law Commission Covering Its Tenth Session," 53 *AJIL* 239-52 (1959).

United Nations Secretariat. *Bibliography on Arbitral Procedure*. UN Doc. A/CN.4/29, 20 June 1950. 43 p.

United States Department of State, Claims Commission United States and Mexico. *Opinions of Commissioners under the*

Convention concluded September 8, 1923. 3 vols. Washington, DC: GPO, 1927, 1929, 1931.

Urrutia, F. J. *La evolución del principio de arbitraje en América.* Bogota, 1908. 192 p.

Verdross, Alfred. "L'excès de pouvoir du juge arbitral dans le droit international public," 55 *RDILC* 225-42 (1928).

Wang, Erik B. "Adjudication of Canada-United States Disputes," 19 *CanYIL* 158-228 (1981).

Wehberg, Hans. "Restrictive Clauses in International Arbitration Treaties," 7 *AJIL* 301-14 (1913).

Wetter, J. Gillis (ed.). *The International Arbitral Process: Public and Private.* 5 vols. Dobbs Ferry, NY: Oceana, 1979.

_____. "Pleas of Sovereign Immunity and Act of Sovereignty before International Arbitral Tribunals," 2 *JIArb* 7-20 (1985).

Wilson, George Grafton. *The Hague Arbitration Cases: Compromises and Awards with Maps.* Boston: Ginn, 1915. 525 p.

Wolf, de, F. C. *General Synopsis of Treaties of Arbitration.* Washington, DC: 1933. 201 p.

Wühler, Norbert. *Die internationale Schiedsgerichtsbarkeit in der völkerrechtlichen Praxis der Bundesrepublik Deutschland.* Berlin: Springer Verlag, 1985. 239 p.

_____. "London Agreement on German External Debts (1952), Arbitral Tribunal and Mixed Commissions," in Bernhardt (ed.), *EPIL* 1 (1981) 140-6.

Zoller, Elisabeth. "Observations sur la révision et l'interprétation des sentences arbitrales," 24 *AFDI* 327-51 (1978).

17. ARBITRATION: CASES

"The *Alabama* Claims Award," in 1 Moore. *I. Arb.* 653-59 (1898).

Anand, R. P. "The Kutch Award," 24 *India Quarterly* 183-212 (1968).

Anderson, C. P. "The Final Outcome of the Fisheries Arbitration," 7 *AJIL* 1-16 (1913).

Anzilotti, Dionisio. "Le questioni di diritto sollevate dagli incidenti del 'Carthage' e del 'Manuba'," 7 *RDI* 200-36, 398-413 (1913).

Apollis, Gilbert. "Le règlement de l'affaire du 'Rainbow Warrior'," 91 *RGDIP* 9-43 (1987).

Balch, Thomas W. *The Alabama Arbitration.* 1900.

Benedek, Wolfgang. "Canevaro Claims Arbitration," in Bernhardt (ed.), *EPIL* 2 (1981) 41-2.

_____. "North American Dredging Co. of Texas Arbitration," in Bernhardt (ed.), *EPIL* 2 (1981) 201-2.

Beyerlin, Ulrich. "German External Debts Arbitration (Greece v. Federal Republic of Germany)," in Bernhardt (ed.), *EPIL* 2 (1981) 109-11.

Böckstiegel, Karl-Heinz. "France-United States Air Transport Arbitration," in Bernhardt (ed.), *EPIL* 2 (1981) 101-3.

Bollecker-Stern, Brigitte. "L'Argentine et le Chili," 83 *RGDIP* 7-52 (1979).

Borchard, F. M. "The North Atlantic Coast Fisheries Arbitration," 11 *ColLR* 1-23 (1911).

Bowett, Derek W. "The Arbitration between the United Kingodm and France Concerning the Continental Shelf Boundary in the English Channel and South-Western Approaches," 49 *BYIL* 1-28 (1978).

_____. "Libyan Nationalization of American Oil Companies' Assets," 37 *CambLJ* 5-8 (1978).

Brown, E. D. "The Anglo-French Continental Shelf Case," 16 *San Diego LR* 461-530 (1979).

Bülck, Hartwig. "Tinoco Concessions Arbitration,"in Bernhardt (ed.), *EPIL* 2 (1981) 275-6.

_____. "El Triunfo Case," in Bernhardt (ed.), *EPIL* 2 (1981) 84-5.

Burdeau, Geneviève. "L'épilogue de l'affaire de Taba: La sentence

340

arbitrale du 29 septembre 1988 entre Israël et l'Egypte," 34 *AFDI* 195-208 (1988).

"Chaco Arbitral Award, October 10, 1938," in 33 *AJIL* 180 (1939).

Cohen Jonathan, Gérard. "L'arbitrage Texaco-Calasiatic contre Gouvernement Libyen (sentence au fond du 19 janvier 1977)," 23 *AFDI* 452-79 (1977).

Colliard, Claude-Albert. "Le différend franco-canadien sur le 'filetage' dans le Golfe du Saint-Laurent (sentence arbitrale du 17 juillet 1986)," 92 *RGDIP* 273-304 (1988).

Colson, David A. "The United Kingdom-France Continental Shelf Arbitration," 72 *AJIL* 95-112 (1978).

_____. "The United Kingdom-France Continental Shelf Arbitration: Interpretive Decision of March 1978," 73 *AJIL* 112-20 (1979).

Conrad, Dieter. "Rann of Kutch Arbitration (Indo-Pakistan Western Boundary)," in Bernhardt (ed.), *EPIL* 2 (1981) 240-2.

David, Eric. "La sentence arbitrale du 14 février 1985 sur la délimitation de la frontière maritime Guinée-Guinée Bissau," 31 *AFDI* 350-89 (1985).

Davidson, J. Scott. "The Rainbow Warrior Arbitration Concerning the Treatment of the French Agents Mafart and Prieur," 40 *ICLQ* 446-57 (1991).

Decaux, Emmanuel. "La sentence du tribunal arbitral dans le différend frontalier concernant l'enclave de Taba (Egypte-Israël, 29 septembre 1988)," 93 *RGDIP* 599-622 (1989).

Derains, Yves. "Chronique des sentences arbitrales," 117 *JDI* 1017-63 (1990).

Doehring, Karl. "Casablanca Arbitration," in Bernhardt (ed.), *EPIL* 2 (1981) 45-6.

_____. "Savarkar Case," in Bernhardt (ed.), *EPIL* 2 (1981) 252-54.

Dolzer, Rudolf. "Abu Dhabi Oil Arbitration," in Bernhardt (ed.), *EPIL* 2 (1981) 1-2.

_____. "ARAMCO Arbitration," in Bernhardt (ed.), *EPIL* 2 (1981) 19-22.

_____. "British Petroleum v. Libya Arbitration," in Bernhardt (ed.), *EPIL* 2 (1981) 40-1.

_____. "Libya-Oil Companies Arbitration," in Bernhardt (ed.), *EPIL* 2 (1981) 168-71.

_____. "Norwegian Shipowners' Claims Arbitration," in Bernhardt (ed.), *EPIL* 2 (1981) 211-3.

_____. "Revere Copper Arbitral Award," in Bernhardt (ed.), *EPIL* 8 (1985) 461-2.

Duléry, F. "L'affaire du Lac Lanoux," 62 *RGDIP* 469-516 (1958).

Dutheil de la Rochère, Jacqueline. "L'affaire du Canal de Beagle (sentence rendue par la Reine d'Angleterre le 22 avril 1977)," 23 *AFDI* 408-35 (1977).

Ferlito, Sergio. "La Santa Sede e il mantenimento della pace: il caso del Beagle," *Il Diritto ecclesiastico e Rassegna di Diritto Matrimoniale* 60-97 (1985).

Fischer, Peter. "LIAMCO-Libya, Petroleum Concessions Arbitration (1977)," in Bernhardt (ed.), *EPIL* 8 (1985) 358-61.

Fitzmaurice, Gerald G. "The Case of the *I'm Alone*," 17 *BYIL* 82-111 (1936).

Gervais, A. "L'affaire du Lac Lanoux," 6 *AFDI* 372-434 (1960).

Gherari, Habib. "La sentence arbitrale du 31 juillet 1989 entre la Guinée-Bissau et le Sénégal," 3 *AJICL-RADIC* 41-60 (1991).

Gómez Robledo, Antonio. *México y el Arbitraje Internacional: El Fondo Piadoso de las Californias; la Isla de la Pasión; El Chamizal.* México, DF: Editorial Porrúa, 1965. 412 p.

Götz, Volkmar. "Ottoman Debt Arbitration," in Bernhardt (ed.), *EPIL* 2 (1981) 220-1.

Greig, D. W. "The Beagle Channel Arbitration," *Australian YIL* 332-85 (1976-77).

Hackett, Frank Warren. *Reminiscences of the Geneva Tribunal of Arbitration 1872: The Alabama Claims.* Boston: Houghton Mifflin, 1911. 450 p.

Hambro, Edvard. "The Ambatielos Arbitral Award," 6 *AVR* 152-73 (1957).

Handl, Günther. "Gut Dam Claims," in Bernhardt (ed.), *EPIL* 2 (1981) 126-8.

Hofmann, Rainer. "Costa Rica Packet Arbitration," in Bernhardt (ed.), *EPIL* 2 (1981) 64-5.

Höpfner, Matthias. "Behring Sea Arbitration," in Bernhardt (ed.), *EPIL* 2 (1981) 36-7.

_____. "Delagoa Bay Arbitration," in Bernhardt (ed.), *EPIL* 2 (1981) 73.

_____. "Orinoco Steamship Co. Arbitration," in Bernhardt (ed.), *EPIL* 2 (1981) 219-20.

Hyde, Charles Cheney. "The Adjustment of the *I'm Alone* Case," 29

AJIL 296-301 (1935).

Jessup, Philip C. "El Chamizal," 67 *AJIL* 423-45 (1973).

_____. "The Palmas Island Arbitration," 22 *AJIL* 735-52 (1928).

Juste Ruiz, José. "Delimitaciones marinas en Africa occidental: El laudo arbitral sobre la delimitación de la frontera marítima entre Guinea y Guinea-Bissau," 42 *REDI* 7-41 (1990).

Kaiser, Joseph H. "Grisbadarna Case," in Bernhardt (ed.), *EPIL* 2 (1981) 124-5.

_____. "Timor Island Arbitration," in Bernhardt (ed.), *EPIL* 2 (1981) 274-5.

Katte, Christoph von. "Hungarian-Romanian Land Reform dispute," in Bernhardt (ed.), *EPIL* 2 (1981) 132-3.

Kerley, E. L. & C. F. Goodman. "The Gut Dam Claims: A Lump Sum Settlement Disposes of an Arbitrated Dispute," 10 *VirJIL* 300-27 (1970).

Kewenig, Wilhelm A. "Young Plan Loans Arbitration," in Bernhardt (ed.), *EPIL* 2 (1981) 296-8.

Khan, Rahmatullah. "Relinquishment of Title to Territory. The Rann of Kutch Award: A Case Study," 9 *IJIL* 157-76 (1969).

Klein, Eckart. "Mergé Claim," in Bernhardt (ed.), *EPIL* 2 (1981) 185-7.

Klemm, Ulf-Dieter. "Continental Shelf Arbitration (France/United Kingdom)," in Bernhardt (ed.), *EPIL* 2 (1981) 58-61.

Lagergren, Gunnar. "The Taba Tribunal," 1 *AJICL-RADIC* 525-32 (1989).

Lagoni, Rainer. "Palmas Island Arbitration," in Bernhardt (ed.), *EPIL* 2 (1981) 223-4.

Lalive, J.-F. "Un grand arbitrage pétrolier entre un Gouvernement et deux sociétés privées étrangères," 104 *JDI* 319-49 (1977).

Lamers, Karl. "Pious Fund Arbitration," in Bernhardt (ed.), *EPIL* 2 (1981) 229-30.

Lane, Robert C. "The Rose Mary," in Bernhardt (ed.), *EPIL* 8 (1985) 462-3.

Madders, Kevin J. "The Lusitania," in Bernhardt (ed.), *EPIL* 2 (1981) 177-80.

_____. "Trail Smelter Arbitration," in Bernhardt (ed.), *EPIL* 2 (1981) 276-80.

Magiera, Siegfried. "Wal Wal Arbitration," in Bernhardt (ed.), *EPIL* 2 (1981) 290-1.

Martens, Ernst K. "Sapphire Arbitration," in Bernhardt (ed.), *EPIL* 2 (1981) 250-2.

McRae, D. M. "Delimitation of the Continental Shelf between United Kingdom and France: The Channel Arbitration," 15 *CanYIL* 173-97 (1975).

Mehren, Robert B. von & P. Nicholas Kourides. "International Arbitrations between States and Foreign Private Parties: The Libyan Nationalization Cases," 75 *AJIL* 476-552 (1981).

Merrills, J. G. "The United Kingdom-France Continental Shelf Arbitration," 10 *CalifWILJ* 314-64 (1980).

Meyer-Lindenberg, Hermann. "Gran Chaco Conflict," in Bernhardt (ed.), *EPIL* 2 (1981) 120-2.

Mosler, Hermann. "Austro-German Arbitration Award under the Treaty of Finance and Compensation of 1961," in Bernhardt (ed.), *EPIL* 2 (1981) 27-9.

Münch, Fritz. "Buraimi Oasis Dispute," in Bernhardt (ed.), *EPIL* 2 (1981) 41.

_____. "North Atlantic Coast Fisheries Arbitration," in Bernhardt (ed.), *EPIL* 2 (1981) 202-5.

Münch, Ingo von. "Clipperton Island Arbitration," in Bernhardt (ed.), *EPIL* 2 (1981) 53-4.

Oellers-Frahm, Karin. "Argentina-Chile Frontier Case," in Bernhardt (ed.), *EPIL* 2 (1981) 24-6.

_____. "Beagle Channel Arbitration," in Bernhardt (ed.), *EPIL* 2 (1981) 33-7.

_____. "France-United States Air Transport Arbitration," in Bernhardt (ed.), *EPIL* 2 (1981) 103-4.

Palmisano, Giuseppe. "Sulla decisione arbitrale relativa alla seconda fase del caso 'Rainbow Warrior'," 73 *RDI* 874-910 (1990).

Panella, Lina. "Controversia tra Cile e Argentina sul canale di Beagle: Dai precedenti tentativi di soluzione alla mediazione della S. Sede," 35 *ComI* 664-84 (1980).

Partsch, Karl Josef. "Naulilaa Arbitration (Portugal v. Germany)," in Bernhardt (ed.), *EPIL* 2 (1981) 199-200.

Pinto, Roger. "L'affaire du Rainbow Warrior. A propos de la sentence arbitrale du 30 avril 1990 (Nouvelle Zélande c. France)," 117 *JDI* 841-96 (1990).

Quéneudec, J. P. "L'affaire de la délimitation du plateau continental entre la France et le Royaume-Uni," 83 *RGDIP* 53-103 (1979).

"La questione del Canale Beagle (lodo arbitrale britannico)," 1 *IusG* 137-85 (1983).

Rama Rao, T. S. "An Appraisal of the Kutch Award," 9 *IJIL* 143-56 (1969).

Rauschning, Dietrich. "Lac Lanoux Arbitration," in Bernhardt (ed.), *EPIL* 2 (1981) 166-8.

Read, J. "The Trail Smelter Dispute," 1 *CanYIL* 213-29 (1963).

Redfern, D. N. "The Arbitration between the Government of Kuwait and Aminoil," 55 *BYIL* 65-110 (1985).

Regelsperger, G. "L'affaire du Costa Rica Packet et la sentence arbitrale de M. de Martens," 4 *RGDIP* 735-45 (1897).

Rigaldies, F. "L'affaire de la délimitation du plateau continental entre la République française et le Royaume-Uni de Grande Bretagne et d'Irlande du Nord," 106 *JDI* 506-31 (1979).

Robin, R. "Un différend franco-anglais devant la Cour d'arbitrage de la Haye," 18 *RGDIP* 303-52 (1911)

Rousseau, Charles. "L'affaire franco-hellénique des phares et la sentence arbitrale du 24 juillet 1956," 63 *RGDIP* 248-92 (1959).

Rubin, A. P. "Pollution by Analogy: The Trail Smelter Arbitration," 50 *Oregon Law Review* 259-82 (1971).

Rüster, Bernd. "Das britisch-französische Schiedsverfahren über die Abgrenzung des Festlandsockels: Die Entscheidungen vom 30. Juni 1977 und vom 14. März 1978," 40 *ZaöRV* 803-40 (1980).

Ruzé, R. "Un arbitrage franco-italien. L'affaire du 'Carthage' et l'affaire du 'Manouba'," 46 *RDILC* 101-36 (1914).

Schulte-Braucks, Antonella. "Cerrutti Arbitrations," in Bernhardt (ed.), *EPIL* 2 (1981) 47-8.

_____. "Chevreau Claim Arbitration," in Bernhardt (ed.), *EPIL* 2 (1981) 51-2.

Seidel, Peter. "The Alabama," in Bernhardt (ed.), *EPIL* 2 (1981) 11-13.

_____. "The *Carthage* and the *Manouba*," in Bernhardt (ed.), *EPIL* 2 (1981) 43-5.

_____. "The *I'm Alone*," in Bernhardt (ed.), *EPIL* 2 (1981) 133-4.

_____. "The Muscat Dhows," in Bernhardt (ed.), *EPIL* 2 (1981) 196-7.

Seidl-Hohenveldern, Ignaz. "Flegenheimer Claim," in Bernhardt (ed.), *EPIL* 2 (1981) 98-9.

_____. "Russian Indemnity Arbitration," in Bernhardt (ed.), *EPIL* 2

(1981) 246-7.

_____. "Zum Urteil des Schiedsgerichtshofes für das Abkommen über deutsche Auslandsschulden zur Young-Anleihe," 23 *GYIL* 401-13 (1980).

Shaw, Malcolm. "The Beagle Channel Arbitration Award," 6 *International Relations* 415-45 (1978).

Silagi, Michael. "Preferential Claims against Venezuela Arbitration," in Bernhardt (ed.), *EPIL* 2 (1981) 234-5.

Steiner, Otto. "Spanish Zone of Morocco Claims," in Bernhardt (ed.), *EPIL* 2 (1981) 271-3.

Suratgar, P. "The Sapphire Arbitration Award, The Procedural Aspects: A Report and a Critique," 3 *Col/TransnL* 152-209 (1965).

Untawale, M. G. "The Kutch-Sind Dispute: A Case Study in International Arbitration," 23 *ICLQ* 818-39 (1974).

Varma, A. "Petroleum Concessions in International Arbitration: Texaco Overseas Petroleum Company v. Libyan Arab Republic," 18 *Col/TransnL* 259-88 (1979).

Verosta, Stephan. "Salem Case," in Bernhardt (ed.), *EPIL* 2 (1981) 248-50.

Visscher, Charles De. "L'arbitrage de l'Ile de Palmas (Miangas)," 56 *RDILC* 735-62 (1929).

Weil, Prosper. "Some Observations on the Arbitral Award in the Taba Case," 23 *Israel Law Review* 1-25 (1989).

Wetter, J. Gillis. "The Rann of Kutch Arbitration," 65 *AJIL* 346-57 (1971).

White, Robin A. "Expropriation of the Libyan Oil Concessions - Two Conflicting International Arbitrations," 30 *ICLQ* 1-19 (1981).

Williams, W. "Reminiscences of the Behring Sea Arbitration," 37 *AJIL* 562-84 (1943).

Wright, Quincy. "The Arbitration of the Aaroo Mountain," 33 *AJIL* 356-9 (1939).

Wühler, Norbert. "German Secular Property in Israel Case," in Bernhardt (ed.), *EPIL* 2 (1981) 116-8.

_____. "Honduras-Nicaragua Boundary Dispute," in Bernhardt (ed.), *EPIL* 2 (1981) 130-2.

18. INTERNATIONAL CENTRE FOR SETTLEMENT OF INVESTMENT DISPUTES

Agyemang, A. A. "African States and ICSID Arbitration," 21 *Comparative and International Law Journal of Southern Africa* 177-89 (1989).

Amerasinghe, Chittharanjan F. "The Jurisdiction of the International Centre for the Settlement of Investment Disputes," 19 *IJIL* 166-227 (1979).

_____. "Submissions to the Jurisdiction of the International Centre for the Settlement of Investment Disputes," 5 *Journal of Maritime Law & Commerce* 211-50 (1974),

Baker, James C. & Lois J. Yoder. "ICSID Arbitration and the U.S. Multinational Corporation. An Alternative Dispute Resolution Method in International Business," 5 *JIArb* 81-95 (1988).

Bouchez, Leo J. "The Prospects for International Arbitration: Disputes between States and Private Enterprises," 8 *JIArb* 81-115 (1991).

Broches, Aron. "The Convention on the Settlement of Investment Disputes between States and Nationals of Other States," 136 *RCADI* 331-410 (1972-II).

Carabiber, Charles. "L'arbitrage international entre gouvernements et particuliers," 76 *RCADI* 217-318 (1950-I).

Cherian, Joy. *Investment Contracts and Arbitration: The World Bank Convention on the Settlement of Investment Disputes.* Leyden: Sijthoff, 1975. 275 p.

Delaume, Georges R. "Le Centre International pour le Règlement des Différends relatifs aux Investissements (CIRDI)," 109 *JDI* 775-843 (1982).

_____. "Le CIRDI et l'immunité des Etats," *RevArb* 143-61. (1983).

_____. "ICSID Arbitration and the Courts," 77 *AJIL* 784-803 (1983).

_____. "State Contracts and Transnational Arbitration," 75 *AJIL* 784-819 (1981).

Gaillard, Emmanuel. "Centre International por le Règlement des Différends relatifs aux Investissements (C.I.R.D.I.)," 118 *JDI* 165-

88 (1991). *See also* 113 *JDI* 197-252 (1986); 114 *JDI* 135-91 (1987).

Gopal, Gita. "International Centre for Settlement of Investment Disputes," 14 *Case WRJIL* 591-611 (1982).

International Centre for Settlement of Investment Disputes. *ICSID Cases: 1972-1984.* Washington, DC, 1985.

Lynch, Stephen T. "The International Centre for the Settlement of Investment Disputes: Selected Case Studies," 7 *ITLJ* 306-26 (1982/83).

Mehren, Arthur T. von & Eduardo Jiménez de Aréchaga. "Arbitration between States and Foreign Enterprises," 63 *Annuaire de l'Institut de Droit International* 31-204 (1989).

O'Keefe, Patrick J. "The International Centre for Settlement of Investment Disputes," 34 *YWA* 286-304 (1980).

Reisman, W. Michael. "The Breakdown of the Control Mechanism in ICSID Arbitration," 4 *Duke LJ* 739-807 (1989).

Soley, David A. "ICSID Implementation: An Effective Alternative to International Conflict," 19 *ILawyer* 521-44 (1985).

19. IRAN-UNITED STATES CLAIMS TRIBUNAL

Audid, Bernard. "Les Accords d'Alger du 19 janvier 1981 tendant au règlement des différends entre les Etats-Unis et l'Iran," 108 *JDI* 713-87 (1981)

Badaruddin, Schandor S. "Choice of Law Decisions in the Iran-U.S. Claims Tribunal," 4 *Emory ILR* 157-84 (1990).

Baker, Steward A. & Mark D. Davis. "Arbitral Proceedings under the UNCITRAL Rules - The Experience of the Iran-United States Claims Tribunal," 23 *GWashJIL&Econ* 267-347 (1989).

_____. "Establishment of an Arbitral Tribunal under the UNCITRAL Rules: The Experience of the Iran-United States Claims Tribunal," *ILawyer* 81-135 (1989).

Belland, Stanton P. "The Iran-United States Claims Tribunal: Some Reflections on Trying a Claim," 1 *JIArb* 237-53 (1984).

Caron, David D. "Interim Measures of Protection: Theory and Practice in Light of the Iran-United States Claims Tribunal," 46 *ZaöRV* 465-518 (1986).

_____. *The Iran-United States Claims Tribunal and the International Arbitral Process.* Leyden: Rijkuniversiteit, Dissertation, 1990. 326 p.

_____. "The Nature of the Iran-United States Claims Tribunal and the Evolving Structure of International Dispute Resolution," 84 *AJIL* 104-56 (1990).

Corten, Olivier, Alain Daems & Eric Robert. "Les questions monétaires devant le tribunal des différends irano-américains," 21 *RBDI* 142-83 (1988).

Crook, John R. "Applicable Law in International Arbitration: The Iran-U.S. Claims Tribunal Experience," 83 *AJIL* 278-311 (1989).

"Decisions of the Iran-United States Claims Tribunal," 78 *ASIL Proc.* 221-40 (1984) (various authors).

Gillespie, Kate. "US Corporations and Iran at The Hague," 44 *Middle East Journal* 18-36 (1990).

Hamel, Willem A. "The Iran-United States Claims Tribunal," 2 *HYIL* 274-350 (1989).

_____ *et al.* "The Iran-United States Claims Tribunal," 1 *HYIL* 358-462 (1988).

Hanessian, Grant. "'General Principles of Law' in the Iran-U.S. Claims Tribunal," 27 *ColJTransnL* 309-53 (1989).

Iran-United States Claims Tribunal Reports (Iran-U.S.C.T.R.). Serial. 10 vols. in 1990. Cambridge: Grotius Publications, Ltd.

"Iran-United States Litigation," 77 *ASIL Proc.* 3-31 (1983) (various authors).

Jones, David Loyd. "The Iran-United States Claims Tribunal: Private Rights and State Responsibility," 24 *VirJIL* 259-85 (1984).

Khan, Rahmatullah. *The Iran-United States Claims Tribunal: Controversies, Cases and Contribution.* Dordrecht: Nijhoff, 1990. 343 p.

Lewis, Robert P. "What Goes Around Comes Around: Can Iran Enforce Awards of the Iran-U.S. Claims Tribunal in the United States?" 26 *ColJTransnL* 515-52 (1988).

Lillich, Richard B. (ed.). *The Iran-United States Claims Tribunal, 1981-1983.* Charlottesville, VA: UP of Virginia, 1985. 175 p.

Mahoney, Peter E. "The Standing of Dual Nationals before the Iran-United States Claims Tribunal," 24 *VirJIL* 695-728 (1984).

Mangård, Niles. "The Hostage Crisis, the Algiers Accords, and the Iran-United States Claims Tribunal," in *Festskrift till Lars Hjerner* 363-418. Stockholm, 1990.

McLaughlin, Gerald T. & Ludwik A. Teclaff. "The Iranian Hostage Agreements: A Legal Analysis," 4 *Fordham ILJ* 223-64 (1980/81).

Pellonpää, M. & M. Fitzmaurice. "Taking of Property in the Practice of the Iran-United States Claims Tribunal," 19 *NYIL* 53-178 (1988).

Radicati di Brozolo, Luca. "La soluzione delle controversie fra Stati e stranieri mediante accordo internazionale: gli accordi fra Stati Uniti ed Iran," 65 *RDI* 299-343 (1982).

Reduine, J. M. "The Effect of Duress on the Iranian Hostage Settlement," 14 *VandJTransnL* 847-90 (1981).

Riesenfeld, Stefan A. "United States-Iran Agreement of January 19, 1981 (Hostages and Financial Arrangements)," in Bernhardt (ed.), *EPIL* 8 (1985) 522-6.

Selby, Jamison M. & David P. Steward. "Practical Aspects of Arbitrating Claims before the Iran-United States Claims Tribunal," 18 *ILawyer* 211-44 (1984).

Stein, Ted L. "Jurisprudence and Jurists' Prudence: The Iranian-Forum Clause Decisions of the Iran-U.S. Claims Tribunal," 78 *AJIL* 1-52 (1984).

Steward, David P. & L. B. Sherman. "Developments at the Iran-United States Claims Tribunal:1981-1983," 24 *VirJIL* 1-53 (1983).

Swanson, Steven R. "Iran-U.S. Claims Tribunal: A Policy Analysis of the Expropriation Cases," 18 *Case WRJIL* 307-60 (1986).

"Symposium on the Iran-United States Claims Tribunal," 16 *Law & Policy in International Business* 667-962 (1984) (various contributors).

Van Hof, Jacomijn J. *Commentary on the UNCITRAL Arbitration Rules: The Application by the Iran-U.S. Claims Tribunal.* Deventer: Kluwer Law & Taxation Publishers, 1992. 357 p.

Westberg, John A. *Case Law of the Iran-United States Claims Tribunal.* Washington, DC: International Law Institute, 1992. 412 p.

_____. *International Transactions and Claims Involving Government Parties. Case Law of the Iran-United States Claims Tribunal.* Washington, DC: International Law Institute, 1991. 392 p.

20. CANADA-UNITED STATES FREE TRADE AGREEMENT: DISPUTE SETTLEMENT

Apuzzo, A. M. & W. A. Kerr. "International Arbitration - The Dispute Settlement Procedures Chosen for the Canada-U.S. Free Trade Agreement," 5 *JIArb* 7-15 (1988).

Castel, J.-G."The Settlement of Disputes under the 1988 Canada-U.S. Free Trade Agreement," 83 *AJIL* 118-128 (1989).

Hage, Robert. "Dispute Settlement under the Canada-U.S. Free Trade Agreement," 28 *CanYIL* 361-78 (1991).

Horlick, G., G. Oliver & D. Steger. "Dispute Resolution Mechanism," in J. Schott & M. Smith (eds.). *The Canada-U.S. Free Trade Agreement.* (1988) 65-100.

Rugman, Alan M. & Andrew Anderson. "The Dispute Settlement Mechanisms Cases in the Canada-U.S. Free Trade Agreement: An Economic Evaluation," 24 *GWashJIL&Econ* 1-43 (1990).

"Summary of Proceedings of the Seminar on Dispute Resolution under the Canada-U.S. Free Trade Agreement," 26 *Stanford JIL* 153-64 (1989).

21. INTERNATIONAL COMMERCIAL ARBITRATION

Aaron, Sam. "International Arbitration II: The Main Centers," 108 *South African Law Journal* 93-117 (1991).

Académie de Droit International de la Haye-Centre d'Etude et de Recherche de Droit International et de Relations Internationales. *L'arbitrage transnational et les contrats d'Etat.* Dordrecht: Nijhoff, 1988. 129 p.

_____. *Transnational Arbitration and State Contracts; Selective Bibliography.* The Hague, 1987. 69 p.

Ader, Menno. *Internationale Handelsschiedsgerichtsbarkeit: Kommentar zu d. Verfahrensordnungen.* Heidelberg: Verlag Recht und Wirtschaft, 1988. 249 p.

Ahrens, Helen & Jürgen Samtleben. "Schiedsgerichtsbarkeit in Paraguay," 36 *RIW-AWD* 721-26 (1990).

American Arbitration Association. "International Arbitration Rules," 2 *World Arb&Medi Rep* 78-90 (1991).

_____. *Survey of International Arbitration Sites.* New York: AAA, 1984. 107 p.

Amoussou Guenou, Roland. "La réforme de l'arbitrage en République fédérale du Nigeria," *RevArb* 445-65 (1989).

Avenessian, Aida B. "The New York Convention and Denationalised Arbitral Awards," 8 *JIArb* 5-29 (1991).

Balladore Pallieri, Giorgio. "L'arbitrage privé dans les rapports internationaux," 51 *RCADI* 287-403 (1935-I).

Béguin, Jacques. *L'arbitrage commercial international.* Montreal: Blais, 1987. 279 p.

Berger, Klaus Peter. "The Modern Trend towards Exclusion of Recourse against Transnational Arbitral Awards: A European Perspective," 12 *Fordham ILJ* 605-57 (1989).

Blessing, Marc. "The Major Western and Soviet Arbitration Rules. A Comparison of the Rules of UNCITRAL, UNCITRAL MODEL LAW, LCIA, ICC, AAA and the Rules of the USSR Chamber of Commerce and Industry," 6 *JIArb* 7-76 (1989).

Böckstiegel, Karl-Heinz. "International Commercial Arbitration. Arbitration between Parties from Industrialized and Less Developed Countries," 60 *ILA Rep* 269-302 (1982).

Broches, Aron. "The 1985 UNCITRAL Model Law on International Commercial Arbitration: An Exercise in International Legislation," 18 *NYIL* 3-67 (1987).

Brown, William. "Commercial Arbitration and the European Economic Community," 2 *JIArb* 21-44 (1985).

Bucher, Andreas & Pierre-Yves Tschanz. *International Arbitration in Switzerland.* Basel: Helbing & Lichtenhahn, 1989. 230 p.

Butler, William E. *Arbitration in the Soviet Union.* Dobbs Ferry, NY: Oceana, 1990. 256 p.

Carbonneau, Thomas E. "American and Other National Variations on the Theme of International Commercial Arbitration," 18 *Georgia JI&CL* 143-238 (1988).

_____. "Arbitral Adjudication: A Comparative Assessment of Its Remedial and Substantive Status in Transnational Commerce," 19 *TexILJ* 33-114 (1984).

_____ (ed.). *Resolving Transnational Disputes through International Arbitration.* Charlottesville, VA: UP of Virginia, 1984. 301 p.

Chatterjee, S. K. (ed.). *Lloyd's Arbitration Reports, 1989.* London: Lloyd's of London, 1989. 338 p.

Chiu, Julie C. "Consolidation of Arbitral Proceedings and International Commercial Arbitration," 7 *JIArb* 53-76 (1990).

Cohn, Ernest J, Martin Domke, & Frédéric Eisemann (eds.). *Handbook of International Arbitration in International Trade. Facts, Figures and Rules.* Amsterdam: North Holland, 1977. 301 p.

Coulson, Robert. "A New Look at International Commercial Arbitration," 14 *Case WRJIL* 359-75 (1982).

Craig, W. Laurence, William W. Park & Jan Paulsson. *International Chamber of Commerce Arbitration.* 2d ed. Dobbs Ferry, NY: Oceana, 1990. 832 p.

Cremades, Bernardo. "Commercial Arbitration," in Bernhardt (ed.), *EPIL* 8 (1985) 82-5.

_____. *Estudios sobre arbitraje.* Madrid: Pons, 1977. 239 p.

"Current Issues in International Commercial Arbitration (Symposium, 5 Articles). 12 *Northwestern Journal of International Law and Business* 1-123 (1991).

Dahl, Enrique & Alejandro M. Garro. "Cuba's System of

International Commercial Arbitration: A Convergence of Soviet and Latin American Trends," 15 *Lawyer of the Americas* 441-66 (1984).

Danilowicz, Vitek. "The Choice of Applicable Law in International Arbitration," 9 *Hastings I&CLR* 235-84 (1986).

Dasser, Felix. *Internationale Schiedsgerichte und lex mercatoria: rechtsvergleichender Beitrag zur Diskussion über ein nichtstaatliches Handelsrecht.* Zurich: Schulthess, 1989. 408 p.

Davidson, Fraser P. "International Commercial Arbitration: The United Kingdom and UNCITRAL Model Law," 11 *JBL* 480-94 (1990).

Delaume, Georges R. "L'arbitrage transnational et les tribunaux nationaux," 111 *JDI* 521-47 (1984).

Deshpande, V. S. "International Commercial Arbitration and Domestic Courts in India," 2 *JIArb* 45-66 (1985).

DeVries, Henry P. "International Commercial Arbitration: A Transnational View," 1 *JIArb* 7-20 (1984).

Domke, Martin. *Commercial Arbitration.* Englewood Cliffs, NJ: Prentice-Hall, 1965. 116 p.

Dore, Isaak I. *Arbitration and Conciliation under the UNCITRAL Rules: A Textual Analysis.* Norwell, MA: Kluwer Academic, 1986.

_____. *Theory and Practice of Multi-Party Commercial Arbitration, with Special Reference to the UNCITRAL Framework.* London: Graham & Trotman, 1990. 201 p.

Doty, Mary Celeste. "An Evaluation of the People's Republic of China's Participation in International Commercial Arbitration," 12 *CalifWILJ* 128-53 (1982).

El-Ahdab, Abdul Hamid. "Le Centre arabe d'arbitrage commercial à Rabat. Convention arabe d'Amman sur l'arbitrage commercial (1987)," *RevArb* 631-40 (1989).

Enein, Aboul. "Arbitration under the Auspices of the Cairo Regional Centre for Commercial Arbitration (an AALCC Centre)," 2 *JIArb* 23-44 (1985).

Farina, Anne Judith. "Talking Disputes into Harmony: China Approaches International Commercial Arbitration," 4 *AUJIL&Pcy* 137-71 (1989).

Gaja, Giorgio (ed.). *International Commercial Arbitration. The New York Convention.* (looseleaf), 7 Parts, 3 vols. Dobbs Ferry, NY: Oceana, 1979----.

Garro, Alejandro M. "Enforcement of Arbitration Agreements and Jurisdiction of Arbitral Tribunals in Latin America," 1 *JIArb* 293-321 (1984).

Gautama, S. "Recognition and Enforcement of Foreign Judgments and Arbitral Awards in the ASEAN Region," 32 *MalLR* 171-88 (1990).

"General Principles of Law in International Commercial Arbitration," 101 *Harvard LR* 1816-34 (1988).

Graving, Richard J. "The International Commercial Arbitration Institutions. How Good a Job Are They Doing?" 4 *AUJIL&Pcy* 319-76 (1989).

Greig, Robert T. "International Commercial Arbitration in Japan: A User's Report," 6 *JIArb* 21-5 (1989).

Grenner, William B. "The Evolution of Foreign Trade Arbitration in the People's Republic of China," 21 *NYUJIL& Politics* 293-327 (1989).

Holtzmann, H. & J. Neuhaus. *A Guide to the UNCITRAL Model Law on International Commercial Arbitration*. 1988.

Houzhi, Tang. "Arbitration - A Method Used by China to Settle Foreign Trade and Economic Disputes," 4 *Pace LR* 519-36 (1984).

International Chamber of Commerce. *Arbitration Law in Europe*. Paris: ICC Services, 1981. 368 p.

_____. *Rules of the ICC Court of Arbitration*. Paris: ICC Services, 1980.

Jalili, Mahir. "Amman Arab Convention on Commercial Arbitration," 7 *JIArb* 139-52 (1990).

_____. "International Arbitration in Iraq," 4 *JIArb* 109-30 (1987).

Jarvin, Sigvard. "L'arbitrage commercial international," 63 *ILA Rep.* 464-504 (1988).

Kahn, Philippe. "Les principes généraux du droit devant les arbitres du commerce international," 116 *JDI* 305-27 (1989).

Kennedy, Lionel. "Enforcing International Commercial Arbitration Agreements and Awards Not Subject to the New York Convention," 23 *VirJIL* 75-101 (1982).

Kerr, Michael. "Arbitration and the Courts: The UNCITRAL Model Law," 34 *ICLQ* 1-24 (1985).

Kos-Rabcewicz-Zubkowski, Ludwik. *Commercial and Civil Law Arbitration in Canada*. Ottawa: U of Ottawa P, 1978. 140 p.

_____ & Paul J. Davidson. *Commercial Arbitration Institutions: An*

International Directory and Guide. Dobbs Ferry, NY: Oceana, 1986. 186 p.

Kui-Nung Cheung, Andrew. "Enforcement of Foreign Arbitral Awards in the People's Republic of China," 34 *AJCL* 295-347 (1986).

Lalive, Pierre A. "Problèmes relatifs à l'arbitrage international commercial," 120 *RCADI* 569-714 (1967-I).

_____ & Emmanuel Gaillard. "Le nouveau droit de l'arbitrage international en Suisse," 116 *JDI* 905-63 (1989).

Lelewer, Joanne K. "International Commercial Arbitration As a Model for Resolving Treaty Disputes," 21 *NYUJIL& Politics* 379-402 (1989).

Lew, Julian D. M. *Applicable Law in International Commercial Arbitration. A Study in Commercial Arbitration Awards*. Alphen aan den Rijn: Sijthoff & Noordhoff, 1978. 632 p.

_____ (ed.). *Contemporary Problems in International Arbitration*. 1987.

_____ & Yves Poillet. *International Commercial Arbitration: A Selected Bibliography*. Dobbs Ferry, NY: Oceana, 1979. 108 p.

Lowry, Houston Putnam. "The United States Joins the Inter-American Arbitration Convention," 7 *JIArb* 83-90 (1990).

Lucio, Saturnino E. "The UNCITRAL Model Law on International Commercial Arbitration," 17 *UMiami I-ALR* 313-38 (1986).

McClendon, J. Stewart & Rosabel E. Everard Goodman (eds.). *International Commercial Arbitration in New York*. New York, The World Arbitration Institute. Dobbs Ferry, NY: Transnational Publishers, 1986 326 p.

McNerney, Mary E. & Carlos A. Esplugues. "International Commercial Arbitration: The UNCITRAL Model Law," 9 *Boston Col I&CLR* 47-71 (1986).

Nattier, Frank E. "International Commercial Arbitration in Latin America: Enforcement of Arbitral Agreements and Awards," 21 *TexILJ* 397-424 (1986).

Norberg, Charles R. *Inter-American Commercial Arbitration*. Dobbs Ferry, NY: Oceana, 1990.

O'Keefe, Patrick J. *Arbitration in International Trade*. Sydney: Prosper Law Publ., 1975. 437 p.

Paasivirta, Esa. *Participation of States in International Contracts and Arbitral Settlement of Disputes*. Helsinki: Lakimiesliiton Kustannus, Finnish Lawyers' Publishing Company, 1990. 357 p.

Park, William W. "Judicial Supervision of Transnational Commercial Arbitration: The English Arbitration Act of 1979," 21 *Harvard ILJ* 87-127 (1980).

Parker School of Foreign and Comparative Law. *The 1989 Guide to International Arbitration and Arbitrators.* 1989----(Annual). Dobbs Ferry, NY: Transnational Juris Publications, 1989. 981 p.

_____. *International Commercial Arbitration and the Courts: A Source Guide.* (Annual). Dobbs Ferry, NY: Transnational Juris Publications, 1990. 460 p.

Paterson, Robert K. & Bonita J. Thompson (eds.). *UNCITRAL Arbitration Model in Canada.* Toronto: Carswell, 1987.

Petersmann, Ernst-Ulrich & Günther Jänicke. *Adjudication of International Trade Disputes in International and National Economic Law.* Fribourg: UP, 1992. 405 p.

Piergrossi, Alberto. *L'arbitrato commerciale negli Stati Uniti d'America e i suoi rapporti con l'ordinamento italiano.* Milan: Giuffré, 1974. 532 p.

Praendl, Felix. "Measure of Damages in International Commercial Arbitration," 23 *Stanford JIL* 263-302 (1987).

Pryles, Michael & Kazuo Iwasaki. *Dispute Resolution in Australia-Japan Transactions.* Sydney: The Law Book Company, 1983. 1985 p.

Real, Gustav K. L. "UNCITRAL-Modellgesetz über die internationale Handelsschiedsgerichtsbarkeit," 89 *ZVglRWiss* 407-440 (1990).

Redfern, Alan & Martin Hunter. *Law and Practice of International Commercial Arbitration.* 2d ed. Scarborough, Ontario: Carswell, 1991. 838 p.

Rubino-Sammartano, Mauro. *L'arbitrato internazionale.* Padua: Cedam, 1989. 932 p.

_____. *International Arbitration Law.* Deventer: Kluwer Law & Taxation Publ., 1990. 537 p.

Sanders, Pieter (general ed.). *Arbitration in Settlement of International Commercial Disputes Involving the Far East.* 9. International Arbitration Congress, Tokyo, 31 May-3 June 1988 (ICCA Congress Series, 4). Deventer: Kluwer Law & Taxation Publ., 1989. 427 p.

_____ (general ed.). *Comparative Arbitration Practice and Public Policy in Arbitration.* Deventer: Kluwer Law & Taxation Publ.,

1987. 402 p.

_____ (ed.). *International Arbitration-Liber Amicorum for Martin Domke*. The Hague: Nijhoff, 1967. 357 p.

_____. "Trends in the Field of International Commercial Arbitration," 145 *RCADI* 205-96 (1975-II).

_____. "A Twenty Years' Review of the Convention on Recognition and Enforcement of Foreign Arbitral Awards," 13 *ILawyer* 269-89 (1979).

Santos Belandro, Ruben B. *Arbitraje comercial internacional: tendencias y perspectivas*. Montevideo: Fundación de Cultura Universitaria, 1988. 392 p.

Sarcevic, Petar (ed.). *Essays on International Commercial Arbitration*. Norwell, MA: Kluwer Academic Publishers, 1989. 256 p.

Schlosser, Peter. *Das Recht der internationalen privaten Schiedsgerichtsbarkeit*. 2d totally revised ed. Tübingen: Mohr, 1989. 791 p.

Schmitthoff, Clive M. & Kenneth R. Simmonds (eds.). *International Commercial Arbitration: Documents and Collected Papers*. (looseleaf). (12 binders). Dobbs Ferry, NY: Oceana, 1975----.

Schütze, Rolf A., Dieter Tscherning, & Walter Wais. *Handbuch des Schiedsverfahrens: Praxis der deutschen und internationalen Schiedsgerichtsbarkeit*. 2d rev. ed. Berlin: de Gruyter, 1990. 719 p.

Shilston, Alan W. "The Evolution of Modern Commercial Arbitration," 4 *JIArb* 45-76 (1987).

Shum, Clement. "International Economic and Trade Arbitration in China," 5 *JBL* 274-80 (1990).

Simmonds, Kenneth R., Brian H. W. Hill, & Sigvard Jarvin (eds.). *Commercial Arbitration Law in Asia and the Pacific*. Paris: ICC Publishing, S.A.; New York: Oceana, 1987. 575 p.

Smit, Hans. "The Future of International Commercial Arbitration: A Single Transnational Institution?" 25 *ColJTransnL* 9-34 (1986).

_____ & Vratislav Pechota (eds.). *The World Arbitration Reporter*. (looseleaf). Vol. I: *International Legal Framework;* Vol. II: *National Legislation*. Austin, Boston, Seattle, St. Paul: Butterworths Legal Publishers. 1986----.

Sornarajah, M. *International Commercial Arbitration*. Singapore: Longman Singapore Publishers, 1990. 306 p.

Storme, Marcel & Bernadette Demenlenaere. *International Commercial Arbitration in Belgium*. Deventer: Kluwer Law and

Taxation Publ., 1989. 306 p.

Summers, L. M. "Arbitration and Latin America," 3 *CalifWILJ* 1-20 (1972).

Szurski, Tadeusz. "Schiedsordnung des Schiedsrichterkollegiums der Polnischen Kammer für Aussenhandel, Warschau," 2 *Jahrbuch für die Praxis der Schiedsgerichtsbarkeit* 213-22 (1988).

Thieffry, Patrick & Christine Lecyer-Thieffry. *Le règlement des litiges civils et commerciaux avec les Etats-Unis.* Paris: Jupiter, 1986. 399 p.

Tiefenbrun, Suzan W. "A Comparison of International Arbitral Rules," 14 *Boston Coll&CLR* 25-49 (1992).

Tschanz, Pierre-Yves. "A Breakthrough in International Arbitration: Switzerland's New Act," 24 *ILawyer* 1107-18 (1990).

Vagts, Detlev F. "Dispute-Resolution Mechanisms in International Business," 203 *RCADI* 9-94 (1987-III).

Van den Berg, Albert Jan. *The New York Arbitration Convention of 1958. Toward a Uniform Judicial Interpretation.* The Hague: T.M.C. Asser Instituut; Deventer: Kluwer, 1981. 466 p.

Walton, Anthony. *Russell on the Law of Arbitration.* 19th ed. London: Stevens & Sons, 1979. 647 p.

Wehringer, Cameron K. *Arbitration Precepts and Principles.* Dobbs Ferry, NY: Oceana, 1969. 115 p.

Williamson, Hugh R. "International Maritime Arbitration: Dispute Settlement without Recourse to the Courts," 7 *Ocean Yearbook* 94-114 (1988).

Yearbook-Commercial Arbitration. Annual. 1976----. General Editor: Pieter Sanders. Published under the auspices of the International Council for Commercial Arbitration. Deventer: Kluwer Law & Taxation Publ.

ABOUT THE AUTHOR

Boleslaw A. Boczek (M.A., L.L.M., S.J.D., Jagiellonian University, Cracow; Ph.D., Harvard University) is Professor Emeritus of Political Science at Kent State University where he has been teaching international law and international organization for nearly 30 years. Prior to that, he had served as a consultant for the United Nations and spent six years doing international legal research at Harvard Law School. Currently, he is a member of the Adjunct Faculty of Case Western Reserve University School of Law where he is teaching international organization. As a Visiting Professor and twice Fulbright Senior Lecturer, he has also taught at universities in a number of foreign countries, including Belgium, Germany, Greece, Mexico, the Netherlands, Poland, and Switzerland. In addition, he has presented papers at many scholarly conferences in the United States and overseas and has published extensively on various international law topics in professional journals in this country and abroad. He is the author of several books and monographs, including the authoritative classic *Flags of Convenience* (Harvard UP, 1962) and (coauthor) *The International Law Dictionary* (ABC-Clio, 1987).